The Ambassadors. 1533 by Hans Holbein the Younger (1497/8–1543). © National
Gallery Picture Library, London.

THE PSYCHOLOGY OF DIPLOMACY

Edited by
Harvey J. Langholtz and Chris E. Stout

Psychological Dimensions to War and Peace

Westport, Connecticut
London

Library of Congress Cataloging-in-Publication Data

The psychology of diplomacy / edited by Harvey Langholtz and Chris E. Stout.
    p.   cm.—(Psychological dimensions to war and peace, ISSN 1540–5265)
   ISBN 0–275–97144–9
   1. Diplomacy—Psychological aspects. I. Langholtz, Harvey J., 1948–
II. Stout, Chris E. III. Series.
JZ1305.P78   2004
327.2'01'9—dc22   2003026356

British Library Cataloguing in Publication Data is available.

Library of Congress Catalog Card Number: 2003026356
ISBN: 0–275–97144–9
ISSN: 1540–5265

First published in 2004

Praeger Publishers, 88 Post Road West, Westport, CT 06881
An imprint of Greenwood Publishing Group, Inc.
www.praeger.com

Printed in the United States of America

The paper used in this book complies with the
Permanent Paper Standard issued by the National
Information Standards Organization (Z39.48–1984).

10 9 8 7 6 5 4 3 2 1

Copyright Acknowledgments

The authors, editors, and publisher gratefully acknowledge permission to reprint the
following:

"Social Psychological Dimensions," Chapter 6 in *Peacekeeping in International
Conflict* (I. William Zartman and J. Lewis Rasmussen, editors). Washington, DC:
Endowment of the United States Institute of Peace, 1993. pp. 194–210. Reprinted
with the permission of the publisher.

Parts of "The Psychology of Diplomacy, as Manifested in the Role of Subregional
and Regional Organizations in Preventing African Conflicts" by Betsie Smith as it
appeared in *A Continent Apart: Kosovo, Africa, and Humanitarian Intervention*
(Elizabeth Sidiropoulos, editor). Copyright © 2001 by Elizabeth Sidiropoulos.
Published by the South African Institute for International Affairs. Reprinted with the
permission of the editor.

The frontispiece, "The Ambassadors" (1533) by Hans Holbein the Younger.
Reprinted with the permission of the National Gallery Picture Library.

Contents

Preface

Some topics can be clearly defined, and in these cases it is not difficult for people to agree on a definition of the topic, assumptions, and the scope of the topic. In the case of the psychology of diplomacy, the definition, assumptions, and scope were not readily apparent.

Part of the explanation for this may be that diplomats and psychologists come from very different backgrounds, traditions, and work environments. Diplomats spend their careers engaged in the reality of the relationships between nations. For most of a diplomat's career, this reality is focused on maintaining the ongoing relationship between his or her nation and other nations. Sometimes this means long postings to remote places, surviving in a bureaucracy, and the tedious and lonely work of adhering to instructions issued by a supervisor who is far away. Most diplomats would not think this has much to do with psychology. Most diplomats will focus on the details of the immediate task to be carried out and the best strategy for reaching the assigned objective.

But, if we examine the writings of psychologists, including those who contributed to this edited volume, the psychology of diplomacy has to deal with perceptions between nations and peoples. It has to do with how diplomats interact. It has to do with some of the fundamental psychological motivations of prejudice, fear, trust, suspicion, greed, and hope. Psychologists—and of course the members of any profession—are concerned about what they see as the current state of international relations. Psychologists are accustomed to dealing with interactions between individuals, and these psychologists may look for ways to address international problems in the same way as interpersonal problems are addressed. These psychologists may hope that by better understanding the psychology of diplomacy we may be able to make a contribution to better relations between nations and between peoples.

The psychologists may be taking too broad and idealistic a view, and the diplomats may be taking a view that is narrowly defined and too bounded by custom. It is not difficult to read the chapters contributed to this edited volume and determine which have been written by diplomats and which have been written by psychologists. The diplomats tend to be focused on the details of reality; the psychologists tend to be focused on ideals and goals.

But perhaps these differences in views are instructive. It is easy for psychologists and others to view diplomacy and international relations from a distance and wonder why so many of the world's conflicts seem intractable. And it is easy for psychologists to wonder if taking a kinder, more conciliatory, stance might lead to mutual respect and accommodation where none now exist.

And it is equally easy for diplomats to reject the idealism of some psychologists as out of touch or uninformed.

The Charter of the United Nations Educational, Scientific, and Cultural Organisation (UNESCO) declares that "Wars begin in the minds of men." There is certainly some face validity to that assertion. And if this is the case, then perhaps wars can be prevented by developing a better understanding of the psychology of diplomacy.

Harvey J. Langholtz

The Psychology of Diplomacy

Harvey J. Langholtz

WHAT IS DIPLOMACY? AND WHAT IS THE PSYCHOLOGY OF DIPLOMACY?

To ask and answer the question, "What is diplomacy?" is to open a long discussion. The answer has changed over history. And the answer can change at any given time based on the context and the specific issue under discussion. To ask and answer the question, "What is the psychology of diplomacy?" is also to open a long discussion, made even longer by different sets of assumptions, wishes, perspectives, and differing answers to the question, "What is psychology?"

To even attempt to address the topic of the psychology of diplomacy, we must first have a sense of what the practice of diplomacy is like in terms of official structure, established protocol, and practical reality. In this introductory chapter we will examine the origins of diplomacy, the goals of diplomacy, how diplomacy is carried out, and some of the day-to-day realities and details that, in sum, start to form the psychology of diplomacy.

There are many useful and valid definitions of diplomacy. One fairly comprehensive such definition is by the U.S. scholar E. Plischke (as cited in Freeman, 1994, p. 75).

Diplomacy is the political process by which political entities (generally states) establish and maintain official relations, direct and indirect, with one another, in pursuing their respective goals, objectives, interests, and substantive and procedural policies in the international environment; as a political process it is dynamic, adaptive, and changing, and it constitutes a continuum; functionally it embraces both the making and implementation of foreign policy at all levels, centrally and in the field, and involves essentially, but is not restricted to the functions of representation, reporting, communicating, negotiating, and maneuvering, as well as caring for the interests of nationals abroad.

Another definition, less comprehensive but more to the point, is by Zhou Enlai (1954): "Diplomacy is war by other means" (Freeman, 1994). For additional and equally valid definitions the reader is referred to Freeman (1994).

So if the definition of psychology is the study of behavior, then of course the psychology of diplomacy is the study of the behavior of diplomats. Or, more precisely, the psychology of diplomacy is the study of the way diplomats will interact as they represent their nations to each other. This interaction will include all forms of communications and negotiations, both formal and informal, in writing, speaking, and any other forms of communication, at both the bilateral and multilateral level, primarily with other diplomats but also including members of the press and media, businesspersons, military personnel, and the general public. It is our goal in examining the psychology of diplomacy to understand how diplomats will interact with each other directly and what sort of psychological environment and assumptions frame this direct interaction. Explicitly not included in this definition are the broader disciplines of international relations, statesmanship, international business, geopolitics, or globalization.

Whichever definition we may accept for diplomacy and the psychology of diplomacy, there will come a point at which a fundamental assumption must be made as part of those definitions. Many spectators of diplomacy, especially idealists who may only view diplomacy from the distance of the general public and through the filtered lens of the media, would wish for diplomacy to be an egalitarian setting in which the appointed representatives of every nation seek equitable and democratic solutions to all problems that may confront the community of nations. This ideal is perhaps best conveyed in the splendid-sounding phrase, "The common benefit of mankind." This concept was first proposed on November 1, 1967, by Ambassador Arvid Pardo of Malta as "the common heritage of mankind" as part of the discussions leading to the UN Convention on the Law of the Sea and was later modified to include the concepts of "the benefit of mankind as a whole" and "the common benefit of mankind." For more discussion of the UN Convention on the Law of the Sea (UNCLOS) and how some of the ideals of UNCLOS have come to be accepted as precedents in international law for subsequent cases of (so-called) commonly held resources, see Borgese (1998) or http://www.unu.edu/unupress/unupbooks/uu15oe/uu15oe0p.htm.

However, in opposition to this inspiring language is the reality that diplomacy is an environment in which nations meet in a zero-sum game, where diplomats maneuver on behalf of their own nations for advantage, and where a gain for one nation can only come at the expense of another. Even UNCLOS itself stands as such an example, in which a large coalition of mostly landlocked and nonseagoing nations developed that was able to dominate the negotiations and maintain language that would have the seagoing nations pay large sums of money to the nonseagoing nations for the privilege of conducting certain operations in international waters—especially deep seabed mining. And when the UN General Assembly adopted Resolution 2749 in 1970, declaring the Common Heritage of Mankind as the principle governing the exploitation of the international seabed, this principle came to serve as a precedent for other international conventions, including the 1972 UNESCO Convention for the Protection of the World Cultural and Natural Heritage, the 1979 Moon Treaty, and others. By its own self-declared language, UNCLOS came into force when it received its 60th national ratification. As it turned out, this distinction fell to Djibouti, when it ratified UNCLOS in 1994. But conspicuously absent from the list of other ratifiers were any of the developed and seagoing nations.

So even when there is a declared effort for diplomats to approach a question with a sense of equality and democracy, the inevitable realities of human nature as expressed through national interest can eventually produce an environment in which each nation is left to look out for itself, and it is the diplomat's responsibility to seek whatever advantage he or she can for his or her own nation. And because diplomats are appointed by and represent their heads of state, and because each head of state is ultimately responsible to his or her own citizenry, it becomes the responsibility of the diplomat to advance the interests of his or her nation's citizens. If we accept Zhou Enlai's previously cited assertion that "diplomacy is war by other means" and combine that with Clausewitz's well-known quote that "war is merely the continuation of policy by other means" (see Rapoport's 1968 translation of Clausewitz's 1832 *On War*), then it follows that diplomacy is a continuation of policy. It is therefore the responsibility of the diplomat to advance his or her nation's policy. A head of state who accepts anything less from appointed diplomats may soon find an erosion of support at home. And so, although at the superficial level the psychology of diplomacy may be one of polite and ritualized discussion, the diplomats know that when they deal with their counterparts from other nations, they do so through a psychology that is at its fundamental level an adversarial one. It is the professional purpose of each diplomat to seek advantage for his or her own nation.

A VERY BRIEF HISTORY OF DIPLOMACY

Throughout history heads of state have sent emissaries to negotiate on their behalf with other heads of state. Often this was done during times of war to negotiate the terms of an end to fighting. These representatives of sovereigns were dispatched to negotiate on specific topics, and when the negotiations ended, so did the ad hoc role of the sovereign's representative. These temporary representatives took two forms. A *nuncius* was a "living letter" authorized to represent a specific point on behalf of his or her sovereign but not authorized to negotiate or enter into a treaty. A *plenipotentiary* had "full powers" and was accorded *plena potestas,* meaning the authority to negotiate terms and sign agreements or treaties on behalf of the sovereign. Both the nuncius and the plenipotentiary were temporary, and when they had concluded the mission for which they had been dispatched, they returned to their nation (Queller, 1967).

This temporary functioning of dispatched emissaries came to an end in the seventeenth century under France's king Louis XIII's first minister from 1624 to 1642, a prince of the church, Armand Jean du Plessis, Cardinal de Richelieu. Richelieu came to power in the midst of the Thirty Years' War (1618–1648). During this war the Habsburg Holy Roman Emperor Ferdinand II was attempting to crush Protestantism, impose Catholic universality, and gain control over the princes of central Europe. Richelieu did not view Ferdinand's goals in terms of religion, but rather in terms of international politics. Richelieu realized that if Ferdinand were successful, he would control Spain to France's southwest, as well as the Northern Italian city–states of Lyon and Savoy and the Netherlands. Not wanting to be surrounded by such a power, Richelieu allied Catholic France with the Protestant enemies of Ferdinand and dispatched permanent emissaries to the Protestant courts. These would not be the ad hoc representatives of sovereigns assigned to negotiate on one particular topic, as had been done in the past, but rather would be living symbols of the alliance of the two courts. He even went so far in his efforts to block Ferdinand's success as to establish an alliance with the Muslim Ottoman Sultan, Shadow of God on Earth in Constantinople (Berridge, 2002; Kissinger, 1994). Richelieu called this permanent presence of representatives *négociation continuelle*, "continuous negotiation" that would be ongoing "in all places" irrespective of war, peace, alliances, or religion (Berridge, Keens-Soper, & Otte, 1991). This continuous negotiation had a way of taking on its own psychological framework and set of assumptions. It was no longer the diplomat's responsibility to negotiate one finite or ad hoc issue. Rather, it was the diplomat's longer-term responsibility to develop a relationship with the influential members of the court to which he was posted. He had to understand the culture and the assumptions of those with whom he spoke. And he had to understand the psychological view of the members of the court and even the citizens of the nation where he represented the interests of his own sovereign and nation.

A separate but related principle that emerged from the thinking of Cardinal de Richelieu was the doctrine of *raison d'état*. Under *raison d'état*, or reason of the state, the interests of the state are considered to be subject to a different set of standards than would be in private morality (Freeman, 1994). This is not to say that states are free to behave in ways that would be considered immoral, rather that states are not bound by the same set of standards that would apply to individuals.

The concept of "resident missions" was at first viewed with suspicion but over time came to be accepted as part of international law. As part of the acceptance of this practice, the ambassador, his family, and his staff came to be accorded certain privileges and immunities to local law, and these diplomatic immunities came to be extended to the home and offices occupied by the foreign envoy under the concept of extraterritoriality (Adair, 1929; Young, 1966).

The French ambassador François de Callières (1645–1717) asserted in *De la manière de négocier avec les Souverains* (On the manner of negotiating with princes) (1716) that international negotiations were too technical and required too much expertise to be left to appointed amateurs. It was the English politician, orator, and philosopher Edmund Burke (1729–97) who in 1796 affixed the label *diplomacy* to what until then was referred to as negotiation (Berridge, 2002, p. 1). With the development of the French system and the French *corps diplomatique* came a professionalization that included admission to the career, a career ladder that included promotion, training, and a salary that could be counted on as long as the career lasted.

In each capital there came to be a community of diplomats with their own set of protocols, a merging sense of professional interests, and also a set of issues on which they and their respective nations took different positions (Berridge, 2002). Although the concept of psychology as a science was still 200 years away, early diplomats in the European capitals developed their own mutually understood ways of interacting and their own set of psychological assumptions.

To support this far-flung community of internationalists and their families, there developed a network of schools to educate their children. To this day there remain worldwide approximately 400 international schools for the children of diplomats (and others), the Lycée Français. These schools typically offer preschool through 12th grade and are academic institutions accredited by local authorities and also the French Ministry of Education. Most classes are conducted in French, and the schools receive substantial financial support from the French government. They typically award a high school diploma (or local equivalent) and prepare students to pass the French baccalaureate. It is their goal to provide an education similar to that provided in a French lycée and still meet the standards of the nation in which they are located. These French lycée schools can be found in New York, San Francisco, and most other large (and some not so large) cities throughout the world. Although they were originated as a way to provide a proper French education for the children of French diplomats, they have come to represent an outpost of European and Western culture in cities worldwide, something important to the diplomatic community. And as an interesting and up-to-date note, this informal diplomatic community now has its own online home at http://www.ediplomat.com/ that caters to both the professional and personal needs of diplomats of all nations posted abroad.

At various times in history—especially during times of war and crisis—diplomacy has been at the forefront of world events. Examples of this include the 1814–15 Congress of Vienna that redrew the map of post-Napoleonic Europe and provided a structure that lasted until the First World War; the 1900 Boxer Rebellion and the defense of Peking's Legation Quarter, home of most foreign diplomats and their families; World War I—as a measure of what can happen when diplomacy fails; the efforts to found the League of Nations and U.S. President Wilson's failure to persuade the U.S. Senate to ratify membership in the League; World War II and especially the negotiations of Churchill, Roosevelt, and Stalin at Tehran and Yalta; the founding of the United Nations in 1945 on the ashes of World War II; the Cold War; the ongoing failure of diplomats to resolve animosities between the Israelis and Palestinians; post–Cold War efforts by the international community to establish peacekeeping missions in Yugoslavia, Somalia, Mozambique, Cambodia, and other areas; and two Persian Gulf Wars and the related maneuvering in the UN Security Council that in one case led to a coalition and support of the Security Council and in the other case did not. In addition to handling the affairs of state during times of war, diplomats have also met to discuss topics of a more general nature: the Hague Convention on how war may be fought and the Geneva Convention on the protection of innocents during times of war, the Kyoto Convention on the Environment, the Rio Convention on Sustainable Development, the International Convention to Ban Land Mines, the Beijing Convention on the Rights of Women, the United Nations Convention on the Law of the Sea, the Committee on the Peaceful Uses of Outer Space, the Nuclear Test Ban Treaty, the Human Rights Convention, and a long list of other international agreements. Even the method and protocol for the practice of diplomacy has been established in a convention itself—the Vienna Convention on Diplomatic Relations of 1961.

Since the days of Richelieu the diplomats who have met at these conferences have included some of their nations' brightest minds as well as elites drawn from the powerful families and high society of their respective nations. These early diplomats came to form a privileged community that, to some extent, has retained its unique characteristics to the present. The diplomats that form this international community attend and send their children to the best colleges in the world. During the early days of the diplomatic community they communicated in Latin; this was replaced with French, and following World War II almost all diplomats came to speak English. (This is English as spoken in the UK. Documents of diplomacy are written in UK English.) Diplomats are, of course, well traveled and know history, geography, science, and culture. They are realists who understand the competing needs of their nations. They understand statesmanship, international politics, the use of the military, and the projection of power. Most of all, they have developed their abilities to communicate, negotiate, threaten, withhold, persuade, and use psychology to get their way on behalf of their nations. (Over the years, some have asked if U.S. diplomats as a group are held to the same standard as those of other nations. The front page of the *Chicago Times* on October 9, 1862, remarked, "[W]ith what care foreign diplomatists [*sic*] are trained, in contrast with the inattention to the whole subject which prevails here." The article went on to point out that in England the candidate for diplomatic service had to "have a good knowledge of the Latin language. He must have an 'accurate knowledge of French grammar, fluency in French conversation . . . a like proficiency in the German tongue . . . a fair knowledge of the political history of Europe, and of North and South America . . . and also a general knowledge of international law.' How many veteran American diplomatists could successfully stand this preliminary examination?")

HOW IS DIPLOMACY PRACTICED?

Decisions about national policy in matters relating to international affairs are made in the capitals of nations. In the case of broad or most-important policy, the decision may be made by the head of state himself or herself, but most decisions will be made by appointed personnel in that nation's ministry of foreign affairs. This ministry will go by different names in each nation. In Canada it is the Department of Foreign Affairs and International Trade; in India it is the Ministry of External Relations; in Russia it is the Ministry of Foreign Affairs; and in the UK it is the Foreign and Commonwealth Office. In the United States it is called the State Department because in September of 1789 it was assigned responsibility for the operation of the Mint, the keeping of the Great Seal of the United States, and the taking of the census, in addition to its responsibility to maintain relations with foreign nations. Although most of the domestic duties were transferred to other departments in the nineteenth century, the name State Department remained (http://www/state.bov/www/about-state/history/depthis.html).

Ministries of foreign relations will maintain a series of offices throughout the world to carry out that nation's foreign policy. When normal diplomatic relations are maintained, each nation will have an embassy located in or near the capital of the other nation, and that is where the ambassador and his or her staff will work, conduct diplomatic affairs that relate to policy and international relations, and often live. (Technically, the office building in which the ambassador and principal staff work is the *chancellery*, and the ambassador's residence is the *embassy*, but somehow in common usage these two words have become reversed.) In addition to the embassy (office) located in the capital, a nation may maintain one or more consulates to handle issues relating to international trade, immigration, visas, and other nondiplomatic activities. For example, large and influential nations such as Germany, Japan, and the UK might maintain consulates in Chicago, Miami, New York, or San Francisco.

In addition to the embassies maintained to conduct relations with other nations, nations will also maintain *missions* to conduct relations with international organizations. These will include missions to the United Nations, NATO, and so on.

For some smaller nations the sheer cost and burden of maintaining embassies or missions to all other nations and international organizations may become simply too high. With almost 200 nations in the world (189 members in the UN), it is not possible to maintain full-time representation in all nations, and in these cases one ambassador may represent his or her nation at the capital of two or more nations as may be convenient. In addition, the staff may be very small, sometimes consisting only of the ambassador alone. As an example,

I once had the occasion to meet with the ambassador of Uruguay to Australia's capital of Canberra where, with a staff of one, he represents his nation to both Australia and New Zealand. The permanent mission of the Republic of Seychelles to the United Nations has one ambassador and a staff of one, whereas the permanent missions of Japan and the United States maintain staffs of more than 50 and 120, respectively.

Diplomats are almost always kept under close control by their capitals, and this will be truer for the larger developed nations but sometimes less true for the smaller or developing nations. Diplomats are not free to make up their own foreign policy as they go along but are instead told what to say through *instructions*. The instructions will be carefully reviewed in the capital and sent by encoded means to the nation's embassy or mission abroad. Sometimes there will be an internal conflict in the capital regarding a particular issue, and different departments will take different positions. For example, in the United States, the State Department may not always take the same view as other departments that have an interest in international relations—the Defense Department, NASA, the Environmental Protection Agency, or the Commerce Department. These internal differences must first be settled in the capital before the diplomat in some foreign city can be issued instructions. And it occasionally happens that internal disagreements in the capital have left the lonely diplomat having to attend a scheduled meeting without instructions or not knowing what he or she is authorized to say or negotiate.

Once a diplomat has received his or her instructions, he or she will be ready to present a *démarche* to their host nation or organization. As an official representation of a nation's view, a *démarche* will be presented and received in a manner intended to enhance the psychological perception of its importance. It will usually be presented in speaking by a diplomat on behalf of his or her own nation and presented to a diplomat (usually of equal rank) from the host nation (or organization) duly authorized to receive a *démarche*. If the *démarche* is presented by one ambassador to another, each ambassador will usually be accompanied by an aide, whose job it is to take notes on the *démarche* and how it is received. The *démarche* will usually request a reply, decision, or action from the diplomat's government. The response to the *démarche* may be provided immediately to the diplomat who presented it, or there may be a delay. Although the word *démarche* is a noun, diplomats will often use it as a verb (i.e., "I need to *démarche* the Austrians").

If a diplomat is not posted to an embassy where he or she is to represent his or her nation at the capital of another nation but instead is posted to a mission to an international organization (i.e., the United Nations or NATO), he or she may be instructed to give an *intervention* at a meeting. This intervention will be a statement that is to be delivered at a meeting (i.e., the Security Council, General Assembly, or subordinate committee of the General Assembly) in speaking verbatim and may sometimes also be distributed in writing.

In some cases it will not be necessary to provide a diplomat with the specific wording of a formal intervention, and in such cases the capital may instead provide talking points, which are, of course, specific concepts to convey and guidelines on what may be represented. Where meetings are informal or dynamic, or where a diplomat will need some flexibility and maneuvering room, talking points will be more appropriate than the text of a preapproved intervention.

Once the *démarche* or intervention has been delivered, the diplomat will draft a *reporting cable* back to the capital to report on how the message was received by the representative of the host nation and any immediate response that was provided. When a diplomat is engaged in a series of ongoing meetings, this can easily mean daily reporting cables and, of course, daily instructions that guide the diplomat based on what was contained in the diplomat's reporting cable. Because the capital is often in a time zone different from the location where the meetings are being held, this can mean overnight exchanges of reporting cables and instructions.

BILATERAL DIPLOMACY AND MULTILATERAL DIPLOMACY

When one nation maintains an embassy in the capital of another nation, this is bilateral diplomacy. In the case of two large nations playing an active role in international affairs (i.e., the UK and the United States), there can be much to discuss. There will almost certainly be a long list of issues that will include topics pertaining to politics, the military, economics and trade, technical issues, finances, academics, cultural exchanges, transportation, and other areas. There can be a constant stream of important and senior visitors from the home capital to the host capital. There is a need to continually report to the home capital on both the official and public sentiment in the host country on a variety of topics. And there is the occasional visit by the home country's head of state to the host country (and vice versa), and of course these can be the cause of administrative overload as the embassy staff, from the ambassador on down, will want things to go well.

In the case of bilateral relations between nations that recognize each other but whose interests are just in different spheres, the frequency and intensity of interactions can become slower and more predictable. I once had the occasion to see the embassy of France to Paraguay, and things certainly seemed well under control. But even where the two nations in question may not have much to discuss about their own relations with each other, they will both be members of the international community and therefore may be actively seeking the other's support in matters relating to multinational diplomacy. They will each know that there may come some future time when they will need to call on each other for support. This can be especially true in the case of the rotating nature of the nonpermanent members of the United Nations Security Council (see following). Even very small nations may find themselves on the Security Council for two years, and during that period they will carry a great deal of responsibility and wield a great deal of power. So although the psychology of bilateral diplomacy may take the form of sustaining positive relations between two nations, multilateral diplomacy will be more complex.

Multilateral diplomacy is typically more active and dynamic than bilateral diplomacy. Although the general public may only be aware of the occasional meeting at the UN General Assembly or Security Council, there are meetings and discussions that go on almost constantly throughout the year, and there are days when seven or eight official meetings can be underway concurrently with informal meetings and discussions taking place on the margins. Chapter III of the United Nations Charter establishes six "principal organs" of the United Nations: "a General assembly, a Security Council, an Economic and Social Council, a Trusteeship Council, an International Court of Justice, and a Secretariat." Chapter IV sets the composition, functions and powers, and procedures of the General Assembly; Chapter V sets the composition, functions and powers, voting, and procedures of the Security Council. Other principal organs are discussed in other chapters of the UN Charter.

The Security Council is without question the body in which the most important and difficult decisions are taken. The Security Council may meet any time, 24 hours a day, 365 days a year, on one hour's notice, but in reality most of the council's work is done during normal business hours (including some evenings) Monday through Friday. The Security Council has 15 members, of which five are permanent members—China, France, Russia, the UK, and the United States. In addition, 10 nonpermanent members are elected to serve two-year terms, with half of these beginning on January 1st of each year. In order for a resolution to pass the Security Council, it must have nine affirmative votes (votes of *yes*) but a vote of *no* by any of the permanent members will veto a resolution. Council members may vote either *yes* or *no* or they may *abstain.* On the most rare occasions they may not vote or be absent from a vote, but such cases are very unusual.

Most of the actual negotiating over language for a resolution of the Security Council is discussed before entry to the large and formal Security Council Chamber. In many cases nations' permanent representatives (ambassadors) to the UN or their assistants will convene privately in bilateral meetings to discuss areas of mutual interest. There is a small room called the Security Council Consultation Chamber located across a small hall from the main Security Council Chamber, and this is where most of the actual discussions take place. The Consultation Chamber is approximately 20 feet wide and 40 feet long and has room for the 15 permanent representatives, plus the UN secretary-general and one other person to sit at a U-shaped table, and there is room for two assistants to sit behind each permanent representative. Meetings in the Consultation Chamber are strictly private, records are not kept, the press is never admitted, and representatives of nations not on the Security Council are not included. Representatives of nonmember nations may be briefed by colleagues of member nations in a nearby lounge.

It is in this Consultation Chamber that most of the actual discussion takes place. Although permanent representatives will usually begin with prepared interventions that have been approved by their capitals, once discussion begins they will often speak without prepared text or notes. The discussion is always polite and respectful, but there is no question that the topics under discussion are very serious and clearly involve matters of war and peace, life and death. Meetings are called and presided over by the president of the Security Council but this presidency rotates on a monthly basis among the permanent and non-permanent members.

The nature and structure of the Security Council can produce its own psychological environment and set of dynamics. Alliances are quickly formed between like-minded nations. Perhaps the strongest alliance is between the UK and United States, and as two permanent members, this alliance takes on additional strength. Representatives of the UK and United States will often consult before council meetings to compare notes. Where there are differences, these will be recognized and dealt with, but where there are areas of mutual support, a coordinated approach will be planned. Once these two allies are in agreement, they will usually seek additional support from other permanent members, and these are usually (but certainly not always!), in order, France, Russia, and China. The permanent representatives and staffs of these nations will work together on issues for months and sometimes years, and they get to know each other well. For any specific issue additional allies will be sought from the nonpermanent members. Although the permanent representatives of the nonpermanent members represent their own nations, they are often mindful that they have been elected by their regional nations and may consult with nations from their regions.

Although the so-called informal meetings in the Security Council Consultation Chamber are private and not recorded, it is the ultimate goal of these meetings to compose a draft resolution the council may vote on in formal session. Once the language of such a draft resolution has been agreed upon, it is printed using blue ink, and the council members refer to this as a resolution being *in blue*. A resolution in blue has not been voted on, but it provides a clear and concrete document to debate, and it affords an opportunity for diplomats to fax copies to their capitals so their governments may instruct them how to proceed with negotiations or how to vote. Once capitals have had time to react to the resolution in blue, the president of the Security Council will call a formal meeting in the Security Council Chamber. These formal meetings are open to other members of the diplomatic community from all nations and are also open to the public (subject to security limitations). Permanent representatives will once again speak on behalf of their nations and voice their positions on the resolution as drafted in blue, but at this point the meeting is mostly a scripted event, and there is little in the way of negotiation or the exchange of views. Once all nations have had an opportunity to give their interventions, the president of the Security Council will call for a vote. Voting is done by the raising of hands, first those who vote yes, then those who vote no, and then those who abstain. The raising of hands will quietly be recorded by UN photographers. The president of the council will declare if the resolution has passed, and if it has it is assigned a consecutive number, by which it will forever be referred, and it is distributed.

Whereas the UN Security Council is the body that debates issues of war, peace, and security, the General Assembly considers issues of broader social, political, and economic scope, and therefore the psychological environment in the General Assembly does not have the same sense of gravity and urgency as that of the Security Council. The General Assembly and its subcommittees also consider resolutions governing the administration of the UN Secretariat. Although the wording of Chapter IV of the UN Charter positions the General Assembly to "discuss any questions relating to the maintenance of international peace and security . . ." (Chapter IV Article 11), in reality, these topics have become the purview of the Security Council, not the General Assembly. The General Assembly, referred to informally by delegates as the "GA," meets each year from September through December. It may convene outside these months but rarely does.

The first few weeks of the GA are taken up with interventions by heads of state, and this period is known as the "General Debate." When the heads of state are at the UN for the General Debate, they typically bring with them their most senior personnel from their ministries of foreign affairs, and with so many high-ranking diplomats in New York City, it is a frenetic time of bilateral meetings (bilats), networking, and photo opportunities, and the staffs at the missions work hard to ensure that the visit by their head of state goes well. Brief meetings between heads of state may be held at the United Nations but are more commonly held at the nearby Waldorf Astoria Hotel or other hotels in the area. These bilats are carefully orchestrated events designed to provide the proper psychological sense of dignity and power to the heads of state, and this will include strict agreement on who will attend, seating, and topics to be discussed. The reason the attendance is prenegotiated is for protocol and so the heads of state will meet on equal terms without one being outstaffed by the other. The bilats will often be no more than a few minutes, long enough to say hello and snap some photos for use in newspapers back home and showing heads of state seated in armchairs next to each other. What is not included in these photographs will be the three-person sofas facing each other and immediately adjacent to the heads of state. Seated on these sofas by prior agreement will be the nations' senior diplomats, usually the minister of foreign affairs and two others. Interpreters, if needed, stand to the side of the heads of state and are not included in each nation's agreed-upon attendance list.

Each member nation of the UN has a seat in the General Assembly, and each nation has one vote. Resolutions on important issues, such as those relating to peace and security, admission of new members, and budget issues, require a two-thirds majority. Resolutions on other issues may be reached by a simple majority but in reality these issues are often accepted by consensus. Although the decisions of the General Assembly are not legally binding, they do represent a measure of international agreement on specific issues.

The work of the General Assembly is divided among six committees:

1st Committee: Disarmament and International Security

2nd Committee: Economic and Financial

3rd Committee: Social, Humanitarian, and Cultural

4th Committee: Special Political and Decolonization

5th Committee: Administrative and Budgetary

6th Committee: Legal

The current fourth committee includes the former unnumbered "Special Political Committee."

Each annual GA is numbered, starting with number 1 in 1945. The 58th GA was in the autumn of 2003. Various other committees will meet throughout the year, and their work will feed into the General Assembly.

Interventions at all official meetings of the UN are simultaneously translated from the language in which they are delivered into the other five official languages so diplomats in attendance may listen through their earpieces. The sheer complexity of this simultaneous translation can sometimes be taken for granted. With six official languages, there are at any given time five translations occurring but a total of 15 language pairs that could require translation. And considering that each language pair potentially requires translations in two directions, the interpreters on staff must be ready at any given meeting to conduct translation in 30 different directions. The interpreters who do this high-speed translation must often cope with highly technical issues, arguments that are complex both in terms of logic and grammar, and the subtle shadings of language and nuanced meanings by which diplomats will communicate. In some rare cases diplomats will give their interventions in one language while listening through their earpiece to another language (usually English) to ensure the interpreter has represented exactly the meaning the diplomat intended. Occasionally diplomats will switch their language in midintervention, sometimes to make a point more clearly, sometimes to be better understood by the speakers of one language, or perhaps sometimes to show that they have the personal capability of expressing complicated thoughts in multiple languages.

Seating at all UN meetings is in alphabetical order in English. This seating can lead to some uncomfortable arrangements, as throughout the Iran–Iraq War their diplomats always sat next to each other (often sharing a two-nation table) with Israel next to Iraq. As a diplomat from the United States I came to know well my colleagues from the United Republic of Tanzania to my left and

Uruguay to my right. The United Kingdom of Great Britain and Northern Ireland was never far off, and before the Union of Soviet Socialist Republics was replaced by Russia, they were also in easy reach at meetings.

THE SUBTLE LANGUAGE OF DIPLOMATIC DISCOURSE

Successful career diplomats will develop excellent communications skills, and they seem to be able to both send and receive with a level of precision and detail not found in normal discussion. They do not interrupt each other. They listen carefully. At the end of listening to a 15- or 20-minute intervention, a practiced diplomat may respond by saying something like, "I believe there were seven points you made and while I agree with your second and fifth points I would like to address some of the assumption in your other points," and with that he or she will enumerate and summarize all seven points, agreeing and disagreeing along the way.

Diplomats will use the precise word in their interventions that conveys the meaning that was intended. They will differentiate between words such as *would, will, could,* or *should.* They will say *persuade* or *dissuade* as appropriate. When they write a reporting cable, they will report if the intervention they listened to indicated the speaker indicated his or her nation would oppose, object, or be disappointed, as each of these would be taken differently (*oppose* means they would work to block it; *object* means they would not like it but would reserve any commitment in terms of action; and *be disappointed* means they do not like it, but they would accept it without blocking it).

In some cases, subtle shifts of policy or concessions within negotiations are signaled by the change of language from one meeting to the next. In the case of the UN General Assembly, with its annual debate of topics, this means that the listener must know that last year a nation indicated it would oppose a proposal whereas this year it would only object.

Diplomats understand logic and the way to use reasoning in an argument. They know the differences between inductive and deductive reasoning, and they will structure their arguments accordingly. They understand the effective use of the subjunctive, and in cases where there seems little hope for overall agreement, they know how to isolate the points of agreement and build on them. In some cases, where they each want to come to an agreement over language that each of their capitals will find acceptable, they use what is called constructive ambiguity so each may claim the meaning of the language was what they intended.

Diplomats do not like to simply say "no" on something. A diplomat might respond to a proposal by saying "maybe," but it is understood that this means "no." If the topic is more complicated, they may say, "This is something that requires careful study and consideration." If a proposal is so annoying and complicated as to not even merit study, the diplomat might say, "We will need more time to give this the level of attention that it deserves," which of course means "none."

Diplomatic language is understated, and the delivery of spoken interventions is almost always done in a polite unemotional voice. When a diplomat refers to "all means necessary" or "face serious consequences," these are understated ways of referring to the use of force—war. During multilateral meetings diplomats will typically not address each other directly, especially if there is disagreement. An intervention will typically start out with the words "Mr. Chairman" or "Madam Chairwoman," and the grammar of all sentences spoken will be framed so the speaker is addressing the chairman, not the other diplomats. If the French delegate wishes to challenge the U.S. delegate, he or she will not say "I disagree with the U.S. position that . . ." but will instead say (in French) "I would take exception to the position voiced by one nation that. . . ." Where there is agreement the diplomats will be more direct and say, "I wish to echo the views expressed by my distinguished colleague from Russia that. . . ." When a diplomat wishes to make it completely clear that he or she is about to express the key points of an official position he or she will preface these points with "on behalf of my delegation," but when he or she wants to signal that the views about to be expressed are official but not necessarily to his or her liking, the diplomat may interject "on instructions from my capital . . . " When the intervention is over, the diplomat will close with "Thank you Mr. Chairman" or "Thank you Madam Chairwoman." If a diplomat is speaking at the United Nations and his or her native language is one if the six official languages at the UN (Arabic, Chinese, English, French, Russian, and Spanish), he or she will essentially always speak in that language, even if he or she is fluent in one or more other languages. If a speaker comes from a nation where one of these six languages is not spoken, he or she is still required to use one of these six. So diplomats from Brazil, Germany, Israel, Italy, Japan, Portugal, the Scandinavian nations, much of Africa, and many other nations, must all be prepared to speak in a language that is not their native tongue.

Although all of this subtlety of language and nuanced meaning may seem at first an impediment to clear communications, the opposite is true. Diplomats develop a keen sense of the psychology of communications. They understand each other. They are able to communicate across different languages, different cultures, and perhaps different sets of psychological assumptions and get to the heart of complicated issues. Rarely, if ever, are wars fought over misunderstandings between diplomats. The diplomats from different nations may see things differently, and they may represent opposing views, but they are able in their own way to represent their own nation's position, gain access to the position of the other nation, and represent the other nation's position to their own capital in language that can be understood. This is perhaps the most important skill of diplomats—the ability to understand each other's cultural and psychological differences and still communicate clearly.

CURRENT TRENDS, VIRTUAL DIPLOMACY, AND
THE FUTURE: THE PSYCHOLOGY OF DIPLOMACY

Cardinal de Richelieu's form of continuous negotiation between nations—diplomacy—has been in place for over 350 years. For most of those years diplomacy was practiced one-on-one between diplomats representing their own nations and serving as conduits between their nations. But with the arrival in turn of radio, telephone, international travel, cable television, and the Internet, diplomacy is carried out more and more between capitals directly, bypassing the ambassador and the embassy located in the host capital. In recent years there has been an expanding interest in how the use of the Internet can provide what has come to be known as virtual diplomacy—raising Richelieu's "continuous negotiation" to a new level. With jet airplanes and the ease of travel, summitry is more common, and heads of state can easily meet face-to-face, undermining the notion that reliance on ambassadors was the only way for sovereigns to communicate. In addition, even if the head of state himself or herself does not attend a meeting, such near-summitry can be left to the minister of foreign affairs, who, of course, is the immediate supervisor of the ambassador. And on technical or domain-specific issues, working-level bureaucrats will often travel to a capital to liaise directly with their counterparts, again bypassing the ambassador. Indeed, some departments within government (DOD, NASA, and others) develop their own international relations branches, often to the chagrin of the State Department. Additionally, these technical-level experts from the various nations tend to remain active in their fields for years, and they can come to form their own informal personalized networks with their own agendas separate from the priorities of their nations.

And of course, cable television brings the actual citizenry of each nation into closer contact with citizens of other nations and problems around the world. People everywhere watched live as the World Trade Center Towers fell, as Palestinian youths threw rocks at Israeli tanks, and as embedded reporters covered U.S. troops fighting their way to Baghdad. Viewers can also be brought to the locations of famine and massacres. This phenomenon, known as the CNN effect (Livingston & Eachus, 1995), has made "people everywhere more aware of situations that seem to cry out for intervention and more familiar with the human tragedies that accompany these horrible calamities" (Blechman, 1996, p. 288). Debates in the UN Security Council are occasionally carried live on cable, and Internet users can receive daily updates on a variety of topics under discussion at the United Nations. Whereas in the past this level of access to international affairs was the exclusive purview of diplomats, the changing technology has at least provided the general public increased access to international relations on an up-to-the-minute basis. It remains to be seen what the long-term psychological impact of this exposure will be. Some argue that this increased exposure to things international will lead to a wider acceptance of different cultures and people from different nations. Events of recent years do not yet bear out this view. So it remains to be seen how these recent developments will affect the psychology of international relations and the psychology of diplomacy.

REFERENCES

Adair, E. (1929). *The exterritoriality of ambassadors in the sixteenth and seventeenth centuries.* London: Longman.

Berridge, G. R. (2002). *Diplomacy theory and practice.* Hampshire, UK: Palgrave.

Berridge, G., Keens-Soper, M., & Otte, T. (1991). *Diplomatic theory from Machiavelli to Kissinger.* Basingstoke, UK: Palgrave.

Blechman, B. (1996). Emerging from the intervention dilemma. In C. Crocker & F. Hampson (Eds.), *Managing global chaos, sources and responses to international conflict.* Washington, DC: United States Institute of Peace Press.

Borgese, E. (1998). *The oceanic circle: Governing the seas as a global resource.* New York: United Nations Publications.

Callières, F. (1716). De la manière de négocier avec les Souverains. In H. Keens-Soper, & K. Schweizer (Eds.). (1994), *The art of diplomacy.* Lanham, MD: University Press of America.

Chicago Times, October 9, 1862.

Freeman, C. W. (1994). *The diplomat's dictionary.* Washington, DC: USIP.

Kissinger, H. (1994). *Diplomacy.* New York: Simon & Schuster.

Livingston, S., & Eachus, T. (1995). Humanitarian crises and U.S. foreign policy: Somalia and the CNN effect reconsidered. *Political Communication 12*(4), 415.

Queller, D. (1967). *The office of ambassador in the Middle Ages.* Princeton, NJ: Princeton University Press.

Rapoport, A. (1968). In A. Clausewitz, *On war.* New York: Penguin.

Young, E. (1966). The development of the law of diplomatic relations. *British yearbook of international law 1964.* London and New York: Oxford University Press.

Zhou Enlai. (1954). In C. W. Freeman (1977), *The diplomat's dictionary.* Washington, DC: USIP.

2

A Psychologist in the Diplomat's Court: A Primer

Chris E. Stout

"The psychology of diplomacy." Such a deceptively simple-sounding concept. Seemingly simple and straightforward, yet quite difficult to pin down. In the long process of getting this book together, senior editor Harvey Langholtz and I found this out in his work with diplomats and my work with psychologists. We found elusiveness in thinking about concepts, theory, and application. We found very different perspectives between contributing authors herein and in the manuscripts we could not make use of. We struggled with the concept ourselves (and I still do). Harvey taught me early on that war represents not only a failure of diplomacy, but also a failure of psychology.

The point of this chapter is to explore how this author came to conceptualize "the psychology of diplomacy." By being the junior editor of the book, this author has learned much more than would have been taught in this vastly complex area. However, the exploration of this area has led to the recognition that there are an abundant number of areas and ways within the province of what psychology can offer.

NGOS AND PSYCHOLOGISTS

One of the major forays for this author into this knotty area of work is the honor of being chosen to serve for a year under the guidance of Corann Oko-rududu, EdD, as a special projects representative for Division 9 (Society for the Psychological Study of Social Issues, or SPSSI) of the American Psychological Association to the United Nations (UN). Division 9 had earned the distinction of holding Non-Governmental Status with the United Nations a number of years prior to the American Psychological Association's more recent attainment of such. Furthermore, the division's status is that of a "Non-Governmental Organization in Consultative Status with the United Nations," thus holding even greater regard within the UN.

Prior to the involvement with the UN, this author did not hold much familiarity with Non-Governmental Organizations (NGOs). NGOs perhaps are best explained in the context of what they are not. Obviously, they are not actors, agencies, or operations of the state, country, or nation (i.e., government). But they are also *not* intergovernmental organizations, such as the United Nations Commission on Human Rights (UNCHR). Well-known examples of NGOs currently are Amnesty International or the International Rescue Committee. Schwenninger (2000) notes that "NGOs have delivered more development assistance worldwide than the UN has . . . ," but not including the funds ponied up via the International Monetary Fund (IMF) and the World Bank. (Which is interesting in itself.)

NGOs have supporters from all varieties of political perspectives (conservative to liberal) and causes (environmental, human rights, sustainability, health care, education, and on and on). In a sense, like their governmental counterparts, they all have "political" agendas. This is likely perfectly fine; however, sometimes such a bias may be forgotten or less obviously visible when thinking of NGOs generally.

This author's time at the UN as part of APA Division 9's NGO marked access to many areas and resources to the UN in New York, which can not only be a heady and exciting experience, it can also be sometimes intimidating as well. Protocol is critical, and rules of order seemed to be innumerable—where one can go depending on what meetings are going on, the ability to provide, or limitation from providing, position papers or presentations to members but only after first getting approval from your own internal organization's committees, et cetera. Such are likely needed in order to avoid chaos, but it also seems, as in any bureaucracy, that much could also be done to streamline methods as well.

Perhaps one of the best ways in which to engage in these processes was the expectation that individuals working as representatives would work on a specific project during their tenure. Such provides the opportunity to seek out diplomatic experts, learn the ropes firsthand, and (hopefully) create an end product that may be of some help. With the counsel and direction of Dr. Okorududu and Peter Walker, PhD, it became this author's goal to work on crafting a position paper that would need to be first approved by the Society for the Psychological Study of Social Issues before it ever would see the light of day at the General Assembly Building. Once such approval was gained, the Preparatory Committee for the Special Session of the General Assembly on the Implementation of the Outcome of the World Summit for Social Development and Further Initiatives would have to then approve it.

The paper ran the gauntlet of approvals and after some fine-tuning was accepted for distribution for the Second Preparatory Session of the Preparatory Committee for the Special Session of the General Assembly on the Implementation of the Outcome of the World Summit for Social Development. It was very exciting and quite an honor that shall remain with this author forever.

The topic was "A Mental Health Approach to Enhancing Implementation of the Copenhagen Program for Action." Its focus was on the psychological aspects of a document known as the "Copenhagen Declaration of 1995," which dealt with sustainable development. The perspective this author formulated was that despite its centrality to all facets of human development and functioning, psychosocial well-being and mental health needs have been historically neglected by the international community.

The five-year review of progress on the implementation of commitments to social development made at Copenhagen in 1995 provided an important opportunity to advance implementation of the Copenhagen Declaration and Platform for Action by placing psychosocial well-being and mental health needs of all people at the center of sustainable social development. Broadly speaking, "mental health is a state of well-being in which the individual realizes his or her ability, can work productively and fruitfully, and is able to contribute to his or her community" (Desjarlais, Eisenberg, Good, & Kleinman, 1995). As such, it includes optimal psychosocial functioning—not just the absence of mental and behavioral dysfunctions.

Thus, in a bit of a paradoxical fashion, the document's title somewhat reductionistically suggested that common, ubiquitous threads of psychological factors run through the issues of sustainable development and as such must include psychological considerations in order to be optimally successful. This notion, and thus title, was known as "Mental Health: The Most Common Denominator." In this concept, psychosocial well-being and mental health, economic and social development, and sustainability are interrelated processes of human development. Accordingly, psychosocial well-being and mental health affect and are affected by poverty, unemployment, and social disintegration— all barriers to social development targeted for national and global commitment and action at the 1995 World Summit for Social Development. Mental health is on par with biomedical factors in determining the quality of life, productivity, and mortality rates. Without mental health there is no health. Without health there is no sustainability in social and economic development.

The Copenhagen Declaration recognizes this critical relationship of social development to mental health and human well-being by acknowledging the importance of addressing underlying structural causes and their "distressing consequences" in order to reduce "uncertainly and insecurity" in the life of people; the need for societal responses to both "material and spiritual needs of individuals, families, and communities"; the reciprocal connection between social development and social justice on the one hand and "peace and security" on the other; the conviction that "far too many people, particularly women and children, are vulnerable to stress" and that "the goals and objectives of social development require continuous efforts to reduce and eliminate major sources of social distress.

Accordingly, the review of outcomes of the Copenhagen Declaration and Platform for Action must call attention to actions called for in the platform to address psychosocial and mental health needs as significant factors in social development. These actions include: ensuring the highest attainable standard of physical and mental health and access of all to primary health care (Commitment 6, p. 22); expanding access to health care services and putting into effect public policies that empower people to enjoy good health and productivity throughout their lives, identified as 2 out of 12 features of an enabling environment for people-centered, sustainable development (p. 43, bullets 9 & 11); improving the situation and protecting the rights of children in especially difficult circumstances (p. 75, item e); establishing policies to enhance the equality of status, welfare, and opportunity of girls, especially in regard to health, nutrition, literacy, and education (Commitment 5, item f, p. 21); improving the situation of older persons, including those who are exploited and physically or psychologically neglected or abused (Item 40b, p. 76); and implementing specific public health and social services to prevent and eliminate problems created by all forms of violence, crime, illicit drugs, and substance abuse (F79, p. 107).

In order to set a framework for understanding the problems of unaddressed mental illness, I discussed the social and economic costs of psychosocial distress and mental illness by noting that during the past decade, there has been increasing recognition within the United Nations system of the negative social and economic impact of impaired mental health and mental illnesses. In the Secretary General's first report to the 46th General Assembly on the implementation of the *Guiding Principles for Developmental Social Welfare Policies and Programmes in the Near Future* (A/46/414), he drew attention to the fact that suicide had been found to be a growing problem, particularly among youth. In the 48th session he made recommendations based on empirical findings that served as a basis for courses of action for governments to consider, such as including "social policy components within comprehensive national strategies for dealing with severe dysfunctional conditions, including anxiety, stress, and suicide."

Research findings across a range of studies undertaken in different countries have established that "major mental disorders take an enormous toll, in all societies, in human suffering, disability, and the loss of community resources." The *1993 World Development Report* (World Bank, 1993) estimated that worldwide mental illnesses account for about 15.1 percent in women and 16.1 percent in men aged 15 to 44 of the Global Burden of Disease measured in Disability Adjusted Life Years (DALYs). These rates exceed those of cancer, heart disease, or tuberculosis.

Between 5 and 7 percent of the world's population is estimated to suffer from clinical depression at any given time. Depression is also economically burdensome because it is the primary cause of disability worldwide. Depression's impact is further amplified in that a depressed individual is four times more likely to suffer a heart attack, and those having a heart attack are four times more likely not to survive it. Although the prevalence of depression is remarkably similar across societies, data from a World Bank study (1993) have revealed that depressive disorders account for close to 30 percent of the disability from neuropsychiatric disorders among women in developing countries but only 12 percent of that among men. Moreover, this gender disparity was even more pronounced in underserved populations.

Despite the prevalence of mental illness in developed, developing, and transitional societies, many individuals are reluctant to seek treatment for psychological illness because of stigma. This is compounded by the limited availability of psychosocial and mental health services, especially in developing and transitional societies. Affordable access is of great concern as treatments for mental illness have improved greatly in the past 15 years, as have their scientific bases. Psychological interventions have a broad empirical foundation that demonstrates improved mental health, productivity, biological health, longevity, quality of life, and economic cost savings. In the United States, for example, the National Institute of Mental Health found that the cost of providing mental health services produced a resultant indirect cost savings of $2.5 billion annually.

After establishing a context of perspective, the expectation is to then make recommendations. I crafted the paper to communicate psychology's deep commitment to the betterment of human welfare and well-being and our extensive experience in the research and treatment of mental illnesses. I came to learn that the issues of social development, conflict resolution and peacekeeping, and health status are broad and encompassing areas of concern within the UN's mission. However, it seemed that the Secretariat, member states, and UN agencies needed to further recognize and take action to reduce the breadth and depth of the often-underrecognized linkages of psychosocial distress and mental illness to poverty, unemployment, and social disintegration. Thus I suggested the following further initiatives:

1. Use psychosocial well-being and mental health as indicators of economic and social development, to be employed in all assessments of progress in implementing the Copenhagen Platform for Action. Such assessments should be disaggregated in terms of gender, age, minority group, and other vulnerable group categories.

2. Enhance implementation and monitoring of the impact of General Assembly Resolution 46/119 of December 17, 1991, "The protection of persons with mental illness and the improvement of mental health care," which supports actions to attain full mental health for all people.

3. Encourage and support the adoption and follow-up by the General Assembly of the Resolution on Women and Mental Health (E/CN.6/199/L.8/Revl), with emphasis on special groups, which recognizes that women have significant and growing mental health needs, particularly in underserved populations that have been relatively neglected in the past.

4. Prioritize provision and rehabilitation of medical and psychological services to respond to the needs of individuals recently traumatized or in crisis; to support the rehabilitation of those who have been physically maimed or psychologically trau-

matized; and, whenever adopting measures under Article 41 of the United Nations Charter, to give consideration to their impact on children, in order to provide appropriate humanitarian exemptions.

5. Provide special training on the protection, rights, and welfare of the psychologically traumatized and mentally ill for personnel involved in peacemaking, peacekeeping, and peace-building activities.

6. Monitor situations of armed conflict, humanitarian emergencies, transition to peace in postconflict situations, economic and social development programs, and other forms of intervention in terms of assessments of their impact on mental health/health as well as associated cost savings.

It is this author's belief that the constant and cumulative voice of psychologically trained professionals will do much to inform diplomats as they engage in their craft. Being a part of an NGO provides the opportunity for such, as well as the opportunity to learn much.

But there are instances in which NGOs may engage in wrongdoing. For example, three major Colombian NGOs have been convincingly accused, as reported in the *Wall Street Journal*, of allegedly disseminating through quite proper channels misinformation and false accusations in order to mire and distract government officials in legal wangling (Mendoza, 2001). In some instances, they reportedly aided groups involved in murders, disappearances, letter bombings, planting land mines in farming areas that dismembered children, and bombing waterworks and bridges. Thus, they created a very diabolical effect by using human rights as a weapon against the very people that needed protection.

There are other risks to look out for also. "Some NGOs have developed through grass-roots support to survive intact, but most are highly dependent on the accumulated wealth of the richest one percent of Americans in the foundations created and fueled by their philanthropy. From this angle, global civil society looks more like the product of an emerging plutocratic order than an answer to the question of world order" (Schwenninger, 2000, p. 42). Perhaps NGOs serve best as useful adjuncts supporting state-to-state cooperation through international organizations and direct provision of services.

PSYCHOLOGY'S ROLES

Psychology often finds itself in its varied manifestations—clinical, industrial/organizational, counseling, and so forth dealing with tertiary responses to situations—helping survivors dealing with psychological trauma of war and associated stresses. Many professionals operating within health care venues and public health arenas are able to sometimes infiltrate prevention into systems. Social and political psychology, policy analyst/psychologists, and other specialties construct and/or analyze situations and offer theories and helpful approaches. Daniel Dodgen, from APA's Public Policy Office, shared the following anecdote to make the point of various levels of intervention:

Mary, Bob, and Sue were having a picnic by the river. Suddenly, Mary noticed that there were babies floating down the river. Quickly, she ran to the river and began pulling the babies out before they drowned. She turned to Bob for help, but he was heading upstream. "I'm going to see if I can help these babies learn to swim, or at least give them something to hold onto," he shouted. "Maybe then they won't be so bad off when they get to you." Mary then turned to Sue for help, but noticed that she, too, was heading upstream. "Where are you going?" asked Mary. "I'm going to the head of the river," she replied, "To find out who's throwing the babies in the river and make 'em stop."

So it seems that psychology can intervene likewise at various levels and points. For example, former president Jimmy Carter, in a May 27, 1999, *New York Times* Op-Ed piece, stated, "Because of its dominant role in United Nations Security Council and NATO, the United States tends to orchestrate global peacemaking. Unfortunately, many of these efforts are seriously flawed. We have become increasingly inclined to sidestep time-tested premises of negotiation, which in most cases prevent deterioration of a bad situation and at least offer the prospect of a bloodless solution. Abusive leaders can best be induced by the simultaneous threat of consequences and the promise of reward—at least legitimacy within an international community." Such suggested interventions rely on basic behavioral theory and are set within a context of cultural and political understanding.

On a larger scale, there have been times in which the United States has boxed itself into having to take punitive action against a nation, "the often tragic result of this final decision is that already oppressed citizens suffer, while the oppressor may feel free of further consequences if he perpetuates even worse crimes. Through control of the news media, he is often made to seem heroic by defending his homeland against foreign aggression and shifting blame for the economic or political woes away from himself" (Carter, 1999). Thus, it would appear that some despots have a better grasp of psychological manipulation of a situation than the superpowers that be.

This is not at all to suggest that psychology has all the answers; it is indeed much easier to exercise 20/20 hindsight, but there are already some mechanisms in place. The United States has the National Academy of Sciences model: the National Academy is one of four organizations under the National Academy umbrella that also includes National Academy of Engineering, the Institute of Medicine, and the National Research Council. Each of the four organizations has a government structure composed of distinguished members and an active staff. The National Academy serves in an advisory capacity on matters concerning science and technology. The Institute of Medicine serves this role in the health care arena. Most studies by the academies are conducted in response to requests from government agencies. The studies often provide valuable input about matters of public policy. However, such a model does not fit as well under the circumstances of conflict with lives being lost daily. The luxury of time for diligent research is often unaffordable. But perhaps there could be improvements made on the establishment of principles, procedures, and information/consultative access when needed that would reflexively include psychological input as an integral component, not an appendage nor afterthought. It is then psychology's responsibility to demonstrate evidence for its value.

Kofi Annan (2002) has noted that his vision for the United Nations' priories for the future are to promote democracy, prevent conflict, and lessen the burden of global poverty. But there also needs to be some temperance concerning the concept of democracy. Don Edward Beck notes in his *Stages of Social Development* (2001) that " 'Democracy,' comes in many different variations, hues, and levels of complexity. There are good reasons why humans have created *survival clans, ethnic tribes, feudal empires, ancient nations, corporate states,* and *value communities* in our long bio-psycho-social-spiritual ascent. However, there is support for focusing on diversity and dialogue, and better understanding the needs of individuals." All of these certainly seem to fall within the purview of psychology and provide an opportunity for psychology to help.

TRAINING MODELS

A relatively new kind of graduate program has developed known as whole systems design. The concept behind whole systems design embodies a wholistic perception of the world, both intellectually and experientially. Such programs enable students to gain a better understanding of the natural and social environment in which they live as well as to explore how best to demonstrate their creativity and leadership in a complex interrelated world.

The systems approach enables students to conceptualize, recognize, and describe the complexity and recurring patterns pounding natural and human systems (Antioch University, 2002). Systems theory provides a framework for synthesizing knowledge as opposed to breaking into narrow, isolated areas of study. Design is inclusive of activities ranging from processes for creating new systems to methods of comprehensive problem solving. In the first instance, design deals with creativity and innovation. In the latter it focuses on primarily systems planning and management. Wholism recognizes that systemic wholes are greater than the simple sum of their parts. It promotes a unified way of being in perceiving that integrates all dimensions of one's experience, including ethical and aesthetic. Such models for learning should bode well for understanding the complexities involved in the psychology of diplomacy.

In using systemic understanding applied to complex social, psychological, and political systems, Beck (2001) notes that

we are witnessing new versions of the historic continental drift as our economic, political, technological, and social worlds are, indeed, being pulled closer together. Further, global problems will require global solutions which, of necessity, will require global thinking. The historic past-present-future timelines will need to be understood. Up stream and down stream viewing points must be maintained. Final state paralysis must be replaced by flow state perspectives. Simplistic car-wash solutions must be replaced by a rich understanding and respect for diversities in people, uniqueness in situations, and inevitable steps and stages in human emergence. Rigid rules, a product of fixed state ideologies, must be supplanted by fluctuating algorithms that engage a world full of variables, lifecycles, wild cards and other complex dynamics that lie at the core of life itself. There are no guarantees; no eternal road maps; no inevitable destinations; no blue print etched in permanent ink. Yet, there are equations, formulas, fractals, consequences, flows, and processes. Each new solution will, over time, create new problems. Human motivations will change as our life conditions get better, or get worse. There are systems within us rather than types of us—stratified decision-making stacks that constantly rearrange themselves in terms of priorities and senses of urgency. Different cultures and subcultures, then, are organic entities that lay on new levels of complexity as changes in life conditions warrant.

More specifically to psychology working within ethnopolitical conflict is a task force headed by Ron Fisher, PhD, and comprised of 30 psychologists from the United States, Canada, Northern Ireland, and South Africa, among other places, members from APA Division 9 (SPSSI) and Division 48 (Society for the Study of Peace Conflict and Violence) and Psychologists for Social Responsibility (O'Connor, 2001). The meeting was supported by a grant from U.S. Institute of Peace, the American Psychological Association, and the Canadian Psychological Association. The result was a curriculum that includes two semesters of institutional training, followed by a four-month internship with students in the field providing trauma relief or conflict resolution in regions worldwide. Programs such as this provide much in the way of concretizing tools and methods for specific training opportunities.

DIRECTION

Of course, this is not to suggest that psychology has cornered the market on truth nor is psychology a panacea for diplomatic functionality. But psychology and psychologists in all their various forms and specialties do have much to offer. Is all this then summed up to be the psychology of diplomacy? Perhaps, perhaps not, but regardless, it offers serious consideration of the role psychology has to offer on the world stage.

It is this author's experience to give talks on activism, especially psychological activism. In these rallying calls, different stories are told, and slides are shown from all over the world. There are statistics and pie charts on terrorist attacks, followed by an X-ray of a shrapnel-laced torso of a suicide-bombing victim. There is a photo of a sniper and then a discussion of the morbid reversals of developmental processes in children in Sarajevo, who were particularly targeted because "When you kill and adult, you kill the past; but when you kill a child, you kill the future." There are the photos of massive graves of the genocide victims and related stories of this author's travel and work in Rwanda. Child soldiers. Civilian casualties of war. Abandoned land mines. Torture victims. Collateral damage. Story after story. Image after image.

This approach was chosen because, as Sante points out,

[A] photograph can enter the mind and reach the heart with the power of immediacy. It affects that part of the psyche where meaning is less dependent upon words and makes an impact more visceral, more elemental, closer to raw experience. People are moved by what they see and read. They respond emotionally, intellectually, and morally, and they realize that there are millions of others who react in a similar way. Around these shared responses a constituency forms. My job is to help reach a broad base of people who translate their feelings into an articulate stance, then through the mechanisms of political and humanitarian organizations bring pressure to bear on the process of change. This dynamic is very difficult to quantify, but I believe it has become part of our collective responsibility. (2000, p. 469)

It is this author's hope that this book has helped to encourage readers to get involved or to do more. Victor Hugo once said: "If a soul is left in the darkness, sins will be committed. The guilty one is not he who commits the sin, but he who causes the darkness." Psychology must do its part to shed light.

REFERENCES

Annan, K. A. (2002). Strategies for world peace: The view of the UN Secretary-General. *The Futurist*, 18–21.

Antioch University. (2002). Program description, WSD Program. Seattle, WA: Author.

Beck, D. E. (2001). Stages of social development: The cultural dynamics that spark violence, spread prosperity, and shape globalization. Personal communication.

Carter, J. (1999, 27 May). Have we forgotten the path to peace? *New York Times*, 27.

Desjarlais, R., Eisenberg, L., Good, B., and Kleinman, A. (1995). *World mental health*. New York: Oxford University Press.

Mendoza, P. A. (2001, 15 June). How Colombia's rebels use "human rights" as a weapon. *Wall Street Journal*, A15.

O'Connor, E. M. (2001, September). From classroom to conflict resolution. *Monitor on Psychology*, 26–27.

Sante, L. (2000). *Inferno*. New York: Phaidon Press.

Schwenninger, S. R. (2000). NGOing global: Can civil society on international scale compensate for the anarchy of world affairs? *Civilization*, 40–41.

World Bank. (1993). *World development report 1993 investing in health*. New York: Oxford University Press.

World Summit for Social Development. (1995). *The Copenhagen declaration and programme of action*. New York: United Nations.

3

Reconciliation between Nations: Overcoming Emotional Deterrents to Ending Conflicts between Groups

Arie Nadler and Tamar Saguy

TWO PERSPECTIVES ON ENDING CONFLICTS: CONFLICT RESOLUTION AND RECONCILIATION

Within psychology the theory and research on the antecedents of conflicts and their ending is subsumed under the term *conflict resolution.* This research and theory assumes that conflict is attributable to actors' disagreement on how to divide valuable resources between them. When the rivals are two countries, the contested resource may be land, and when the rivals are two individuals, this resource may be money. Regardless of the nature of the resource or the identity of the rivals, this perspective implies that the way to end conflict is to negotiate an optimal formula for the division of these resources. Thus, the conflict resolution perspective views the end of conflict as the outcome of the calculus of opposing interests between rational actors.

This general view on the end of conflict has dominated relevant discussions in social psychology in particular (Pruitt, 1998; Pruitt & Carnevale, 1993) and the social sciences in general (Blau, 1964; Homans, 1961). It has found expression in the methodologies that have been used to study these processes (e.g., Prisoner's Dilemma Game, Colman, 1982; Rapoport & Chammah, 1965) and the theoretical explanations that have been offered to account for the ability or lack of ability of the parties to resolve the conflict (Emerson, 1981). Diplomacy can be viewed as the attempt to put these principles into action in the international arena. Although both practitioners (Savir, 1998) and scholars of international relations (Crawford, 2000) acknowledge the role of emotional–psychological factors in the diplomatic process, they view them as background factors and secondary in importance to the actual differences that separate the parties. Operating under these assumptions, diplomats have focused their efforts on ending or preventing conflicts between nations trying to find a formula that will be accepted by the rivals on the division of the contested resources between them.

Another perspective on the end of conflict is the empirical and theoretical discussions that are subsumed under the concept of reconciliation (Bar-Tal, 2000; Itoi, Ohbuchi, & Fukuno, 1996; McCullough, Worthington, & Rachal, 1997). As defined elsewhere (Nadler, 2002; Nadler & Liviatan, in press) the reconciliation perspective views the end of conflict as the result of the removal of the *emotional barriers* that exist between the rivals. These include the emotions that are associated with the parties' perceptions of having been *victimized* by their adversary and feelings of *distrust* that have accumulated during years of conflict. Discussions within this tradition tell us that if these emotional barriers are not removed, the likelihood of reaching an agreement will be relatively low, and that even if an agreement had been reached, it is not likely to hold. When distrust dominates, the parties are unlikely to rely on their adversary's commitments and may refuse to sign an agreement with them, even if the contours of such an agreement are well known and accepted. Regarding feelings of victimization, when parties' attention is focused on past pains inflicted on them by their adversary, they are unable to center on actions that will advance the prospects of future coexistence (Scheff, 1994).

Beyond the potential inhibitory role on parties' ability to reach an agreement, the emotional barriers between the parties may put to naught an agreement after it has already been signed. If parties harbor feelings of distrust toward each other, their postagreement relations are likely to be fraught with misinterpretations and misperceptions of the rival's behavior and intentions. Moreover, the viability of an agreement that had been laboriously achieved will be threatened if the parties do not address feelings that are associated with the past of victimization, such as a need for revenge and lingering feelings of humiliation. This is likely to find expression in reignition of violence. Nowhere is this reality more evident than in 2002 in Tel-Aviv—the time and place in which these words are written. In fact, the Oslo agreements signed in 1993 deliberately avoided addressing issues of the parties' responsibility for past wrongdoings. These agreements were based on the assumption that after some years of gradual building of trust between the two parties they will be more ready to address these thorny emotional issues. The hostilities between Israelis and Palestinians that began in the summer of 2000 suggest that this assumption may have been inaccurate. In fact, the violence that started in October 2000 has deepened the distrust between the two parties and created new memories of pain and victimization. All this serves to again remind us that the end of conflict must be built on two pillars: finding a solution to the actual problems that separate the parties (e.g., division of land) through processes of *conflict resolution,* and addressing the emotional barriers that separate them through processes of *reconciliation.*

The focus of the present chapter is on reconciliation. We shall center on the removal of the emotional barriers on the road to ending international conflicts.

Although our analysis is a general analysis of processes of reconciliation, the examples and the research findings are situated within the context of the conflict between Israelis and Palestinians. In the following sections we shall elaborate on a distinction between two categories of reconciliation: *socioemotional reconciliation* and *trust building reconciliation* and present research that is relevant for each.

TWO ROUTES TO RECONCILIATION: SOCIOEMOTIONAL AND TRUST-BUILDING RECONCILIATION

Two emotional blocks that are grounded in the reality of conflict need to be removed if the parties are to move from a reality of conflict to one of more harmonious relations. The first is made up of feelings that originate from the parties' perceived victimization by their adversary and center on the parties' wish to avenge past wrongdoings done to them. This motivation is driven by the victims' desire to restore perceptions of self-control and self-worth that have been shattered by the experiences of victimization (Frijda, 1993). Such feelings originate from specific events that had occurred during the conflict in which one party views itself as having been unjustifiably victimized by the other. It should be emphasized that being a victim or perpetrator is viewed as psychologically construed and changeable as a function of relevant situational variables that affect an individual or group's construal of itself or its rival as one or the other. This active construal of self and other as victim or perpetrator has a key role in determining the course of conflict and the prospects of ending it. An example of this is the observation made by the first author (Nadler, 2002) and others (Rouhana & Bar-Tal, 1998) that one of the reasons for the protracted nature of the Israeli–Palestinian conflict is the fact that both Israelis and Palestinians view themselves as the only legitimate victim in the conflict. These emphases on active construal of victimhood that is affected by situational variables is consistent with social psychology's basic tenets that social reality is actively construed by actors and that this construal is situationally determined (Ross & Nisbett, 1991).

One way in which feelings of victimhood can be dealt with is by taking revenge on one's rival—the perpetrator. Yet, although revenge is likely to have positive effects on the victim's feelings of self-worth and control (Akhtar, 2002), it is associated with the danger of instigating a new round of violence in the form of revenge that is met by counterrevenge. The emotional barriers that are associated with feelings of victimization can be dealt with more constructively when the adversary apologizes to the victim, who in turn may reciprocate by granting forgiveness to the perpetrator. This route has been discussed by Tavuchis (1991) under the heading of the apology–forgiveness cycle and is labeled in this context of intergroup relations as *socioemotional reconciliation*. In relations between nations and groups it is likely to take on the form of public apologies from leaders who assume responsibility for their nation's wrongdoing. We shall expand on the nature of socioemotional reconciliation and the conditions under which it may be more or less efficient in promoting reconciliation in subsequent sections.

The other emotional block on the road to securing conflict-free relations is the distrust that exists between the adversaries after years of conflict and animosity. To remove this emotional block, the parties must rebuild the trust between them in a prolonged and gradual process. This commonly occurs when the adversaries learn to trust each other as a consequence of successfully cooperating on joint projects. This process has been labeled by students of international relations as peace building (Lederach, 1997) and is labeled here as *trust-building reconciliation.* In their recent review of the place of trust in intergroup negotiations, Kramer and Carnevale (2001) wrote that much of the literature has recognized the circular relation between trust and cooperation. They write: "Trust tends to beget cooperation and cooperation breeds further trust. Therefore, if a cycle of mutual cooperation can be initiated and sustained, trust will develop" (p. 441).

There are several key differences between these two routes toward reconciliation. These are differences in (a) the temporal focus of socioemotional and trust-building reconciliation, (b) the nature of change that each addresses, and (c) the goal that each aims for. Regarding the temporal focus, socioemotional reconciliation suggests that addressing *past wrongdoings* is the only way to build a reconciled future. In fact, this approach to reconciliation suggests that reconciliation between enemies is predicated on the perpetrator's willingness to accept responsibility for past wrongdoings and the victim's willingness to let go of this painful past by granting forgiveness to the perpetrator. Trust-building reconciliation, on the other hand, is not concerned with the painful past. Its emphasis is on *cooperation in the present* as a vehicle to achieve a more trustworthy and reconciled future. It makes the implicit assumption that to let bygones be bygones is the most effective strategy for reconciliation between enemies. Thus, whereas socioemotional reconciliation holds that confronting the painful past is the key to a reconciled future, trust-building reconciliation suggests that cooperation in the present is the key for such a future.

A second difference between these two routes to reconciliation is the nature of change that each implies. Socioemotional reconciliation implies an immediate change in relations between victim and perpetrator once the apology–forgiveness cycle has been completed. After the perpetrator of evil has accepted responsibility for past transgressions and the victim has granted forgiveness, the relations between the two former enemies are said to be transformed from enmity and hatred to reconciled relationships almost instantaneously. Trust-building reconciliation does not assume such a psychological transformation. It is viewed as a gradual and long learning process in which former enemies learn to slowly replace the belief that the adversary holds sinister intentions toward them with the belief that its intentions are benign and that one can base one's own words and actions on the other's promises (Kramer & Carnevale, 2001).

Third, trust building and socioemotional reconciliation aim for different outcomes. Socioemotional reconciliation aims to allow social *integration* between two former enemies, whereas trust-building reconciliation aims to allow conflict-free *separation* between them. Processes of socioemotional reconciliation are intended to heal the rift between two conflicted parties so that they can live together harmoniously within the perimeters of the same social unit. The goal of trust-building reconciliation is more modest. It aims to engender enough trust between the two parties that will allow them to coexist next to each other. To make this difference more concrete, let us use an example of relations between a person and his or her estranged spouse. To end a conflict the two spouses must first decide whether their aim is integration or separation. If they want to be reunited as a family, they may want to address past pains and suffering that they inflicted on each other through a process of socioemotional reconciliation. If, however, they aim to separate, they may want to center on processes of trust-building reconciliation, which will allow them to coexist separately and cooperate on issues that still bind them (e.g., visitation rights for children). This a priori decision on integration or separation as determining the applicability of trust-building or socioemotional reconciliation is not limited to the case of interpersonal conflicts. For example, the nations of the former Yugoslavia must first determine whether they envisage a future of living in the same integrated sociopolitical unit or coexisting as separate sociopolitical units before they embark on socioemotional or trust-building reconciliation.

We will revisit this issue of the links and differences between trust-building and socioemotional reconciliation in a later section when we discuss the applications of the present analysis. Before we move to a more detailed discussion of each of these two routes toward reconciliation and present relevant data, it should be noted that their separate discussion is for the sake of conceptual clarity. In reality these two processes are interdependent. The ability to openly confront the pains of the past (i.e., socioemotional reconciliation) is likely to impact favorably on the trust between the two groups, and the existence of trust will facilitate a confrontation with the painful past.

SOCIOEMOTIONAL RECONCILIATION: REVENGE OR APOLOGY AND FORGIVENESS?

When people and groups have been in conflict they have usually humiliated and harmed each other. Because of this, at the end of conflict the perpetrator has a debt that he or she owes to the victim. This debt must be paid if relations between the former two adversaries are to become more harmonious (Exline & Baumeister, 2000; Hebl & Enright, 1993). This debt is also said to be behind the victims' motivation for revenge. Frijda (1993) has made the observation that revenge is an empowering experience that helps the victim to overcome the feelings of helplessness that are related to having been victimized. The problematic nature of revenge is that because victimhood is actively construed, in many intergroup conflicts *both* parties view themselves as the legitimate victim. They are therefore equally motivated to take revenge of their adversary, and one act of revenge may institute a cycle of revenge that will intensify rather than quell conflict. Nowhere is this process more painfully clear than at the time and place in which these words were written. The violence between Israelis and Palestinians since 2001 and 2002 seems to follow a consistent pattern. A Palestinian's terror attack becomes the impetus for the retaliation that the Israeli army takes, which then becomes the cause for the Palestinian next act of violence, and so it continues to spiral into what seems like an uncontrollable string of loss and destruction.

In commenting on the nature of the apology–forgiveness cycle, Tavuchis writes: "An apology, no matter how sincere or effective, does not and cannot undo what has been done. And yet, in a mysterious way, and according to its own logic, this is precisely what it manages to do" (p. 5). What is the nature of this mystery that Tavuchis refers to? How can words that are exchanged between victim and perpetrator remove the emotional deterrents to ending a conflict? The answer to this lies in the way in which apology and forgiveness fulfill the emotional needs of the perpetrator and the victim, respectively. Regarding the perpetrator, Tavuchis (1991) and Scheff (1994) suggest that the perpetrators of wrongdoings are threatened with being expelled from the moral community to which they belong. Using a similar logic, Baumeister, Stillwell, and Heatherton (1994) suggest that the arousal of guilt is because of a person's fear of being excluded from meaningful close relations with others. By apologizing and accepting responsibility, the perpetrator acknowledges a debt to be repaid to the victim for having perpetrated these wrongdoings. The victim then may forgive, in which case the debt is canceled, or he or she may seek material compensation that will allow the cancellation of this debt. In either case, however, the threat to the perpetrator's membership in the moral community is lessened. Regarding the victims, they hold the key to canceling the perpetrator's debt. They can grant or withhold forgiveness or make it conditional on some form of material compensation. In either case, the victim is empowered by this and gains greater equality with the perpetrator.

The research on the effects of perpetrators' apologies and the determinants of the victims' willingness to forgive has focused on interpersonal relations. We shall briefly review this empirical evidence and its implications for the intergroup reconciliation.

Research has found that apologies have positive effects on the victim's perceptions of the perpetrator (Baron, 1990) and the victim's feelings of self-worth (Obhuci & Sato, 1994). Further, independent observers who viewed a transgressor that had apologized for his transgressions viewed him more positively than those who viewed a transgressor who had not apologized (Darby & Schlenker, 1982). Regarding the operational definition of apology, this research suggests that apologies must contain (a) the perpetrator's expression of empathy for the suffering of the victim, and/or (b) acceptance of responsibility for having caused these sufferings. Yet, sometimes apologies do not exert such positive effects on the victim and his or her relations with the perpetrator. Research indicates that when the perpetrator who apologized is perceived as being untrustworthy, the offended party is not likely to accept the apology, and the likelihood that it will reciprocate by granting forgiveness is relatively low (Obhuci & Sato, 1994). Moreover, when the perpetrators are perceived as untrustworthy, they are regarded less positively if they had apologized than if they had not (Darby & Schlenker, 1989). Similar emphases on the role of trust as a prerequisite to apology to promote reconciliation have been made by Tavuchis (1991) and Scheff (1994). Taken together, this highlights the fact that in the absence of a basic level of trust between the perpetrator and the victim, apologies are likely to be perceived by the victim as a manipulative ploy and are likely to reduce the prospects for reconciliation.

Applied to the arena of international conflict, the preceding suggests that genuine apologies in the form of acceptance of responsibility or expression of empathy for the rival's conflict-related suffering can contribute to the removal of the emotional barrier of feelings of victimization and contribute to reconciliation between the parties. This has been well understood by political leaders. In the last three decades there have been numerous examples in which a leader of one nation or group has apologized for the wrongdoings that had been perpetrated by his or her group. A famous example is the memorable gesture of the then German chancellor, Willy Brandt, who during a visit to a Nazi concentration camp fell to his knees and asked the forgiveness of the Jewish victims of the Nazi regime. Another prominent example is President Alwyn of Chile's famous speech on Chilean national TV in which he apologized for the crimes committed by the Pinochet regime. A third, and more recent, example is the apology of Pope John Paul II to women, Jews, and other minorities that were the victims of persecution by the Catholic Church. In all these examples leaders have tried to deal with the emotional barriers that were attributable to past victimization by accepting responsibility for these wrongdoings and apologizing for them. This has been done with the belief that perpetrators must openly accept responsibility for past wrongdoings and apologize to the victim if they wish to reconcile with them. This phenomenon has been aptly labeled the "politics of apology" (Cunningham, 1999).

In spite of this, social psychological research and theory has remained mute regarding the role of apologies in reducing tensions between groups. One reason for this may be the theoretical emphasis in social psychology on cognitive, as opposed to affective, processes that govern social behavior in general and intergroup behavior in particular. Another reason may be the religious overtones that are associated with concepts such as forgiveness or reconciliation from which social scientists wish to disassociate themselves (Akhtar, 2002).

To study these processes we conducted experimental investigations of the effects of a Palestinian leader's acceptance of responsibility for Israeli conflict-related suffering and his expression of empathy for these sufferings on Israelis' readiness to reconcile with Palestinians. In these studies Israeli students read what they believed to be a speech made by a Palestinian leader that had been delivered to the Palestinian parliament. This two-page speech consisted of an analysis of the situation in the Middle East and ended differently for different participants, according to the experimental conditions to which they were assigned. Half the participants read a speech that ended with an expression of empathy for the conflict-related suffering of Israelis, whereas the other half were not exposed to such expressions of empathy. Further, half the participants were exposed to statements in which the Palestinian leader accepted Palestinian responsibility for having caused these sufferings whereas the other half were not. This allowed us to experimentally assess the relative effects of expressions of empathy and acceptance of responsibility on willingness to reconcile with the enemy. Importantly, half the Israeli participants were designated, on the basis of a premeasure, as having relatively high trust in Palestinians whereas the other half was designated as low trust. Finally, we ran two parallel experiments. The first was conducted in June–July 2000, about 4 months before the outbreak of the current wave of hostilities between Israelis and Palestinians, and the second 18 months later, at the height of these hostilities.

The results of the two experiments indicate that high-trust Israelis who had been exposed to expressions of empathy for their compatriots' suffering perceived the speaker, Palestinians in general, and prospects for reconciliation with Palestinians more favorably than high-trust Israelis who had not been exposed to similar expressions of empathy. An opposite pattern indicates that low-trust Israelis who had been exposed to similar expressions of empathy had worse perceptions of the speaker, Palestinians in general, and prospects for reconciliation with them than low-trust Israelis who had not been exposed to similar expressions of empathy. In other words, for low-trust Israelis apology in the form of expression of empathy backfired.

A number of points should be emphasized here. First, these findings provide an empirical demonstration of the power of apology as a vehicle to reduce tensions in the international arena. Second, these effects were obtained during times of relative calm as well as during times when the conflict between Israelis and Palestinians has been red and glowing. Third, in these studies expression of empathy for the pains of one's adversary, rather than acceptance of responsibility for these conflict-related pains, was a more potent determinant of reconciliation. It has been suggested that this is because of the fact that the recipients of apology were the stronger party in the conflict, Israelis, for whom expressions of empathy may be more psychologically important than acceptance of responsibility. This is because such expressions, which acknowledge Israeli suffering and victimhood, reduce the threat to membership in the "moral community" more effectively than do statements about accepting responsibility for these sufferings. It may be that for the weaker side in the conflict, acceptance of responsibility, which acknowledges a debt to them, would be more psychologically important than expression of empathy (for a fuller discussion see Nadler & Leviatan, in press). Finally, the findings highlight the important role of trust in this context. On the background of lack of trust, attempts to lower the socioemotional barriers between parties to a conflict through apology may create higher barriers rather than removing them. This brings us to a discussion of trust and trust-building reconciliation. We shall first consider the concept of trust and its links with socioemotional and trust-building reconciliation and then continue to a more detailed discussion of trust-building reconciliation.

TRUST-BUILDING RECONCILIATION: LEARNING TO TRUST THROUGH COOPERATION

Trust: Definition and Links with Socioemotional and Trust-Building Reconciliation

Trust is thought of as the "glue that holds relationships together" (Lewicki & Wiethoff, 2000, p. 86). Within psychology, personality researchers have viewed the tendency to trust others as a stable personality disposition that is rooted in early learning experiences (Rotter, 1971) and psychosocial development (Erikson, 1963). Social psychologists have focused on situational conditions that can either destroy or build trust (Kramer & Carnevale, 2001). A common thread to these, and other theoretical perspectives on trust (e.g., sociology, Gambetta, 1998; political science, Hardin, 1992), is the idea that when one has a high level of trust in others, he or she attributes to them positive intentions and is willing to base judgments and actions on their words and deeds. Distrust implies that one attributes sinister motivations to the other and desires to protect the self from the other's conduct (Kramer & Carnevale, 2001).

There are different bases on which trust can be based. Two bases of trust are relevant to the present discussion of socioemotional and trust-building reconciliation (Lewicki & Wiethoff, 2000). The first is labeled calculus-based trust and is determined by the outcomes that the parties obtain from maintaining the relationship relative to the costs of severing it. This trust is built slowly and gradually in many interactions that test the other's trustworthiness. Calculus-based trust is fragile in that it can be destroyed by one or a few actions that imply that the other cannot be trusted. A second basis of trust is identification-based trust. This type of trust is characteristic of parties who are in a unit relationship and share a common group identity (e.g., familial or organizational identity). Parties whose relations are based on this type of trust perceive that their interests are fully protected and represented by the other, and therefore there is no need for ongoing monitoring of the other's behavior toward oneself or one's group.

There is a conceptual link between the distinction of trust-building and socioemotional reconciliation and the distinction between identification-based and calculus-based trust. Trust-building reconciliation is a process that aims to yield calculus-based trust. It is aimed to enable two adversarial parties to coexist in a conflict-free environment in which parties do not attribute malevolent intentions to their counterpart and believe that they can base their conduct on the other's words and deeds. Socioemotional reconciliation is conceptually correlated with identification-based trust in that both emphasize the goal of social integration between two actors who share a common group identity. Finally, Lewicki and Wiethoff suggest that oftentimes calculus-based trust must be established before identification-based trust can be built. In a similar way, the data on the role of trust as a determinant of the effects of the perpetrator's expression of empathy and acceptance of responsibility on the victim's willingness to reconcile tell us that a sufficient level of trust must exist before acts of socioemotional reconciliation can proceed.

Conflict is likely to put a strain on the trust between two rivals, and protracted and intense intergroup conflict (e.g., the Israeli–Palestinian conflict) is likely to destroy it completely. During such times each party seeks to maximize its gains at the expense of the other, commits acts of violence against its rival, and engages in much deception and concealment to further its goals. These actions reinforce each side's perception of the other as having negative intentions toward one's group and encourages the view that one cannot one's own conduct on the promises and commitments made by the adversary. The end of conflict is predicated on the willingness to base action on the commitments that the rival undertakes. When distrust dominates, this is difficult if not impossible. In their recent review of the literature on trust, Lewicki and Wiethoff write: "[A]crimonious conflict often serves to increase distrust which makes conflict resolution even more difficult and problematic" (2000, p. 85).

Conditions for Effective Trust-Building Reconciliation

How can trust be rehabilitated? Research on the antecedents of conflict and cooperation indicates that trust is likely to replace distrust when the parties engage in successive interactions in which they are concerned simultaneously with their own interests and the welfare of their counterpart (Pruitt, 1998). This dual-concern model suggests that "self" and "other" concerns are not opposites of the same continuum, but two independent dimensions, and it is likely to dominate when both parties work toward achieving a common goal. In successive interactions of this kind parties learn to be aware of and sensitive to the concerns of the "other" and to gradually become more willing to base their own behavior on the other's words and deeds. In a similar vein, Sherif et al. (Sherif, Harvey, White, Hood, & Sherif, 1961) indicate that successive events in which rival groups had cooperated to achieve a common goal (i.e., superordinate goal) resulted in reduction in the level of intergroup conflict.

These findings suggest that when members of two rival groups work jointly to achieve a common goal, they are, temporarily at least, embracing a larger group identity that subsumes their separate identities, and this reduces intergroup conflict. This idea that cognitive redrawing of the boundaries of the two rival groups that produces a large and inclusive group reduces intergroup conflict has received more recent and direct support in the work of Gaertner and his colleagues on recategorization. They report less negative perceptions and behavior toward a rival group when members of groups A and B had been induced to see themselves as members of an inclusive group C (Gaertner, Mann, Dovidio, Murrell, & Pomare, 1990; Gaertner, Mann, Murrell, & Dovidio, 1989). Applied to the present context of trust-building reconciliation, this research suggests that trust can be enhanced through successive experiences of cooperating to achieve a common goal, which induces members of the rival groups to view themselves, albeit temporarily, as members of an inclusive common in-group. Research on the contact hypothesis indicates that such cooperation between rivals will lessen intergroup tensions and lead to more trust when it is a *sustained* cooperation between *equals* to achieve *common goals* in a *supportive* context (Pettigrew, 1998).

Applying this to the relations between the rival nations in the Middle East, the multilateral negotiations that were established at the 1991 Madrid conference seem to have been based on a similar logic. In these multilateral negotiations, parties from the region negotiated issues that were common to all of them. Issues such as water shortages in the Middle East, quality of the environment in the region, or the promotion of tourism to archeological sites in the Middle East were discussed. Such experiences could have encouraged Israelis and Arabs living in the region to view themselves as equal peoples in the Middle East who share common problems. This work should have increased the trust between the rival sides and allowed them to tackle the thorny bilateral issues in an atmosphere of greater trust.

Trust Building between Israelis and Palestinians: A Study on Key Factors in the Success of Trust-Building Reconciliation

To explore the processes of trust building between enemies we studied the perceptions of Israelis and Palestinians who were involved in trust-building projects. These were common in the period between the signing of the Oslo agreement in 1993 and the outbreak of hostilities between Israelis and Palestinians in October 2000. Yet, they did not disappear. Even at the end of 2002, when these words were written, when trust between the parties was at its lowest, Israelis and Palestinians continued to cooperate in various areas. The projects that our interviewees were involved in included joint activities in the fields of education, commerce, agriculture, medicine, arts, science, and culture. The interviews were conducted in the second half of 2001 and the first half of 2002. Each lasted about 90 minutes, and interviewees were 10 Israelis and 4 Palestinians. Due to the tensions between Israelis and Palestinians during this time and the fact that the interviewee, the second author, is an Israeli, the number of Palestinian interviewees is smaller than that of Israeli interviewees. The purpose of the interviews was to learn more about the conditions that facilitate or hinder trust-building reconciliation.

The interviews were half structured and consisted of open conversations that were designed to obtain information on specific issues. On the basis of pilot interviews and literature on peace building (Kelman, 1998; Lederach, 1997), we sought to obtain data on our interviewees' perceptions on the role of (a) power relations, (b) social identity processes, (c) cultural factors, and (d) third party's involvement in making cooperation on joint project an effective trust-building mechanism. We shall briefly describe some of the major findings.

The critical factor for the success of common projects as trust-building mechanisms is the existence of equality between the parties. Consistent with similar emphases in the relevant literature (Amir & Ben-Ari, 1986; Cook, 1985; Pettigrew, 1998), intergroup cooperation led to greater trust and improved relations only when it was based on equality between interactants. When there is an objective power asymmetry between the parties, as is the case between Israelis and Palestinians, equality needs to be deliberately planned and systematically implemented. Thus, for example, decisions about the design and implementation of the project must be made jointly, and a successful project is one that is administered jointly. Our interviewees also stressed that equality must have concrete expressions. A majority noted that the place of meeting should alternate between Israeli and Palestinian cities and that the budget should be either split evenly or administered jointly with full exposure. When inequality dominates, common projects seem to deepen distrust.

The second issue that our interviewees focused on was the role of social identity processes in trust-building reconciliation. There is tension between two approaches in this context. On the basis of relevant research and theory in social psychology (Brown, 1995), we have labeled one as the recategorization approach and the other as the subcategorization approach. Briefly stated, the recategorization approach seeks to de-emphasize the two conflicting identities and suggests that a cooperative contact will lead to greater trust when two conflicting identities are contained within a larger common identity. The subcategorization approach seeks to emphasize the meeting between two distinct identities and suggests that cooperative contact will lead to greater trust when the identities of the two groups are made salient. Thus, for example, when a group of Palestinian and Israeli cardiologists meet to work on a common medical project the recategorization approach suggests a de-emphasis of the distinct national identities of the two groups and an emphasis on their common identity as physicians instead. The subcategorization approach, on the other hand, would suggest framing the project as one in which Israelis and Palestinians meet to cooperate on a medical project. This would retain, and even emphasize, the separate national identities of the two groups.

Our interviews suggest that the preference of one model over the other is linked to the group's power position. Palestinians show a preference for a sub-categorization model in which each group retains its distinct national identity whereas Israelis have a preference for a recategorization model in which separate national identities are de-emphasized and a premium is placed on the common and inclusive group identity (e.g., physicians). One reason for this differential preference may be the fact that the Palestinians, as the weaker party, desire a sociopolitical change, and to that end they want to accentuate the differences that exist between the groups. The Israelis, as the stronger group, are motivated to maintain the existing status quo between the two groups, and embracing a common identity lessens the conflict and with it the need for sociopolitical change.

Our interviewees have also referred to the equalizing role of a third party in trust-building projects. In fact, when a relatively powerful third party is involved in a project (e.g., American, European, UN), the perceived power position of the two adversarial groups becomes more equal relative to this more powerful third party. Finally, cultural differences play a significant role in the success of trust-building projects. Different cultural definitions on what constitutes a binding commitment (e.g., a signed agreement, an oral agreement, etc.) can result in misunderstandings and deepen mistrust. Cultural differences are also linked to the issue of power. Some of our interviewees noted that the discourse that places an emphasis on conflict resolution is a Westernized discourse with which Israelis feel more comfortable than do Palestinians. This has resulted in the perception that Palestinians are often put in a disadvantage in such a cultural context. These perceptions reinforce Hubbard's (1999) observation that past discussion on intergroup contact has disregarded the link between equality and cultural differences.

In all, our interviews highlight the role of equality as a prerequisite for the success of trust-building reconciliation. Equality can be introduced directly into a project, as when parties decide on an even split of the budget between them, or indirectly, as when the parties include a more powerful third party as their partner. This critical role of *equality* in the *cooperation* between adversaries is consistent with the emphases garnered from five decades of research on the contact hypothesis (Pettigrew, 1998, 2001). The role of the other two conditions of *supportive context* and a *psychologically meaningful contact* are demonstrated in the responses of our interviewees regarding the fate of those trust-building projects that continued during the period of violent clashes between Israelis and Palestinians.

During the first seven years after the signing of the Oslo agreements there was a *supportive context* for trust-building efforts between Israelis and Palestinians. This allowed the creation of many such projects. Since October 2000 the context has been much less supportive and the number of such projects has been reduced dramatically. We asked our interviewees what they thought accounted for the survival of the projects that did continue. A recurring theme in the answers was the quality of interpersonal relations between Israelis and Palestinians who stood at the helm of a particular project. When relations were close and trustworthy a project continued in spite of the nonsupportive context. Other reasons seem to be related to the content of the project. Those that were relevant to real and pressing needs (e.g., food-related agricultural projects) stood a better chance of survival than those that focused on less-concrete and less-pressing needs (e.g., cultural projects). We conclude by again noting that *cooperation* that is done on an *equal basis* in a *supportive context* and allows for the creation of *meaningful interpersonal relations* is likely to result in successful trust-building reconciliation.

CONCLUSIONS AND IMPLICATIONS

The present chapter departs from other discussions on the psychology of conflict by focusing on reconciliation rather than on conflict resolution. We focused attention on socioemotional reconciliation, which is anchored in the apology-forgiveness cycle, and trust-building reconciliation, which is the slow process in which adversaries learn to trust each other by cooperating to achieve common goals. In the concluding section we would to like to center attention on the conditions under which one is more or less appropriate than the other.

Trust—a necessary condition: If there is a high level of distrust between the two parties, socioemotional reconciliation may do more harm than good. Our findings suggest that under such conditions apologies may do more harm than good. The intent behind the perpetrator's acceptance of responsibility and expression of empathy may be misconstrued, and intergroup relations may be worse than they would have been had no apology been made. Under such conditions trust-building reconciliation is more appropriate, and only after a degree of intergroup trust is established can the parties embark on the path of socioemotional reconciliation through the apology-forgiveness cycle. This two-stage approach is consistent with Lewicki and Weithoof's (2000) suggestion that only after calculus-based trust has been established can identification-based trust be built.

Consensus on the victim and perpetrator?: A second condition that determines the appropriateness of socioemotional or trust-building reconciliation is the degree to which there is a consensus on which group is the perpetrator and which is the victim (Nadler, 2002). Some conflicts come to an end when there is a consensus on who is the victim and who is the victimizer. For example, the conflict between black and white South Africans ended with a consensual agreement that the apartheid regime was the perpetrator of crimes against black South African victims. Other conflicts, however, end when both parties view themselves as the victim and the other as the perpetrator. This may be more characteristic of postconflict relations between the nations in the former Yugoslavia or in relations between Israelis and Palestinians. Socioemotional reconciliation is more likely to yield positive results in the first case when there is a clear and consensual agreement on who is the victim and who is the perpetrator. When each side views itself as the only legitimate victim and the other as the perpetrator, both view it as the other's responsibility to apologize and accept responsibility for past wrongdoings. Under these conditions, genuine expressions of empathy and acceptance of responsibility for the other's conflict-related suffering are unlikely. Enough trust must be built first to allow group members to be certain that their apologies will be reciprocated by counterapologies and forgiveness by the adversary.

Goal of reconciliation—separation or integration?: A third variable that is relevant here is the goal of reconciliation (Nadler, 2002). Some reconciliation efforts aim to produce a postconflict reality of social integration between former adversaries, whereas in other situations the goal is separation and coexistence. For example, black and white South Africans determined that they will live together in a united South Africa, and their goal was to make a split society whole again. In other cases, in relations between ethnic communities in the former Yugoslavia, the goal has been the creation of separate national groups that will coexist rather than be integrated into a single national unit. Socioemotional reconciliation is more appropriate when the goal is integration, and trust-building reconciliation is more applicable when the goal is separation (Nadler & Leviatan, in press). In the first case all energies need to be harnessed to ensure that the wounds of the past are healed so that the two parties can become equal partners in the same social unit (i.e., country, organization, or family). The apology–forgiveness cycle is necessary to facilitate this goal. When the goal is separation and coexistence, trust-building reconciliation allows the parties to build enough trust to enable coexistence rather than creating a unit relationship between them.

In conclusion, socioemotional reconciliation should be treated with caution. Apologizing and forgiving is not a magic cure for all conflicts. Sometimes it may backfire. When there is a high level of *mistrust*, when there is a belief by both parties that their group is the *only legitimate victim*, or when the goal of reconciliation is *separation*, trust-building reconciliation is more appropriate to achieve conflict-free relations between groups.

The foregoing discussion suggests that removing emotional deterrents may be an important vehicle of the diplomatic process when it seeks to promote the end of conflict between nations. We already know political leaders conduct politics of apology to further their goals. While noting the importance of this route in bringing about the end of international conflict, the present chapter also cautions against a wholesale adoption of this tactic. The existence of trust has been identified here as a key necessary condition. Our discussion of trust has focused on the fact that trust between adversaries can be rebuilt only in the presence of certain conditions. Chief among these is the equality that needs to be systematically designed and implemented into processes of trust-building reconciliation. Further, our study suggests that the more and less powerful groups have different motivations when cooperating in joint projects. Whereas the more-powerful group seeks to maintain the status quo, the less-powerful group seeks to change it. Finally, our understanding of the emotional barriers that separate nations that have been in conflict needs to be broadened before we can be more confident in devising ways to remove them. Once such a greater understanding is gained, it is likely to inform the practitioners of diplomacy on ways to achieve an end to conflict between nations and facilitate the building of peace between them. The study of the emotional deterrents to the end of conflict between nations and research into the processes of reconciliation that aim to remove them are a heuristic meeting place for scholars of diplomacy and social psychology. This scholarly interaction is likely to bear important fruits that will broaden our knowledge of intergroup behavior and provide useful tools to the practitioners of diplomacy.

REFERENCES

Akhtar, S. (2002). Forgiveness: Origins, dynamics, psychopathology and technical relevance. *Psychoanalytic Quarterly, 71*, 175–212.

Amir, Y., & Ben-Ari, R. (1986). Contact between Arab and Jewish youth in Israel: Reality and potential. In M. Hewstone and R. Brown (Eds.), *Contact and conflict in intergroup encounter* (pp. 45–58). Oxford: Basil Blackwell.

Baron, R. A. (1990). Countering the effects of destructive criticism: The relative efficacy of four interventions. *Journal of Applied Psychology, 75*, 235–245.

Bar-Tal, D. (2000). From intractable conflict through conflict resolution to reconciliation: Psychological analysis. *Political Psychology, 21*, 351–365.

Baumeister, R. F., Stillwell, A. M., & Heatherton, T. F. (1994). Guilt and interpersonal approach. *Psychological Bulletin, 115*(2), 243–267.

Blau, P. M. (1964). *Exchange and power in social life.* New York: Wiley.

Brown, R. (1995). *Prejudice: Its social psychology.* Oxford: Blackwell.

Colman, A. M. (1982). *Game theory and experimental games.* Oxford: Pergamon.

Cook, S. W. (1985). Experimenting on social issues: The case of school desegregation. *American Psychology, 40*, 452–460.

Crawford, N. C. (2000). The passion of world politics. *International Security, 24*, 116–157.

Cunningham, M. (1999). Saying sorry: The politics of apology. *The Political Quarterly, 10*, 285–293.

Darby, B. W., & Schlenker, B. R. (1989). Children's reactions to transgressions: Effects of the actor's apology, reputation and remorse. *British Journal of Social Psychology, 28*, 353–364.

Darby, B. W., & Schlenker, B. R. (1982). Children's reactions to apologies. *Journal of Personality and Social Psychology, 43*, 742–753.

Emerson, R. M. (1981). Social exchange theory. In G. M. Rosenberg and H. R. Turner, *Social psychology: Sociological perspectives.* New York: Basic Books.

Erikson, E. H. (1963). *Childhood and society.* New York: Norton.

Exline, J. J., & Baumeister, R. F. (2000). Expressing forgiveness and repentance: Benefits and barriers. In M. E. McCullough, K. Pargament, & C. E. Thoresen (Eds.), *Forgiveness: Theory, research and practice.* New York: Guilford Press.

Frijda, N. H. (1993). The lex talionis: On vengeance. In S. H. M. van Goozen, N. E. van de Poll, & J. A. Sergeant (Eds.), *Emotions: Essays on emotion theory* (pp. 263–289). Hillsdale, NJ: Erlbaum.

Gaertner, S. L., Mann, J. A., Dovidio, J. F., Murrell, A. J., & Pomare, M. (1990). How does cooperation reduce intergroup bias? *Journal of Personality and Social Psychology, 59,* 692–704.

Gaertner, S. L., Mann, J. A., Murrell, A. J., & Dovidio, J. F. (1989). Reduction of intergroup bias: The benefits of recategorization. *Journal of Personality and Social Psychology, 57,* 239–249.

Gambetta, D. (1998). Can we trust trust? In D. Gambetta (Ed.), *Trust: Making and breaking cooperative relationships.* Oxford, UK: Blackwell.

Hardin, R. (1992). The street level epistemology of trust. *Annals der kritikal, 14,* 152–176.

Hebl, J. H., & Enright, R. D. (1993). Forgiveness as a psychotherapeutic goal with elderly females. *Psychotherapy, 30,* 658–667.

Homans, G. C. (1961). *Social behavior: Its elementary forms.* New York: Harcourt Brace & World.

Hubbard, A. S. (1999). Cultural and status differences in intergroup conflict resolution: A longitudinal study of a Middle East dialogue group in the United States. *Human Relations, 5* (3), 303–325.

Itoi, R., Ohbuchi, K., & Fukuno, M. (1996). A cross-cultural study of preference of accounts: Relationship closeness, harm severity, and motives of account making. *Journal of Applied Social Psychology, 26,* 913–934.

Kelman, H. C. (1998). Social-psychological contributions to peacemaking and peacebuilding in the Middle East. *Applied Psychology, 47*(1), 5–28.

Kramer, R. M., & Carnevale, P. J. (2001). Trust and intergroup negotiation. In R. Brown & S. Gaertner (Eds.), *Intergroup processes* (pp. 431–450). Malden, MA: Blackwell Publishing.

Lederach, J. P. (1997). *Building peace: Sustainable reconciliation in divided societies.* Washington, DC: U.S. Institute of Peace.

Lewicki, R. J., & Wiethoff, C. (2000). Trust, trust development and trust repair. In M. Deutch & P. T. Coleman (Eds.), *The handbook of conflict resolution: Theory and practice* (pp. 86–108). San Francisco: Jossey Bass Publishers.

McCullough, M. E., Worthington, E. L., & Rachal, K. C. (1997). Interpersonal forgiving in close relationships. *Journal of Personality and Social Psychology, 73,* 321–336.

Nadler, A. (2002). Post resolution processes: An instrumental and socio-emotional routes to reconciliation. In G. Salomon & B. Nevo (Eds.), *Peace education: The concept, principles and practices around the world* (pp. 127–143). Mawhah, NJ: Erlbaum.

Nadler, A., & Liviatan, I. (in press). Inter-group reconciliation: Theoretical analysis and empirical findings. In N. R. Branscombe & B. Doosje (Eds.), *Collective guilt: International perspectives.* New York: Cambridge University Press.

Ohbuchi, K., & Sato, K. (1994). Children's reactions to mitigating accounts: Apologies, excuses and intentionally of harm. *Journal of Social Psychology, 134*, 5–17.

Pettigrew, T. F. (1998). Inter-group contact theory. *Annual Review Psychology, 49*, 65–68.

Pettigrew, T. F. (2001). Intergroup Relations and National and International Relations. In R. Brown & S. Gaertner (Eds.), *Intergroup processes* (pp. 514–532). Malden, MA: Blackwell Publishing.

Pruitt, D. G. (1998). Social conflict. In D. T. Gilbert, S. T. Fiske, & G. Lindzey (Eds.), *The handbook of social psychology* (4th ed., pp. 470–503). New York: McGraw-Hill.

Pruitt, D. G., & Carnevale, P. J. (1993). *Negotiation in social conflict.* Pacific Grove, CA: Brooks/Cole.

Rapoport, A., & Chammah, A. (1965). *Prisoner's dilemma: A study in conflict and cooperation.* Ann Arbor: University of Michigan Press.

Ross, L., & Nisbett, R. E. (1991). *The person and the situation: Perspectives on social psychology.* New York: McGraw-Hill.

Rotter, J. B. (1971). Generalized expectancies for interpersonal trust, *American Psychologist, 26*, 443–452.

Rouhana, N., & Bar-Tal, D. (1998). Psychological dynamics of intractable conflicts: The Israeli-Palestinian case. *American Psychologist, 53*, 761–770.

Savir, U. (1998). *The process: 1,100 days that changed the Middle East.* New York: Random House.

Scheff, T. J. (1994). *Bloody revenge: Emotions, nationalism and war.* Boulder, CO: Westview Press.

Sherif, M., Harvey, O. J., White, B. J., Hood, W. R., & Sherif, C. W. (1961). *Inter-group conflict and cooperation: The Robber's Cave experiment.* Norman: University of Oklahoma Press.

Tavuchis, N. (1991). *Mea culpa: A sociology of apology and reconciliation.* Stanford, CA.: Stanford University Press.

4

The Psychology of Diplomatic Conflict Resolution

Stuart Seldowitz

Some time ago a relative bought me a coffee cup containing the inscription "Diplomacy: The ability to tell someone to go to hell so that he'll look forward to making the trip." Although pithy, the saying captured the essence of diplomacy—the ability to convince foreign leaders that doing what you want is in their interest. By necessity, convincing sometimes requires credible threats of dire consequences if not followed. Nevertheless, diplomacy's essence is the art of persuasion. Not surprisingly, whether as individuals or as representatives of governments, we are more likely to succeed if we have a clear psychological understanding of the person we are trying to convince.

Yet, when diplomats gather and talk about their craft, the psychology of the political relations between states rarely comes up. Diplomats do not typically think that psychology has any relevance to diplomacy and rarely think of the behavior of states or their leaders in psychological terms. To a large degree this is because of the backgrounds that almost all diplomats share.

Most members of the U.S. Foreign Service have university degrees in international affairs, political science, economics, or law. Almost none have studied psychology, and very few have even taken university-level courses in psychology or related disciplines. Even worse, diplomats are notorious for being creatures of habit, meaning that they are likely to continue to ignore psychological factors in international affairs because they have always done so. Nevertheless, even a cursory analysis of attempts to resolve regional conflicts indicates that diplomats ignore psychological factors of conflicts at their peril.

Psychology plays two related but different roles in international affairs. Psychological factors influence what states or their leaders believe is important. In other words, during substantive negotiations psychology plays a role in determining the objectives of the sides. An understanding of the other side's outlook can also give a party insight into how to approach the negotiations. This tactical dimension is the focus of this chapter.

Nations, like individuals, have their own characters, patterns of behavior, and histories. Like individuals, no two states react to the same set of circumstances the same way. Like individuals, states can suffer from psychological disorders such as paranoia, stunted development, or dependency syndrome, and like individuals, abnormal behavior by states can be traced to some traumatic event in their pasts. Thus, what might seem like a rational compromise that protects both sides' vital interests to an outside mediator is perceived differently by the parties themselves. A recent example was the failure of Israeli and Palestinian negotiators at the June 2000 Camp David summit to resolve the question of sovereignty over the Temple Mount. According to both Israeli and Palestinian press reports, the American mediators put forward a number of compromise proposals. All of these ideas seemed reasonable in the corridors of the State Department, but none of them were acceptable to the parties.

That said, there are two major differences in the way psychologists approach abnormal behavior by individuals and how diplomats react to abnormal behavior by states. First, to say that a state is behaving abnormally is not to say that every, or even most, citizens of that state are mentally ill. In fact, one of the first points of analysis that diplomats must address is whether the abnormal behavior is the product of a particular leader or reflects ideas shared by the general population. It has been widely reported that the United States intelligence community prepares psychological profiles on major world leaders and that these profiles are used by analysts and others to predict behavior. But abnormal patterns of behavior by leaders are much more dangerous if they are shared by their publics. Second, psychologists and diplomats react very differently to evidence of abnormal behavior. A psychologist's objective is to cure the patient. In the short run the diplomat's goal is more modest, and perhaps more Machiavellian. Ideally diplomats try to turn another state's abnormal behavior to their advantage, or at worst view it as something that must be overcome. Attempts to change deeply rooted behavior is usually reserved for long-term programs intended to slowly change popular attitudes.

I heard about an example of a diplomat turning irrational attitudes to his advantage during my diplomatic assignment in the early 1980s to a U.S. consulate in northern Mexico. At the time Mexican politics were dominated by the Institutional Revolutionary Party (PRI). Although the PRI was a broad tent that included different factions, many PRI leaders had an exaggerated and sometimes paranoid view of U.S. influence in Mexico. In one meeting with the U.S. ambassador, a group of PRI leaders accused the United States of conspiring with the Mexican opposition to undermine the Mexican government. Rather then engaging in a fruitless effort to refute the accusation in the usual way by arguing that Washington did not take sides in internal Mexican matters, the ambassador decided to turn his Mexican companions' paranoia against them. "If the United States supported the opposition," he said, "the opposition would surely be in power." The Mexicans thought about it for a few seconds, and blurted out, "But that means that since we are in power you must support us." The ambassador smiled but did not respond.

The dissolution of the Socialist Federal Republic of Yugoslavia (SFRY) in 1991 and the wars in Croatia, Bosnia, and Herzegovina that followed provide an opportunity to examine how psychological factors affected an international crisis and how diplomats eventually learned to use those same factors to resolve it. The destruction of Yugoslavia had many causes, and it is perhaps unfair to focus on only one or two. It is true that ethnic hatreds and conflicts were not a new phenomenon in the south Balkans in the late 1980s and early 1990s. It is also true that the transition from communism exacerbated an already fragile political and social structure. But neither ancient ethnic hatreds nor the end of the Cold War made the violent breakup of Yugoslavia inevitable or unavoidable. Rather, Yugoslavia was destroyed by the psychological makeup of its key leaders at a moment of instability and vulnerability and their ability to manipulate the psychological weakness of its publics.

It is more controversial to blame a country's national psychology for the nationalist fanaticism that swept through the Balkans in the early and mid 1990s. Some will interpret even raising the issue as an attempt to blame all Serbs and Croats for what happened. That is not my intention. But it is also inaccurate to portray Serbs and Croats as the innocent victims of bad or criminal leaders. Leaders do not appear in a vacuum, and neither Serb president Milosevic nor Croat president Tudjman would have gained power or been able to implement their programs without substantial public support. In fact, like Germans who lived under the Third Reich, most Serbs or Croats either supported policies that were morally indefensible or acquiesced to them. Only a small minority bravely joined the opposition.

Many nations have a key moment in their histories, one that defines them as a nation. The battle of Kosovo in June 1389 between Serb and Turkish armies remains the key to understanding the Serb nationalist view of the world. Americans find it difficult to understand why Serbs take their history this seriously. It remains a major factor in the way they view current events. As is true for many "nationalist myths," the truth of what actually happened during the battle is less important than what most Serbs believe occurred. Many historians have pointed out that the battle was a draw, and that some Serbs fought on the Turkish side whereas non-Serbs, including some Muslims, fought on the Serb side. Nevertheless, Serb nationalists have turned the battle into a heroic, but ultimately futile, stand against the barbaric Turks. According to the myth, the battle led directly to 500 years of domination by the Muslim Turks, but helped save Christian Europe from being overwhelmed. The fact that the Christian world has never recognized the debt they owe the Serb nation has imbued Serb nationalism with a sense that the outside world is either hostile or ungrateful. Moreover, during the wars in Bosnia and Croatia, Serb nationalists pointed to the sacrifices Serbs made in saving Christianity and later siding with the Allies in World War I and fighting the Nazis during World War II as excuses for the mass murder of innocent non-Serbs.

A personal experience from my tour with the U.S. Mission to the United Nations demonstrates the degree to which Serbs are obsessed with their history and assume others are as well. Coming out of the Security Council after the council passed the latest anti-Serb resolution, I was stopped by a member of the Yugoslav delegation who asked how the United States could take such a strong position condemning Serb atrocities in Bosnia and Croatia. "Don't you remember," I was asked, "that the Kingdom of Serbia was the first European state to recognize the United States *de jure*?" He was shocked when I responded that most Americans had no idea when and how the Serbs recognized the United States, and even if his claim was correct, few Americans believed that events in the late 1700s could be used as an excuse for genocide today.

My colleagues and I were constantly amazed when seemingly rational, well-educated Serb representatives would revert to paranoid conspiracy theories to explain the dissolution of Yugoslavia. The common thread in these explanations was that an innocent, misunderstood Serbia was once again the victim of forces it could not control. Two examples illustrate this point: The same Serb diplomat who had raised Serb recognition of the early United States once told me that he "knew" that the United States was taking a hard line in condemning Belgrade because we had been duped by a German-Catholic-Muslim conspiracy that saw Serbia as the key obstacle to world domination. At about the same time our embassy in Belgrade sent in a cable quoting from a column in a leading Belgrade newspaper. The columnist, too, thought he had figured out what was behind international isolation of Serbia, but his explanation was slightly different. According to this theory the United States had secretly invented and put into orbit a sophisticated camera that could see what was under the Earth's surface. From that device we learned that huge mineral and oil deposits lay under Serbia. In order to get our greedy little capitalist hands on this mineral wealth the United States had first engineered the destruction of Yugoslavia and was now seeking to bring Serbia to its knees.

It is not clear to what extent Serbian president Milosevic shared the paranoid fantasies that were stoked by his public statements and government-controlled press. Milosevic's evolution from orthodox communist to Western-leaning banker to Serb nationalist to "friend of the West," to nationalist again has been well documented. It is unlikely he ever truly believed in any of these ideologies. Rather, Milosevic was the amoral manipulator, ready to say or do anything that would advance his political career. Devoid of core beliefs, Milosevic had the great advantage of being able to plan his next moves solely based on what was likely to advance his personal interests. Like others who worked on the Balkans in the early 1990s, I assume that the suicide of both his parents had a profound impact on Milosevic's personality and outlook. (Milosevic's father was a Serbian Orthodox priest who committed suicide when his son was four years old. Milosevic's mother was a schoolteacher who committed suicide several years later.) Whatever its cause, those who dealt with him closely have commented on Milosevic's lack of empathy for human suffering, even of his own people, isolation, and ability to switch immediately from warm hospitality to clinically cold discussion of events.[1]

In his 1996 book, *Origins of a Catastrophe,* Warren Zimmermann, the last U.S. ambassador to Yugoslavia, quoted from a facetious cable he had written about Milosevic's character. Zimmermann said he had reported that

there were really two Milosevics. Milosevic One was hard-line, authoritarian, belligerent, bent on chaos, and wedded to the use of force to create a Greater Serbia. Personally he was apoplectic, he hated Westerners, and he spoke in Serbian.

Milosevic Two was polite, affable, cooperative, and always looking for reasonable solutions to Yugoslavia's problems. He was calm, he liked to reminisce about his banking days in New York, and he spoke good English.[2]

Richard Holbrooke commented on the same aspect of Milosevic's personality in his 1998 book, *To End a War.* Holbrooke wrote that "Milosevic could switch moods with astonishing speed, perhaps to keep others off balance. He could range from charm to brutality, from emotional outbursts to calm discussions of legal minutiae. When he was angry, his face wrinkled up, but he could regain control of himself instantly."[3]

I will leave it to others to try to determine the clinical causes for Milosevic's own views and explain the fantasies that drove Serb nationalism. Whatever the reasons behind Milosevic's behavior, the objective of the Bush and Clinton administrations was to stabilize the Balkans and put an end to the atrocities that Milosevic and his even more radical compatriots were responsible for. Although the crisis in the Balkans might have been, as former secretary of state Christopher called it, the "problem from Hell," its resolution was not nearly as difficult as some policy makers assumed. Finding a solution required hardheaded analysis of Milosevic's character and political goals and the political will to take the necessary strong measures.

The failure to understand Milosevic's psychological makeup and the effect it would have on the development of the crisis was a major factor in the West's failure to confront Milosevic before events spiraled out of control. By the summer of 1992 it was clear that Milosevic had committed aggression against Croatia and Bosnia and supported the mass murder of non-Serbs in his drive to unite all Serbs into a Greater Serbia. Faced with a ruthless opponent who was unconcerned about the human consequences of his actions and was willing to use brutal methods to accomplish his goals, the Bush administration should have realized that there was a credible threat, and if necessary, that use of force was the only way to dissuade Milosevic from continuing down the road he was clearly on.

Nevertheless, the Bush foreign policy team never caught on. In retrospect the Bush administration's failure in the Balkans is surprising in view of its success in reversing the Iraqi invasion of Kuwait and managing the collapse of the Soviet Union. David Gompert, a senior official on the staff of the Bush administration's National Security Council, later wrote that the administration knew "a year before the fighting began that Yugoslavia was being led toward the abyss by a few demagogic politicians [but] simply knew of no way to prevent this from occurring. . . . The Bush national security team that performed so well in other crisis was divided and stumped."[4] As war became increasingly inevitable in the summer of 1991, Secretary of State Baker made his only trip to Belgrade, a short day trip. Baker's brief visit in which he failed to threaten strong action to arrest Yugoslavia's slide into chaos confirmed what Milosevic must have already suspected—that the United States was disengaged. Although Baker never intended to give Milosevic a green light, the Serb leader undoubtedly interpreted Baker's actions as an indication that the administration was not prepared to take strong measures to restrain him. Baker's later statements giving our European allies the lead in organizing the Western response to the war in Croatia must have further strengthened Milosevic's conviction that he had nothing to fear from the United States or its allies.

The first major lost opportunity to arrest Yugoslavia's slide toward the abyss came in the autumn of 1991. War had already broken out in Croatia, and events were giving the West an indication of what lay ahead if hostilities spread to Bosnia. On October 1, the Serb-dominated Yugoslav Army (JNA) began shelling the Croatian town of Dubrovnik from sea and surrounding hills. Until then the army had claimed that it was acting to protect Croatia's Serb minority, but no Serbs lived in Dubrovnik, and it was not a legitimate military target. The decision to shell it anyway was an early sign that civilians were fair game. Also in October the army tightened it siege of the town of Vukovar. On November 20, after Vukovar fell, Serb troops entered the town's hospital and took away 261 patients. They were never seen again, and three Serb officers were later indicted by the International Criminal Tribunal for the former Yugoslavia for being responsible for their deaths. A decision by NATO to use force in response to either of these events would have demonstrated Western resolve and could have averted the war in Bosnia. Instead, the Bush administration continued to hide behind the Europeans and limited its response to additional UN resolutions calling for an end to hostilities.

Zimmermann later wrote that "[t]he refusal of the Bush administration to commit American power early in the Bosnian war—even though that refusal was based on an honest perception of the U.S. national interest—was our greatest mistake of the entire Yugoslav crisis. It made an unjust outcome inevitable and wasted the opportunity to prevent over a hundred thousand deaths."[5] In Gompert's words, "Predictably, the attempt to hold the Yugoslav crisis at arm's length did not spare the United States the effects of, or responsibility for, the failure that followed."[6]

The Bush administration's hands-off policy toward the Balkans might be explainable if they had not known they were dealing with an opponent as determined as Slobodan Milosevic, or if they had failed in similar crises else-where in the world. Once the use of force was taken off the table, Milosevic knew that diplomatic isolation and perhaps economic sanctions were the strongest measures he had to worry about. Neither scared him. Moreover, the Bush administration, including President Bush, Secretary of State Baker, Secretary of Defense Cheney, and Chairman of the Joint Chiefs Powell had shown in their response to the Kuwait crisis that they knew how to deal with world leaders who only understood the use of force.

The Bush administration's passivity toward the Balkans can be explained one of two ways. One is that they grossly misread Milosevic's psychological makeup and overestimated the likelihood that he would be constrained by threats other than force, while seriously underestimating the lengths he was prepared to go to accomplish his goals. A second more cynical explanation is that the Bush team might have determined that chaos in the Balkans, where American oil interests were not at risk, was not worth the risk to U.S. forces or to the president's upcoming reelection campaign. In either case, the Bush administration's lack of resolve amounted to a lost opportunity to restrain Milosevic early on and has led to charges of U.S. complicity in the Bosnian genocide that followed.

For most of its first three years in office the Clinton administration suffered from the same inability to understand Slobodan Milosevic and the Bosnian Serb leadership. The Clinton team could rightly argue that the Bush administration's failure to use force early on was a lost opportunity that allowed the situation to seriously deteriorate. Nevertheless, until the summer of 1995 the Clinton team made many of the same mistakes as its predecessor and largely failed to follow the tough policy that was needed. The one exception to this rule was then U.S. ambassador to the United Nations Madeleine Albright. Albright, who spent part of her childhood living in Yugoslavia and who made the study of Eastern Europe her academic specialty, understood the psychology of the region. Sometimes alone, sometimes with Leon Fuerth of Vice President Gore's office, Albright consistently argued that halfhearted measures would not work in the Balkans. Although sometimes a lonely voice in the wind, the administration's eventual success in the Balkans owes much to her perseverance and courage. After becoming secretary of state in the second Clinton administration, Albright again demonstrated her understanding of the region, courage, and determination by insisting on a strong response to Serbian actions in Kosovo.

The Bosnian Serb massacre of over seven thousand Bosnian Muslims after conquering the town of Srebrencia in July 1995 finally spurred the administration to take effective action. Although conceived in the White House, the U.S. peace initiative was led by Assistant Secretary of European Affairs Richard Holbrooke. Unlike a long series of international mediators who had tried and failed to end the Bosnian conflict, Holbrooke understood the psychology and negotiating styles of the region's leaders. When the Europeans, UN command-ers, and some members of our own military pushed for a premature end to NATO's bombing campaign against the Bosnian Serbs, Holbrooke successfully argued that the bombing was necessary for a successful negotiation because it demonstrated the West's political will. Holbrooke understood that rather than the fanatic fighters others thought them to be, the Bosnian Serbs were really school yard bullies, and the best way to defeat bullies was to confront them. As he later wrote,

I was beginning to get a sense of the Pale (Bosnian) Serbs; headstrong, given to empty theatrical statements, but in the end essentially bullies when their bluff was called. The Western mistake over the previous four years had been to treat the Serbs as rational people with whom one could argue, negotiate, compromise, and agree. In fact, they respected only force or an unambiguous and credible threat to use it.[7]

Holbrooke led the American team at the Dayton Peace Conference, where he was able to broker an agreement that provided for the peaceful reintegration into Croatia of Eastern Slavonia, the last part of Croatia still held by the Serbs, and the Dayton Peace Accords, which ended the war in Bosnia. Holbrooke's understanding of Milosevic's psychological makeup was demonstrated in a ca-ble he sent to Washington during the Dayton Conference. Holbrooke wrote:

Milosevic seems to be enjoying himself at Dayton Place, although he likes to intimidate people. Standing up to him when he attacks is the key; he respects people who act as tough as him. He is always testing us. In order to move him, we must lay down very firm markers and not move them unless we know exactly what we are getting in return.[8]

If Slobodan Milosevic was the mad genius most responsible for Yugoslavia's violent dissolution, Croatian president Franjo Tudjman must also shoulder some of the blame. Tudjman was a strong Croat nationalist and had been jailed for his political beliefs during the Tito period. Thus, he differed from Milosevic, whose nationalism was primarily a means to gain and then keep power. If Milosevic was the master manipulator who truly believed in nothing, Tudjman was an authoritarian, intolerant leader who had a strong sense of his future place in Croatia's history and knew exactly what he wanted. Ambassador Zim-mermann wrote that Tudjman reminded him of a strict schoolmaster whereas Milosevic conjured up images of a con man.[9]

During World War II Tudjman joined Tito's partisans and rose to the rank of general. After the war he became the Yugoslav Army's Head Political Com-missar but by 1967 had become converted to the nationalist cause. Tudjman had been jailed twice for nationalist activities and quickly became a leader of Croatia's nationalist movement. Having spent a significant part of his life as a partisan fighting the Nazis and their Croatian allies and then in Tito's prisons, Tudjman was not easily intimidated by diplomats or Western politicians. His success in fulfilling a thousand-year-old dream of Croatian independence gave him an exaggerated sense of his destiny and place in history.

As was the case with Milosevic, negotiating successfully with Tudjman required an understanding of his psychological background. Tudjman's willingness to sacrifice for his beliefs made attempts to intimidate him futile. The key to dealing with Tudjman was the ability to understand his view of history and Croatia's role in it. At one time or another, every foreign diplomat who dealt with Tudjman was subjected to his "clash of civilizations" speech. In Tudjman's view Catholic Croatia was at the forefront of a clash of civilizations with Islam and to a much lesser extent Orthodox Christianity. In Tudjman's view, the battle for dominance in the Balkans between the Austro-Hungarian Empire and the Ottoman Turks had never really ended. Muslims were inherently violent, prone to religious extremism, and they posed a present danger to Christian civilization in Europe. In a January 14, 1992, meeting with Ambassador Zimmermann he predicted that the Bosnian Muslims would first flood Bosnia with half a million Turks disguised as Bosnians to become a majority and then establish a fundamentalist state. They would then seek common cause with Muslims in Serbia and Kosovo to establish a greater Bosnia that would stretch from the Croatian border to Libya. Serbs and Croats in Bosnia would be "eradicated."[10] Croatia's location, on the fault line with Orthodox southeast Europe and bordering on Bosnia, made it the main bulwark against these ambitions. Tudjman never gave up on the belief that the Bosnian Muslims' ultimate intention was to establish a fundamentalist Muslim state that would threaten not only Bosnian Croats and Serbs, but also the rest of Europe.

Tudjman's relationship with the West was complicated and mirrored his psychological outlook. On the one hand he believed that the United States and Western Europe owed Croatia a special thanks for being at the front line of the conflict with Islam. On the other, he sincerely wanted to be accepted as a Western statesman and for Croatia to be accepted as a Western nation. Tudjman lost few opportunities to remind visitors of Croatia's historical ties with Austria and central Europe. Being accepted as a historic figure was important to Tudjman, and his attempts to mimic Tito's uniforms and lifestyle sometimes assumed comic proportions.

Obviously, Western diplomats who dealt with him found Tudjman's paranoid fantasies about a Muslim conspiracy and Croatia's role as Europe's first line of defense ridiculous and not a little bit frightening. Although Tudjman's background made it hard to intimidate or threaten him, his vanity and exaggerated view of Croatia's importance would provide Western diplomats with an opening to exploit. Unfortunately, not all Western mediators understood that Tudjman's paranoia and exaggerated sense of importance, although exasperating, could be turned to their advantage.

The negotiations in March of 1995 over the continued presence of a United Nations force in Croatia provides a clear example of taking psychological factors into account when approaching a foreign leader. On January 2, 1992, both the

Croatian government and the JNA agreed to a ceasefire brokered by UN mediator Cyrus Vance.

Both sides also agreed that a UN peacekeeping force, to be known as the UN Protection Force (UNPROFOR), would be deployed in the approximately one-third of Croatian territory controlled by the Yugoslav Army and their Croatian Serb allies. The deployment of UN forces created an anomalous situation—on the one hand, the UN Security Council and Secretariat recognized Croatia's territorial integrity, meaning that the Serb-held territories would have to be reintegrated into Croatia. On the other, the UN presence was increasingly seen in Zagreb as freezing the status quo and de facto creating a new international border. The continued displacement of Croat refugees who had been expelled from their homes in the Serb-held zones also rankled Zagreb, as did UNPROFOR's carefully drawn neutrality between the Croatian government and the Croatian Serb authorities. Zagreb's frustration grew as time passed without any change in the status quo and as international attention shifted to the war in Bosnia.

UNPROFOR's mandate had to be renewed every six months. During the lead-up to the renewal scheduled for March 31, 1995, Tudjman announced that his government would demand UNPROFOR's withdrawal. Under UN peacekeeping practice, which required the agreement of the state on which a peacekeeping force was to be deployed, Zagreb's withdrawal of consent would force UNPROFOR's withdrawal. European reaction to Tudjman's implied threat was harsh. The British and French, who had the two largest contingents in UNPROFOR and who therefore were sensitive to any criticism of the peacekeeping force, advocated that Tudjman's warning be ignored. Not surprising, considering his psychological makeup, this only served to force Tudjman to dig himself in deeper that UNPROFOR would have to withdraw. Preoccupation with Bosnia caused the situation to drift until Holbrooke went to Zagreb to talk to Tudjman.

Unlike his European colleagues, Holbrooke understood that threatening Tudjman with dire consequences if he forced the UN to withdraw would not work. Instead, Holbrooke used a much more effective strategy. Well aware of Tudjman's psychological prejudices, Holbrooke decided to exploit them to allow the UN to stay and thereby avert the crisis. Knowing Holbrooke's reputation for tough talk, Tudjman undoubtedly expected to hear the usual arguments on how expelling the UN would lead to another Croat/Serb war, which Croatia would lose, and how precipitating such a conflict would severely damage Croatia's relations with the West. Instead, Holbrooke took a different approach. Shortly after sitting down with Tudjman, Holbrooke matter of factly told him that Croatia faced a momentous choice in the days ahead. Croatia was at a crossroads, he said, and had to choose one of two paths. The first led to Croatia's integration into Western Europe, including eventually the European Union and NATO. The second, Holbrooke said, would bring Croatia toward the Ottoman Empire. If Croatia wanted to join Western Europe, it had to remain engaged with the UN and EU mediators and allow a UN peacekeeping force to stay. In recognition of the fact that Tudjman's public statements demanding that UN-PROFOR leave made it difficult for him to back down, Holbrooke agreed to a face-saving formula. UNPROFOR would technically be withdrawn but would be replaced by a UN peacekeeping force with essentially the same force structure and chain of command but with a different name. Thus was born the United Nations Confidence Restoration Operation in Croatia, known as UNCRO.

By taking advantage of Tudjman's ambition that Croatia be seen as a Western European country and his hatred and disdain for the Ottoman Turks, Holbrooke was able to get Tudjman to agree to a continued UN presence in Croatia. By agreeing to a formula that allowed Tudjman to back down gracefully, Holbrooke allowed him to retain his self-image of the tough nationalist who refused to bend to foreign pressure.

In her 1997 book, *Yugoslavia—Death of a Nation*, Laura Silber relates a similar episode in 1994. At the time about 70 percent of Bosnia was controlled by the Bosnian Serbs, and vicious fighting had broken out between the Muslim-led Bosnian government and the Bosnian Croats. Faced with this bleak situation the United States decided to try to broker a Muslim/Croat agreement that would create a Muslim/Croat federation. Tudjman, as usual, held the key. Silber wrote that in January 1994, U.S. mediator Charles Redman had lunch with a "senior Croat" who explained how Tudjman saw his role in history. If Redman could persuade Tudjman that an agreement establishing a federation would confirm his role in history, he might agree. Redman took the advice on how to approach Tudjman and in February 1994, after intensive negotiations, the Muslim/Croat federation was born.[11]

Many factors were responsible for the dissolution of the former SFRY, and many ingredients were necessary for peace to be restored. In the end, the willingness to use force in response to Serb provocations was the most important factor. Nevertheless, our belated understanding of the psychological outlook of the region's leaders made it easier to negotiate the final peace settlement. Only after understanding Milosevic's worldview were we able to find a successful strategy to make peace. If Milosevic and Tudjman had been common citizens with the same psychological makeup and behavior, they would have been advised to undergo psychological treatment. Unfortunately for the citizens of the former Yugoslavia, they were not just members of the general public. Rather, their psychological abnormalities and the inability of Western Europe and the United States to understand what drove them were responsible for the suffering of millions of innocents on all sides.

NOTES

The views expressed in this chapter are those of the author and not necessarily those of the Department of State or the U.S. government. This article is based principally on my recollections from 1991 to 1996 when I worked at the U.S. Mission to the United Nations. Those recollections were supplemented by reference to three of the best books published on the Yugoslav crisis. They are: *To End a War* by Richard Holbrooke, *Origins of a Catastrophe* by Warren Zimmermann, and *Yugoslavia—Death of a Nation* by Laura Silber and Allan Little.

1. Warren Zimmermann, *Origins of a Catastrophe—Yugoslavia and Its Destroyers* (New York: Times Books, 1996), p. 24.

2. Zimmermann, p. 26.

3. Richard Holbrooke, *To End a War* (New York: Random House, 1998), p. 114.

4. As quoted in Holbrooke, p. 26.

5. Zimmermann, p. 216.

6. As quoted in Holbrooke, p. 28.

7. Holbrooke, p. 152.

8. Holbrooke, p. 285.

9. Zimmermann, p. 72.

10. Zimmermann, p. 181.

11. Laura Silber and Allan Little, *Yugoslavia—Death of a Nation* (London: Penguin Books, 1997), p. 320.

REFERENCES

Holbrooke, R. (1998). *To end a war.* New York: Random House.

Silber, L. & A. Little (1997). *Yugoslavia—death of a nation.* London: Penguin Books.

Zimmermann, W. (1996). *Origins of a catastrophe—Yugoslavia and its destroyers.* New York: Times Books.

5

The Nature of International Conflict: A Social–Psychological Perspective

Herbert C. Kelman

The purpose of this chapter is to discuss four propositions about the nature of international conflict that flow from a social–psychological perspective and that have clear implications for conflict resolution. These propositions expand on the view of international conflict provided by the realist or neorealist schools of international relations or other, more traditional approaches focusing on structural or strategic factors. The four propositions can be summed up as follows.

First, international conflict is *a process driven by collective needs and fears*, rather than entirely a product of rational calculation of objective national interests on the part of political decision makers. Second, international conflict is *an intersocietal process*, not only an interstate or intergovernmental phenomenon. Third, international conflict is *a multifaceted process of mutual influence*, not only a contest in the exercise of coercive power. And fourth, international conflict is *an interactive process with an escalatory, self-perpetuating dynamic*, not merely a sequence of action and reaction by stable actors.

Thus, a social–psychological perspective—without denying the importance of objectively anchored national interests, the primacy of the state in the international system, the role of power in international relations, and the effect of structural factors in determining the course of an international conflict— enriches the analysis in a variety of ways: by exploring the subjective factors that set constraints on rationality; by opening the black box of the state as unitary actor and analyzing processes within and between the societies that underlie state action; by broadening the range of influence processes (and, indeed, of definitions of power) that play a role in international politics; and by conceiving international conflict as a dynamic process, shaped by changing realities, changing interests, and changing relationships between the conflicting parties.

CONFLICT AS A PROCESS DRIVEN BY COLLECTIVE NEEDS AND FEARS

International or ethnic conflict must be conceived as a process in which collective human needs and fears are acted out in powerful ways. Such conflict is typically driven by nonfulfillment or threats to the fulfillment of basic needs. These include not only such obvious material needs as food, shelter, physical safety, and physical well-being, but also, and very centrally, such psychological needs as identity, security, recognition, autonomy, self-esteem, and a sense of justice (Burton, 1988). *Need*, as used here, is an individual-level concept; needs are attributes of individual human beings. But insofar as these needs become driving forces in international and intergroup conflict, they are needs of individuals articulated through important identity groups. The link to groups—the collective aspect—is indeed an important and almost ubiquitous feature of human needs. The fulfillment of needs takes place to a considerable extent within the context of groups of different sizes. The ethnic group, the national group, and the state are among the collectivities that serve as important vehicles for the fulfillment and protection of fundamental needs.

Closely related to these basic needs in intergroup conflict situations are fears about the denial of the needs—fears focusing, for example, on perceived threats to security or identity. In protracted conflicts between identity groups, such fears often take on an existential character, turning the conflict into a struggle over group survival. The Israeli–Palestinian conflict, for example, can be described as an existential conflict between two parties, each of which sees its very existence as a national group at stake in the conflict (Kelman, 1987).

Needs for identity and security and similarly powerful collective needs, and the fears and concerns about survival associated with them, are often important causal factors in intergroup and intercommunal conflict. The causes of conflict generally combine objective and subjective factors, which are related to each other in a continuingly circular fashion. Conflicts focusing, for example, on issues like territory and resources almost invariably reflect and further magnify underlying concerns about security and identity. But, whatever their role in the causation of a conflict, subjective forces linked to basic needs and existential fears contribute heavily to its escalation and perpetuation. It is such needs and fears that create resistance to change, even in those situations in which both parties, or significant elements of both parties, have come to the conclusion that it is in their best interest to put an end to the conflict. Despite this perceived interest, the parties are often unable to extricate themselves from the escalatory dynamic in which they are caught up.

Exploration of collective needs and fears is particularly helpful in understanding why it is so difficult for parties to change course in conflicts that have become increasingly destructive and detrimental to their interests. Although they may recognize that it is to their advantage to find a negotiated solution, they are afraid to go to the negotiating table. Or, having reluctantly gone to the table, they are afraid to make the concessions or accommodations that are necessary for the negotiations to move forward. They worry that once they enter negotiations or—having entered negotiations—once they make certain concessions, they will find themselves on a slippery slope: that they will inexorably be moving, concession after concession, into a situation that in the end will leave their very existence compromised. In short, the sense that their identity, security, and very existence as a national group are at stake contributes heavily to resistance to negotiation or to accommodation in the course of negotiations.

The role of such existential fears and needs is more pronounced in ethnic conflicts than in the kinds of interstate conflicts with which traditional theories of international politics have been concerned. But collective needs and fears play a part in all international conflicts and lie behind what is usually described as national interests. National interests—which are essentially the interests perceived by the elites that control the operative definition of the national interest—are heavily influenced by objective factors. The fact that a state, for example, lacks certain essential resources, or has an ethnically divided population, or has no access to the sea obviously plays a role in how the elites define its interests. But these objective factors always combine with subjective factors in determining how different segments of a society perceive state interests and what ultimately becomes the national interest as defined by the dominant elites. The subjective determinants of perceived national interests are the collective needs and fears of the society, as interpreted by the political leadership.

Similarly, it can be assumed that all conflicts represent a combination of rational and irrational factors. Ethnic conflicts, though often portrayed as uniquely irrational, resemble conflicts between states and even between superpowers in containing both rational and irrational elements. Moreover, in each type of conflict the mix may vary from case to case. Some ethnic conflicts may be preponderantly rational, just as some interstate conflicts may be preponderantly irrational.

In all international conflicts, the needs and fears of populations are mobilized and often manipulated by the leadership. Collective needs and fears are often linked to individual needs and fears. For example, in ethnic conflicts characterized by a high level of violence, the fear of annihilation of one's group is often (and for good reason) tied to a fear of personal annihilation. Insofar as these personally tinged collective needs and fears are mobilized, they become the focus of collective action within a society. The mobilization and manipulation of collective needs and fears vary in the degree of demagoguery and cynicism that they involve, but they are always seen as necessary tasks of leaders in a conflict situation. Furthermore, though mobilized and often manipulated, collective needs and fears must be viewed as real and authentic reactions within the population.

What does this conception of conflict as a process driven by collective needs and fears imply for conflict resolution? First, it follows from this view that genuine conflict resolution must address these needs and fears. If a conflict is to be resolved, in the sense of leading to a stable peace that both sides consider just and to a new relationship that is mutually enhancing and contributes to the welfare and development of the two societies, the solution must satisfy the fundamental needs and allay the deepest fears of the populations. The objective of conflict resolution is not to eliminate the conflict entirely, which is neither possible nor desirable as a general goal (because conflicts are potentially constructive forces within a society or region and serve as the basis for necessary social change); rather, it is to eliminate the violent and otherwise destructive manifestations of conflict. But even these destructive elements of conflict cannot be made to disappear overnight in conflicts that have been pursued for many years and sometimes for generations and are marked by accumulated memories that are constantly being revived by new events and experiences. Conflict resolution does not imply that past grievances and historical traumas have been forgotten and a consistently harmonious relationship has been put in place. It simply implies that a process has been set into motion that addresses the central needs and fears of the societies and establishes mechanisms to continue confronting them.

From a normative point of view, the ultimate criterion for a successful, mutually satisfactory solution of a conflict is that it has addressed the fundamental needs of both parties. Thus, what negotiation theorists mean by a win–win solution in a protracted conflict between identity groups is a solution that has, in fact, spoken—however imperfectly—to such needs and the fears associated with them: a solution in which neither side is required to sacrifice what it considers to be a vital need, and both are reassured with respect to their deepest fears. It is in the search for such solutions that justice enters the picture in nonadversarial approaches to conflict resolution, such as interactive problem solving (see Fisher, 1997; Kelman, 1986, 1992b, 1998; Rouhana & Kelman, 1994). The problem-solving workshops that my colleagues and I organize, for example, are governed by a no-fault principle, which eschews efforts to establish who is right and who is wrong from a legal or a moral point of view. Although the parties' differing views of rights and wrongs must be discussed because they contribute significantly to the dynamics of the conflict, the assumption is that the parties cannot find a solution by adjudicating these differing views. Rather, they must move toward a solution by jointly discovering mutually satisfactory ways of dealing with the issues that divide them. Insofar as they arrive at a solution that addresses the fundamental needs of both parties, justice is being done—not perfect justice, but enough to ensure the prospects for a durable peace. Thus, commitment to a solution that is responsive to the basic concerns of the two parties is the operationalization of justice in a problem-solving approach.

An interesting implication of a human-needs orientation, first noted by John Burton (1988), is that the psychological or ontological needs on which it focuses—needs like identity, security, or recognition—are not inherently zero-sum. There is no necessary reason why one party must gain its identity or security at the expense of the other. In fact, much of the new thinking about security—exemplified by the concept of common security—is based on the proposition that each party's security is enhanced by the security of the other. Similarly, in a context of mutual recognition, the identity of one is enhanced by the identity of the other (Kelman 1987, p. 358). In intense conflicts, of course, there is a strong tendency to see these needs as zero-sum and to assume that one's own security and identity can be protected or enhanced only by depriving the other of security and identity. But because these needs are not by nature mutually exclusive, addressing them may offer possibilities for a mutually satisfactory solution. If the parties can push behind their incompatible positions and explore the underlying needs that engender these positions, they may be able to shape an integrative solution that satisfies both sets of needs. Once such underlying needs have been addressed, issues such as territory or resources—which are more inherently zero-sum in nature (although also susceptible to creative reframing)—can then be settled through distributive bargaining.

A final implication of the view of conflict as a process driven by collective needs and fears relates to the question of when the individual becomes the appropriate unit of analysis in international relations. Though the needs and fears that drive conflict are collectively expressed and must be satisfied at the collective level, they are experienced at the level of individual human beings. To address such needs and fears, therefore, conflict resolution must, at some stage, provide for certain processes that take place at the level of individuals and the interaction between individuals. One such process is empathy, or taking the perspective of the other, which is essential to any effort to move toward an accommodation that takes account of the needs and fears of both parties. Empathy develops in the interaction between individuals, and it is in the minds of individuals that the perspective of the other has to be somehow represented. Creative problem solving is another example of a process essential to conflict resolution that takes place in the minds of individuals and the interaction between them, as they move from analysis of the causes of the conflict to generating new ideas for resolving it. Insight and learning are further examples of individual-level processes that need to be part of a larger effort at conflict resolution. Problem-solving workshops and similar conflict-resolution activities provide a setting in which such processes can occur. They contribute to the larger process of conflict resolution by creating, through the interaction between the participating individuals, a product that can be exported into the political arena—a product in the form of new insights and new ideas, which can then enter into the political debate and the decision-making process within the conflicting societies. Thus, a problem-solving workshop can be thought of as a laboratory—indeed, as a workshop in the literal sense of the word—where a product is being created for export. Essentially, workshops represent a special microprocess that provides inputs into the macroprocess of conflict resolution.

CONFLICT AS AN INTERSOCIETAL PROCESS

A focus on the needs and fears of the population involved in conflict readily brings to mind a second social–psychological proposition: that international conflict is not merely an intergovernmental or interstate phenomenon, but an intersocietal phenomenon. The conflict, particularly in the case of protracted ethnic struggles, becomes an inescapable part of daily life for the members of the two communities. The conflict pervades the whole society and its various component elements—not only when it takes the form of explicit violence, but even at times when the violence is muted. Thus, analysis of conflict requires attention, not only to its strategic, military, and diplomatic dimensions, but also to its economic, psychological, cultural, and social-structural dimensions. Interactions along these dimensions, both within and between the conflicting societies, shape the political environment in which governments function. Intrasocietal and intersocietal processes define the political constraints under which governments operate and the resistance to change that these produce. For example, the leaders' attempts to respond to public moods, to shape public opinion, and to mobilize group loyalties often feed the conflict and reduce the options for conflict resolution.

A view of conflict as a process that takes place between two societies immediately prompts us to examine what is happening *within* each society. In particular, this view alerts us to the role of internal divisions within each society. Although theories of international relations often treat states as unitary actors, the societies that states or other political organizations represent are never monolithic entities. Every political community is divided in a variety of different ways, and these internal divisions often play a major role in exacerbating or even creating conflicts *between* such political communities. The course of an intergroup conflict typically reflects the intragroup conflicts that exist within both conflicting groups, which impose constraints on the political leaders. Leaders pursuing a policy of accommodation have to consider the reactions of opposition elements, which may accuse them of betraying the national cause or jeopardizing national existence. They also have to be responsive to the anxieties and doubts within the general population, which the opposition elements both foster and draw support from. In all of these ways, internal divisions introduce severe constraints on efforts at conflict resolution.

Although the intersocietal nature of conflict contributes to its perpetuation, it also creates certain necessities and opportunities for conflict resolution. The internal divisions within each society do indeed impose serious constraints on decision makers in the pursuit of peaceful solutions, but they also provide them potential levers for change. Such divisions challenge the monolithic image of the enemy that parties in conflict tend to hold and enable them to deal with each other in a more differentiated way. They can come to recognize that even in a community mobilized to engage actively in a violent conflict, there may be elements amenable to an alternative approach who are potential partners for negotiation. This reality provides the opportunity, for example, for forming coalitions across the conflict lines—coalitions between those elements on each side that are interested in negotiation. Indeed, problem-solving workshops and related activities can be conceptualized as part of a process of forming precisely such a coalition (Kelman, 1993). A coalition across conflict lines, however, must of necessity remain an uneasy coalition. If it became overly cohesive, its members would lose their ability to influence the political decision making within their respective communities. By becoming too closely identified with their counterparts on the other side, they might become alienated from their own conationals, lose credibility at home, and hence forfeit their political effectiveness and their ability to contribute to another important precondition for conflict resolution: the development of a new consensus for a negotiated solution within their own community. If coalitions across conflict lines remain sensitive to the need to maintain the members' separate group identities and protect their credibility at home, they represent a potentially effective way of capitalizing on the divisions within the conflicting societies in the interest of conflict resolution, peacemaking, and ultimately building a new relationship between the former enemies.

Another implication of an intersocietal view of conflict is that negotiations and third-party efforts should ideally be directed not merely to a political *settlement* of the conflict in the form of a brokered political agreement, but to its *resolution*. A political agreement may be adequate for terminating relatively specific, containable interstate disputes, but it is an inadequate response to conflicts that engage the collective identities and existential concerns of the societies involved. Conflict resolution in this deeper and more lasting sense implies arrangements and accommodations that emerge out of the interactions between the parties themselves, that address the needs of both parties, and to which the parties feel committed. An agreement that is not widely accepted within the two societies is unlikely to make for a durable peace. What is required, in short, is a gradual process conducive to structural and attitude change, to reconciliation, and to the transformation of the relationship between the two societies—the development of a new relationship cognizant of the interdependence of the conflicting societies and open to cooperative, functional arrangements between them. The real test of conflict resolution in deep-rooted conflicts is how much the process by which agreements are constructed and the nature of the resultant agreements contribute to transforming the relationship between the parties.

Finally, a corollary of an intersocietal analysis of conflict is a view of diplomacy as a complex mix of official and unofficial, formal and informal efforts with complementary contributions. The peaceful termination or management of conflict requires binding agreements that can only be achieved at the official level. But insofar as we think of conflict as not only an interstate, but also an intersocietal affair, many different sectors of the two societies have to be fruitfully involved in a more elaborate, integrated process of diplomacy. In this context, unofficial, noncommittal interactions can play a constructive comple-mentary role by exploring ways of overcoming obstacles to conflict resolution and helping to create a political environment conducive to negotiation and other diplomatic initiatives (Saunders, 1988).

CONFLICT AS A MULTIFACETED PROCESS OF MUTUAL INFLUENCE

Much of international politics entails a process of mutual influence, in which each party seeks to protect and promote its own interests by shaping the be-havior of the other. Conflict occurs when these interests clash: when attainment of one party's interests (and fulfillment of the needs that underlie them) threat-ens, or is perceived to threaten, the interests (and needs) of the other. In pur-suing the conflict, therefore, the parties engage in mutual influence, designed to advance their own positions and to block the adversary. Similarly, in conflict resolution—by negotiation or other means—the parties exercise influence to induce the adversary to come to the table, to make concessions, to accept an agreement that meets their interests and needs, and to live up to that agree-ment. Third parties also exercise influence in conflict situations by backing one or the other party, by mediating between them, or by maneuvering to protect their own interests.

The typical influence process in international conflict relies on a mixture of threats and inducements, although the balance between negative and positive incentives varies considerably from case to case. Political analysts and decision makers often rely heavily, if not exclusively, on the use and threat of force as the means of exerting influence on adversaries. Thus, the U.S.–Soviet relation-ship during the Cold War was predominantly framed in terms of an elaborate theory of deterrence—a form of influence designed to keep the other side from doing what you do not want it to do. In other conflict relationships, the em-phasis may be on compellence—a form of influence designed to make the other side do what you want it to do. Such coercive strategies are part of the repertoire of influence processes in all domains of social life, but they entail serious costs and risks, and their effects may be severely limited. For example, they are likely to be reciprocated by the other side and thus lead to escalation of the conflict, and they are unlikely to change behavior to which the other is committed.

Thus, the effective exercise of influence in international conflict requires a broadening of the repertoire of influence strategies, at least to the extent of combining "carrots and sticks"—of supplementing the negative incentives that typically dominate international conflict relationships with a variety of positive incentives (cf. Baldwin, 1971; Kriesberg, 1981, 1982). Positive incentives may take the form of economic benefits, sharing essential resources, international approval, integration in regional or global institutions, or a general reduction in the level of tension. They are particularly effective if they represent ways of meeting the other's interests or responding to the other's security concerns that are at the heart of the conflict and if they are part of a concerted strategy that invites reciprocation. An example of an approach based on the systematic use of positive incentives is Osgood's (1962) GRIT (Graduated and Reciprocated Initiatives in Tension Reduction) strategy. President Anwar Sadat of Egypt, in his 1977 trip to Jerusalem, used a variant of the GRIT strategy by undertaking a unilateral initiative, based on the expectation (partly prenegotiated) of Israeli reciprocation (Kelman, 1985). But unlike the GRIT strategy, which starts with small concessions and gradually builds on them, Sadat's strategy in effect started at the end: "he made a massive, fundamental concession by accepting the basic principles of Israel's position . . . in the anticipation that negotiations would fill in the intervening steps" (Kelman, 1985, p. 216). GRIT, the Sadat initiative, and other strategies based on positive incentives have the potential of transforming the conflict into a new relationship in which both parties' needs and interests are met and continuing differences are resolved by peaceful means.

The view of influence in conflict relationships as a multifaceted process emphasizes positive inducements as a useful complement to the negative inducements that predominate in international conflict—as a strategy that often entails smaller short-term risks and greater long-term benefits than the use or threat of force. But it goes further: it also provides a framework for identifying the *types* of positive inducements that are most likely to be effective. Effective use of positive incentives requires more than offering the other whatever rewards, promises, or confidence-building measures seem most readily available. It requires actions that address the fundamental needs and fears of the other party. Thus, the key to an effective influence strategy based on the exchange of positive incentives is *responsiveness* to the other's concerns: the parties influence each other by actively exploring ways in which they can help meet each other's needs and allay each other's fears. Responsiveness also implies sensitivity to the other's constraints: it requires both parties to explore ways to help each other overcome the constraints within their respective societies against taking the actions that each wants the other to take. Responsiveness to the other's needs and fears is a fairly common form of influence in normal social relations. It is not, however, a strategy that parties in conflict are normally inclined to use because it requires them to explore and carry out actions designed to benefit the adversary.

The advantage of a strategy of responsiveness is that it alerts the parties to ways of exerting influence on the other through their own actions—through positive steps (not threats) that are within their own capacity to take. The process is greatly facilitated by communication between the parties to identify actions one party can readily take—actions that are politically feasible for that party and perhaps not even especially costly—but that are likely to have an impact on the other. Ultimately, the effectiveness of a strategy of responsiveness depends on careful adherence to the principle of reciprocity. One-sided responsiveness cannot sustain itself for long.

A key element in an influence strategy based on responsiveness is *mutual reassurance*, which is particularly critical in any effort to resolve an existential conflict. How, for example, can the parties to such a conflict be induced to come to the negotiating table and, once there, to make the concessions necessary to reaching an agreement? Because they are afraid that negotiations and concessions might jeopardize their national existence, mutual reassurance is a major motivating force—along with a mutually hurting stalemate and mutual enticement.

Negative incentives clearly play a significant role: the negotiation literature suggests that parties are often driven to the table by a mutually hurting stalemate, which makes negotiations more attractive than continuing the conflict (Touval & Zartman, 1985, p. 16; Zartman & Berman, 1982). Thus, one way of inducing an adversary to negotiate is to make the conflict more painful through the use of threats, military pressure, or other coercive means. But reliance on such negative incentives has many liabilities: it may push the parties to the table but does not necessarily make for productive negotiations once they get there, and it may reduce the likelihood of achieving an agreement that is mutually satisfactory and desirable. Therefore, negative incentives must at least be complemented by positive ones (cf. Zartman & Aurik, 1991)—by what Zartman has called "mutual enticement."

But parties engaged in existential conflicts are afraid to move to the negotiating table and to make concessions at the table, even when the status quo has become increasingly painful and they recognize that a negotiated agreement is in their interest. They worry that negotiations may lead to a series of ever more costly concessions that will ultimately jeopardize their security, their national identity, and their very existence. To advance the negotiating process under such circumstances, it is at least as important to reduce the parties' fears as it is to increase their pain.

Mutual reassurance can take the form of acknowledgments, symbolic gestures, or confidence-building measures. To be maximally effective, such steps need to address the other's central needs and fears as directly as possible. When Egyptian president Sadat spoke to the Israeli Knesset during his dramatic visit to Jerusalem in November 1977, he acknowledged that in the past Egypt had rejected Israel, refused to meet with Israelis, refused to exchange greetings. By clearly acknowledging the past hostility and thus validating Israelis' own experiences, he greatly enhanced the credibility of the change in course that he was announcing. These remarks helped to reassure the Israeli public that his offer was sincere and not just an elaborate trick to extract concessions that would weaken Israel's position in the continuing confrontation.

At the opening of this visit, Sadat offered a symbolic gesture that had an electrifying effect on Israelis: as he stepped off the plane, he engaged in a round of cordial handshakes with the Israeli officials who had come to greet him. The refusal of Arab officials to shake their hands had been profoundly disturbing to Israelis throughout the years of the conflict. It symbolized Arab denial of Israel's legitimacy and of the very humanity of its people. Sadat's gesture spoke directly to this deep hurt and signaled the beginning of a new relationship.

Confidence-building measures may consist of any acts that respond to the other's demands or accrue to the other's benefit. Again, however, they are particularly effective when they address major grievances and demonstrate sensitivity to the other's fundamental concerns. Thus, for example, the closing of military installations and removal of Israeli troops anywhere in the occupied territories—even if limited in scope—are concrete indicators to Palestinians that the peace process might in fact ultimately lead to an end to the occupation and thus reassure them that their leadership has not embarked on a course that threatens their national aspirations.

Acknowledgments often have a powerful psychological impact in opening the way to negotiation and accommodation, even though they are verbal statements that may not be immediately translated into concrete action steps. *Acknowledgment* in this context refers to a party's public acceptance or confirmation of the other party's view of its status, its experience, its reality. Thus, one party may acknowledge the other's humanity, the other's nationhood, the other's national rights, the other's suffering, the other's grievances, the other's interpretation of its history, the other's authentic links to the land, or the other's commitment to peace. Such acknowledgments do not constitute acceptance of the other's position or accession to the other's claims, but they recognize that there is some legitimacy to these positions and claims and some basis for them in the other's experience. Acknowledgments have such a potentially powerful impact because the history of the conflict is often marked by a systematic denial of the other's experience, authenticity, legitimacy, and even membership in the human family. These denials are a source of profound fear and insecurity because they undermine the very foundations of the group's claim to nationhood and challenge its right to national existence. Acknowledgment of what was heretofore denied is thus an important source of reassurance because it signals that the other, having accepted the legitimacy of one's claims, may indeed be ready to negotiate an agreement that addresses one's fundamental concerns. Under these circumstances, the parties are more likely to deem it safe to enter negotiations, despite the risks and uncertainties, and to make significant concessions. A good example of this kind of acknowledgment was the mutual recognition of Israel and the PLO in the Oslo accords of September 1993, which helped create the initial breakthrough in Israeli–Palestinian negotiations.

Apart from persuading the parties that their fundamental concerns will be addressed in the negotiations, acknowledgments may play a more subtle role in reassuring them that it is now safe to end the conflict, even if it requires major concessions. Acknowledgments do so insofar as they confirm the parties' national narratives. A central element of the Palestinian narrative, for example, is that the establishment of Israel created a profound injustice to the Palestinian people, who were displaced, dispossessed, dispersed, and deprived of their society and their future. An Israeli acknowledgment of that injustice, by confirming the Palestinians' national narrative, might allow them to let go of the conflict and accept a compromise solution, even though it would not fully remove the injustice they feel. It would vindicate their view of history, thus providing a justification for accepting a pragmatic approach so they can end the struggle and go on with their lives. By contrast, a central element of the Israeli national narrative holds that the establishment of Israel was an act of historical justice that enabled the Jewish people to return to its ancestral homeland after centuries of dispersion and persecution. A Palestinian acknowledgment of the Jewish people's historic roots in the land, by confirming the Israelis' national narrative, might enable them to let go of their claim to exclusive ownership of the land and accept a formula for sharing it with the Israelis. Again, the acknowledgment would vindicate their view of history and thus provide a justification for accepting the reality of the Palestinian presence and putting an end to the conflict.

In sum, acknowledgments provide reassurance both at the level of security and at the level of identity. By signaling acceptance of the other's legitimacy, each party reassures the other that negotiations and concessions no longer constitute mortal threats to its security and national existence. By confirming the other's narrative, each reassures the other that a compromise does not represent an abandonment of its identity, which is articulated by its national narrative.

Acknowledgments with the capacity to reassure the other are difficult to formulate because the national narratives of the conflicting parties typically clash. In confirming the narrative of the other, each party risks undermining its own narrative. Therefore, the parties often need to negotiate their acknowledgments with each other (perhaps in the context of a problem-solving workshop)—to engage in a joint process of formulating statements that will serve to reassure the recipient without threatening the issuer (Kelman, 1992a). The effectiveness of other forms of mutual reassurance, such as symbolic gestures and confidence-building measures, may be similarly enhanced if they are generated through such an informal negotiation process, in which the impact on the recipient and the constraints of the issuer can be jointly considered and balanced. A critical criterion for the maximal effectiveness of acknowledgments, gestures, and confidence-building measures is careful adherence to the principle of reciprocity. Reassuring the other is rarely cost free; the reassurance involves some concession—or at least is perceived to do so—and it often generates some domestic criticism. Thus, it is important that it be done in a context in which the initiator receives a visible return. Reciprocity itself is a source of mutual reassurance in that it signals to the parties that their concessions will not simply be pocketed by the other, but are likely to advance their own interests.

An influence strategy based on responsiveness to each other's needs and fears and the resulting search for ways of reassuring and benefiting each other has important advantages from a long-term point of view. It does not merely elicit specific desired behaviors from the other party, but it can contribute to a creative redefinition of the conflict, joint discovery of mutually satisfactory solutions, and transformation of the relationship between the parties. In terms of my earlier distinction between three processes of social influence (Kelman, 1961; Kelman & Hamilton, 1989; see also Rubin, 1989), a strategy of mutual responsiveness is likely to have an impact that goes beyond *compliance*, inducing changes at the level of *identification* and potentially *internalization*.

Positive incentives per se have an advantage over negative incentives in that they create an atmosphere more conducive to negotiation and provide greater opportunities for building a new relationship. But if promises, rewards, and confidence-building measures are offered randomly—essentially as "bribes"—without reference to the recipient's underlying needs and fears, they are likely to induce change only at the level of compliance (i.e., a relatively unstable change in public behavior without accompanying changes in private beliefs).

On the other hand, if positive incentives are used as part of a systematic strategy of responsiveness and reciprocity, they help develop a working trust and a valued relationship between the parties. The relationship becomes an incentive in its own right, in that the parties will be inclined to live up to each other's expectations to maintain and extend their new relationship. In this case, the resulting influence can be said to be at the level of identification: the parties are likely to change not only their public behavior, but also their private beliefs—at least as long as the relationship remains salient.

As parties develop a relationship based on responsiveness and reciprocity, they become better able to approach their conflict as a shared dilemma that requires joint efforts at analysis and problem solving. A joint problem-solving approach is conducive to agreements that are inherently satisfactory to the parties because they meet their fundamental needs and that are lasting because they create a sense of ownership and commitment. The negotiation and implementation of such agreements can be characterized as changes at the level of internalization: changes in behavior and beliefs that are congruent with the parties' own values and are relatively stable and enduring. The gradual transformation of the relationship between the parties, which makes these changes possible, itself becomes a key element of the mutually satisfactory and stable (i.e., the "internalized") outcome of a successful negotiation.

CONFLICT AS AN INTERACTIVE PROCESS WITH AN ESCALATORY, SELF-PERPETUATING DYNAMIC

Conflict is an interactive process, in which the parties change as they act and react in relation to each other. In intense conflict relationships, the natural course of the interaction tends to reinforce and deepen the conflict, rather than reduce and resolve it. The interaction is governed by a set of norms and guided by a set of images that create an escalatory, self-perpetuating dynamic. This dynamic can be reversed through skillful diplomacy, imaginative leadership, third-party intervention, and institutionalized mechanisms for managing and resolving conflict. But, in the absence of such deliberate efforts, the spontaneous interaction between the parties is more likely than not to increase distrust, hostility, and the sense of grievance.

The needs and fears of parties engaged in intense conflict impose perceptual and cognitive constraints on their processing of new information, with the resulting tendency to underestimate the occurrence and the possibility of change. In normal human relations, social interaction is the way in which people determine what the other needs and expects, assess the occurrence and possibility of change in these needs and expectations, and adjust their own behavior accordingly. By accommodating to each other's needs and expectations, both participants are able to advance the achievement of their respective goals. An essential feature of social interaction is the effort to take account of the other's purposes, perceptions, intentions, and expectations by implicitly taking the role of the other—on the assumption that the other has a mind like one's own, with similar kinds of purposes, perceptions, intentions, and expectations. In intense conflict relationships, this ability to take the role of the other is severely impaired. Dehumanization of the enemy makes it even more difficult to acknowledge and access the perspective of the other.

The inaccessibility of the other's perspective contributes significantly to some of the psychological barriers to conflict resolution described by Ross and Ward (1995). The dynamics of conflict interaction tend to entrench the parties in their own perspectives on history and justice. Conflicting parties display particularly strong tendencies to find evidence that confirms their negative images of each other and to resist evidence that would seem to disconfirm these images. Thus, interaction not only fails to contribute to a revision of the enemy image, but also actually helps to reinforce and perpetuate it. The combination of demonic enemy images and virtuous self-images leads to the formation of mirror images (cf. Bronfenbrenner, 1961; White, 1965), which greatly contributes to the escalatory dynamic of conflict interaction, as exemplified by the classical pattern of an arms race: When one side increases its arms and takes other actions that it considers defensive, the other interprets these steps as preparation for aggression and proceeds to increase its arms—presumably in defense against the other's intended aggression. The first side, however, interprets these steps in turn as preparation for aggression and further increases its arms, which further persuades the second party of the other's aggressive intentions—and thus a conflict spiral is set into motion. Interaction guided by such mirror images of enemy and self create self-fulfilling prophecies by inducing the parties to engage in the hostile actions they expect from one another.

Self-fulfilling prophecies are also generated by the conflict norms that typically govern the interaction between parties engaged in an intense conflict. Expressions, in word and action, of hostility and distrust toward the enemy are not just spontaneous manifestations of the conflict but are normatively pre-scribed behaviors. Both leaders and publics operate under a set of norms that require them to be militant and unyielding vis-à-vis the other side, to accuse the other of misdeeds, to be suspicious of their intentions, to deny all justice to their cause. Political leaders assume that their public's evaluation of them depends on their adherence to these norms and may go out of their way to avoid appearing weak or gullible. These tendencies are reflected in their tactical and strategic decisions, in the way they approach negotiations with the other side, in their public pronouncements, and ultimately, in the way they educate their own publics. For the publics, in turn, adherence to these norms is often taken as an indication of group loyalty; those who acknowledge that there may be some justice on the other side or propose a conciliatory posture may expose themselves to the accusation of treason or at least naiveté. In short, the dis-course in deep-rooted conflicts is marked by mutual delegitimization and de-humanization. Interaction governed by this set of norms—at the micro and the macro levels—contributes to escalation and perpetuation of the conflict. Parties that systematically treat each other with hostility and distrust are likely to become increasingly hostile and untrustworthy.

The dynamics of conflict interaction create a high probability that oppor-tunities for conflict resolution will be missed. As realities change in the inter-national, regional, or domestic environment, the parties in a long-standing conflict may well become amenable to a compromise solution. There may be possibilities for resolving the conflict in ways that are mutually satisfactory—or at least preferable to continuing the struggle and maintaining the status quo. But parties caught up in the conflict dynamics, whose interaction is shaped by the norms and images rooted in the history of the conflict, are systematically constrained in their capacity to respond to the occurrence and possibility of change. The nature of their interaction makes it difficult to communicate the changes that have occurred on their own side or to notice the changes on the other side and to explore the possibilities for change that would serve both sides' interests. Conflict resolution efforts, therefore, require promotion of a different kind of interaction, capable of reversing the escalatory and self-perpetuating dynamics of conflict: an interaction conducive to sharing per-spectives, differentiating the enemy image, and developing a language of mutual reassurance and a new discourse based on the norms of responsiveness and reciprocity.

IMPLICATIONS FOR CONFLICT RESOLUTION

In discussing each of the four propositions about the nature of international conflict offered here, I have pointed to some of its implications for conflict resolution. This concluding section draws together the implications of the anal-ysis for the macroprocess of peacemaking. In doing so, it also points to the special contributions that the microprocess of interactive problem solving (see

Fisher, 1997; Kelman, 1986, 1992b, 1998; Rouhana & Kelman, 1994) can make to the larger diplomatic enterprise.

The view of conflict as a process driven by collective needs and fears serves as a sharp reminder that a conflict cannot be genuinely resolved until these needs and fears of the parties are addressed. Even though the solution to a deep-rooted conflict may require painful compromises on both sides, it is likely to be perceived as just insofar as it satisfies the fundamental needs and allays the deepest fears of each. Only such a solution can serve as the basis of a stable, long-term peace, and a cooperative, mutually enhancing relationship.

Unofficial, interactive approaches to conflict resolution, such as problem-solving workshops, can contribute to resolving contentious issues in ways that meet the basic needs of one party without raising the fears of the other. They do so by enabling unofficial but politically involved representatives of the two parties to engage in exploratory, noncommittal communication, in which they can enter into each other's perspective, gain insight into the other's (and indeed their own) main concerns, and jointly shape creative new ideas for mutually satisfactory solutions to the conflict. The insights and ideas generated by this process can then be injected into the political debate and the decision-making process within the two societies.

The view of conflict as an intersocietal process points to the limits of political agreements signed by governments, often under the pressure or with the mediation of outside powers or international organizations. At least in the case of protracted, existential conflicts between identity groups, a durable peace requires movement beyond *settlement* of the conflict to its *resolution*. The agreement must address both parties' basic concerns. It must be widely accepted within the two societies, and the two populations must feel committed to it. It must reflect and further promote structural and attitude change and lead to a transformation of the relationship between the societies.

Another implication of the intersocietal nature of conflict is a view of diplomacy as a complex array of official and unofficial processes with a complementary relationship to each other. Unofficial interactions make it possible to explore possible openings for mutual accommodation and help to create a political atmosphere conducive to negotiation. Furthermore, awareness of the intersocietal nature of conflict helps to counteract the monolithic image that parties in conflict tend to have of each other by encouraging them to attend to what is happening within the other society and to the diversity of tendencies that it encompasses. More differentiated mutual images provide a basis for forming coalitions between the pro-negotiation elements on the two sides, dedicated to the search for common ground in the two sides' pursuit of their respective interests.

Problem-solving workshops and related fora for interactive conflict resolution can be seen as precisely such coalitions across conflict lines (Kelman, 1993, 1997a). They engage in a process of direct interaction, designed to generate ideas for resolving the conflict that address the needs of both parties and to which both parties can feel committed—essential conditions for agreements that will be widely accepted within the two societies and thus conducive to a durable peace. Binding agreements can only be reached at the official level, but unofficial interactions can contribute to enhancing the probability and the quality of the official agreement. Moreover, interactions within problem-solving workshops both promote and model the new relationship between the conflicting societies on which a long-term peace must ultimately rest.

The third proposition, positing conflict as a multifaceted process of mutual influence, suggests which strategies and tactics of influence between conflicting parties are most conducive to conflict resolution and to the development of a long-term peaceful relationship. Coercive strategies, which are the dominant mode of influence in conflict relationships, entail serious costs and risks and tend to produce only short-term effects. There is a need, therefore, for a shift of emphasis from the use of force or the threat of force to the use of positive incentives. Moreover, positive inducements are most effective when they are deliberately chosen to be responsive to the needs, fears, and constraints of the other party. A key element of an influence strategy based on responsiveness is mutual reassurance, which can take the form of acknowledgments, symbolic gestures, or confidence-building measures. A strategy of responsiveness and reassurance is most effective when it addresses the other's most basic concerns about identity and security and when it adheres to the principle of reciprocity.

The unofficial, noncommittal setting of problem-solving workshops can be particularly useful in identifying and formulating acknowledgments, gestures, and confidence-building measures that each side can offer to the other. Through a process of joint thinking, the parties can help each other devise steps of mutual reassurance that would be meaningful to the recipient without entailing unacceptable costs to the actor. This process often involves some informal negotiation, including "negotiation" of national identities and national narratives (Kelman, 1992a). Parties cannot be expected to abandon their identities or their national narratives, but they may be able to adjust their identity so that it is no longer contingent on denial of the other's identity, and to accommodate their own narrative to the narrative of the other.

Finally, the view of conflict as an interactive process with an escalatory, self-perpetuating dynamic suggests that conflict resolution efforts must be designed to counteract and reverse this conflict dynamic. A conflict relationship generates images and norms that entrench the conflict and create barriers to change that inhibit conflict resolution. Therefore, conflict resolution efforts must be geared to discovering the possibilities for change, identifying the conditions for change, and overcoming the resistances to change. Openness to change and reversal of the conflict dynamic depend on the establishment of a new discourse among the parties, characterized by a shift in emphasis from power politics and threat of coercion to mutual responsiveness, reciprocity, and invitation to a new relationship.

At the microlevel, problem-solving workshops and similar approaches to conflict resolution are designed to contribute to the reversal of the escalatory dynamic of conflict interaction by promoting a different kind of interaction, characterized by a de-escalatory dynamic. To this end, workshops encourage the parties to penetrate each other's perspective, to differentiate their image of the enemy, to develop a de-escalatory language and ideas for mutual reassurance, and to engage in joint problem solving designed to generate ideas for resolving the conflict that are responsive to the fundamental needs and fears of both sides.

ACKNOWLEDGMENT

This chapter is based in large part on pages 194–210 of Kelman (1997b). This material is reprinted here by permission of the original publisher and editors.

REFERENCES

Baldwin, D. (1971). The power of positive sanctions. *World Politics, 24,* 19–38.

Bronfenbrenner, U. (1961). The mirror image in Soviet-American relations: A social psychologist's report. *Journal of Social Issues, 17*(3), 45–56.

Burton, J. W. (1988). Conflict resolution as a function of human needs. In R. A. Coate & J. A. Rosati (Eds.), *The power of human needs in world society* (pp. 187–204). Boulder, CO: Lynne Rienner.

Fisher, R. J. (1997). *Interactive conflict resolution.* Syracuse, NY: Syracuse University Press.

Kelman, H. C. (1961). Processes of opinion change. *Public Opinion Quarterly, 25,* 57–78.

Kelman, H. C. (1985). Overcoming the psychological barrier: An analysis of the Egyptian-Israeli peace process. *Negotiation Journal, 1,* 213–234.

Kelman, H. C. (1986). Interactive problem solving: A social–psychological approach to conflict resolution. In W. Klassen (Ed.), *Dialogue toward interfaith understanding* (pp. 293–314). Tantur/Jerusalem: Ecumenical Institute for Theological Research.

Kelman, H. C. (1987). The political psychology of the Israeli-Palestinian conflict: How can we overcome the barriers to a negotiated solution? *Political Psychology, 8,* 347–363.

Kelman, H. C. (1992a). Acknowledging the other's nationhood: How to create a momentum for the Israeli-Palestinian negotiations. *Journal of Palestine Studies, 22,* 18–38.

Kelman, H. C. (1992b). Informal mediation by the scholar/practitioner. In J. Bercovitch & J. Z. Rubin (Eds.), *Mediation in international relations: Multiple approaches to conflict management* (pp. 64–96). New York: St. Martin's Press.

Kelman, H. C. (1993). Coalitions across conflict lines: The interplay of conflicts within and between the Israeli and Palestinian communities. In S. Worchel & J. Simpson (Eds.), *Conflict between people and groups* (pp. 236–258). Chicago: Nelson-Hall.

Kelman, H. C. (1997a). Group processes in the resolution of international conflicts: Experiences from the Israeli-Palestinian case. *American Psychologist, 52,* 212–220.

Kelman, H. C. (1997b). Social–psychological dimensions of international conflict. In I. W. Zartman & J. L. Rasmussen (Eds.), *Peacemaking in international conflict: Methods and techniques* (pp. 191–237). Washington, DC: U.S. Institute of Peace.

Kelman, H. C. (1998). Social–psychological contributions to peacemaking and peace-building in the Middle East. *Applied Psychology: An International Review, 47,* 5–28.

Kelman, H. C., & Hamilton, V. L. (1989). *Crimes of obedience.* New Haven, CT: Yale University Press.

Kriesberg, L. (1981). Non-coercive inducements in U.S.–Soviet conflicts: Ending the occupation of Austria and nuclear weapons tests. *Journal of Military and Political Sociology, 9,* 1–16.

Kriesberg, L. (1982). Non-coercive inducements in international conflict. In C. M. Stephenson (Ed.), *Alternative methods for international security* (pp. 105–120). Washington, DC: University Press of America.

Osgood, C. E. (1962). *An alternative to war or surrender.* Urbana: University of Illinois Press.

Ross, L., & Ward, A. (1995). Psychological barriers to dispute resolution. In M. P. Zanna (Ed.), *Advances in experimental social psychology* (Vol. 27, pp. 255–304). New York: Academic Press.

Rouhana, N. N., & Kelman, H. C. (1994). Promoting joint thinking in international conflicts: An Israeli-Palestinian continuing workshop. *Journal of Social Issues, 50*(1), 157–178.

Rubin, J. Z. (1989). Some wise and mistaken assumptions about conflict and negotiation. *Journal of Social Issues, 45*(2), 195–209.

Saunders, H. H. (1988). The Arab-Israeli conflict in a global perspective. In J. D. Steinbruner (Ed.), *Restructuring American foreign policy* (pp. 221–251). Washington, DC: Brookings Institution.

Touval, S., & Zartman, I. W. (Eds.) (1985). *International mediation in theory and practice.* Boulder, CO: Westview Press.

White, R. K. (1965). Images in the context of international conflict: Soviet perceptions of the U.S. and the U.S.S.R. In H. C. Kelman (Ed.), *International behavior: A social-psychological analysis* (pp. 238–276). New York: Holt, Rinehart & Winston.

Zartman, I. W., & Aurik, J. (1991). Power strategies in de-escalation. In L. Kriesberg & S. J. Thorson (Eds.), *Timing the de-escalation of international conflicts* (pp. 152–181). Syracuse, NY: Syracuse University Press.

Zartman, I. W., & Berman, M. R. (1982). *The practical negotiator.* New Haven, CT: Yale University Press.

6

Diplomacy in an Era of Intrastate Conflict: Challenges of Transforming Cultures of Violence into Cultures of Peace

Michael Wessells

Diplomacy is one of the oldest instruments of statecraft and of violence prevention. In the current security environment, its basic tools such as negotiation, mediation, conciliation, and coercion remain important elements of efforts to build peace. In the post–Cold War world, diplomatic treaties, state policies, and trained cadres of professional diplomats remain key elements of comprehensive efforts to build peace.

In the current security environment, however, official diplomacy is limited by its emphases on state actors and on top-down strategies of building peace via agreements between leaders and governments. The dominance of intrastate conflict is a key feature of the security environment. The number of armed conflicts increased steadily from the 1970s to the early 1990s (Renner, 1999), and although the number has decreased, there continue to be approximately 25–35 wars fought each year (Wallensteen & Sollenberg, 2000). Overwhelmingly, the conflicts are intrastate, as only 6 of 103 armed conflicts fought between 1989 and 1997 were international (Renner, 1999). This contrasts with the start of the twentieth century, when interstate fighting was the dominant pattern.

For traditional diplomacy, intrastate conflicts present compelling political challenges. Contested state legitimacy is central in these conflicts, which feature nonstate actors such as opposition groups, guerrillas, warlord-led groups, and paramilitaries. Not infrequently, state actors resist meeting with leaders of opposition groups because meetings could produce image loss and imply recognition of the other as having legitimate claims and status. State actors often distrust nonstate actors, which may not regard themselves as bound by the laws of an unjust state or by international treaties. Similarly, nonstate actors may resist diplomatic solutions because they accept violence as an instrument of liberation, want to use violence to gain political control, or fear that meetings will either make them appear soft or lend credibility to the state. Diplomacy is often blocked by massive doubt that official settlements will work, and in some contexts, these doubts have considerable basis in reality. In Angola, for example, a diplomatically constructed cease-fire collapsed in 1992 when the opposition group (UNITA) rejected the results of the first democratic elections, thereby plunging the country back into war. In addition, peace processes have served as breathing spaces in which armies increase their strength. In December 1998, for example, when war reerupted, UNITA unleashed greater firepower than anyone had expected, revealing the failures of a UN monitoring mission and increasing doubt that a diplomatic solution would ever be constructed.

Psychologically, the changing nature of the conflicts poses significant challenges to diplomacy. Even following a cease-fire or the signing of a peace agreement, communities on the ground remain deeply divided, harbor lingering hatreds, and confront persistent root causes of violence such as poverty and oppression. Left behind are cultures of violence that cannot be transformed by signed peace agreements and urgings by leadership into cultures of peace. In this context, social injustices and cycles of violence are likely to continue, damaging the prospects for peace.

The purpose of this chapter is to identify key psychological obstacles to official diplomacy that are associated with the rise of long-term, intrastate conflicts and that require expanded, integrated views of diplomacy. It analyzes the manner in which the psychosocial wounds of communalized war and the systemic nature of violence limit what official diplomacy can accomplish. It argues that official diplomacy, which both institutionally and conceptually has been kept distinct from issues of humanitarian assistance, development, and social justice, cannot by itself repair divided societies, mitigate protracted conflicts, or perform the wide array of peace-building tasks that are needed to establish peace. Diplomacy needs to be supplemented by tight linkages with humanitarian assistance, peacemaking, and peace building. The holistic approach recommended suggests that effective diplomacy will focus less on leader-designed treaties and arrangements and more on multilevel processes of social transformation and long-term development that help to convert cultures of violence into cultures of peace. Recognizing the multidisciplinary nature of peace building, the chapter also identifies psychological tools and processes that complement those of official diplomacy.

EMOTIONAL AND SOCIAL WOUNDS

The shift toward intrastate war brought with it changes in the nature of fighting that have powerful psychological implications. In previous centuries, war was mostly a matter of armies clashing on relatively well-defined battlefields, and nearly 90 percent of the casualties were combatants. But in intrastate wars, former neighbors often fight each other in and around communities, destroying homes and means of livelihood, displacing large numbers of people, and leaving behind large numbers of land mines and unexploded ordnance that ruin the prospects of agriculture and resumption of normal activities around homes and communities. As evident in the brutal conflicts in Rwanda, Bosnia, Kosova, and East Timor, among many others, contemporary wars target mostly civilians and include mass rapes, group murders, genocide, and human rights abuses on a massive scale. Approximately 90 percent of the casualties are civilians, thereby reversing the pattern evident in previous centuries.

TRAUMA, SHATTERED SOCIAL TRUST, AND SOCIAL IDENTITY

Intercommunal wars leave a distinctive psychological footprint centered around trauma and the shattering of social trust (Wessells, 1998a, 1998b). Because the fighting directly targets communities and civilians, large numbers of people experience attack, loss of loved ones, separation from family, destruction of home and property, displacement, sexual violence, and continued threats from land mines. Because most of the wars occur in the developing world, these stresses interact with and add to already severe stresses associated with poverty, environmental degradation, violence, and failed government. Fatigued by decades of struggle against repressive regimes, many people who live in contemporary war zones report feeling overwhelmed by their experiences, loss, and trauma, and many abandon hope. Remarkably, even in the worst circumstances, people exhibit significant resilience, cautioning against simplistic images of war-traumatized populations.

Trauma heightens people's sense of the world as a dangerous place, increasing their desire to take steps, including the use of violence, to protect themselves (Staub, 2001). The personal wounds and memories of the horrible things that happened often create desire for revenge, spreading seeds of violence that political leaders may manipulate. The residues, however, are communal as well as individual. Communities engaged in armed conflict often create narratives of trauma and victimization—collective memories—that enshrine the communal suffering and create shared images of unwarranted victimhood (Volkan, 1997). In communities in Palestine, Northern Ireland, Kosovo, and many others, communities integrate the belief that they and their ethnic, religious, or cultural group have been victimized into their social identities. The social construction of one's own group as victims who have been unjustifiably assaulted or mistreated by the out-group becomes a psychological warrant for revenge, counterattack, or militarization to protect one's group. In this manner, prevalent war trauma helps to set the stage for ongoing cycles of violence.

Betrayal contributes to the heightened sense of vulnerability and the shattering of social trust. In interstate conflicts, the combatants usually are soldiers who do not know each other and whose fighting is government controlled. In many interstate conflicts, citizens view themselves and the citizens of the rival country as pawns in a struggle orchestrated by politicians. Personally felt animosity toward people on the other side may be low because the bad things that happen are attributed to the governments, not to the people themselves (cf. White, 1984).

A different attributional pattern, however, occurs in intercommunal conflicts in which one recognizes former neighbors as the people who killed one's family, burned one's home, or raped one's sister. Often, highly personal attributions are made, as it is assumed that the neighbors had only pretended to be friendly and had violated ordinary customs of decency toward others who are recognized and have done no harm. When apparent friends turn out to be enemies, the capacity to trust others is a major casualty. This distrust acquires strong ethnic loading where fighting occurs along ethnopolitical fault lines, and the perceptions are that it is the members of the particular ethnic group who did bad things. In this context, ethnic markers carry greater salience, and harm inflicted on a member of one's own group is perceived as harm done toward all members of the group. Suspicion of the out-group, no matter how peaceful they might have appeared, becomes a familiar pattern that seems warranted by one's life experiences. Seeing members of the out-group living in the community or walking in the streets can evoke powerful fears, trigger horrifying memories, and incite violent behavior. Even peace becomes threatening. After all, it is during times of peace that members of other groups build their strength and plan their deadly attacks. What heightens fear the most is the ambiguity regarding who the enemy is. The enemy is not just the soldiers or political leaders but neighbors, workers, and other people in the community.

Social distrust also stems from destabilization, dislocation, and local competition between warring groups. As always, war disrupts familiar social routines that add stability and meaning to life. But in intrastate fighting the destruction is often focused on civilians, meaning that schools, roads, health posts, and homes may be destroyed on a large scale. As witnessed in Kosovo and East Timor, intrastate wars create large waves of refugees, whose movement across state borders regionalizes the conflict. Conflicts also create equally vast numbers of internally displaced people, whose movement into new areas stretches social support systems beyond their capacity, heightens conflict over scarce resources, and amplifies internal tensions.

Confusion arises also from the activities of a dizzying array of competing groups, which make communities pawns in local power struggles. In Colombia, for example, rural communities are often trapped between the competing demands and violent tactics of paramilitaries, government forces, guerrillas, and narcotraffickers. In Somalia, competing warlords fight for control of different communities. In these and other conflicts, communities see that the government cannot protect their security. This increases fears that the enemy, which comes from within, could be anywhere and that there is no means of stopping them. It also undermines citizens' trust that there remains a government that will defend the people and provide an anchor in an uncertain social world.

These observations suggest the need for multilevel approaches to diplomacy that build a social and psychological platform for both the construction and implementation of official agreements. Without communal healing and reconstruction of social trust, it will be very difficult to rebuild a society such as Kosovo for peace. Even following the signing of an official peace accord, lingering hatreds and fears can spark continued violence that unravels the peace accord and faith in the viability of the wider peace process. In addition, people may feel so overwhelmed by what they have been through that they may not be in a good position to rebuild economically or politically.

Communal healing may help set the stage for negotiated agreements by generating public support and increasing "ripeness" for a negotiated settlement. In the absence of communal healing, people may be vulnerable and manipulable, giving extremists a fertile emotional climate in which to stir hatreds and generate backlash against a peace process. Public sentiments against peace proposals can tie leaders' hands, make them fearful for their survival, and pressure them into taking relatively hawkish stances that impede the construction of peace. To induce the systemic change that is needed, diplomacy needs to be coordinated with multilevel programs to support healing and rebuilding of social trust.

HEALING AND REBUILDING SOCIAL TRUST

Healing involves coming to terms with the past and is best understood as a social process. Healing and rebuilding social trust are reciprocal processes, as deep healing requires the reestablishment of social trust and a sense of personal and collective security. In addition, healing often occurs through emotional sharing and reintegration in a group context and through solidarity. Conversely, building social trust requires healing and coming to terms with the past, as excessive fear and traumatic memories make it difficult for people to reconnect.

Diverse psychosocial tools exist for promoting healing and rebuilding social trust. By adapting the tools to the local context, interweaving Western-based methods with indigenous methods, and choosing which tools to use based on a process of local consultation and dialogue, it is possible to avoid the imposition of outsider approaches and to promote sustainable practices (Wessells & Monteiro, 2000). Among the main categories of tools are the following.

Healing Practices

In Western contexts, healing can be achieved through counseling and emotional expression and reintegration in a safe climate, and the healers typically consist of trained professionals. In non-Western contexts, where individualism is not the norm and spirituality is at the center of life, healing is often understood as a communal process and may not be based on emotional expression

(Honwana, 1997). Instead, the emphasis is on the conduct of rituals to restore spiritual harmony and to enable social integration, and the healers often consist of local healers, clergy, or spiritual leaders. In nearly all contexts, healing also occurs through the reestablishment of familiar daily routines and activities that meet basic needs, provide a sense of safety and normalcy, and build continuity between past, present, and future. Community-based activities that support resilience, social healing, solidarity, and hope are key parts of healing (Wessells & Monteiro, 2001).

Truth Commissions

Often the first step toward healing is to enable the truth to be told via truth commissions or other public means (de la Rey, 2001; Hamber, 1998). Truth commissions serve to bring out the truth about hidden injustices, to remove social lies promulgated through state-sponsored violence, and to publicly name and validate the suffering of people who had previously been treated as invisible and less than fully human. Truth is also a precondition for the establishment of justice, though significant debate remains about the value of truth-telling in the absence of steps to end impunity or to provide reparations.

Dialogues

Intergroup dialogues can help to reduce negative stereotypes, to humanize members of a group that had previously been demonized, and to set the stage for cooperation and productive activities across group lines. In heated situations, however, intergroup contact may also occasion negative, damaging behavior that only makes matters worse. Successful cross-conflict dialogue often requires having a skilled facilitator who sets careful ground rules, enables constructive behavior, and weeds out extremists who may amplify destructive conflict.

Interactive Problem-Solving Workshops

A particularly useful tool in facilitating communal change is the interactive problem-solving workshop pioneered by Kelman (1996), Burton, and others (cf. Fisher, 1997). In this approach, a skilled facilitator and his or her third-party team selects from each side moderates who are open-minded and who are politically influential, although they are outside official positions in their respective communities. In a neutral, academic context, groups of approximately four members of each group meet for a period of several days in dialogues assisted by the third party. The dialogues emphasize active listening and joint problem-solving discussions in which both sides consider "what-if" questions, generate possible options for addressing particular problems, and act as collaborators in solving problems at the heart of the conflict. Following the dialogues, the participants return to their respective communities, planting the seeds of their learning about the other side on a wider basis.

Superordinate Goals

Another useful tool in building communal change entails cooperation on superordinate goals (Sherif, 1966), defined as goals that are held by all the parties, that can be achieved through intergroup cooperation, but that cannot be accomplished by one group acting by itself. Difficult issues such as addressing poverty, HIV/AIDS, and environmental degradation provide fertile ground for collaboration. The process of cross-conflict cooperation can mitigate against zero-sum thinking; build a sense of common ground; reduce hostility, stereotypes, and polarization; and help to construct wider social identities than the narrow identities that had featured victimization and fueled violence.

Tolerance Building

In divided societies, it is vital to build tolerance between conflicting groups. This can be particularly challenging in the aftermath of violent conflict, when strong tensions and high risks of violence make it impossible to bring together conflicting groups or to engender constructive dialogue at the community level. One method used successfully on a limited scale in Kosovo and other war contexts is to conduct community workshops on human rights. A human rights focus strengthens belief in the dignity of all human life, moves discourse beyond the frame of political conflict, and reinforces commitment to fundamental principles that ought to protect people everywhere but that frequently get pushed off the screen by war. A related, reflective methodology entails stimulation of internal reflection by asking questions such as, "Is this what we want to become?" In environments such as Kosovo, where wounds are too close to the surface to discuss reconciliation and where daily abuse of Serbs and other minorities occurs, this reflective approach can bypass questions regarding politics and one's own victimization.

PSYCHOSOCIAL ASSISTANCE IN EMERGENCIES

The process of healing, although long term, cannot wait until the work of official diplomacy is done. Instead it needs to begin during or shortly following the acute phase of emergencies and to integrate seamlessly with long-term development. This important point has not always been recognized and is still not embodied in the practice of many humanitarian agencies. Consistent with the ideas of Maslow (1968), many humanitarians have held that basic, subsistence needs must be met first. The initial work in an emergency is to provide food, clothing, shelter, and other biological necessities, whereas psychosocial intervention comes later. This approach is not unreasonable as people cannot heal when they have empty stomachs or no shelter.

This approach, however, overlooks the fact that the way in which aid is administered has a powerful psychological impact. If refugees, for example, are treated as passive victims who must be fed like cattle, as occurs when relief agencies throw food off the back of a truck to the starving masses, already severe problems of dehumanization and helplessness may be exacerbated. In contrast, if refugees are empowered and help to make decisions about how aid is distributed, this can begin the process of reasserting control, thereby reducing trauma and laying a psychological foundation for long-term development. Increasingly, the humanitarian assistance community recognizes that healing is not something to be accomplished through stand-alone, psychosocial activities. What are needed are holistic approaches that meet basic human needs and into which psychosocial dimensions are integrated. In this view, psychosocial assistance is less a separate program intervention than a methodology—a way of doing things—that builds dignity, respect for human rights, and emotional and social well-being.

The need for integrated approaches is evident in emergencies such as that created by the massive reprisal attacks on East Timor by Indonesian paramilitaries in 1999. Following decades of brutal occupation, the East Timorese people had voted in favor of independence from Indonesia. Indonesian paramilitaries promptly ravaged the country, scattered hundreds of thousands of people in the mountains and drove over one hundred thousand more across the border into West Timor, and damaged or destroyed nearly 80 percent of homes and buildings (Taylor, 1999). Following the attack, displacement, and living with little food or water and in fear of one's life, many people reported feeling overwhelmed, in shock over what they had been through, and hopeless and unable to control their circumstances.

Situations such as this require an empowerment approach that integrates material assistance, community rebuilding, and emotional and social support. This integrated approach is at the heart of a consortium program being implemented in seven districts by three international NGOs—Christian Children's Fund, International Rescue Committee, and Save the Children Federation. The material assistance consists mostly of shelter reconstruction activities in which communities decide which homes to rebuild, and East Timorese workers, including people from the local communities, build the shelters, with materials provided mostly by the UN High Commission on Refugees. Basic materials for children's activities—balls, sewing materials, musical instruments, and so forth—are provided to enable groups to organize structured, normalizing activities for war-affected children. Small grants enable community projects and support activities of social groups in small business activities. In communities, groups of parents and concerned citizens conduct dialogues on tolerance building and human rights. This approach recognizes that healing is communal and involves restoration of normal patterns of living (Gibbs, 1997). In addition, some of the greatest stressors relate to material deprivation, and healing, empowerment, and material reconstruction go hand in hand. It embodies the view that the tasks of diplomacy and state building that lie ahead require a foundation of planful communities, healthy civil society, social healing, and tolerance.

More broadly, this work recognizes that the success of diplomacy will likely be limited unless it is coupled with emergency assistance to displaced people. Mass displacements in armed conflict create impetus for more fighting because many displaced people want to return home and are willing to use violence to do so if necessary. In addition, displaced people often live in difficult conditions and experience isolation and stigmatization, which contributes to divided societies. In contemporary conflicts, diplomacy remains an art but it is not the art of statesmanship so much as the art of coordinating interventions at different social levels, of uniting fractured communities, and of integrating humanitarian, emergency assistance with long-term development.

SYSTEMIC VIOLENCE

In conflicts such as those in Bosnia, East Timor, and Kosovo, the most brutal acts of organized fighting—the ethnic cleansing, massacres, and mass rapes—receive the most attention. Less-visible aspects of the conflict system, however, are often equally deadly and problematic for the construction of peace. In war zones, violence becomes normalized and saturates different levels of society such as family, school, and community. Acts of physical violence are often rooted in systems of oppression, inequity, poverty, and various other forms of social injustice. To build peace, it is essential to address these root causes through interventions at multiple levels. In the broadest sense, the challenge is to convert cultures of violence into cultures of peace (Brenes & Wessells, in press).

STRUCTURAL VIOLENCE

Contemporary conflicts are intextricably interconnected with problems of structural violence (Galtung, 1969), which entails the failure of socially constructed institutions to meet basic human needs (Christie, Wagner, & Winter, 2001). Structural violence is manifest in oppression, social injustice, denial of human rights, and preventable deaths because of denial of basic services such as health care. In intrastate conflicts, the struggle for power, coupled with existential fear, desire for revenge, and zero-sum identity processes, often creates divided societies in which one identity group systematically oppresses others. Control over scarce resources is used as a tool of domination, and the resulting relative deprivation and victims' identity help to fuel ongoing conflict.

A powerful case in point is the 1994 Rwandan genocide, in which the massive, direct violence was rooted in systemic oppression and injustice. During the Belgian colonial rule that preceded independence, Tutsis enjoyed a privileged role, and the system denied most Hutus equal wealth, land, education, and access to political power (Prunier, 1995). Reaction against this asymmetry and oppression was largely responsible for the rise following independence of Habyarimana's Hutu-led regime, which turned the tables and systemically privileged Hutus. By the 1990s, Hutus and Tutsis, who were defined as much by social class as ethnicity (Smith, 1998), feared each other not only because of the current situation but also because of the large-scale killings that had occurred along ethnic lines and without accountability both in Rwanda and neighboring Burundi. Discrimination against Tutsis and bouts of politically motivated violence within Rwanda created hundreds of thousands of mostly Tutsi refugees, who concentrated in Uganda and organized militarily to return home and regain power. Extremists in Habyarimana's own party are believed to have murdered Habyarimana, unleashing a well-planned genocide that killed approximately 800,000 Tutsis and moderate Hutus.

Structural violence is often exacerbated by environmental degradation and resource scarcity, a connection Renner (1996) has outlined in regard to Rwanda. Between 1954 and 1993, the population of Rwanda tripled, making it the most densely populated country in Africa. Because of land scarcity, the explosive population growth was not matched by expansion of cropland, leading to overcultivation and declining fertility. In addition, farming in places vulnerable to erosion became even more prevalent. The net result was a sharp decline in per capita food production and increased reliance on imports. Favoring the northwest, which was his home and political center, President Habyarimana channeled development assistance in ways that divided the country further. As Rwanda faced rising foreign debt, foreign lenders encouraged coffee cultivation and export to pay the debt. But when the international coffee market collapsed in the late 1980s, Rwanda suffered huge losses of export revenues. Rising economic pressures and powerful fears of local people that they would lose their land created an environment ripe for exploitation by extremist politicians within Habyarimana's regime. A key lesson is that environmental degradation can engender economic hardships that become part of the conflict system and help to set the stage for violence. Increasingly, resource scarcities not only amplify privileging of the dominant groups but also create desperation and a sense of crisis that give political leaders a powerful card to play.

Beyond Rwanda, the interplay between structural violence and armed conflict is visible in intrastate conflicts around the world. The September 1999 violence in East Timor, for example, erupted following the vote of the East Timorese people for independence. If the vote for independence was the spark, the kindling was the Indonesian military's 25 years of severe repression of the East Timorese people (Taylor, 1999). Similarly, the liberation struggle in countries such as South Africa and the Philippines followed decades of brutal oppression, which planted seeds for conflict. Further, conflicts such as those in

Sudan or Northern Ireland (Cairns & Darby, 1998) grow out of systems of oppression that privilege one identity group over others. Worldwide, nearly two-thirds of minority groups, distinguished from dominant groups by ethnicity, religion, social class, and other features, experience economic and political discrimination (Gurr, 1992). Minority group members often view themselves as victims, and they see the discrimination and mistreatment as transgressions that warrant action, including violence, to change the system or to avenge their losses. In contrast, dominant group members, clinging to their privileges, typically adopt a stance of self-righteous defense of the status quo. On both sides, violence becomes seen as a necessary instrument. Because of this linkage between structural violence and armed conflict, peace processes must address root causes of violence and end structural as well as direct violence (Christie et al., 2001).

VIOLENCE NORMALIZATION AND PREVALENCE

The durability of many conflicts creates a system of beliefs and practices that weave violence into the fabric of daily life, making it difficult for leaders to change. Approximately 40 percent of contemporary armed conflicts have been going on for over a decade (Smith, 1997). The protracted nature of armed conflict, which owes to the cyclical nature of the fighting, means that societal violence becomes part of the social horizon, and entire generations grow up in a situation in which violence is the norm. In countries such as Angola, where the conflict is 40 years old, the concept of peace seems quite alien to many people as it is a condition that they have never experienced directly. Throughout society, the prominence of war as a daily feature of one's social landscape cements cognitive scripts that portray violence as an acceptable instrument for achieving one's goals.

In addition, war zones become cultures of violence via the spread of stress and desperation and the spilling over of values and practices supportive of violence. As poverty and the hardships of daily living escalate as a result of the fighting, family stresses and violence increase (Walker, 1999). In the 10 war zones the author has worked in over the past decade, one of the most frequent reports made by women is that wife beating increased in and around the periods of intense fighting and hardships. Further, war creates such difficult conditions that many people turn to crime as a means of meeting their basic needs, and violence, the tool that many had learned well through participation in the war, becomes their main instrument. In war zones, a weakened police force, the corrosion of law and order, and increasing desperation typically enables an upsurge in violent crime. The result is a blurring of boundaries between war and peace that makes the postconflict environment as dangerous as the war itself.

Youth militarization and political socialization contribute to as well as grow out of the normalization of violence. In war-torn societies, war games are commonplace, as children act out on playgrounds and in the streets scenes that they have seen, heard about, or imagined. Youth have many models of fighting to emulate, as on a daily basis they may see the troops of governments, paramilitaries, or opposition groups in and around their communities. Through social learning, many youth come to value the prestige of the uniform, which of course is associated with the power of the gun. In families and even in schools, children hear war stories, learn the communally constructed myths about history and the horrible things done by members of the other side, and learn to fear and even hate the other.

At a time in their lives when they are defining their identity, youth may be attracted by ideology and liberation struggles that actively engage them in violence, even if they are not part of organized military units. As illustrated in the current fighting between Israelis and Palestinians, youths are increasingly political actors who may take fighting into their own hands. The evolution of norms toward fighting, coupled with widely held belief systems that undergird the violence (Rouhana & Bar-Tal, 1998), make the violence very difficult to control from the top by leaders and by treaties. In the streets, the fighting takes on a life of its own and is initiated by many sources without direct orders. As people are wounded physically and emotionally in the fighting, their sense of victimization increases, leading to additional fighting.

Worse, local military commanders frequently recruit young people as soldiers in violation of the Convention of the Rights of the Child and its recently developed Optional Protocol that boosts the minimum recruitment age to 18 years. Worldwide, there are approximately 300,000 child soldiers who may perform a variety of roles such as combatants, cooks, porters, spies, and sex slaves (Boothby & Knudsen, 2000; Brett & McCallin, 1996; Wessells, 1997). Children become soldiers for many different reasons such as glory seeking, money, security, desperation to survive, family honor, and excitement. Not infrequently, children are abducted, brutalized, and either terrorized or forced to commit murders as means of ensuring they will not try to escape. Youth militarization strips societies of some of its potentially richest social capital. Following the fighting, youth who had formerly been soldiers have no job skills or education, know the power of the gun, and are at risk of banditry and crime that strengthens the culture of violence.

THE NEED FOR HOLISTIC APPROACHES

In this context, official diplomacy is limited in several respects. First, in systems of communal violence, psychological and political pressures may thwart the construction of peace agreements. Popular pressures may constrain severely whether negotiations can take place, who can participate, which options can be brought to the table, and how much progress can occur during the talks. Second, psychological and political pressures often thwart implementation of agreements achieved through diplomacy. The problem cannot be reduced to backlash from extremist political leaders alone. Often, agreements reached at the top are not supported by strategies to address the reticence of community leaders, the fears and hatreds felt by community people, and the influence of local norms, values, and socialization practices that support violence. Because most conflicts are intercommunal, they are unamenable to top-down approaches but require steps to change the intergroup hostilities and the normalized violence that exists at community levels.

Both dynamics are illustrated clearly by the current al-Aqsa Intifada in the Israeli–Palestinian conflict, in which Palestinian youths throw stones at Israeli troops, leading to violence escalation and what many regard as disproportionate use of force by Israeli Defense Forces. The intense animosity and fighting in the streets make it difficult to convene official peace talks, and eruptions of violence during any talks derail them. More important, the violence is not necessarily leader driven but is initiated at the grassroots level by Palestinian youth who take matters into their own hands. Having a momentum of its own, the violence is difficult to control from the top. Although local Palestinian leaders may have some ability to contain violence, their influence is limited. Once stones have been thrown, Israeli Defense Forces respond, and people are injured or killed, which the Palestinian community regards as yet another transgression that sparks additional rage and violence. Leader-driven processes are ill suited for enabling changes in the hearts and minds of Palestinian youth. Top-down processes need to be complemented by changes at the grassroots level, leading analysts such as Lederach (1997) to call for middle-out approaches. These target changes on midlevel leaders who then spread key messages and build nonviolent norms both at the grassroots level and at the higher policy-making levels.

Official diplomacy is also not well suited to addressing structural violence and the root causes of armed conflict. Diplomacy can open the door for change by carving agreements to end discrimination and oppression, to redistribute resources in a more equitable manner, or to protect the local environment. Ultimately, though, diplomacy needs to be linked to effective strategies and interventions that promote long-term, sustainable development and the social justice that is inseparable from peace.

Psychologists have numerous methodologies and tools to contribute to work aimed at transforming cultures of violence into cultures of peace. The tools outlined in the preceding section on healing are relevant. Truth commissions, for example, help to bring injustices to light, establish an atmosphere of honesty, and provide a platform for building social justice. Further, methods such as interactive problem solving are particularly well suited to addressing communal violence. At the local level, one can bring together community leaders on opposing sides to build understanding and to analyze various options for handling problems of violence and its causes. Following the problem-solving workshops, leaders return to their communities and talk with others, spreading what they had learned and planting seeds of nonviolent conflict management throughout the community. Similarly, the method of superordinate goals is highly useful in building cooperation and a sense common ground at the community level. Other psychologically informed approaches include the following.

Reduction of Discrimination

Discrimination is at the heart of structural violence and has psychological components as well as institutional ones. Psychologists have numerous tools for reducing racism, negative stereotypes, enemy images, and denigrating images that enable and rationalize the mistreatment of out-groups (Hewstone & Greenland, in press; Pettigrew, 1998). Longer-term work to reduce the injustices associated with sexism, classicism, and other -isms is also needed. Useful psychological tools include empowerment, positive role modeling, mentoring, and social support in times of transition. This includes processes of peace building, in which groups such as women have been marginalized and relatively invisible (McKay & Mazurana, 2001).

Layered Work on Conflict Resolution

To address systemic violence, methods of nonviolent handling of conflict need to be established, made normative, and supported at multiple levels. Within families, efforts to reduce spouse abuse and child abuse are relevant, as is wider work oriented toward enabling constructive conflict management (Abrahams, 2001; Cahn, 1994). Similarly, much work is needed in schools, workplaces, and communities to encourage nonviolent conflict resolution (Deutsch & Coleman, 2000). In communities, it is valuable to mobilize peace committees and to activate and support indigenous processes of conflict resolution (Fry & Bjorkqvist, 1997).

Education for Peace

Education for peace is both formal and nonformal. In schools, it entails methods such as peer mediation, cooperative learning, training of teachers and administrators in nonviolence, curriculum reform to remove demonic images of the other, and changing the norms, values, and culture of the school in the direction of nonviolence (Coleman & Deutsch, 2001). Universities can provide not only research but also education that analyzes the war system, dialogue about nonviolent options, and practica that give students firsthand experience in peace building. Outside school, it involves conducting community dialogues on human rights, the value of nonviolence, and nonviolent options for handling conflict. In protracted conflicts where "peace" has disappeared from public discourse, getting it back into public discussion can itself change the psychological horizon.

Media Activity

Media such as television often show excessive violence that contributes to normalization by desensitizing viewers, encouraging cognitive scripts of violence, modeling of violent behavior, and heightening viewers' sense of danger (Donnerstein, Slaby, & Eron, 1994). Still, media such as radio and television can be powerful means of promoting tolerance, respect for human rights, and peace. Public radio, for example, can air drama that shows the harmful effects of violence and the benefits of handling conflicts nonviolently. Similarly, peace radio can promote constructive discussion across the lines of conflict, tell stories of peacemakers, and provide independent information that counteracts war propaganda.

Youth Development

The best way of preventing structural and direct violence is through prevention efforts that create positive developmental pathways for young people, particularly adolescents who have the capacity to do enormous good or significant harm. Too often, youth feel marginalized and have no positive role within the community. Keeping them involved in quality education, providing training in basic life skills, and enabling leadership and participation in community development activities can reduce the risks that youth will participate in violence. Vocational training, apprenticeships, and mentoring can help youth find employment and meaningful work, thereby helping to reduce poverty, desperation, and alienation that fuel criminal activity and to build hope for a positive future.

CONCLUSION

The current era of intrastate conflict does not spell the death of diplomacy—far from it. Diplomacy will continue to be a vitally important approach for conflict prevention and mitigation and for the construction of peace. To maximize its contributions to peace, however, diplomacy needs to become more holistic, integrated, and psychologically informed. In both concept and practice, stronger bridges must be built between diplomacy, humanitarian assistance, long-term development, peacemaking, and peace building. In the field, great need exists for increased cooperation and coordination across agencies and tasks, moving beyond the current state of fragmentation. Leader-led peace processes need to be complemented and supported by grassroots processes that alter oppositional identities, norms of violence, oppression, fear, and hatred. Psychologically informed approaches that address emotional and social wounds and that promote nonviolence at multiple levels need to be integrated into the holistic approach suggested. Psychological changes need to be complemented with macrostructural changes to end oppression and injustice. Because violence is systemic, efforts to build peace in an era of intrastate conflict must be equally systemic.

REFERENCES

Abrahams, N. (2001). Intimate violence. In D. Christie, R. Wagner, & D. Winter (Eds.), *Peace, conflict and violence: Peace psychology for the 21st century* (pp. 19–27). Upper Saddle River, NJ: Prentice Hall.

Boothby, N. G., & Knudsen, C. M. (2000). Children of the gun. *Scientific American, 282*(6), 60–66.

Brenes, A., & Wessells, M. (in press). Building cultures of peace. *Peace and Conflict: Journal of Peace Psychology.*

Brett, R., & McCallin, M. (1996). *Children: The invisible soldiers.* Vaxjo, Sweden: Radda Barnen.

Cahn, D. (Ed.). (1994). *Conflict in personal relationships.* Hillsdale, NJ: Erlbaum.

Cairns, E., & Darby, J. (1998). The conflict in Northern Ireland: Causes, consequences, and controls. *American Psychologist, 53*(7), 754–760.

Christie, D., Wagner, R., & Winter, D. (Eds.). (2001). *Peace, conflict and violence: Peace psychology for the 21st century.* Upper Saddle River, NJ: Prentice Hall.

Coleman, P., & Deutsch, M. (2001). Introducing cooperation and conflict resolution into schools: A systems approach. In D. Christie, R. Wagner, & D. Winter (Eds.), *Peace, conflict and violence: Peace psychology for the 21st century* (pp. 223–239). Upper Saddle River, NJ: Prentice Hall.

de la Rey, C. (2001). Reconciliation in divided societies. In D. Christie, R. Wagner, & D. Winter (Eds.), *Peace, conflict and violence: Peace psychology for the 21st century* (pp. 251–261). Upper Saddle River, NJ: Prentice Hall.

Deutsch, M., & Coleman, P. (Eds.). (2000). *The handbook of constructive conflict resolution: Theory and practice.* San Francisco: Jossey-Bass.

Donnerstein, E., Slaby, R., & Eron, L. (1994). The mass media and youth aggression. In L. Eron, J. Gentry, & P. Schlegel (Eds.), *Reason to hope* (pp. 219–250). Washington, DC: American Psychological Association.

Fisher, R. J. (1997). *Interactive conflict resolution.* Syracuse, NY: Syracuse University Press.

Fry, D., & Bjorkqvist, K. (Eds.). (1997). *Cultural variation in conflict resolution: Alternatives to violence.* Mahwah, NJ: Erlbaum.

Galtung, J. (1969). Violence, peace and peace research. *Journal of Peace Research, 3,* 176–191.

Gibbs, S. (1997). Postwar social reconstruction in Mozambique: Reframing children's experiences of trauma and healing. In K. Kumar (Ed.), *Rebuilding war-torn societies: Critical areas for international assistance* (pp. 227–238). Boulder, CO: Lynne Rienner.

Gurr, T. (1992). Third World minorities at risk since 1945. In S. J. Brown & K. M. Schraub (Eds.), *Resolving Third World conflict: Challenges for a new era* (pp. 52–90). Washington, DC: U.S. Institute of Peace.

Hamber, B. (1998). *Past imperfect: Dealing with the past in Northern Ireland and societies in transition.* Derry: INCORE.

Hewstone, M., & Greenland, K. (in press). Intergroup conflict. *International Journal of Psychology.*

Honwana, A. (1997). Healing for peace: Traditional healers and post-war reconstruction in southern Mozambique. *Peace and Conflict: Journal of Peace Psychology, 3,* 293–305.

Kelman, H. C. (1996). The interactive problem-solving approach. In C. Crocker, F. Hampson, & P. Aall (Eds.), *Managing global chaos* (pp. 501–520). Washington, DC: U.S. Institute of Peace Press.

Lederach, J. P. (1997). *Building peace: Sustainable reconciliation in divided societies.* Washington, DC: U.S. Institute of Peace Press.

Maslow, A. (1968). *Toward a psychology of being.* Princeton, NJ: Van Nostrand.

McKay, S., & Mazurana, D. (2001). Women, girls and structural violence: A global analysis. In D. Christie, R. Wagner, & D. Winter (Eds.), *Peace, conflict and violence: Peace psychology for the 21st century* (pp. 341–349). Upper Saddle River, NJ: Prentice Hall.

Pettigrew, T. (1998). Intergroup contact theory. *Annual Review of Psychology, 49,* 65–85.

Prunier, G. (1995). *The Rwanda crisis.* New York: Columbia University.

Renner, M. (1996). *Fighting for survival.* New York: Norton.

Renner, M. (1999). Ending violent conflict. *Worldwatch Paper 146.* Washington, DC: Worldwatch.

Rouhana, N., & Bar-Tal, D. (1998). Psychological dynamics of intractable ethnonational conflicts: The Israeli-Palestinian case. *American Psychologist, 53*(7), 761–770.

Sherif, M. (1966). *Group conflict and cooperation.* London: Routledge.

Smith, D. (1997). *The state of war and peace atlas,* 3rd ed. London: Penguin.

Smith, D. N. (1998). The psychocultural roots of genocide. *American Psychologist, 53*(7), 743–753.

Staub, E. (2001). Genocide and mass killing: Their roots and prevention. In D. Christie, R. Wagner, & D. Winter (Eds.), *Peace, conflict and violence: Peace psychology for the 21st century* (pp. 76–86). Upper Saddle River, NJ: Prentice Hall.

Taylor, J. G. (1999). *East Timor: The price of freedom.* London: Zed Books.

Volkan, V. (1997). *Bloodlines.* New York: Farrar, Straus & Giroux.

Walker, L. (1999). Psychology and domestic violence around the world. *American Psychologist, 54,* 21–29.

Wallensteen, P., & Sollenberg, M. (2000). Armed conflict, 1989–99. *Journal of Peace Research, 37*(5), 635–649.

Wessells, M. (1997). Child soldiers. *Bulletin of the Atomic Scientists, 53*(6), 32–39.

Wessells, M. G. (1998a). The changing nature of armed conflict and its implications for children: The Graça Machel/U.N. study. *Peace & Conflict: Journal of Peace Psychology, 4*(4), 321–334.

Wessells, M. G. (1998b). Children, armed conflict, and peace. *Journal of Peace Research, 35*(5), 635–646.

Wessells, M. G., & Monteiro, C. (2000). Healing wounds of war in Angola: A community-based approach. In D. Donald, A. Dawes, and J. Louw (Eds.), *Addressing childhood adversity* (pp. 176–201). Cape Town: David Philip.

Wessells, M. G., & Monteiro, C. (2001). Psychosocial intervention and post-conflict reconstruction in Angola: Interweaving Western and traditional approaches. In

D. Christie, R. Wagner, & D. Winter (Eds.), *Peace, conflict and violence: Peace psychology for the 21st century* (pp. 262–275). Upper Saddle River, NJ: Prentice Hall.

White, R. K. (1984). *Fearful warriors: A psychological profile of U.S.–Soviet relations.* New York: Free Press.

7

Multitrack Diplomacy: Global Peace Initiatives

Tyrone F. Price and Linda A. Price

INTRODUCTION

Destructive intergroup conflict is the most costly enigma facing humankind. It is the preeminent social issue of our time in that it ruthlessly saps the resources required for human development and productivity and in the extreme threatens global survival. Poorly handled cleavages occur in a variety of settings—organizational, communal, and international—and the costs of destructive escalation are readily apparent to all. In organizational settings, badly managed conflict between workers and management and among various departments and units result in lost time, lowered morale, and wasted energy. In communal settings, racial prejudice, discrimination, and tension among ethnic groups breeds inequality and debilitates the quality of life for many. At the international level many parts of the world are aflame with violence whereas other parts of the world smolder, all against the backdrop of an impending nuclear holocaust.

We must also acknowledge the functional aspect of intergroup conflict as a source of necessary social change and the movement toward justice and equality. Developed and sustainable societies, although still harboring noticeable inequities, are those that have found apparently adequate means of addressing conflicting group interests. Many other societies are racked by cleavages between various interests and class groups. The ideal is that differences are confronted and resolved nonviolently and in ways that are mutually acceptable to the groups involved. Nevertheless, this approach is seldom used.

Conflict prevention activities aim to mitigate mass violence between or within countries. This field of endeavor mainly involves governments, multilateral agencies like the United Nations, and nongovernmental organizations (NGOs). Conflict specialists describe many methods and strategies to resolve international, global conflict: conflict prevention, conflict resolution, conflict management, preventive action, preventive peace diplomacy, and so on. These proactive preventive strategies should be implemented to prevent destructive action at an early stage so that the conflict is manageable.

Theorists who study the history of war describe a cyclic progression of conflict: early signs of trouble between antagonistic groups, hostile actions, warfare, and postconflict cleanup. At each stage, specific interventions by conflict specialists may be appropriate to prevent the conflict from escalating.

In recent years, NGOs have begun to play a significant role in conflict prevention. These groups, part of the larger blossoming of civil society around the world, now number in the thousands and use a wide variety of methods. Advocacy and public interest organizations, the news media, humanitarian relief providers, academia, or private actors have initiated unofficial intervention.

A typical initiative by an NGO would convene meetings between unofficial representatives of disputing parties to build confidence between sides, a process often referred to as "track two diplomacy" because it works just below the official, or track one level. Often, only an NGO can convene such parties and create such a space for dialogue because of the politically sensitive nature of such meetings. This approach has, for example, been quite fruitful in addressing the Israeli–Palestinian conflict until most recently because of escalated conflict.

A culture of peace consists of the set of values, attitudes, and behaviors that reflect and inspire social interaction and sharing and solidarity that rejects violence and endeavors to prevent conflicts by tracking their roots. Problems are solved through dialogue and negotiations that guarantee to everyone the full exercise of all rights and the means to participate fully in the endogenous development of their society. This research will address global peace and conflict resolution strategies from a diplomatic and social–psychological approach with implications for social scientists.

CONFLICT: A SOCIAL PSYCHOLOGICAL PERSPECTIVE

The problem of conflict is certainly one of the most relevant in the present state of affairs of the world. With the destruction of the West-East division, the exacerbation of North-South differences, and the challenges of globalization, which further pressure Third World economies, new conflicts are arising, and in some cases their solution is not met with diplomatic means, and force is employed. Destructive intergroup conflict is the most complex and costly enigma facing humankind. It is the preeminent social issue of our time in that it ruthlessly saps the resources required for human development and productivity and in the extreme threatens our very survival. Poorly handled cleavages occur in a variety of settings—organizational, communal, and international—and the costs of destructive escalation are readily apparent to all.

We must also acknowledge the functional aspects of intergroup conflict as a source of necessary social change and the movement toward justice and equality. Developed and sustained societies, although still harboring noticeable inequalities, are those that have found apparently adequate means of addressing conflicting group interests. Many other societies are racked by cleavages between various interests and class groups, each seeking "a place under the sun." Thus, on the moral question of the desirability of intergroup conflict, there are initially two answers. The first is that conflict simply exists and as such it is neither good nor bad. It is a central fact of human existence, and the first task of social scientists is to describe and explain it. The second answer is that conditional intergroup conflict can be either good or bad, depending on whether it is handled constructively or destructively. The ideal is that differences are confronted and resolved nonviolently and in ways that are mutually acceptable to the groups involved (Fisher, 1990).

The threat of violence is pervasive in our era, having reached what might be its highest level in human history. Domestic and street violence is an immediate fact of life in most societies. Collective violence between ethnic and racial groups and among nations brings about destruction on a catastrophic scale. The threat of this kind of violence is not new; indeed, some earlier societies may have faced even higher levels. What is new is that the threat is of almost unimaginable scope; virtually any outbreak could trigger vast cataclysms of violence (Scheff & Retzinger, 1991).

The Jekyll and Hyde sides of conflict are nowhere more evident than in group and intergroup relations. Conflict and its most extreme disguise, competition, have been identified as the cause of intergroup hostility and discrimination (Dovidio, Mann, & Gaertner, 1989). The roots of war are often deeply embedded in conflict over territory or basic attitudes and values (Glad, 1990; Kaplan & Markus-Kaplan, 1983).

Nevertheless conflict may initiate broad and important social change. Looking within the United States, open and sometimes violent conflict between blacks and whites served as the stepping stone for reform of nearly every facet of life, including education, voting, political districting, employment, and law. Similar reforms are analogous to conflict involving people of different genders, religions, ages, and sexual orientations. It is a matter of speculation whether these changes would have occurred without open confrontation. However, it is a matter of record that the confrontation was a motivating source for these changes (Worchel & Simpson, 1993).

Efforts to avoid or ignore conflict can have disastrous effects on group process and productivity. Encouraging mainstream, minority, or deviant members to openly express their alternative viewpoints can play a very positive role in group decision making (Worchel, Coutant-Sassic, & Grossman, 1991).

Conflict has often served as an elixir. Sherif (1961) found that two enemies would become temporary allies if the conflict widened to include a common foe. Politicians have long recognized the common enemy approach as a means of consolidating power.

SOURCES OF CONFLICT

The Latin word *confiftus,* a "striking together with force," implies disagreement, discord, and actions to produce disruptive effects. When conflict occurs in a group, the actions or beliefs of one or more members of the group are unacceptable and are resisted by one or more of the other group members. In many instances conflict in a group occurs because members must compete for limited resources. Intragroup conflict has many causes. Some theorists prefer to emphasize communication difficulties, organizational structures, and social and psychological factors (Blake & Mouton, 1984).

Two drug gangs attack each other with semiautomatic rifles in a struggle over territory. Striking miners attack police and state troopers when they try to move the strikers' picket lines. University students complain that faculty members are not committed to teaching and assign grades unfairly, and the faculty believes that students are intellectually lacking. The Israeli and Arab conflict is also an example of intergroup conflict.

Intergroup conflict occurs at all levels of social organization, from discord within families to organized disputes in industrial settings and riots stemming from breakdowns in racial relations to conflicts between nations. Although conflicts between groups are one of the most complicated phenomena studied by social scientists, the goal of greater understanding and the promise of reduced tensions are challenging (Forsyth, 1990).

Conflict theory maintains that intergroup conflicts occur because of competition among groups over limited resources. This theory notes that the things people value, including food, territory, wealth and power, natural resources, and energy, are so limited that if the member of one group manages to acquire a scarce commodity, the members of another group will go without it. Naturally, groups would prefer to be haves rather than have-nots, so they take steps to achieve two interrelated outcomes: attaining the desired resources and preventing the other group from reaching its goals (LeVine and Campbell, 1972). Competition-based theories of conflict explain class struggles (Marx & Engels, 1947), rebellions (Gurr, 1970), international warfare (Deutsch, 1985; Streufert & Streufert, 1986), racism (Bobo, 1983), and tribal rivalries in East Africa (Brewer & Campbell, 1976).

Intergroup conflict arises in many forms, and there are a number of topologies for categorizing it. Galtung (1965) distinguishes conflict at the individual level from that at the collective level, which may be either intrasystem or intersystem. Thus, collective conflict may be intranational or international, and Galtung notes that the introduction of a group level to the scheme would account for conflict within and between classes or ethnic, racial, or other interest groups. Beres and Schmidt (1982) distinguish four predominant areas of conflict research: (1) social conflict involving structures of dominance and inequity between class or interest groups within a society, (2) industrial conflict between organized labor and management groups within an established adversarial system, (3) organizational conflict involving small groups (units, departments, etc.) and conflict within a cooperative system, and (4) international conflict between nations within the loosely defined global system. Dahrendorf (cited in Angell, 1965) delineates conflict between various levels of social units including groups (e.g., males), sectors (e.g., the army and the navy), and societies (e.g., Protestants and Catholics). Suprasocial relations involve conflict between countries or blocks. Dahrendorf's scheme also distinguishes among conflicts between equals and unequals and between the whole versus a part (e.g., the state versus the corporation).

Building on these schemes, the current analysis distinguishes various systems. Intergroup conflict primarily can be located at the organizational, communal, societal, and international levels. Intergroup conflict in organizations occurs between various structural groupings such as departments, between labor and owners, and managers, as in classic industrial conflict. In communal settings, intergroup conflict is often expressed between ethnic, racial, religious, and gender groups and is usually noticeable through the existence of prejudice and discrimination as well as the occasional outburst of violence. These intergroup cleavages may also be expressed at the societal level in the form of social issues (i.e., racism, poverty) and are joined by conflict between classes, political groups, or other broad sectors of society, such as the military industrial complex, the environmental lobby, and various other social movements. Finally, at the international level there is conflict between nations and blocks that is often intermixing with intergroup cleavages at the societal and communal levels. It is this intermixing of levels and issues that produces the most enigmatic and irresolvable form of intergroup cleavage, protracted social conflict.

There exists in the world today a number of intense intergroup conflicts, some between and some within nations, that appear intractable. A continuing state of tension is heightened by episodes of escalation often involving violence, which is typically determined by mutual exhaustion and/or some form of peacekeeping. Traditional approaches to conflict management prove ineffective, and the underlying issues move no closer to resolution. Examples of such conflicts at various points of longevity and expression include those in the Middle East, Northern Ireland, Cyprus, Lebanon, India, Pakistan, Kampuchea, Sri Lanka, Iraq–United States, and the Horn of Africa. Numerous other conflicts of a similar but less-intense nature exist throughout the world, awaiting the process of escalation to increase their intensity and visibility.

This type of seemingly intractable intergroup conflict has recently been labeled "protracted social conflict" by Azar (1983) to denote its ongoing and seemingly irresolvable nature. The sources of protracted social conflict are not to be found in the traditional loci of economics or power but in the frustration of compelling needs, including those for security, identity, and participation, which are essential to human development. Protracted social conflict is there-fore typically rooted in a combination of economic underdevelopment, struc-tural inequality, and unintegrated political systems. Historical intergroup cleavages are often combined with continuing inequity to produce the irre-pressible nature of protracted social conflict. In a similar vein, Burton (1987a) speaks of "typically rooted conflicts," which are not based on interests that are negotiable, but on underlying needs that cannot be compromised. The most conspicuous of these are violent conflicts between communities and nations over the preservation of cultures, values, and needs for identity. Traditional methods of conflict management, which deal only with surface issues, simply suppress underlying needs and help lay the seeds for more intense conflicts in the future.

The particular humanistic value base of applied social psychology asserts that individuals and social groups have undeniable needs and rights for security, dignity, and respect in both physical and psychological terms, involving iden-tity, recognition, participation, and control over their own destiny. Denial or suppression of these needs and rights creates a dynamic for social change that must be considered in conjunction with traditional sources of intergroup and international conflict in the areas of economics and power (Fisher, 1990).

THE NATURE OF INTERNATIONAL CONFLICT

A social–psychological perspective to conflict suggests that certain proposi-tions about the nature of international conflict emerge from more traditional approaches such as the realist school of international relations. The first prop-osition holds that international conflict is a process driven by collective needs and fears, rather than entirely a product of rational calculation of objective national interest on the part of political decision makers. Second, internal con-flict is an intersocietal process, not only an interstate or intergovernmental phenomenon. Third, international conflict is a multifaceted process of mutual influence, not only a contest in the exercise of coercive power. And fourth, in-ternational conflict is an interactive process with an escalating, self-perpetuating dynamic, not merely a sequence of action and reaction by stable actors.

International or ethnic conflict must be conceived as a process in which col-lective human needs and fears are acted out in powerful ways. Such conflict is typically driven by nonfulfillment or threats to the fulfillment of basic needs. These needs include not only obvious material ones, such as food, shelter, physical safety, and physical well-being, but also psychological needs, such as identity, security, recognition, autonomy, self-esteem, and a sense of justice. These needs become driving forces in international and intergroup conflict. The link of needs to groups, their collective aspect, is an important and almost ubiquitous feature of human nature. The fulfillment of needs takes place to a considerable extent within the context of groups of different sizes. The ethnic group, the national group, and the state are among the collectives that serve as important vehicles for fulfilling and protecting fundamental needs.

Closely related to these basic needs in intergroup conflict situations are fears about the denial of the needs, fears focusing, for example, on perceived threats to security or identity. In protracted conflicts between identity groups, such fears often take on an existential character, turning the conflict into struggle over group survival. The Israeli–Palestinian conflict, for example, can be described as an existential conflict between two parties, each of which sees its very existence as a national group threatened.

Identity, security, and similarly powerful collective needs and the fears and concerns about survival associated with them are often important causal factors in intergroup and intercommunal conflict. The causes of conflict generally combine objective and subjective factors, which are related to others in a circular fashion. Conflicts focusing, for example, on issues such as territory and resources almost invariably reflect and further magnify underlying concerns about security and identity. Whatever their role in the causation of a conflict, subjective forces linked to basic needs and existential fears contribute heavily to its escalation and perpetuation. Such needs and fears create a resistance to change, even in situations in which both parties, or significant elements of both parties, have concluded that it is in their best interest to end the conflict. Despite this perceived interest, the parties are often unable to extricate themselves from the escalating dynamic (Kelman, 1996).

THE THREE DYNAMICS AND CONFLICT RESOLUTION

The essential qualities of the three dynamics are summarized in table 7.1. It focuses on the differences among the three dynamics in regard to eight important factors:

1. How people are viewed
2. How people obtain value
3. How force can and should be used
4. The nature of relationships
5. The nature of attachment
6. The degree of honesty
7. The kind or quality of emotions
8. The effect on conflict resolution

Each dynamic represents a group of psychosocial needs and their method of expression through other people. The chart should become increasingly meaningful as the reader progresses through the chapter.

Table 7.1

The Three Dynamics. Three dynamics typically occur in combination within both individuals and institutions. A person or a religion, for example, may express a mix of themes based on love, liberty, and coercion all at once. The goal is to identify the dynamics, to understand their characteristics and consequences, and, if possible, to encourage shifts toward liberty and ultimately toward love.

	I. LOVE	II. LIBERTY	III. COERCION
1. People:	person, beings	agents, doers	objects subhuman
2. Value	unconditional	earned, acquired	assigned
3. Force:	abhorred, rejected	In self-defense	arbitrary
4. Relationship	gifting, sharing	voluntary, competitive	involuntary, coercive
5. Attachment:	interdependent	independent	detached
6. Honesty:	maximized	contractual	restricted
7. Emotions:	love, joy	esteem, respect	helplessness, emotional pain
8. Conflict:	prevented, resolved	barely controlled	suppressed, exacerbated

Source: Breggin, P. (1992). *Beyond Conflict: From Self-help and Psychotherapy to Peacemaking.* New York: St. Martin's Press.

Three dynamics typically occur in combination within both individuals and institutions. A person or a religion, for example, may express a mix of themes based on love, liberty, and coercion simultaneously. The goal is to identify the dynamics, to understand their characteristics and consequences, and if possible, to encourage shifts toward liberty and ultimately toward love.

Love, with its abhorrence of force and inherent valuing of the other, is the ultimate route to conflict resolution. The deepest conflicts can rarely be prevented or resolved without empathic love for those with whom we are in conflict. Only when people treasure each other and care about each other's basic needs can conflict be turned into mutual cooperation with lasting peace or harmony.

Love is the ultimate source of conflict resolution in every aspect of our lives. To resolve inner or psychological conflict, we must learn to love ourselves; to resolve interpersonal and global conflict, we must learn to understand those with whom we are in conflict and appreciate their differences.

Liberty, with the use of force limited to self-defense, is an important stage in conflict resolution. The principle of equal rights provides the safety people often require before they will dare to become intimate and loving. The principles of reason, self-determination, and equal rights encourage bargaining and mediation.

Liberty without love results in more superficial and temporary solutions, with the regeneration or recycling of conflict at a later date. A married couple bargains over where to go on vacations, and each year one of them is less satisfied with the choice than the other. Annually they must go through tense and competitive negotiations over how to spend their two weeks together. Conflict resolution occurs when they love each other sufficiently to take joy in each other's happiness. They become as delighted with their partner's pleasure as with their own, and now help each other find their ideal vacation spot. When people in conflict work together to identify and to fulfill each other's needs, the result are always a more lasting and profound conflict resolution.

The same is true on an international level. To create a war, a leader must stir up hatred for the enemy. To bring lasting peace, as between the United States and Canada, people must feel affinity for each other. They must seem so alike to each other in terms of their common humanity that they would not dream of resorting to violence to solve their problems.

The most successful policies of the United States, for example, the Marshall Plan that helped reconstruct postwar Western Europe or Douglas MacArthur's successful efforts to bring democracy to Japan, have been based on the principle of empathic caring. In each case, the United States cooperatively assisted other nations to fulfill their basic needs. This mutual effort developed a constructive relationship conducive to peace and harmony.

Coercion all too often seems the preferred method of conflict resolution, but it only leads to suppression and, ultimately, violence. Coercion suppresses and injures the powerless and in the extreme produces totalitarianism in society. It fosters power and control on the part of the perpetrator and submission and helplessness on the part of the victim. Attitudes toward force can be critical in identifying each dynamic and in understanding their outcomes. In love, force is abhorred. We do not wish to injure our loved ones, even in self-defense, but we never initiate force. In coercion, we initiate force to satisfy our needs. Liberty encourages or produces independence in personal relationships and the free market of society. It encourages competition and ranking people according to a hierarchy of achievement or success. Love generates personal bonding and human community; liberty generates personal autonomy and freedom of expression; coercion generates personal oppression and totalitarianism (Breggin, 1992).

MULTITRACK DIPLOMACY

The term *multitrack diplomacy* is based on the original distinction made by Joseph Montville in 1981 between official governmental actions to resolve conflicts (track one) and unofficial efforts by nongovernmental professionals to resolve conflicts within and between states (track two). Later, Louise Diamond coined the phrase "multitrack diplomacy," recognizing that to lump all track two activities into less than one label did not capture the complexity or breadth of unofficial diplomacy. Ambassador John McDonald then wrote an article expanding track two into four separate tracks: conflict resolution professionals, business, private citizens, and the media. This framework, however, still had the four unofficial tracks operating with the exclusive purpose to affect or change the direction of track one.

Track one diplomacy is government-to-government, formal, official interaction between instructed representatives of sovereign states. It can be either bilateral in nature, involving two governments, or multilateral in approach, involving many governments.

Track two, on the other hand, is nongovernmental, informal, and unofficial. It is interaction between private citizens or groups of people within a country or from different countries that are outside the formal governmental power structure.

These people have as their objective the reduction or resolution of conflict, within a country or between countries, by lowering the anger or tension or fear that exist through improved communication and a better understanding of each other's point of view. Track two diplomacy is not a substitute for track one, but rather is in support of parallel track one goals. In fact, a successful track two effort may well lead into track one, especially when specific agreements or treaties or other formal understandings are called for.

Track two diplomacy is a process designed to assist official leaders to resolve or, in the first instance, to manage conflicts by exploring possible solutions out of public view and without the requirements to formally negotiate or bargain for advantage. Track two diplomacy seeks political formulas or scenarios, which satisfy the basic security and esteem needs of the parties to a particular dispute. It seeks to promote an environment in a political community through the education of public opinion that would make it safer for political leaders to take risks for peace.

Track two diplomacy involves at least two and perhaps three interdependent processes. The first process consists of small, facilitated, problem-solving workshops or seminars that bring together the leaders of conflicting nations or groups (or their representatives) to (1) develop workable personal relationships in microcosm, (2) understand the dimensions of the conflict from the perspective of the adversary, and (3) at some point develop joint strategies for dealing with the conflict as a shared problem, the solution of which requires reciprocal and cooperative efforts.

The second process is to influence public opinion. Here the task is a psychological one, which consists of reducing the sense of victimhood of the parties and rehumanizing the image of the adversary. If successful, this process will gradually bring about a climate of opinion within the community or nation that makes it safe for political leaders to take positive steps, perhaps those involved in the small workshops toward resolving the conflict.

In the problem-solving workshops it is quite possible, even common, for leaders to develop a vastly expanded understanding of a conflict and of the psychological tasks to be mastered before it can be solved. It is also possible for them to undergo a personal transformation in which their sense of and approach to the enemy becomes humanized. But these leaders are compelled to reenter the political environment of their constituents who have not had the opportunity to gain insights from the workshop experience (McDonald & Bendahmane, 1986).

Cooperative economic development, the third process, may not be essential to conflict resolution, but it provides incentives, institutional support, and continuity to the political and psychological process. To groups and nations in conflict, cooperative economic activities offer the prospect of growth, enhancement of individual well-being, and a measure of stability for families and communities that have often suffered significant personal loss and endured chronic instability.

The nongovernmental movement toward peacemaking and peace building has grown exponentially in recent years. As a result, the designation of track two no longer describes the variety, scope, and depth of citizen involvement.

Multitrack diplomacy evolved as the process of defining and applying an eclectic approach to resolve international conflict. Today, multitrack diplomacy consists of nine tracks in a conceptual and practical framework for understanding this complex system of peacemaking activities:

1. **Government, or Peacemaking through Diplomacy.** This is the world of official diplomacy, policy making, and peace building as expressed through formal aspects of the governmental process: the executive branch, the State Department, Congress, the U.S. Trade Representative's Office, the United Nations, and others.

2. **Nongovernmental, Professional, or Peacemaking through Conflict Resolution.** This is the realm of professional nongovernmental action attempting to analyze, prevent, resolve, and manage international conflict by nonstate actors.

3. **Business, or Peacemaking through Commerce.** This is the field of business and its actual and potential effects on peace building through the provision of economic opportunities, international friendships and understandings, informal channels of communications, and support for the peacemaking activities.

4. **Private Citizen, or Peacemaking through Personal Involvement.** This includes the various ways that individual citizens become involved in peace and development activities through citizen diplomacy, exchange programs, private voluntary organizations, nongovernmental organizations, and special-interest groups.

5. **Research Training and Education, or Peacemaking through Learning.** This track includes three related words: research, as it is connected to university programs, think tanks and special-interest research centers; training programs that seek to provide training in particular skills such as negotiation, mediation, conflict resolution, and third-party facilitation; and education, including kindergarten through graduate programs that cover various aspects of global or cross-cultural peace order studies and conflict analysis, management, and resolution.

6. **Activism, or Peacemaking through Advocacy.** This track covers the field of peace and environmental activism on such issues as disarmament, human rights, social and economic justice, and advocacy of special-interest groups regarding specific governmental policies.

7. **Religion, or Peacemaking through Providing Resources.** This examines the beliefs and peace-oriented action of spiritual and religious communities and such morality-based movements as pacifism, sanctuary, and nonviolence.

8. **Funding, or Peacemaking through Providing Resources.** This refers to the funding community—those foundations and individual philanthropists that provide the financial support for many of the activities by the other tracks.

9. **Communication and the Media, or Peacemaking through Information.** This is the realm of the voice of the people: how public opinion gets shaped and expressed by the media—print, film, video, radio, electronic systems, the arts.

Each of these nine tracks represents a world unto itself with its own philosophy and perspective, purpose, language, attitudes, activities, diversities, culture, and membership. At the same time, each of these worlds exists within the context of the others. Among and between these miniworlds are numerous places of overlapping, collaborative, and complementary activities; relationships that span the spectrum from close and natural allies to adversaries; and varying degrees of openness for communication and mutual support (Diamond & McDonald, 1996).

PREVENTIVE DIPLOMACY

By their nature and mandate many nongovernmental organizations (NGOs) have an obligation to work to prevent and transform conflicts, overcome injustices, and promote values of dignity and empowerment. Working cooperatively with governments and effectively using the resources that only governments can provide, international NGOs can maximize the personalized assistance during time of conflict and disaster. By implementing programs that emphasize holistic development and the growth of civil society, NGOs can play a critical role in preventing future conflict.

Nongovernmental organizations are privately organized and privately financed agencies formed to perform some philanthropic or other worthwhile task in response to a need that the organizers think is not adequately addressed by public, governmental, or United Nations efforts. Churches, civic groups, labor unions, private foundations, and millions of individuals have established organizations that usually operate as tax-free entities to support some group cause. Although many of these operate within their own borders, a very large number of NGOs have defined their mission as working with people in other countries as an alternative or adjunct to official foreign aid. Examples of NGOs are the Red Cross, Catholic Relief Services, CARE, American Friends Service Committee, Oxfam, Accion, Technoserve, Save the Children Fund, World Vision, NGOs within Inter Action, and many others (Anderson, 1996).

Today's world conflicts are proving difficult to resolve through traditional methods. Instead of wars between nations, states' conflicts often appear as struggles for power and dominance within states, pitting elite, ethnic, and religious groups against one another amid the breakdown of the government (Hackett, 1996). Preventing ethnic strife in divided societies is never certain and always complex. Peacemakers, whether insiders or outsiders, in nongovernmental organizations need to understand fully the roots and political contexts of existing conflicts as well as to define precisely the nature of challenges posed by particular conflicts before attempting to intervene or to prescribe cures.

There are two kinds of crises: those likely to blow over and those likely to blow up. The first kind includes quiet chronic disturbances that do not normally attract international notice and that local communities and indigenous NGOs manage on a daily basis. The second encompasses violent outbreaks that require diplomatic or military intervention. Violent crises also range in intensity from street battles to genocide.

Preventive diplomacy is the concatenation of actions that might be taken to deter disputes from arising between parties, make it more difficult for disputes to escalate into warfare, and limit the spread of ethnic or other conflicts that develop into hostilities. Preventive diplomacy is the instrument that seeks to promote the peaceful settlement of disputes between nations or groups within nations. Preventive diplomacy is what governments do, together or alone, to keep disputes from escalating into warfare.

Preventive diplomacy is the use of coercive or noncoercive means to avoid, deter, deflect, or reduce conflict. It takes three main forms:

- Conflict prevention, averting disputes between states and other parties
- Conflict containment, preventing the horizontal and vertical escalation of hostilities
- Postconflict conciliation, preventing the reemergence of disputes

Nicolaidis offers a similar categorization on the three stages of conflict prevention: early, late, and continuous (or what the United States calls postconflict peace building). She further elaborates on the barriers against as well as the opportunities for prevention during each of these stages.

Techniques of preventive diplomacy, as elaborated by Nicolaidis and Vayrynen and Leatherman, include the following:

- Peace building—the removal or reduction of conditions fostering violence between or among groups or states
- Preventive deployment—the interposition of military or observer forces between contending elements
- Mediation—the resolution of disputes before hostilities emerge, or afterward

Early warning is sounding alarm bells at the right time and in a salutary and appropriate manner. It alerts local and international communities to the likely onset of violence between or among groups or states. It has at least three components: information (which must be accurate), analysis (which must be dispassionate), and communication (which must be accessible and clear). Even so, the concept of early warning is vague and ambiguous. What if nobody is listening? Or what if people respond prematurely or erroneously?

Early warnings and conflict prevention are above all about politics. Politicians seeking to manipulate them for partisan ends invariably filter reports of intranational hostilities. NGOs can serve as valuable independent sources of facts. Yet the more tense the confrontation, the more likely it is that the NGO's efforts to gather information will be viewed as interference (MacFarquhar, Rotberg, & Chen, 1996).

THE CONFLICT PREVENTION CYCLE IN RELATION TO OTHER INTERVENTIONS

The customary approach to defining preventive action operationally is through a categorization of different phases to be addressed in the cycle of conflict. Intrastate conflict prevention can be viewed as occurring during three different phases. First, early prevention action consists of intervening in latent conflicts where disputes have not yet escalated into violent outbreaks. This is sometimes called "conflict prevention," as contrasted with preventive diplomacy. Intervention at this phase attempts to prevent disputes from turning into conflicts. Late preventive action occurs when hostilities have already broken out and when international action is aimed at controlling escalation into increasing violent conflict and the horizontal spread of conflicts across national boundaries. In the field of conflict resolution, intervention at this stage is usually referred to as conflict management. Finally, continuous preventive action, or what the UN now refers to as postconflict peace building, seeks to prevent conflicts from recurring where they have already taken place (the UN does not recognize postconflict reconstruction and preventive diplomacy). To some extent, one can argue that all early preventive diplomacy is also continuous in that some version of the occurring conflict has at some point in the past already escalated into violence. Under these circumstances resolution is restricted to situations in which prevention is incorporated into an actual reconstruction effort where managing reconstruction and prevention are intimately related (Nicolaidis, 1996).

This focus for conflict prevention helps to clarify some of the prevalent confusion among terms commonly used for intervention into conflicts, including forms of diplomacy and foreign policy. One illustration of the relationships of these forms of action appears in table 7.2. The table depicts the stage in the full life cycle of a typical conflict that preventive diplomacy occupies in relation to action taken at points within the continuum. The conflict in question may be within a state (for example, a civil war) or between states (for example, a border war).

As the table shows, the course of disputes that become violent can be plotted in terms of two dimensions: the degree of operation or hostility that exists between two or more parties or the intensity of the conflict (the vertical axis) and the evolution of the conflict over time (the horizontal axis). The arcing line across the table portrays the course of a typical conflict as the intensity of hostility rises and falls over the period of its life.

Arranged down the far left column of the table are gradations in the amicability or animosity that can exist among two or more parties labeled levels of peace and conflict. These gradations differ according to such factors as the parties' degree of awareness of their dispute and separate identity, polarization, value congruence or divergence, mutual trust, and hostile behavior. All these levels involve some degree of conflict, but with significantly different levels of hostility, including violence. Examples of recent conflicts at roughly these levels and phases are given inside the arc.

As we can see, preventive diplomacy comes into play in the course of conflicts as tensions in the relationships between parties shift from the status of stable

Table 7.2
Levels of Peace and Conflict

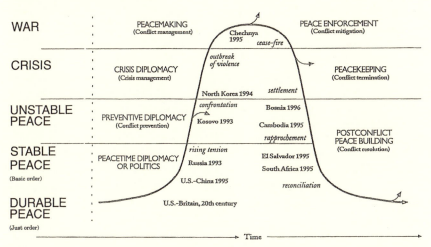

Source: From Lund, Michael S. (1996). *Preventing Violent Conflicts: A Strategy for Preventive Diplomacy* (p. 38). Washington, DC: United States Institute of Peace Press.

peace to that of unstable. Conflict prevention is most operative when ordinary peacetime diplomacy and politics have begun to break down and tensions rise but before crisis management is necessary. Addressing neither peaceable relationships and conditions nor crisis and war, it is activated specifically in troubled unstable places and times when it is likely that regimes or peoples will take up arms or use other forms of coercion such as repression to resolve emerging political differences. The objective is to keep actual disputes from taking the form of confrontation or all-out violence and to return them to the processes of peacetime diplomacy. If conflict prevention fails and the situation deteriorates into a crisis, the notion of preventive diplomacy ceases to apply, at least until the conflict has abated, in which case the process needs to be repeated to avoid a renewal of violent conflict (Lund, 1996).

THE STUDY OF INTERNATIONAL MEDIATION

Conflict is one of the most pervasive and inevitable features of all social systems, however simple or complex they may be and irrespective of their location in time and space. This is true of personal, group, and organizational, as well as international systems. Wherever it occurs, conflict is significant, newsworthy, and challenging. It can lead to mutual satisfaction and growth, or it may produce acrimony, hostility, and violence.

There are a number of ways of managing conflict. These may range from avoidance and withdrawal through bilateral negotiation to various forms of third-party intervention. Third-party intervention in conflict, particularly of the nonbinding, noncoercive kind, is in many ways as old as conflict itself. It has played an important role in industrial and preindustrial societies. Unresolved problems and conflicts create the conditions for third-party intervention (Bercovitch & Houston, 1993).

The practice of settling disputes through intermediaries has had a rich history in all cultures, both Western and non-Western (Gulliver, 1979). Although there are considerable differences in the way mediators from different cultures deal with conflict, all approaches have value in terms of managing or settling disputes. In the international arena with its perennial challenge of escalating conflicts, shrinking resources, rising ethnic demands, and the absence of generally accepted rules of the game, the potential application of mediation is truly limitless.

A cursory review of recent international disputes reveals the extent and heterogeneity of mediation. In the last decade or so, we have seen the involvement of such parties as the United Nations (in the Vietnam–Kampuches dispute, the Iraq–Kuwait dispute, and the Yugoslav dispute), the pope (in the Beagle Channel dispute), the Organization of African Unity (in the Tanzania–Uganda dispute), the Organization of American States (in the Nicaragua dispute), the Arab League and Algeria (in the Iraq–Kuwait dispute), and the United States (in numerous efforts in the Middle East). Less-formal mediation efforts (by the Quakers, for example, or by prominent politicians such as President Carter, Lord Owen, Prince Sihanouk, or Colin Powell) occur on a daily basis.

As a form of international conflict management, mediation is likely to occur when (1) a conflict has gone on for some time, (2) the efforts of the individuals or actors involved have reached an impasse, (3) neither actor is prepared to countenance further costs or escalation of the dispute, and (4) both parties welcome some form of mediation and are ready to engage in direct or indirect dialogue (Bercovitch, 1984).

Whatever its specific characteristics, mediation must in essence be seen as an extension of the negotiation process whereby an acceptable third party intervenes to change the course or outcome of a particular conflict. The third party with no authoritative decision-making power is there to assist the disputants in their search for a mutually acceptable agreement. As a form of conflict management, mediation is distinguishable from the more binding forms of third-party intervention such as arbitration and adjudication in that it is initiated on request, and it leaves the ultimate decision power with the disputants (Folberg & Taylor, 1984).

International disputes are not static or uniform events. They vary in terms of the situation, parties, intensity, escalation, response, meaning, and possible transformation. These features define the context of a dispute and cannot help but affect its course and outcome. Mediation is shaped by the context and characteristics of a situation. The specific rules, beliefs, attitudes, behaviors, and symbols that make up international conflict impinge or perhaps even govern the process of mediation. As a social process, mediation may be as variable as the disputants themselves. To be successful, mediation must be adaptive and responsive. It must reflect different problems, parties, and situations. For mediation to be effective it must relate to and reflect the wider conflict.

Figure 7.1 represents an approach to the study of mediation that does take the context and the other factors into account; we refer to it as the contingency

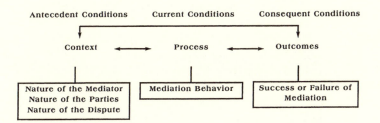

Figure 7.1   A Contingency Model of Mediation

Source: Bercovitch, J., & Lamare, J. (1993, September). *Correlates of Effective Mediation in International Disputes: Theoretical Issues and Empirical Evidence.* Paper presented at the annual meeting of the American Political Science Association, Washington, DC.

approach. This approach was used in a series of earlier studies (Bercovitch, 1986; Bercovitch & Houston, 1993; Bercovitch & Langley, 1993; Bercovith & Wells, 1993). The approach stipulates variables with specific operational criteria, each of which may have an impact on mediation effectiveness. At the heart of this approach are clusters of context, process, and outcome variables. Each cluster refers to specific characteristics of the party, the dispute, the mediator, and the outcome. Mediation outcomes, whether successful or not, are logically seen as the result of the interaction of context and process variables.

This contingency approach offers a useful framework by which to organize and integrate much of the literature on mediation. It also allows us to evaluate the impact of different kinds of mediation, assess the relationships between dispute characteristics and mediation, and evaluate the most successful mediation strategies (Bercovitch & Wells, 1993).

Mediation must not be analyzed or understood in terms of a simple cause-and-effect model in which a particular strategy invariably produces a desired outcome. Mediation in general and international mediation in particular is not merely an exogenous input that can affect or influence the disputants, their behavior, or their perceptions. The relationships between mediators and the disputing parties are reciprocal. Those involved in a dispute wish to influence the mediator, and the mediator certainly hopes to influence the parties. The contingency approach enables us to focus on this reciprocal relationship through a detailed study of a single case or numerous mediation situations.

When conflicts arise between individuals or groups, they can be settled or resolved in a limited number of ways, including third-party intervention, conciliation, and mediation. Mediation has received the most attention among scholars and practitioners working in the field of conflict resolution. Numerous scholarly analyses of mediation theory and research have appeared over the past two decades, including several volumes published by Jossey-Bass in 1994. Simultaneously, mediation practice has emerged as the single most powerful tool in the alternative dispute resolution (ADR) movement designed to create alternatives to litigation. Mediation practice has flourished in the United States (and elsewhere, but to a lesser extent), and is applied in situations from divorce to community conflict to business, labor, and international relations.

Mediation is generally understood (based on its obvious use in the labor field and increasingly international relations) as an informal process in which a neutral third party with no power to impose a resolution helps the disputing parties try to reach a mutually acceptable settlement.

This common formulation captures some of the major features of the process, especially its informality and consensuality. It also reflects the view that the most significant effect of the process is the production of a voluntary settlement of the dispute (Bercovitch, 1992).

Beyond the level described by such conventional definitions, however, the mediation process contains within it a unique potential for transforming people and engendering moral growth by helping them wrestle with difficult circumstances and bridge human differences in the very midst of conflict. This transformation potential stems from mediation's capacity to generate two important effects, empowerment and recognition. In simplest terms, empowerment restores the individual's self-value and ego strength to cope with life's problems. When both of these processes are held central in the practice of mediation, parties are helped to use conflicts as opportunities for moral growth and the realization of transformation potentials.

Peacemaking between nations in current practice typically involves largely public meetings between 10 and 15 opposing groups. In this context, group dynamics and the very architecture of the meeting rooms seem to foster bimodal alienation. For example, the broadcasts of a Madrid conference showed the Arab and Israeli representatives denouncing each other to visibly large audiences. The speakers' awareness of television cameras added an even larger audience to their perception of the situation.

Under such circumstances there is little room for creative ideas and the repair of damaged bonds. Speakers feel constrained to reaffirm their loyalty within their own group and their isolation and hostility toward the other group. To allow room to maneuver a radically different format may be necessary.

One possibility would be to arrange for as many one-on-one private encounters as the disputants would allow. Formal meetings would always be held in the presence of a psychologist with substantial experience in dealing with persons in crisis, as in divorce and custody mediation and other forms of high-conflict disputes. Perhaps the most productive form of single encounters would be between opposite numbers: the leading representatives of each group meeting, the next highest, and so on. Being in the same position might help establish a minimal amount of identification between the opponents, which could be the first step toward building a bond. In current mediation practice, the later group meetings would be organized to emphasize the areas of agreement and the gains toward conciliation made during the conference. The main focus is on the repair of damage to the social and emotional bond between the disputants (Scheff, 1994).

CULTURAL ASPECTS OF INTERNATIONAL MEDIATION

Mediation has always been something of a mysterious art. Behind closed doors, skilled individuals somehow find ways to work out compromises among people who disagree about intense and important matters. Mediators are not passive participants in any sense. Rather, they actively construct the resolution process and behavior protocol expected from the disputants. They define the problem, choreograph the agenda and meetings, exercise control over communication and information, and have direct input into the types of agreements that are possible (Kolb, 1994).

From an ethnographic perspective, disputants look less like competitors in a strategic interaction rationally choosing among strategic and tactical moves and resemble performers in a stylized enactment in which the roles and plays are culturally constructed (Gulliver, 1979, chapter 7). North American mediators are expected to be impartially trained professionals. Their job is not to preach but to provide the protagonists with problem-solving and resolution alternatives. In the international arena their role is infused with a Christian moral imperative: "blessed are the peacemakers." In contrast, the Middle Eastern "Wasta" has an ascriptive, not professional, role and is chosen from local leaders. He is expected to separate the adversaries, scrupulously protect their honor, and restore equilibrium between them if necessary by preferring the claims of the weaker party.

THE PEACE ISSUE AS PART OF THE GLOBAL CRISES ISSUE

Peacemaking is the active process of peace, the behavior of actors and institutions that lead to more peaceful relations. It is subject to understanding and systematization through the standard tools of empirical analysis. Many scholars in the field have come to use the term as a way of linking conflict resolution techniques with achievement of peace (National Conference on Peacemaking and Conflict Resolution 1983, 1984, 1996). Peacemaking is to be distinguished from peacekeeping, which is a narrower and technically specified set of procedures for maintaining a cease-fire, a demilitarized area, or buffer zone.

Conflict occurs at all levels of society, interpersonal, intercultural, and international. In many instances, the origins of conflict are in the nonfulfillment or blockage of fundamental human needs. Conflict may then be defined empirically as escalated natural competition of two or more parties who believe they have incompatible goals and whose aim is to neutralize, injure, or gain advantage over the other party or parties. Struggles over identity, values, power, and scarce resources are at the heart of all social conflicts (Coser, 1956; Kriesberg, 1984).

Resolution is the focus of the U.S. Institute of Peace's mission to "peacefully resolving international conflict." A conflict may be said to be resolved when all the parties freely accept a solution that has the following characteristics:

1. By joint agreement, the solution satisfies the interests and needs underlying the conflict.
2. The solution does not sacrifice any party's important values.
3. The parties will not wish to repudiate the solution, even if they are in a position to do so.
4. The solution meets standards of justice and fairness.
5. The solution is sufficiently advantageous to all the parties so that it becomes self-supporting of self-enforcing (adapted from Azar & Burton 1986, p. 171).

Resolution is only one of a wide range of outcomes that may be preferred. Any party's stance toward a given conflict depends largely on variables such as ideology, power (who has it), and goals (that is, who wishes to maintain or gain what). Low-power groups generally do not call for conflict resolution or peace; they want empowerment, change, and justice. Their typical approach is to agitate conflict. More powerful parties are more likely to deter, suppress, repress, or control conflict. A third-party intervener may aim to resolve, manage, regulate, or settle conflicts whereas academics analyze, teach, and predict. True and lasting resolution of conflicts requires attention in the process to improving the relationship between the parties as well as securing a substantive outcome. Agreement terminates conflicts; relationships implement agreements.

It is widely accepted that the survival of humanity is severely challenged by various global crises (World Commission on Environment and Development, 1987). The prospect of a worldwide war and the grave ecological problems over the planet are only the most prominent symptoms. Hunger crises in various parts of the world, for example, should by no means be forgotten, nor unemployment. All these pose serious political and economic problems. Global crises form the basis for political and economic decisions. Aside from their political and economic importance, they also influence the well-being of humans on a daily basis, even for those not living in a war zone or areas immediately challenged by ecological problems. Although debated by some authors (e.g., Coles, 1986), it seems generally accepted that the prospects of nuclear war (see Fiske, 1987) and of ecological catastrophes pose a serious threat to psychic well-being around the world.

Wagner (1988) distinguishes between negative and positive approaches to the problem of war. He points out that the negative goal of avoidance of war has been a priority because of the increasing nuclear threat posed by both superpowers. Avoiding war is a reactive, concrete, and short-term approach to a serious problem. However, focusing only on the prevention of war precludes us from conceptualizing concrete positive goals in the promotion of peace.

Rappaport (1986) called for a social policy of empowerment over prevention. He discussed how the concept of prevention is grounded in the belief that people are dependent children who need to be helped or protected from the harmful effects of society. This belief leads to interventions that perpetuate the expert-helper stance in which professionals decide what is best for others.

Empowerment, however, has to do with "enhancing the possibilities for people to control their own lives" and views people as "full human beings with both needs and rights" (Rappaport, 1986, p. 154). Whereas prevention suggests the use of professional experts, empowerment suggests collaboration between people, regardless of professional level.

The concept of empowerment is useful as a means of moving away from the negative goal of preventing war to a positive goal of promoting peace. Problems of war can be reframed into solutions of peace. This is a major undertaking within peace research at present and one in which psychology and many other disciplines as well as citizens are playing a role. Wagner (1988) believes that the goals of creating peace may be more easily maintained than the goals aimed at preventing war.

As mentioned earlier, peace is more than simply the absence of war (Brock-Utne, 1985; Galtung, 1985). Peace might be defined in terms of social justice or increased access to social, political, and economic resources for those who have been traditionally denied equality, such as minorities and women (Brock-Utne, 1985). Peace might also be defined as an increased international awareness of and commitment to protecting the environment we share (Milbrath, 1988).

COPING WITH THREATS

There are some golden rules for ensuring security. They are very straight-forward; however, this does not mean they are easy to apply on all occasions and under all circumstances.

1. The first golden rule of security is to free one's adversary from his or her fear. To do so, it is imperative, as soon as a conflict begins to take shape, to rebuild confidence, necessary for all, beneficial for all.

2. The second rule is to guarantee one's own security but not to make it an obsessive, unhealthy, and excessive political concern. I am mindful of Goethe's thought, "He who lives for his security alone is already dead."

3. The third golden rule is that in the age of ballistic missiles, it is a delusion to think that one can protect the inviolability of a frontier. The most secure boundaries are those that separate two friendly countries. One must begin by building cooperation; confidence and friendships must be encouraged to flourish.

4. The fourth golden rule is to see world peace as an indivisible whole. The Conference for Security and Cooperation in Europe (CSCE), which issued its Final Act 20 years ago in Helsinki, seemed to have made a correct assessment of that obvious political imperative. We would now do well to issue with all speed a "Helsinki Final Act for the South" or else organize a conference on security and cooperation in the Mediterranean area having as its guiding principles the following points:

   • Mutual recognition of existing boundaries
   • Necessity to progress toward democratization throughout the region
   • Policy of progressive disarmament
   • Campaign against terrorism, pollution, and drugs
   • At the same time press for other Helsinki-type agreements in all the sensitive areas of the world

5. The fifth golden rule is that security and cooperation is a united couple that does not believe in divorce. One cannot carry on without the other. Cooperation is the indispensable corollary of security (Cahill, 1996).

TRADITIONAL PEACEKEEPING

The Social–Psychological and Diplomatic Focus

Peacekeeping is the deployment of a United Nations presence in the field, hitherto with the consent of all the parties concerned, normally involving United Nations military and/or police personnel and frequently civilians as well. Peacekeeping is a technique that expands the possibilities for both the prevention of conflict and the making of peace (Ghali, 1992).

In today's world, traditional international peacekeeping usually involves the United Nations peacekeeping forces. However, traditional peacekeeping by UN forces has expanded and changed its mission.

Examples of recent peacekeeping activities and locations include patrolling cease-fire lines (Cyprus); protecting humanitarian relief shipments (Rwanda and Somalia); demobilizing troops (Bosnia); disarming militias (Somalia); organizing and supervising elections (Cambodia); instilling respect for human rights in police, soldiers, and government officials (Central Africa); and even functioning as surrogate governments (El Salvador). Intervention in the form of peace enforcement may precede these peacemaking activities. The timing and procedures used in these expanded peacemaking missions involve cultural considerations. These considerations are particularly important in the case of violent conflicts (Montville, 1990).

Conflict management is peace enforcement: the application of military force to separate combatants to restore the status quo when there have been breaches of peace (Wurmser & Drake, 1993). The use of peace enforcement is required when violent conflict is occurring, but violence is malignant and should only be used as last resort. It can corrupt those using it and those that it is used against. It fosters revenge, vengeance, and other negative emotional states in the victimized and provokes aggression and dehumanization in the victimizers (Staub, 2001). It can arouse and reinforce negative cultural identities and promote ethnocentrism.

A more positive conception of peace involves peacemaking. Peacemaking programs are designed to bring potential and former combatants together to manage their differences through negotiation, mediation, and conciliation. Lawyers, diplomats, psychologists, and social scientists that are trained as mediators strive to assist others to work through their problems, reach compromises, and manage their conflicts more constructively (Etheridge, 1979).

The most proactive view of peace is that of the peace builders. Psychologists, sociologists, and anthropologists favoring peace building have as their goal the creative resolution of conflicts without the use of force or coercion (Wagner, 1988). Conflict management depends on building and maintaining personal relations that promote understanding and collaboration among a variety of individuals and groups. Old antagonisms are addressed and reconciled through active programs in forgiveness and reconciliation (Njeri, 1993). The peace-building approach has the most promise for managing current and future cultural conflict productively (Kimmel, 1994). Peace building reinforces positive cultural identities and promotes cultural understanding.

PEACE MAKING IN THE TWENTY-FIRST CENTURY

Like the world order in transition, the conceptual lenses we use to interpret our world and to orient our actions are undergoing remarkable change. Traditional concepts such as state, power, national interest, and diplomacy appear in a much wider frame. The capabilities and foreign policy decisions of individual states must broaden to cover more extensive relationships among bodies politic the world over. This step entails seeing relationships between nations as a political process of continuous interaction between significant elements of whole societies (Saunders, 1990). Given the fact that nations face problems that they are unable to solve by themselves or even within the narrow confines of the interstate system, a broader, more comprehensive approach is needed to guide peaceful change in the international realm.

This approach challenges us to develop a conceptual framework that integrates rather than fragments understandings of the relationships among a variety of international actors, including states, regional organizations, public and private organizations, and individuals. Relations among nations are increasingly a continuous policy influencing communities (Saunders, 1990). Social and political change occurs through many levels of interaction rather than a linear series of governmental actions and responses. The issue is not whether state or nonstate actors are more important (states usually are), but whether more complex coalitions of actors affect more outcomes in contemporary international politics (Nye, 1990). The need to deal with internal protracted conflicts as much as with interstate wars sets the stage for innovative as well as historic measures and approaches and provides the basis for constructing a new system of world order.

Peace operations cover the broad spectrum of actions intended to forestall, diminish, or end outbreaks of violence on the international scene. They encompass six more or less distinct types of civilian, civilian military, or military programs designed essentially to give peace a chance in varying circumstances of violence across the broad front of conflict resolution. Each has defined goals and employs particular techniques; there is much scope for progression from one category to another and a good deal of interaction at each stage. The six forms of peace operations are as follows:

- Peacemaking: an activist role (military, civilian, or both) involving diplomatic negotiations, conferences, early warning procedures, mediation, conflict resolution, and preventive diplomacy techniques to avoid or resolve a conflict or initiate a peace process.

- Peacekeeping: the use of international military personnel, either in units or as individual observers, as part of an agreed peace settlement or truce, generally to verify and monitor cease-fire lines.

- Reconstruction: wide-ranging involvement by civilians, the military, or both in providing assistance of a broad infrastructure after the conclusion of hostilities (often incorrectly called peace building).

- Protective engagement or containment: the use of international military capabilities and the standing of the international community to protect civilian populations, deliver humanitarian relief, or provide a platform for peace negotiations while strife continues.

- Deterrence: the deployment of military forces to dissuade a potential aggressor from pursuing a violent course.

- Peace enforcement: the coercive use of military power to impose a solution to a dispute, to punish aggression, or to reverse its consequences (McLean, 1996).

CONCLUSION

The problem of destructive intergroup and international conflict can be seen as the most significant issue confronting humankind, particularly in the nuclear age. The enigma of destructive intergroup conflict lays down a gauntlet to the social science disciplines that is both complex and urgent. The field of international relations has shown an abiding interest in intergroup conflict among states and/or factions, particularly as expressed in the violence of war.

Conflict is a pervasive, permanent, and inherent feature of world politics. It may be the inevitable consequence of interactions among many groups that have not resolved differences. More specifically, competing demands for scarce resources in a world of inequality and disorder guarantee that conflict will remain at the center of the study of international relations. However, how conflict is conceptualized and what methods are recommended to address it has varied considerably over the history of international discord. The overall threat of violence is pervasive. The immediate question for all disciplines is what unique contribution each might make to the nonviolent and constructive resolution of national and global conflict.

The field of international relations has shown an abiding interest in intergroup conflict among states and/or factions, particularly as expressed in the violence of war. Conflict may be the inevitable consequence of interaction among groups that live in anarchy. More specifically, competing demands for scarce resources in a world of inequality and disorder guarantee that conflict will remain at the center of the study of international relations.

Conflict is one of the most pervasive and inevitable features of all social systems, however simple or complex they may be and irrespective of their location in time and space. This is true of personal, group, and organizational, as well as international systems. Conflict can lead to mutual satisfaction and growth or it may produce acrimony, hostility, and violence. Conflict can be managed in ways that maximize its potential benefits and minimize its destructive consequences.

The concept of empowerment (enhancing the possibilities for people to control their own lives) is useful as a means of moving away from the negative goal of preventing war to a positive goal of promoting peace. Whereas prevention suggests the use of professional experts, empowerment suggests collaboration between people, regardless of professional level. Empowerment is a complex concept that has personal and political implications. On a personal level empowerment refers to a subjective state of mind, feeling competent, and experiencing a sense of control; on a political level, it refers to the objective reality of opportunities in social structures and the reallocation of power through a modification of social structures. Empowerment involves the process of increasing personal, interpersonal, or political power so that individuals, families, and communities can take action to improve their situations.

The international community has come to recognize that once the conflict has been resolved, the warring parties not only require assistance in negotiating peace agreements, but they also urgently require assistance in consolidating peace.

REFERENCES

Anderson, M. (1996). Humanitarian NGOs in conflict intervention. In C. Crocker, F. Hampson, & P. Aall (Eds.), *Managing global chaos: Sources of and responses to international conflict.* Washington, DC: United States Institute for Peace.

Angell, R. C. (1965). The sociology of human conflict. In E. B. McNeil (Ed.), *The nature of human conflict.* Englewood Cliffs, NJ: Prentice Hall.

Azar, E. E. (1983). *The theory of protracted social conflict and the challenge of transforming conflict situations.* (Monograph Series in World Affairs, 20, #M2, 81–99). Denver, CO: University of Denver.

Azar, E., & Burton, J. (1986). *International conflict resolution (EDS): Theory and practice.* Boulder, CO: Lynn Reinner.

Bercovitch, J. (1984). *Social conflicts and third parties: Strategies of conflict resolution.* Boulder, CO: Westview.

Bercovitch, J. (1986). International mediation: A study of incidence, strategies and conditions of successful outcomes. *Cooperation and Conflict, 21,* 155–168.

Bercovitch, J. (1992). The structure and diversity of mediation in international relations. In J. Bercovitch & J. Rubin (Eds.), *Mediation in international relations: Multiple approaches to conflict management.* New York: St. Martin's.

Bercovitch, J., & Houston, A. (1993). Influence of mediator characteristics and behavior on the success of mediation in international religions. *International Journal of Conflict Management, 4,* 297–321.

Bercovitch, J., & Langely, J. (1993). The nature of the dispute and the effectiveness of international mediation. *Journal of Conflict Resolution, 37,* 670–691.

Bercovitch, J., & Wells, R. (1993). Evaluation mediation strategies: A theoretical and empirical analysis. *Peace and Change, 18,* 3–5.

Beres, M. E., & Schmidt, S. M. (1982). The conflict carousel: A contingency approach to conflict management. In G. B. J. Bomers & R. B. Peterson (Eds.), *Conflict management and industrial relations.* Boston: Kluwer-Nijhof Publishing.

Blake, R., & Mouton, J. (1984). *Solving costly organizational conflict: Achieving intergroup trust, cooperation, and teamwork.* San Francisco: Jossey-Bass.

Bobo, L. (1983). White's opposition to busing: Symbolic racism or realistic group conflict? *Journal of Personality and Social Psychology, 45,* 1196–1210.

Breggin, P. (1992). *Beyond conflict: From self-help and psychotherapy to peacemaking.* New York: St. Martin's.

Brewer, M. B., & Campbell, D. T. (1976). *Ethnocentrism and intergroup attitudes. East African evidence.* New York: Halstead Press.

Brock-Utne, B. (1985). *Educating for peace: A feminist perspective.* New York: Pergamon.

Burton, J. (1987a). *World society.* Lanham, MD: University Press of America.

Cahill, K. (1996). *Stopping wars before they start: Preventative diplomacy.* New York: Basic Books.

Coles, R. (1986). *The political life of children.* Boston: Atlantic Monthly Press.

Coser, L. (1956). *The functions of social conflict.* Toronto: Free Press.

Deutsch, M. (1985). *Distributive justice: A social psychological perspective.* New Haven, CT: Yale University Press.

Diamond, L., & McDonald, J. (1991). *Multitrack diplomacy: A systems guide and analysis.* Grinnell: Iowa Peace Institute.

Diamond, L., & McDonald, J. (1996). *Multitrack diplomacy: A systems approach to peace,* 3rd ed. Hartford, CT: Kumarian Press.

Dovidio, J. F., Mann, J., & Gaertner, S. L. (1989). Resistance to affirmative action: The implications of aversive racism. In F. A. Blanchard & F. J. Crosby (Eds.), *Affirmative action in perspective.* New York: Springer-Verlag.

Etheridge, A. (1979). *Images of conflict.* New York: St. Martin's.

Fisher, R. (1990). *The social psychology of intergroup and international conflict.* New York: Springer-Verlag.

Fiske, S. (1987). People's reaction to nuclear war: Implications for psychologists. *American Psychologist, 42*(3), 207–217.

Folberg, J., & Taylor, A. (1984). *Mediation: A comprehensive guide to resolving conflicts without litigation.* San Francisco: Jossey-Bass.

Forsyth, D. (1990). *Group dynamics.* Pacific Grove, CA: Brooks/Cole.

Galtung, J. (1965). Institutionalized conflict resolution. A theoretical paradigm. *Journal of Peace Research, 6,* 167–191.

Galtung, J. (1985). Twenty-five years of peace research: Ten challenges and some responses. *Journal of Peace Research, 22*(2), 141–158.

Ghali, B. (1992, June). Agenda for peace. In *United Nations Document A/47/277 S/ 24111.*

Glad, B. (1990). *Psychological dimensions of war.* Newbury Park, CA: Sage.

Gulliver, P. H. (1979). *Disputes and negotiations: A cross-cultural perspective.* New York: Academic Press.

Gurr, T. R. (1970). *Why men rebel.* Princeton, NJ: Princeton University Press.

Hackett, R., & Karlberg, M. (1996). *Decision-making and conflict resolution.* Paper presented at the Conference on Consultation, Landegg Academy, Wienacht, Switzerland.

Kaplan, K. J., & Markus-Kaplan, M. (1993). Walls and boundaries in Arab relations with Israel: Interpersonal distancing model. *Journal of Conflict Resolution, 17,* 457–472.

Kelman, H. (1996). Social-psychological dimensions of international conflict. In I. W. Zartman & J. L. Rasmussen (Eds.), *Peace making in international conflict: Methods and techniques.* Washington, DC: U.S. Institute of Peace Press.

Kimmel, P. (1994). Cultural perspectives on international negotiation. *Journal of Social Issues, 50* (1), 179–196.

Kolb, D., and Associates. (1994). *When talk works: Profiles of mediators.* San Francisco: Jossey-Bass.

Kriesberg, L. (1984). *Research in social movement, conflict and change* (Vol. 7). Greenwich, CT: Jai Publishers.

LeVine, R. A., & Campbell, D. T. (1972). *Ethnocentrism: Theories of conflict, ethnic attitudes, and group behavior.* New York: Wiley.

Lund, M. (1996). *Preventing violent conflicts,* Washington, DC: U.S. Institute of Peace.

MacFarquhar, E., Rotberg, R., & Chen, M. (1996). In R. Rotberg (Ed.), *Vigilance and vengeance. NGOs preventing ethnic conflict in divided societies.* Cambridge, MA: Brookings Institution Press.

Marx, K., & Engels, F. (1947). *The German ideology.* New York: International Publishers.

McDonald, J., & Bendahmane, D. (1986). *Conflict resolution: Track two diplomacy.* Washington, DC: U.S. Government Printing Office.

McLean, D. (1996). Peace operations and common sense. In C. Crocker, F. Hampson, & P. Aall (Eds.), *Managing global chaos: Sources of the responses to international conflict.* Washington, DC: United States Institute of Peace Press.

Milbrath, L. (1988, July). *Making connections: The common roots giving rise to the environment, feminist, and peace movements.* Paper presented at the annual meeting of the International Society for Political Psychological.

Montville, J. (Ed.). (1990). *Conflict and peacemaking in multiethnic societies.* Lexington, MA: Lexington Books.

National Conference on Peacemaking and Conflict Resolution. (1983, 1984, 1986). *Conference Reports.* Fairfax, VA: George Mason University.

Nicolaidis, K. (1996). International preventive action: Developing a strategic framework. In R. Rotberg (Ed.), *Vigilance and vengeance: NGOs preventing ethnic conflict in divided societies.* Cambridge, MA: Brookings Institution Press.

Njeri, I. (1993). Sushi and grits: Ethnic identity and conflict in a newly multicultural America. In G. Early (Ed.), *Lure and loathing: Essays on race, identity, and the ambivalence of assimilation* (pp. 13–40). New York: Penguin Press.

Nye, J. (1990). *Bound to lead: The changing nature of American power.* New York: Basic Books.

Rappaport, J. (1986). In praise of paradox: A social policy of empowerment over prevention. In E. Seidman & J. Rappaport (Eds.), *Redefining social issues* (pp. 141–164). New York: Plenum.

Saunders, H. (1990). A historic challenge to rethink how nations relate. In V. Volkan, J. Montville, & O. Julius (Eds.), *The psychodynamics of international relationships* (Vol. 1, pp. 1–30). Lexington, MA: Lexington Books.

Scheff, T. J. (1994). *Bloody revenge: emotions, nationalism, and war.* Boulder, CO: Westview Press.

Scheff, T., & Retzinger, S. (1991). *Emotions and violence.* Lexington, MA: Lexington Books.

Sherif, M. (1961). *Intergroup conflict and cooperation. The robber's cave experiment.* Norman: University of Oklahoma.

Staub, E. (2001). Genocide and mass killing: Their root and prevention. In D. Christie, R., and D. Winter (Eds.), *Peace, conflict, and violence: Peace psychology for the 21st century,* (pp. 76–86). Upper Saddle River, NJ: Prentice Hall.

Streufert, S., & Streufert, S. C. (1986). The development of interaction conflict. In S. Worchel & W. G. Austin (Eds.), *Psychology of intergroup relations* (2nd ed., pp. 134–152). Chicago: Nelson-Hall.

Wagner, R. (1988). Distinguishing between positive and negative approaches to peace. *Journal of Social Issues, 44,* 1–15.

Worchel, S., Coutant-Sassic, D., & Grossman, M. (1991). A developmental approach to group dynamics: A model and illustrative research. In S. Worchel, W. Wood, & J. Simpson (Eds.), *Group process and productivity.* Newbury Park, CA: Sage.

Worchel, S., & Simpson, J. (1993). *Conflict between people and groups: Causes, processes, and resolutions.* Chicago: Nelson-Hall.

World Commission on Environment and Development. (1987). *Our common future.* Oxford: Oxford University Press.

Wurmser, D., & Dyke, N. (1993). *The professionalization of peacekeeping.* U.S. Institute of Peace.

8

The Psychology of Diplomacy, as Manifested in the Role of Subregional and Regional Organizations in Preventing African Conflicts[1]

Betsie Smith

The chapter discusses the psychology of diplomacy as observed within the context of conflict prevention and resolution in Africa and within the ambit of Africa's colonial history and the aftereffects of the Cold War. It then focuses on traditional African methodology of conflict prevention and resolution. The importance of community and relationships, of councils of elders, as well as the distortion of Africa's cultural and psychological heritage by postcolonial leaders and systems are highlighted. The Organization of African Unity (OAU), as continental organization tasked with conflict resolution and of late also economic integration, is discussed with an overview of historical factors that impacted on its development. Information is provided with respect to conflict resolution mechanisms in regional organizations in east, west, and southern Africa, with specific reference to The Economic Community of West African States (ECOWAS) intervention in Sierra Leone. A brief parallel is drawn between Sierra Leone and Kosovo in respect of the legality of these interventions. Reference is made to the role of specific individuals and to ways in which governments and civil society can complement each other with respect to conflict resolution. The notion of disorder as political instrument is considered, together with the retraditionalization of Africa,[2] as they impact on a prognosis for conflict resolution. The chapter concludes with an argument in favor of professional diplomacy to give substance to the efforts of heads of state and other leaders in their endeavors to prevent and resolve conflicts in Africa. Professional diplomacy is also championed as a way in which to counterbalance the negative effects of the informalization of politics[3] on the conducting of interstate relations, proper governance, and delivery.

INTRODUCTION

The concept of conflict prevention and resolution in Africa cannot be discussed in isolation from Africa's history. Of particular relevance are the effects of the colonial legacy and the Cold War (and its end) on indigenous psyches, in particular the cultures of conflict resolution, but also on the functioning of states in general.

Postcolonial Africa had to grapple with myriad foreign cultures and structural arrangements that had superimposed themselves onto indigenous methods. The process of accommodating the remnants of foreign cultures within reemerging African practices is still continuing. To complicate matters, post–Cold War African countries have had to find ways in which to manage their achievements since independence with new demands posed by globalization, internal conflict, and developments within African regional organizations and structures that are themselves in transition.

The "deconstructive" effect of colonialism on African identity and the challenge to "reconstruct" after the Cold War cannot be overemphasized. Of course, the conduct of diplomacy and conflict resolution is of particular importance in this respect. Bernard Lewis's perspectives about identity in the Middle East are of equal relevance to Africa and warrant an extensive quotation:

If [we] compare the political map of the Middle East with that of, say Europe, certain significant differences emerge. Of the twenty-five or so states that make up the map of Europe, all but a few small exceptions, such as Belgium, Switzerland and now Cyprus, have one important characteristic in common. The name of the country or nation is also the name of the dominant—sometimes the sole—ethnic group; it is also the name of the principal language used in that country, sometimes indeed only in that country. Czechoslovakia and Yugoslavia were only apparent exceptions, since these were modern names for old-established national and cultural entities. Both have since broken up—Czechoslovakia into Czech and Slovak states, Yugoslavia into its ethno-religious components.

This European combination of ethnic, territorial and linguistic nomenclature has existed for many centuries . . . but even many which did not become sovereign states had names, languages and cultures of their own, and a strong sense of territorial and national identity expressed in the cult of national history and the pursuit of national aims. . . .

In Europe the names, and for the most part the entities which they designate, are old, with a continuous history dating back at least to the Middle Ages and sometimes to antiquity. This is true even of those countries which, like Germany and Italy, did not attain political unity until the nineteenth century, or those others, like Poland and the Baltic states, which did not recover or attain independence until the twentieth. The lines on the map—many of them, as in much of North America, obviously drawn with a ruler—which divide the present day Middle East into sovereign states are, with few exceptions, new. And some of the entities which they designate are new, without precedent in the medieval or ancient past. The difference in the character of the names themselves is even more remarkable. The names by which the European states are known derive from their own languages and from their own history, and designate continuing and self-conscious entities.[4]

Unlike Europe's development of identity and statehood over millennia, Africa's colonial heritage, combined with mistakes that followed independence and the Cold War, has brought about enormous disparities in political, economic, linguistic, judicial, institutional, and administrative cultures within a relatively short period of time. A particular dilemma is how to harmonize all these disparities within and among states and between organizations/structures. To borrow Nandini Patel's phrase, all these influences have "throttled the process of state building in Africa."[5]

Another imperative is bridging the largely artificial gap between North and sub-Saharan Africa, implementing the new objectives of the OAU as they have been formulated post-1989, and rationalizing the objectives and membership of subregional organizations. Finding common ground with respect to initiatives specifically related to conflict resolution underpins all these responsibilities.

The development of effective conflict resolution mechanisms and techniques has been particularly affected by Africa's history and influenced by Africa's cultural and psychological heritage. While having to find their feet as individual states, regional integration has been a crucial factor in Africa's response to the challenges posed by raging conflicts, ever-accelerating globalization and the marginalization of Africa. As will be seen, in uniquely African fashion, such efforts have mostly been driven and managed from the top, mainly by heads of state.[6]

Some may argue that the decision to send African leaders to the G8 Okinawa Summit has little to do with conflict prevention and resolution. Africa's argument, and increasingly that of other international players, is that Africa's debt burden has a direct bearing on its ability to address poverty and the conflicts that result from it. The secretary-general of the United Nations put it well in his 1998 *Report on the Causes of Conflict and the Promotion of Durable Peace and Sustainable Development in Africa:*

The prevention of conflict begins and ends with the promotion of human security and human development. . . . When tensions rise or conflict threatens, many African countries do not have the basic resources to meet critical needs. . . . Addressing the threat that an unsustainable debt burden poses to the economic security and long-term stability of Africa requires comprehensive and decisive action by the international community.[7]

Another view is that the very fact that African decision making (and by implication diplomacy) is largely being driven from the top and very often informally, without substantiation by professional diplomats and a meritocracy, is one of the most important reasons why decisions are rarely implemented and why the African state is all but an "empty shell, façade and décor."[8]

THE PSYCHOLOGY BEHIND REGIONAL INTEGRATION AND CONFLICT RESOLUTION IN AFRICA

Historically, regional integration within Africa, and with it conflict resolution, has always been managed by senior members of the community, unlike in other parts of the world where integration was driven from the bottom upward, starting with specific issues and developing into larger entities and encompassing more issues. In the traditional context, Africans have also shown a preference to resolve conflicts in an informal way with an emphasis on "group-centredness"[9] and with a consideration to "ongoing social relations and internal solidarity."[10] In order to understand the psychology behind conflict resolution in Africa, Jannie Malan advises thus:

Throughout all the complexity and variety in Africa's history of conflict resolution, there seems to be an elemental warp and weft [or matrix]:
The one is the tradition of family or neighbourhood negotiation facilitated by elders.
And the other is the attitude of togetherness in the spirit of humanhood *(ubuntu)*. [Emphasis the author's.]
Both of these are clear manifestations of a committedness to the community concerned and an orientation to a comprehensive view of life. . . . Both these elements can be traced back to methods used since the earliest days of group, tribal and national leaders working together with their councils of elders. . . . But both can also be discerned in present-day methods which are used either independently of imported structures, or alternatively to such structures. . . . The emphasis is on association and relationships . . . [Even by] looking at some of the constituents of the total life context one by one . . . our mindset should not be one of analysing and classifying, but rather one of synthesising and integrating.[11]

Malan goes on to warn against "indoctrinated individualism."[12]

In most traditional African settings, conflicts are thus not dealt with on a one-on-one basis, but collectively in the presence of the most respected members of the community, the elders. Consequently, it is also unusual to wash dirty linen in public and confront people causing, or involved in, a conflict situation directly, especially in front of outsiders.

Sadly, at a time when regained independence was being savored, sovereignty was elevated to the point where legitimate avenues for cooperation were regarded as a potential threat to hard-won freedom. Similar to other parts of the world (perhaps even in Yugoslavia), the personal identity of the head of state was subsumed into the identity of the state so that he could no longer distinguish between his identity as individual and the identity of the country he was governing. Fernand Braudel uses the example of Louis XIV, but also ascribed at least once to Elizabeth I of England, who is reported to have said "L'etat, c'est moi."[13] Africa (with many other countries all over the world) is replete with heads of state who have misused the resources and security apparatuses of their states for their personal benefit, thereby creating "conflict generating centres,"[14] particularly in one-party systems. Malan sees the formation of one-party systems as the development of an "African democracy . . . inspired by an allergy to foreign and imperfect models of democracy, and by a desire to reinstate a traditional African model oriented towards consensus and unity."[15]

With respect to multiparty responses to one-partyism, "[p]olitical leaders and parties were tempted to narrow their perspectives to tunnel visions of their own policies and positions, thereby ignoring the needs and interests of the people of their countries. Many became trapped in restricted ways of thinking, which often prove to be a sure recipe for conflict."[16] As will be seen in the discussion on the role of individuals, in reality, multiparty is perhaps a misnomer in that these arrangements actually led to one-*person* states.

Coupled with personal rivalries between leaders, efforts for integration and conflict resolution have been fraught with duplication. In turn, it has resulted in an overstretching of human, institutional, structural, and economic capacity to manage initiatives with essentially the same goals.

George Ayittey is less diplomatic about the psychology of some of Africa's postcolonial leaders and contends that most African political systems have exhibited various shades of the "Big Man" patrimonial rule. He distinguishes three types of leadership that surfaced in the postcolonial era: charismatic, patriarchal, and revolutionary or populist prophetic. The latter two resulted in tyrannical rule, characterized by "its coercive, idiosyncratic, and whimsical nature because of chronic feelings of insecurity. . . . But despite outward appearances, the strongman is often weak internally or psychologically. An economic illiterate, he cannot distinguish between a budget deficit and a trade deficit. To cover up his inadequacies, he craves—and demands—veneration, adulation, and obedience. He surrounds himself with followers who constantly reaffirm their faith in his exceptional wisdom and generosity."[17]

Chabal and Daloz develop this aspect further by highlighting the blurred lines in Africa between state and civil society, between state and private enterprise, and between official and private identities. They point out that, in postcolonial Africa, the "actual behaviour of leaders"[18] indicates that the "state was never functionally differentiated from society"[19] and that African societies are "not mass-societies composed of discrete individuals detached from their communal environment."[20] Elaborating on the benefits of the patrimonial system for the African elites, which are not significantly increased in numbers but just "recycled,"[21] they write that "[i]n practice, however, the difference between [business and politics] is more symbolic than real, since the overlap of the world of politics and that of business is one of the most salient features of contemporary Africa. What brings both sides together is the determination to control and contain disorder within manageable, that is instrumentally productive, boundaries. What patrons do not want is for violence to get out of control."[22] By "control" this writer understands it to mean "unprofitable" for both their positions of power and for their economic well-being.

As for the role of *individuals*, removed from their identities as members of a community, the notion of recognition and reward is rare, except for the veneration of the head of state/strongman/patron. (The latter is perhaps afforded in turn for the interdependencies caused by the patrimonial system as described by Chabal and Daloz.)[23]

All these factors have a bearing on diplomacy because an individual may be efficient but not connected to the right patrimonial link to make the contact useful. It is rare to find an African delegate who approaches another delegation individually. In this writer's experience, there is a preference for collective negotiation, lobbying, and drafting and presentation of position papers.[24]

Another aspect that begs attention is the African worldview, which is linked to the notion of the communal. This is a controversial topic because it touches the very core of identity, culture, religion, approaches to responsibility and accountability, response to opportunities and crises, the planning and implementation process, as well as interaction with "the other." However, it is essential to mention this aspect of Africa's heritage because, as in any other part of the world, it dictates behavior.

This writer agrees with Darrow L. Miller,[25] who wrote

All people and cultures have a particular model of the universe, or worldview. Their worldview does more to shape their development, their prosperity or poverty, than does their physical environment or other circumstances.

Too little attention has been given to this aspect of humanity, both in ordinary interaction with people and in formal diplomacy, probably with incalculable damage to relations between people and nations.

What is the most prevalent African worldview? In addition to centuries of Christianity and Islam, many African practices continue to derive from an animist approach to life, "which views reality as essentially spiritual. . . . The physical world is . . . 'animated' by spirits. Animism posits that events come solely from the outside, from the spiritual realm, as do the solutions. To solve a problem, one must appease the spirits."[26]

Veneration of ancestors is important in Africa, and diplomats are well advised to take into account the importance of older people in this society:

Central to African beliefs is the link between the world of the living and that of the dead . . . all inhabit the same world . . . [and] one of the consequences of such belief is that, for Africans, there is a link between identity and locality which goes well beyond the Western notion of what the French call *terroir*. One's locality is where the ancestors are buried. It assumes, therefore, a significance which is more than symbolic—which is, in fact, instrumentally meaningful for the conduct of daily life. . . . Mobutu's compulsive decision to take the bones of his parents on his final journey into exile is exemplary in this respect. Moreover, the universally recognizable tendency of politicians to favour their own may well have to do with more than mere ethnic bias. It may include a religious dimension which has hitherto almost never been taken into consideration but which could turn out to be deeply significant to the reality of politics [and the diplomacy of conflict resolution] in contemporary Africa.[27,28]

This observation is borne out by Sarah W. Gachege's plea for traditional conflict resolution methods. To illustrate her point, she cites several examples of conflict situations in African pastoral settings in which the reconciliation between conflict parties have been or is sanctified by a ceremony involving some form of animal sacrifice and special drink or food.[29] These examples clearly show that the rational and irrational still combine to serve the same purpose. Furthermore, the irrational renders all interaction to have a metaphysical dimension, whereas the rational causes interaction to be political, with a constant interplay between the two.

The Organization of African Unity (OAU)

Before elaborating on conflict resolution within the OAU context, it is useful to contextualize the establishment of the OAU on May 25, 1963. Patel explains,

The process of regional integration in Africa almost corresponds with the emergence of independent African states. It is important to note that much as the African states struggled to cope with the demands of being real sovereigns and nation states, the urge for integration and the establishment of [an] African presence in the world came almost spontaneously.[30]

This was precipitated by the realization that, as young nations, Africa needed to speak with one voice to the rest of the world. The unity of Africa, defense of the sovereignty of individual states, eradication of all forms of colonialism, and the promotion of international cooperation with due regard for the Charter of the UN and the Universal Declaration of Human Rights were all enshrined in the OAU Charter.

With respect to conflict resolution, the Charter made provision for the establishment of two institutions: the Commission on Mediation, Conciliation, and Arbitration and the Defence Commission. The principles of Article III in which member states solemnly affirmed and declared their adherence to, among other things, "peaceful settlement of disputes by negotiation, mediation, conciliation or arbitration" were to guide the work of these two commissions.[31]

Neither of these OAU commissions ever became functional. Differences of opinion about sovereignty, structure, authority, functions, financing, and accountability hampered the implementation of "repeated resolutions"[32] by OAU Heads of State and Government. With respect to the Military Commission, military action was primarily understood in terms of defense against outside interference, and not as a mechanism for inter-African deployment. Financial and logistic impediments were a crucial factor in this commission not getting off the ground, despite accusations in 1970 by the then OAU secretary-general Diallo Telli that Africa was "showing what could be termed indifference to its security."[33]

In view of what was said earlier about indigenous methods of conflict resolution, Ayittey's explanation as to why postcolonial leaders could not agree is logical. He argues that traditional African systems to settle disputes did not include resolution of *intertribal* disputes, except for a few ad hoc measures or attempts at diplomacy.[34] These heads of state may have come to the OAU with their cultural experience of human interaction, hence the preference for collective action, but lacking exposure to the skills necessary for interstate interaction.

A new dynamism made its way through Africa after the Cold War. The demise of one of the superpowers not only confronted Africa's leaders with a completely altered geopolitical situation globally, which in turn has accelerated the marginalization of the continent. It also altered strategic positions of African states internally and among each other and within regions. Many conflicts that were frozen during the Cold War were unfrozen subsequent to the fall of the Berlin Wall. Prevention was therefore almost impossible.

A significant consequence has been a comprehensive rethinking of Africa's approach to conflict resolution. What Ayittey had suggested in 1998 has been receiving increasing attention, namely that, instead of rushing "blindly [to] copy foreign systems they did not understand, [African nationalists and elites should have] looked in their own backyard [where] they would have found the solutions to many of Africa's recurrent crises."[35] Original African techniques of conflict resolution have begun to resurface, bringing home the necessity to analyze, manage, and resolve conflicts in a holistic manner. Although always being acceptable in informal initiatives, formal regional efforts are beginning to accommodate the traditional methodology. Added to the age-old value of *ubuntu*, it was no longer acceptable to deal with political issues divorced from their developmental or economic dimensions. The fact that there is a dialectical link between stability, security, and development found resonance in one of the first African policy documents to be signed after the Cold War.

The Abuja Treaty, in terms of which an African Economic Community was established, was signed in 1991. Although an ambitious vision, the treaty envisaged what other reports recommended long after that. There is hardly an aspect of human endeavor that did not find its way into the Abuja Treaty and that does not beg interaction incrementally between states, regions, and continental bodies.

Subsequent to the Abuja Treaty, the Cairo Declaration of 1993 authorized the establishment of the OAU Central Organ for the Prevention, Management, and Resolution of Conflict. Among other things, it recognized the need to broaden the scope of which set of circumstances would constitute an early warning signal to potential conflict. Other reports that were published internationally may have received more attention, but they all said the same thing.[36]

The most seminal document to come forth on the issue was prepared by an African, Mr. Kofi Annan, Secretary-General of the United Nations. He took the debate much further in his 1998 *Report on the Causes of Conflict and the Promotion of Durable Peace and Sustainable Development in Africa.* In an almost daring fashion, he spelled out the crucial notion of Africa accepting responsibility for itself, which underlies all initiatives to improve the lives of the people on the continent. To paraphrase his argument, he called for a shortening of the line of action between a conflict situation, the people who suffer from it, and the people who try to solve it. Whereas the United Nations has the primary responsibility to maintain international peace and security, governments, regional and subregional organizations, and other institutions from civil society and business should share more of this responsibility in a coordinated, constructive fashion. He has put his conviction into practice by insisting on a much closer relationship between the UN, civil society, and business. (Who would have dreamed, even five years ago, that the UN would have its own UN/NGO and UN/Business Web sites!)

The South African minister of foreign affairs elucidated this integrated approach in a speech delivered in Japan earlier this year:

Our approach is to address the causes of these conflicts in all their manifestations in order to provide the framework for development and good governance. Thus, matters such as sustainable development, environmental security, over-population, crime, the narcotics trade, money laundering, corruption, terrorism, proliferation of small arms and the eradication of landmines take on special importance. Within the ambit of causes of conflict, we also regard as important the effects of poverty, under-development, HIV/AIDS, malaria and tuberculosis. While all these phenomena are prevalent in other parts of the world, they are particularly acute in Africa.[37]

Since 1993, the OAU has come a long way. Whereas it was unheard of not so long ago to talk about the internal problems of individual countries for fear of breaching sovereignty, not a single OAU meeting these days takes place without a list of conflict situations on the agenda. At the OAU Summit in 1999, member countries whose government had come into power by unconstitutional means during the previous year were given a "yellow card."[38] At the OAU Summit in Togo in July 2000, two countries (Comoros and Côte d'Ivoire) were not allowed to participate in the deliberations. Despite some extremely critical words to the summit, the upholding of the "yellow card" principle made the UN secretary-general "look forward to the day when the General Assembly of the United Nations takes the same principled stand and follows the lead of the OAU."[39]

Also during the 2000 OAU Summit, the heads of state and government adopted the "Declaration on the Framework for an OAU Response to Unconstitutional Changes of Government." In the declaration, the leaders express their "grave concern about the resurgence of coup [sic] d'état in Africa," coming "at a time when our people have committed themselves to respect of the rule of law based on peoples [sic] will expressed through the ballot and not the bullet."[40]

The document sets out four elements of a framework for an OAU response to unconstitutional changes of government. They include a definition of what constitutes an unconstitutional change, measures and actions the OAU would progressively take to respond to such changes, and an implementation mechanism.

What started as a nongovernmental initiative in 1990 by President Olusegun Obasanjo of Nigeria as head of the Africa Leadership Forum while he was out of government has now (since his return as president) found its way into the Togo Summit declarations. After a series of conferences, the "CSSDCA Solemn Declaration" is perhaps the most comprehensive and integrated document on peace and security yet to emanate from Africa's leaders. The Conference on Security, Stability, Development, and Cooperation in Africa (CSSDCA) is a consultative process among African leaders. It is designed to "provide a policy development forum for the elaboration and advancement of common values within the main policy organs of the OAU. . . . [T]he interactive approach embedded in the CSSDCA should provide an invaluable tool for the pursuit of the agenda of the OAU in the new millennium, with particular reference to the issues of Security, Stability, Development, and Cooperation."[41] The document makes particular reference to the "interdependence of Member States and the link between their security, stability and development [which makes] it imperative to develop a common African agenda [which] must be based on a unity of purpose and a collective political consensus derived from a firm conviction that Africa cannot make any significant progress without finding lasting solutions to the problem of peace and security."[42]

The "Constitutive Act of the African Union," also adopted at the Togo 2000 Summit, is the result of an initiative by Colonel Muhammar Ghadaffi from Libya. Frustrated by lack of progress with the review of the OAU Charter, he hosted an Extraordinary OAU Summit meeting in Sirte during 1999 in which he recommended the formation of a "United States of Africa." After much deliberation, especially by legal experts, the objectives of the union have now been formulated, among others, to "accelerate the political and socio-economic integration of the continent"[43] . . . and "coordinate and harmonize policies between existing and future Regional Economic Communities."[44] In other words, the OAU and African Economic Community (AEC) will eventually be collapsed into one organization.

The act does not mention conflict resolution as such, but the principles according to which the union will function include the "right of the Union to intervene in a Member State pursuant to a decision of the Assembly in respect of grave circumstances, namely war crimes, genocide and crimes against humanity,"[45] and the "right of Member States to request intervention from Union in order to restore peace and security."[46]

One would hope that the strides made to operationalize the Conflict Management Centre of the OAU since its establishment in 1993 will be recognized and strengthened once the African Union is constituted. The Central Organ of the OAU, which functions at the level of heads of state (with one meeting per year), the Council of Ministers (with biannual meetings) and ambassadors (once a month) remotely reflects the characteristics of a "security council." A major difference with the UN Security Council (*and* obstacle to implementation of decisions) is the Central Organ's infrequent meetings, that it has no implementation arm similar to the various agencies of the UN, and that it does not have something similar to the Department of Peacekeeping Operations (DPKO) that can plan at the scale required for proper peacekeeping.[47]

One of the most remarkable OAU achievements in terms of conflict resolution in recent years, albeit not on the African continent, has been the resolution of the Lockerbie issue. By sheer force of its collective action to ignore the air sanctions against Libya, the UK and the United States were compelled to compromise and let justice take its course according to a deal brokered by former president Mandela and Saudi Arabia. The ability of the OAU to force a revision of a long-held Security Council position, which had been dominated by the only remaining superpower, bears testimony to Africa's ability to mobilize action on a matter of principle.

The OAU and Peacekeeping

Peacekeeping under an OAU banner has always been difficult. The organization's very history and nature dictated against peacekeeping in a collective fashion. The problems that beset the OAU during the peacekeeping effort in Chad between 1981 and 1982 are still prevalent today, despite the end of the Cold War. In fact, the nature of the conflict in Chad is reminiscent of the types of conflicts in Africa today. Amato writes,

The problems that beset the OAU peacekeeping force in Chad were a practical demonstration of all that the opponents of the pan-African high command or any other form of a pan-African military force had been saying all along. Even if the OAU had been sufficiently prepared, which it was not, for the peacekeeping task that it had taken upon itself in Chad, its chances of success were much less than fifty-fifty. A civil war situation was the worst situation in which to test the viability of an inexperienced international peacekeeping force. Its only chances of possible success depended on taking sides with the government of the day against the dissident forces that were seeking to overthrow it. In that case, the intervention force would have to plunge itself into the conflict in a way that would enable it to achieve a decisive victory—and pull out immediately thereafter, if it was not to get itself bogged down by an interminable guerilla warfare.[48]

After 17 years, Amato's insights seem to have been almost prophetic. Although not under the OAU banner, subsequent missions in Liberia and Sierra Leone are chilling reminders of the same dilemma.

The most pertinent drawback of the OAU's ability to plan and oversee peace-keeping missions has been the lack of mechanisms and resources to implement decisions and monitor progress. The OAU has always been a *policy* body with its main focus on extracontinental threats and representing collective African positions in larger fora such as the UN and NAM. The establishment of the Central Organ for Conflict Prevention, Management, and Resolution, coupled with the Conflict Management Centre, which serves as its secretariat, has witnessed a fundamental shift in OAU thinking. It is true to say that the OAU still does not have implementing, financial, or logistic capacity, but the regular meetings of the Central Organ, specifically at ambassadorial level, have put conflict prevention, management, and resolution, as well as peacekeeping, firmly on the OAU's agenda in a much more structured way. The OAU in recent years has also dispatched observer missions to Burundi, Rwanda, and the Comoros. OAU teams have also monitored elections in most of the countries that held elections since 1993. These measures present another dimension of what Michael Lund calls the "creeping institutionalization of the culture of prevention."[49]

Capacity has always been the biggest problem for African peacekeeping. In 1997, under the auspices of the Central Organ, the OAU Chiefs of Staff made some pertinent recommendations that include the following:

- The OAU should undertake preliminary **preventive action** in an emergency situation and then approach the UN to deploy a peace operation. The focus, therefore, is to react in limited time to a crisis situation.

- Only peace operations should be undertaken, **excluding peace enforcement,** unless with a clear mandate from the UN Security Council.

- Initially one brigade per subregion could be earmarked as a contribution to a **standby arrangement** from each of the five subregions.

- All **training** should be conducted according to UN doctrine and standards but also complimented by African needs.

- Joint peace support **exercises** should be organized under the auspices of the OAU at subregional level.

- The OAU Conflict Management Centre, especially, and its **early-warning** capacity should be strengthened.

- The OAU should adopt a structure to regulate **command, control, and communications** as well as effective **logistics** within the context of a peace support operation.[50]

These recommendations should be seen in the context of Africa's reaction to proposals that came from abroad, in particular the American idea of an "African Crisis Response Force," ultimately converted into the "African Crisis Response Initiative" (ACRI). Given Africa's deeply rooted culture of consultation, Africans were angered by the idea that the "quick fix" for African conflicts lay in the training, by outside forces (and in the American case special forces), of rapid deployment of *African* forces. Worse, it was believed that such would take place without participation of the countries that had trained them. Whereas in the past the OAU had eschewed international forces in Africa because of their colonial and Cold War connotations, the organization now insists that African peacekeeping should not be "ghetto-ized." Although there is recognition that Africa's capacity should be strengthened, the international community's reneging on its responsibilities in Somalia, Rwanda, and Sierra Leone have informed the current position of the OAU. The *leitmotiv* since 1994 has been that the ultimate responsibility for international peace and security lies with the UN and *all* its members. Whereas sovereignty used to be sacrosanct in the past, the responsibility of the UN to commit itself equally to Africa is now underpinning all African deliberations on peacekeeping.

With respect to the notion of a common doctrine for peacekeeping, initial debates within Africa were bedeviled by semantics. In some quarters, "doctrine" was understood to have ideological connotations.[51] Of late, research initiatives such as that of the Institute of Security Studies (ISS) have done much to remove the reluctance to use certain terminology. Leading figures that represent the African peacekeeping fraternity have since 1997 participated in their personal capacity in seminars organized by a variety of institutions. These seminars have encouraged frank debate on issues of particular relevance to doctrinal and operational aspects and are bound to influence official positions in future.[52]

Subregional Organizations

For the sake of brevity, the following organizations are discussed:

- The Southern African Development Community (SADC)
- The Economic Community of West African States (ECOWAS)
- The Intergovernmental Authority on Development (IGAD)

Until about 1994, most of these organizations left the political work pertaining to the management and resolution of conflicts to the continental organization, the OAU, while concentrating on economic integration. However, all the subregional organizations have taken initiatives to bring together their efforts aimed at socioeconomic development and the strengthening of peace and stability within their regions.

Intractable conflicts within all the subregions of Africa, as well as the common realization that political stability and security must be fostered within the context of sustainable development, compelled these organizations to revisit the artificial separation of objectives and activities. Some are further developed than others, but all these organizations now have mechanisms in place or afoot to deal with conflict resolution in their regions.

SADC

A final resolution is still outstanding on whether the Organ on Politics, Defence, and Security should be part of SADC or an independent informal entity, as was the case with the Frontline States. Nonetheless, this issue should not detract from the numerous initiatives, formal as well as informal, that are underway to augment the region's activities and interoperability with respect to security in the subregion. These initiatives range from constant meetings, formal and informal, between heads of state, to capacity building to strengthen institutional structures, to the building of partnerships with the donor community and civil society.

A prime example is capacity building for peacekeeping, crime prevention, and the curbing of illicit trafficking in small arms under the auspices of the Interstate Defence and Security Committee (ISDSC)[53] and the Southern African Regional Police Chiefs Co-operation Organisation (SARPCCO). Together with a variety of nongovernmental organizations, military officers, and civilian personnel from SADC, countries receive regular training in conflict prevention and management, peacekeeping, and crime prevention. Where deeper government involvement is required, such as the holding of full-scale peacekeeping exercises, SADC provides the overall mandate and political guidance. Two such exercises have been held: Blue Hungwe in Zimbabwe in 1998 and Blue Crane in South Africa in 1999.

ECOWAS

In West Africa, the Heads of State of ECOWAS in December 1999 adopted the protocol for their own "mechanism for the prevention, management, settlement of conflicts, and the maintenance of peace and security."[54] This meeting also endorsed the establishment of the West African Court of Justice and confirmed that a Community Parliament had to be established within the shortest possible time. Furthermore, a code of conduct was agreed on that compels member states "to declare all dedicated light weapons and ammunition to the ECOWAS Secretariat at the beginning of international peace operations."[55] Member countries have to seek permission from ECOWAS before importing light weapons for purposes of hunting or sporting activities.[56] Although there is a moratorium[57] within ECOWAS on the importation, export, and manufacture of small arms, this code of conduct will enable countries to import these arms for the purposes as stated previously. At their Silver Jubilee meeting of May 28–29, 2000, in Abuja, Nigeria, the ECOWAS leaders continued their institutionalizing of conflict resolution measures:

- They expressed satisfaction with the entry into force of the protocol on the Community Parliament.
- Information was requested with a view to adopt concrete measures on controlling child trafficking.

• The executive secretary of ECOWAS was requested to work closely with the Ghanaian authorities to draft the statutes of the proposed Criminal Intelligence Bureau to be submitted for adoption by the community.[58]

On July 21, 2000, Reuters reported about the first meeting of the ECOWAS Defence and Security Commission in Accra on July 19–20, 2000. The report stated that ECOWAS was to set up four early-warning conflict observatories to improve the prevention of civil tension and upheavals in and among member countries. The first such observatory was expected to open in Abuja, Nigeria, to be followed by Ghana, Burkina Faso, and Benin. According to the report, the commission will be expected to provide technical advice to regional leaders for the deployment of a now "permanent composite standby military unit in place of the ad-hoc Economic Community Cease-Fire Monitoring Group (ECOMOG) force."[59]

The interventions by ECOMOG in Liberia and Sierra Leone have been both lauded and criticized, depending on commentators' interpretations with respect to international law. Those with an orthodox view of international law argue that ECOMOG, just like NATO in Kosovo, did not have a Security Council mandate to intervene in terms of Chapter VIII of the charter (with Chapter VII rules of engagement). Proponents of this argument say it is better to err on the right side of the law.[60] In the case of Sierra Leone, mandates were mostly obtained ex post facto, whereas in Kosovo's case, no such mandate (not even ex post facto) was obtained. The current Security Council mandates for Sierra Leone and Kosovo also point to significant differences with respect to legal mandates and responsibilities. The mandate for Kosovo differentiates between the security aspects of the mission to be carried out under the NATO umbrella, and the administrative, humanitarian, human rights, and development aspects of the mission to be carried out by a rainbow of UN and European civilian organizations. The current mandate for Sierra Leone provides one mandate for all activities under a collective UN banner.

The counterargument, also similar to Kosovo, is for a justifiable defense against violations of the Geneva Conventions and the duty to support justified defense. As is the case with Kosovo, the argument is that the Security Council may not have granted the mandate for a UN intervention in Sierra Leone (and Kosovo)[61] in the first place. With respect to Sierra Leone, Africans have always argued that their underrepresentation in the Security Council, combined with permanent member politics, has rendered Africa to be its stepchild. ECOWAS argued in favor of an intervention because the dire humanitarian and human rights situation in the country necessitated firm and urgent action.

IGAD (formerly IGADD)

When the Intergovernmental Authority on Drought and Development (IGADD) was formed in 1986, it had a very narrow mandate around the issues of drought and desertification. Since then, and especially in the 1990s, IGADD has become the accepted vehicle for regional security and political dialogue. Today, IGAD stands for the Intergovernmental Authority on Development and has three priority areas of cooperation:

- Conflict prevention, management, and resolution and humanitarian affairs
- Infrastructure development (transport and communications)
- Food security and environment protection

Article 18 of the agreement establishing IGAD states that members shall act collectively to preserve peace, security, and stability, which are essential pre-requisites for economic development.[62] It is in this context that IGAD has been involved in activities to facilitate the peace processes in Somalia and the Sudan.

In Somalia, IGAD was the guarantor for the process taking place in Djibouti to forge national reconciliation in Somalia. An interesting feature of the efforts to restore a functional and properly constituted government to that country is the active involvement of civil society. At their meeting in November 1999, the IGAD Heads of State and Government "called on the international community as a whole to co-operate more effectively with IGAD with the view to enhancing the role of Civil Society in Somalia for making a difference for peace in that country and for national reconciliation."[63] Interestingly enough, the leaders "reiterated once again that there is no alternative for peace in Somalia to *pushing forward with the building block and the bottom-up approach in which the role of warlords is contained and that of Civil Society is enhanced.*"[64]

On all these platforms, topics such as economic development and integration are being interspersed by debates and programs to prevent unconstitutional changes of government, the strengthening of administrative and political struc-tures, environmental security, the issue of illicit small arms trafficking, land mines, and how to improve the access of women to a better life. Many of these topics were untouchable a few years ago, but Africa's political liberation has made it possible for these organizations to tackle them now. The end of colo-nialism only signaled a virtual liberation because it was followed immediately thereafter by the devastating proxy wars in Africa that were the manifestations of superpower politics. Only after the Cold War could Africa attend to its problems without the entanglements of colonialism and the Cold War.

ROLE OF INDIVIDUALS IN AFRICAN CONFLICT RESOLUTION

In line with earlier remarks about the traditional African approach to conflict resolution, it is interesting to note how senior African statesmen are using their stature or positions within African organizations to address conflict sit-uations. Limited space allows for only a few cursory remarks.

Because of his unique moral standing in the international world, former president Nelson Mandela of South Africa has been able to utilize his "African wisdom" (derived from the title of Jannie Malan's publication)[65] to sterling effect. During his tenure as head of state, his approach to collective problem solving and nation building made him a singularly popular figure among all South Africans, irrespective of their political persuasions. He has been able to contribute to conflict resolution elsewhere in the most remarkable way, including the Lockerbie issue and Burundi. What distinguishes his conflict resolution technique is his ability to merge his all-inclusive approach with the guiding of opposing parties to come straight to the point. Professor Jakes Gerwel, chairperson of the Nelson Mandela Trust and witness to Mr. Mandela's methods, explains it as follows:

Although he insists on inclusivity, he gets singularly impatient with grand-standing. According to Mr. Mandela, an over-emphasis about the historical context of a conflict also holds the danger of becoming irrelevant to its resolution. He believes that, no matter how right a party may have been at some point during the conflict, any conflict reaches a stage where none of the parties have exclusive claim to being right or has to carry all the blame for being wrong.[66]

Another African leader who has contributed much to forging a synergy between the political and developmental aspects of conflict resolution is Dr. Salim Ahmed Salim, secretary-general of the OAU. His efforts to establish and manage the OAU Central Organ and the Centre for Conflict Management are well documented. His particular emphasis has been on early warning and early action.

The resolution of the conflict between Ethiopia and Eritrea, which culminated in the signing of the Cessation of Hostilities Agreement on June 14, 2000, may be attributed in large measure to President Abelaziz Bouteflika of Algeria. During the signing of the agreement, both the Ethiopian and Eritrean presidents insisted on retaining President Bouteflika as guarantor of the agreement, despite the fact that he was no longer the OAU chair. His term as chairperson of the OAU during 1999/2000 saw the OAU taking the leading role in ending the Ethiopia/Eritrea war. The wording of Article 2 of the agreement, that a "[p]eacekeeping [m]ission shall be deployed by the United Nations under the auspices of the OAU"[67] should be interpreted in terms of the political significance played by the OAU in the person of President Bouteflika as well as Africa's emphasis on collectivity.

These examples are in stark contrast to other leaders who did not "establish political systems that bore any resemblance to indigenous systems" but instead adopted personalized methods of ruling that border on "sultanism," to use Ayittey's analysis.[68]

This writer proposes that a more useful analysis may be to compare the duties of traditional African leaders with the governing style of most postcolonial leaders, even to the present day. In the former, to quote Ayittey again, he "was the political, social, judicial, and religious head of the tribe. As such, he had wide-ranging powers [but was kept in check] by various bodies and institutions to prevent an abuse of power and corruption. A chief with despotic tendencies was first reminded of the oath he took upon assumption of power."[69] And "destoolment" (removal from office) did happen!

In contrast, Richard Sandbrook (1993) paints a frightening, but correct, picture of what Ayittey calls "the typical African tyrant and how he rules."[70]

The strongman, usually the president, occupies the centre of the political life. Front and centre stage, he is the centrifugal force around which all else revolves. Not only the ceremonial head of state, the president is also the chief political, military and cultural figure: head of government, commander-in-chief of the armed forces, head of the governing party (if there is one) and even chancellor of the local university. His aim is typically to identify his person with the "nation."[71]

Surely these latter leaders must have been informed by their original heritage and adapted, or rather distorted, it to a style of leadership and diplomacy that suited their current needs or, more correctly, their political and economic appetites.

CIVIL SOCIETY AND CONFLICT RESOLUTION IN AFRICA

During the Kosovo Seminar at South African Institute of International Affairs (SAIIA), other papers focused specifically on the role of civil society in conflict resolution in Africa, but a few remarks in this chapter may be appropriate. African leaders in general have come to accept the necessity to interact with civil society. All three major declarations of the Lome OAU Summit include references to civil society, nongovernmental organizations, and in particular the fact that the role of women should receive special attention.[72] The earlier observations about the IGAD process in Somalia also bear witness to this, as do recent activities in Angola[73] and Burundi.[74] In Angola, church organizations seem to be spearheading a groundswell of civilian demands that the war be stopped.[75] In Burundi, women's organizations have held various conferences to sensitize negotiators about the role they can play in resolving the conflict.

Numerous civilian organizations are beginning to contribute to conflict resolution in Africa. Their most important value is in detecting the signals that may prompt armed conflict in the long term. The contribution of experts from civil society has been significant in initiatives emanating from the OAU ranging from the land mine issue and children in armed conflict to illegal proliferation of small arms, early warning, and peacekeeping. In South Africa, civil society was actively involved in the drafting of the White Paper on South African Participation in Peace Missions. They are also assisting in the implementation of the White Paper.

The delineation of roles between government and civil society was clarified as follows by the South African minister of foreign affairs in her speech in Japan:

By creating the environment for civil society to grow and establish strong institutions, governments and regional organisations are stimulating the formation of relationships based on partnership.[76]

The Sirte Declaration aims to establish a pan-African parliament "to provide a common platform for our peoples and their grass-root organizations to be more involved in discussions and decision-making on the problems and challenges facing our continent."[77]

What this means is that in order to facilitate the roles of subregional organizations and NGOs, both governments and civil society need to cooperate closely. Although civil society is crucial in playing a supportive role to government initiatives, governments have to bear ultimate responsibility for their actions. Governments and regional organizations can offer the following strengths:

- They can provide the political framework for peace, security, stability, and development.
- They can lend the weight of international law to our work.
- They can facilitate access to other international human, financial, and infrastructural resources.
- They can develop the necessary structural and institutional "skeleton" from which processes can be developed to put flesh onto this skeleton in order to complete the full body.

NGOs, on the other hand, can help to supplement the efforts of governments in several ways:

- They can assist governments to build human resource capacity through training in especially management and administration.
- They can supplement early warning mechanisms to prevent conflict.
- They can function as a sounding board for policy initiatives.
- They can contribute to policy formulation. In South Africa there was excellent cooperation with regard to the international campaign to ban land mines and with initiatives to eradicate the scourge of illicit trafficking of small arms.[78]

CONCLUSION

It has been the purpose of this chapter to provide information about the cultural and psychological foundations of Africa's approach to diplomacy and conflict resolution. The fact that many African organizations and structures do not function according to Western standards and logic does not mean that conflict prevention and resolution does not happen. Informality and a behind-the-scenes methodology seems to be the preferred method, although more is being done to put in place the necessary mechanisms and build capacity to provide for early warning, for early action, and to hold parties in conflict with each other accountable to their undertakings.[79]

What is most needed, though, is for leaders in the top echelons of decision making to integrate their efforts with growing capacity at other levels within governments and in civil society. The phenomenon of what Ayittey calls "functional illiteracy" is very real. It is not uncommon to find leaders and officials with impressive academic qualifications but little practical experience, understanding of (and sympathy for) administrative processes, and technical institutional background. This is usually obscured by a healthy dosage of arrogance, perhaps to hide their insecurity. Only by fostering professionalism can implementation be guaranteed. In any case, an organic functioning between government, bureaucracy, and civil society is fundamental to good governance, which in itself prevents conflicts. African leaders have made repeated and specific commitments in this respect, the latest of which is to be found in the Solemn CSSDCA Declaration:

The active and genuine participation of citizens of every country in the decision-making processes and in the conduct of public affairs must be fostered and facilitated.[80]

The Algiers Declaration of 1999 is even more specific:

We are convinced that the increase in, and expansion of the spaces of freedom and the establishment of democratic institutions that are representative of our peoples and receiving their active participation, would further contribute to the consolidation of modern African States underpinned by the rule of respect for the fundamental rights and freedoms of the citizens and democratic management of public affairs.[81]

Heads of state have the authority to adopt resolutions, make commitments, and agree to certain actions. However, they need the support from lower levels to translate vision into reality. In this respect, I agree with the former British foreign secretary, Mr. Douglas Hurd, who makes a strong case for professional diplomacy:

In the world of immortal but incompetent nations states professional diplomacy becomes more not less important. . . . Their first task is the accumulation and use of relevant information. On the whole, embassies are not now needed to report immediate and dramatic events. The news of a coup, a terrorist attack, even a substantial famine, will be flashed across the world without benefit of ambassadors. But the modern media are far less competent in the routine reporting of ordinary events. . . . Professional diplomacy is thus needed to provide not facts and figures but the relationship between those facts and figures, together with insights into the likely behaviors of those taking the resulting decisions.[82]

Diplomacy is as old as humanity. Conflict prevention, management, and resolution in Africa is not a new phenomenon either. What is new is the fact that it is being formalized into structures that encompass the whole continent, subregions, and local entities. However, all of us still suffer from what M. Scott Peck calls "simplistic"[83] thinking. His comments of these phenomena are extremely relevant:

Although people are different, an all-too-common flaw is that most tend to believe they somehow instinctively know how to think and communicate. In reality, they usually do neither well because they are either too self-satisfied to examine their assumptions about thinking or too self-absorbed to invest the time and energy to do so or how they make their decisions. And when challenged, they show very little awareness of—or become easily frustrated by—the dynamics involved in truly thinking and communicating well. . . . If we don't begin to think well, it's highly likely that we may end up killing ourselves.[84]

Conflicts begin in the minds of people. They can be prevented and stopped only in the minds of people.

It is hoped that the arguments put forward in this chapter will make a small contribution to better diplomacy and more enduring conflict resolution.

NOTES

1. The original version of this article was delivered under the title *The Role of Sub-Regional and Regional Organisations in Preventing Conflicts in Africa*. It was presented during the seminar staged by the South African Institute for International Affairs (SAIIA) at the Fifth Meeting of the Independent International Commission on Kosovo, University of the Witwatersrand, Johannesburg, August 25–26, 2000. It has been reworked to emphasize perspectives more relevant to the current publication. Permission by SAIIA to publish this article in its new form is acknowledged. The views expressed in this article are her own and do not necessarily reflect the views of the South Africa government.

2. Patrick Chabal and Jean-Pascal Daloz, *Africa works: Disorder as political instrument* (Bloomington: Indiana University Press, 1999), 45–47.

3. Ibid., 1–2, 14–15.

4. Bernard Lewis, *The multiple identities of the Middle East* (London: Phoenix, 1998), 59–61.

5. Nandini Patel, *Conflict resolution through regional organisations in Africa*, paper presented at the 40th Annual Conference of the Africa Institute of South Africa, Pretoria, May 30 to June 2, 2000.

6. Recent initiatives have illustrated how collective initiatives by African leaders can successfully change foreign positions for the benefit of all parties concerned. When the EU approached the OAU for an "EU/Africa" Summit, the idea was to talk only about

development issues and exclude conflict resolution and debt relief from the agenda. The Europeans also seemed reluctant to put in place follow-up mechanisms. At the insistence of the Africans, the title was changed to the Africa-Europe Summit to properly reflect the participants in the meeting. The resultant Cairo Declaration reserves 5 out of 16 pages to conflict resolution and debt relief, and a Plan of Action was negotiated to secure follow-up. Another example is the OAU decision to delegate three African heads of state to present Africa's case on the debt issue to the G8 Okinawa Summit.

7. Secretary-general of the United Nations, Report to the General Assembly: The causes of conflict and the promotion of durable peace and sustainable development in Africa, S/1998/318, 1, 24.

8. Patrick Chabal and Jean-Pascal Daloz's analysis of the African state is relevant also in any discussion about diplomacy because it addresses the very heart of interstate relations. See *Africa works: Disorder as political instrument,* The International African Institute in association with James Currey (Oxford) (Bloomington: Indiana University Press, 1999), 4–16. Also important are the views about the decision-making process by African leaders as expressed by George B. N. Ayittey in his *Africa in chaos* (New York: St. Martin's Press, 1998), 163, 164.

9. Jannie Malan, *Conflict resolution wisdom from Africa* (Durban, South Africa: ACCORD, 1997), 32.

10. Ibid., 30.

11. Ibid., 17, 18.

12. Ibid., 19.

13. Fernand Braudel, *A history of civilisations* (New York: Penguin, 1993), 324.

14. Malan, op. cit., 34.

15. Ibid., 34.

16. Ibid., 35.

17. George B. N. Ayittey, *Africa in chaos* (New York: St. Martin's Press, 1998), 158, 159.

18. Chabal and Daloz, 31.

19. Ibid., 13.

20. Ibid., 19.

21. Ibid., 31–35.

22. Ibid., 80.

23. Ibid., 37–44.

24. Someone with a Western understanding of individualism may find this practice time consuming and even frustrating. The integration of the diplomatic *corps* in South Africa, which is in the process of transformation after its democratization in 1994, should provide interesting material for research. Of specific value would be the adaptation process of diplomats from a Western background and those with mostly Western academic qualifications, but an African cultural background, and how this transformation process is influencing the methodology of diplomacy.

25. Darrow L. Miller with Stan Guthrie, *Discipling nations: The power of truth to transform cultures* (Seattle: YWAM Publishing, 1999), 32.

26. Ibid., 34. In relation to diplomacy and conflict resolution, this would be a simplistic notion. Efforts to interact with Africans (or for that matter with any other part of the world) should not discard all other aspects that may have caused a conflict; the point is merely that peoples' worldview is important and should form part of the entire repertoire of diplomacy and conflict resolution.

27. Chabal and Daloz, 65, 66, 67.

28. South Africa's experience during the Truth and Reconciliation Commission is a good example. Perpetrators of atrocities against political activists had to indicate to family members where they had buried the bones of their loved ones. This reveals the deep-seated belief that the spirits of the ancestors have to be appeased and respected by proper burial at the proper place. If we are serious about conflict resolution in Africa, research on how to resolve conflicts about land issues urgently needs to factor in this aspect of the continent's psyche.

29. Sarah W. Gachege, *The marginalization of indigenous approaches of peace making and reconciliation*, paper presented at the 40th Anniversary Conference of the African Institute of South Africa, Pretoria, May 29–June 2, 2000.

30. Patel, op. cit., 3.

31. The ancient African preference for mediation and arbitration, as opposed to "more adversarial and adjudicative procedures of conflict resolution and reconciliation" is highlighted by Sarah W. Gachege in her paper, see footnote 29.

32. C. O. C. Amate, *Inside the OAU: Pan-Africanism in practice* (New York: St. Martin's Press, 1986), 176. Amate provides a vivid rendition of the histories of these two commissions until 1983.

33. Ibid., 175.

34. Ayittey, 83.

35. Ibid.

36. In its 1997 report, the Carnegie Commission on Preventing Deadly Conflict put the emphasis on the integration of structural, financial, political, economic, and social approaches to ensure peace and development. The Organisation for Economic Coordination and Development (OECD), in its "Development assistance committee guidelines on conflict, peace and development cooperation" of 1997, also recognized the link between development and conflict.

37. Dr. Nkosazana Dlamini Zuma, minister of foreign affairs of South Africa, speech at seminar, *The Roles of sub-regional and non-governmental organisations in conflict prevention and peace initiatives in Sub-Sahara Africa*, Tokyo, March 28, 2000.

38. 35th Assembly of Heads of State and Government of the OAU, Algiers, July 12–14, 1999, AHG/Decl. 141 (XXXV). African leaders decided that member states whose governments came to power through unconstitutional means after the Harare Summit (of 1997) should restore constitutional legality before the next summit.

39. Mr. Kofi Annan, Secretary-General of the UN, *Address to the annual assembly of heads of state and government of the OAU*, Togo, July 10, 2000.

40. 36th Ordinary Session of the OAU Assembly of Heads of State and Government, *Declaration on the framework for an OAU response to unconstitutional changes of government*, Togo, July 2000, AHG/Draft/Decl. 5 (XXXVI) Rev. 1, p. 1.

41. 36th Ordinary Session of the OAU Assembly of Heads of State and Government, *CSSDCA solemn declaration*, Togo, July 2000, AHG/Draft/Decl. 4 (XXXVI) Rev. 1, p. 2.

42. Ibid., 3.

43. 36th Ordinary Session of the OAU Assembly of Heads of State and Government of the OAU/4th Ordinary Session of the AEC, *Constitutive act of the African Union*, Togo, July 10–12, 2000, Article 3 (c).

44. Ibid., Article 3 (l).

45. Ibid., Article 4 (h).

46. Ibid., Article 4 (j).

47. At the level of planning for peacekeeping, there have been some recent productive developments in that the OAU Central Organ and UN Department of Peacekeeping Operations (DPKO) have established a joint coordinating committee to coordinate their responsibilities with respect to the UN Mission in Ethiopia/Eritrea. Military liaison officers representing the OAU are stationed in both Addis Ababa and Eritrea to interlink the OAU's planning activities with those of the UN.

48. Amato, op. cit. 187–189.

49. Michael Lund, *Creeping institutionalization of the culture of prevention: Recent progress and next step*, paper delivered at the seminar "Preventing Violent Conflict— The Search for Political Will, Strategies and Effective Tools," Stockholm, June 2000.

50. OAU Secretariat, Report of the Second Meeting of the chiefs of Defence Staff of the Central Organ of the OAU Mechanism for Conflict Prevention, Management and Resolution, Harare, 25 October 1997.

51. Mark Malan, *Towards an integrated doctrine for peace support operations in Africa*, ISS Monographs Series No. 46, Pretoria, February 2000.

52. Of particular importance is the "Prague to Pretoria" process under the auspices of the Institute for Security Studies, Pretoria, and the Institute of International Relations, Prague.

53. The ISDSC is a remnant of the informal Frontline States grouping of Southern African heads of state who were responsible for conflict management prior to South Africa's democratization in 1994. Although not a formal body in terms of international law, it remains an extremely effective instrument to mobilizing Southern African cooperation on matters relating to security and crime-prevention. All SADC countries are members and are represented by ministers of defence, public security (police) and state security (intelligence). It also functions effectively at officials level. Also important to note is that the good work done by the "informal" ISDSC is an indication that, in Africa, "informal" does not necessarily mean "illegitimate."

54. BBC Monitoring Service, English translation of Radio Togo text of *Communiqué issued after ECOWAS Summit*, Togo, 10 December 1999.

55. ECOWAS Code of Conduct for the implementation of the moratorium on the importation, exportation and manufacturing of light weapons, signed in Lome, 10 December 1999, art. 8, 9 (1).

56. Ibid. Art. 9 (3).

57. ECOWAS Declaration of a moratorium on importation, exportation and manufacture of light weapons in West Africa, signed in Abuja, 31 October 1998.

58. ECOWAS Silver Jubilee Anniversary Celebration, *Final Communiqué*, Abuja, 28–29 May 2000, Articles VII (ii)14, VIII and X.

59. Kwaku Sakyi-Addo, *ECOWAS to establish early-warning conflict units*, reported for Reuters, 21 July 2000. At the time of finalizing this article, no details were available. Pertaining to the standby force, pertinent issues to be finalized will probably include regional leadership, composition, and capacity of the to be established regional standby force, command and control, finances and logistics.

60. A strong case against the NATO intervention in Kosovo is made by Robert Hayden, University of Pittsburgh, *Humanitarian hypocrisy*. See also contribution of Raju G. C. Thomas from Marquette University, *NATO and international law*. Both comments are available on Kosovo & Yugoslavia: Law in Crisis, JURIST: The Law Professor's

Network, date of comments not specified. See other comments on Web site http://www.jurist.law.pitt.edu/hayden.htm.

61. See in particular the article by Fred Halliday, "Are NATO actions prudent and are they legal?," *The Irish Times*, 1 April 1999, accessed on Web site address http://www.ireland.com/newspaper/opinion/1999/0401/opt3.htm. See also Antonio Cassess, "*Ex iniuria ius oritur:* Are we moving towards international legitimation of forcible humanitarian countermeasures in the world community?," *European Journal of International Law*, Vol. 10. (1999) no. 1, accessed on Web site address http://www.ejil.org/journal/Vol10/No1/com.html.

62. IGAD Charter, Art. 18, Nairobi, 21 March 1996.

63. 7th IGAD Summit of Heads of State and Government, *Declaration*, Djibouti, 26 November 1999, 3.2.

64. Ibid. Emphasis mine.

65. Jannie Malan, op. cit.

66. Prof. Jakes Gerwel, chairperson of the Nelson Mandela Trust, in a telephonic interview with author, August 11, 2000.

67. Agreement on cessation of hostilities between the Government of the Federal Democratic Republic of Ethiopia and the Government of the State of Eritrea, signed in Algiers on June 18, 2000.

68. Ayittey, 92–94.

69. Ibid., 87, 89.

70. Ibid., 94.

71. Richard Sandbrook, *The politics of Africa's stagnation* (New York: Cambridge University Press, 1993), as quoted by Ayyitey, 94.

72. 36th Ordinary Session of the Assembly of Heads of State and Government of the OAU, *Draft Lome Declaration*, AHG/Draft/Decl. 2 (XXXVI) Rev. 1, introductory par. 2 and operative par. 24; the *CSSDCA Solemn Declaration*, op. cit., par. 10(b), 11(b) and 14 (Stability, par. C); *Declaration on the framework for an OAU response to unconstitutional changes of government*, op. cit., 3.

73. Lara Pawson, "Angolan opposition seek united voice," BBC News, 9 August 2000, accessed on Web site http://news6.thdo.bbc.co.uk/hi/english/world/africa/newsid%5F872000/872588.stm. See also article on IRIN, "Church Ready to Help Mediate," accessed on Web site http://www.allafrica.com/stories/200008010022.html.

74. See article by Mary Kimani, "All party Burundi women peace conference," *Internews* (Arusha Tanzania), 18 July 2000, accessed on Web site http://www.allafrica.com/stories/200007180552.html.

75. See also article by Virginie Ladisch, "Civil society play their tole in the Angolan peace process," *Conflict Trends* 3(2000).

76. Zuma, op. cit.

77. 4th Extraordinary Session of the OAU Assembly of Heads of State and Government, *Sirte Declaration*, Sirte, September 8–9, 1999, par. 8 i (b).

78. For a contrasting view of civil society in Africa, see the chapter, *The illusions of civil society*, in Chabal and Daloz, 17–30.

79. Chabal and Daloz provide a fascinating analysis of the nature of African institutions as they exist at present. Their insights in the book quoted in this article should be required reading for any analyst.

80. CSSDCA Solemn Declaration, op. cit., par. 11(b).

81. 35th Ordinary Session of Heads of State and Government of the OAU, Algiers, July 12–14, HAG/Decl. 1 (XXXV) 3.

82. Douglas Hurd, *The search for peace, A century of peace diplomacy* (London: Warner Books, London, 1997), 168, 170.

83. M. Scott Peck, *The road less travelled and beyond* (London: Rider, 1997), 25.

84. Ibid., 25, 26.

9

The Psychology of Middle Eastern Water Conflicts

Matthew F. Shaw and Jeff Danielski

Even the most seemingly straightforward positions contain a tangled web of coexisting interests, needs, and fears (Fisher & Ury, 1991; Kelman, 1990). These factors bring depth and complexity to all conflicts. Consider a father and daughter arguing about a homework assignment. The father claims the daughter should complete her work before socializing with friends. The father's position, like all positions, is based on myriad conscious and unconscious needs, fears, and interests. For example, the father may want to assert his authority, ensure that she receives good grades, or prevent her from following her brother's example. The daughter claims she should be allowed to complete her homework after returning from a movie. Her position may contain within it desires to spend time with friends, assert her independence, or belittle her father.

All conflicts are overdetermined. Whether a dispute involves a parent and child or a group of sparring nation states, it contains multiple layers of interests that lie beneath the avowed positions. Each layer is associated with specific fears, wishes, and expectations that produce a type of psychological valence. Observers and participants often describe conflicts in simplistic terms, focusing on the positions rather than the interests and disavowing pertinent psychological factors. It is common to hear international disputes described as simple disagreements over occupation of a territory or access to a resource. Such analyses sometimes neglect relevant economic, cultural, and sociopolitical concerns and usually ignore the psychological investment that leads to the conflict's perpetuation. This oversimplification can be envisioned as an attempt to contain the anxiety associated with highly complicated issues. The ability to tolerate ambiguity and complexity is a developmental achievement that is undoubtedly compromised during times of intense threat, and yet it is essential to the resolution of seemingly intractable conflicts.

There is a profound need to develop a more sophisticated understanding of the multifaceted nature of international conflicts and the cooperative, interdependent interventions that lead to their resolution. The study of water disputes, perhaps more than any other realm of conflict, enables one to develop such an understanding. To emphasize the relevance of studying the distribution and allocation of water is to highlight the obvious. Water is an essential resource. It not only provides mobility, security, and in some cases communal identity, it also sustains life. Daniel Moynihan, former senator from New York State, aptly said, "You can live without oil, and you can even live without love. But you can't live without water" (McGuire, 2001).

Although more than 70 percent of the world's surface is covered with water almost seven miles deep, most of the 5.8 billion humans living on it do not have access to clean, reliable water supplies (McGuire, 2001). Approximately 97 percent of the earth's water is seawater, and nearly 2 percent is held within glaciers and ice caps. Many of the freshwater reserves that lie beneath the earth's surface are too deep and therefore too expensive to tap (Postel, 1992). If all the planet's water were held within a gallon jug, one tablespoon would represent the amount of available freshwater. Furthermore, prohibitively expensive water delivery systems, poor water management strategies, expanding populations, and increased water usage by industry, agriculture, and domestic households tax already depleted reserves (McGuire, 2001).

The water that is available is not distributed equitably among communities. Some communities have excess resources, have little motivation to conserve, and prove to be poor stewards of their supplies. Other communities live amid such scarcity that desperation leads to extreme and violent means. Water conflicts uniquely emphasize interdependency and its denial. Rivers flow through communities and across borders. To alter the river is to affect the water one's downstream neighbors receive. Irrigation techniques in one location may raise the water tables in a neighboring region and therefore change the salinity of their soil. Whereas global interdependency is subtle and readily disavowed in relation to many issues, the unique physical and symbolic attributes of water make it glaringly obvious.

The centrality of water in violent, protracted conflicts is exemplified in the Middle East. No region in the world has suffered from a more perilous water crisis. Though roughly 5 percent of the world's population lives within the Middle East and North Africa, the region contains only 0.9 percent of the world's water resources (World Bank, 1996 cited in Berman & Wihbey, 1999). Between 1955 and 1990, the number of water-scarce countries in this region increased from 3 to 11 and is anticipated to increase to 18 by 2025 (Darwish, 1994 cited in Berman & Wihbey, 1999). The amount of water available per capita in the Middle East is the lowest in the world. It is only 15 percent of African and 33 percent of Asian levels (World Bank, 1996 cited in Berman & Wihbey, 1999). As populations grow exponentially and the need for agricultural production expands, the intensity of water conflicts will continue to escalate.

When confronted with scarce resources, anxiety arises and often leads to rigid coping styles and vigilant cognitive orientations (Bar-Tal, 2001). Within such a context, it is little wonder that communities hoard resources, act out against neighboring communities, and attempt to deny their interdependency. Rather than searching for cooperative and mutually beneficial solutions, fear and anxiety create a climate of reactivity. Furthermore, once a conflict escalates and eventually becomes protracted, communities develop societal beliefs to help members cope with the traumas and make sense of their suffering. These same beliefs that provide solace and endurance also engender a psychological investment that in turn perpetuates the conflict (Bar-Tal, 1998). To relinquish one of these beliefs (e.g., the delegitimacy of one's opponent) is to open oneself to memories of the original traumas without the buffering influence of the belief.

Three models of conflict resolution are particularly relevant to understanding the resolution of international water disputes. The distributive bargaining model was developed in the context of labor negotiations and proposes a set of strategies for allocating a fixed pool of resources (Walton & McKersie, 1965 cited in Cross & Rosenthal, 1999).

Distributive bargaining is a competitive, position-based, agreement-oriented approach to dealing with conflicts that are perceived as win–lose or zero-sum gain disputes. The negotiators are viewed as adversaries who reach agreement through a series of concessions (Bartos, 1995 cited in Cross & Rosenthal, 1999).

The negotiations occur in a temporal vacuum in which the negotiator's sole preoccupation is with maximizing self-interest (Pruitt & Carnevale, 1993 cited in Cross & Rosenthal, 1999). Within the distributive bargaining model, one strengthens one's position and weakens the adversary's position through making threats, holding firmly to one's stance, and withholding information (Cross & Rosenthal, 1999). In short, one assumes that a win for the adversary is a loss for oneself.

The second model, the interactive bargaining approach, "is a cooperative, interest-based, agreement-oriented approach to dealing with conflicts that are intended to be viewed as 'win/win' or mutual-gain disputes" (Cross & Rosenthal, 1999, p. 564). Rather than working with a fixed sum of resources, negotiators attempt to increase the amount and methods for distributing available resources (Fisher & Ury, 1981). Negotiators use techniques such as clearly defining the problem, sharing information openly, and exploring feasible solutions collaboratively to address the unique interests of each party (Cross & Rosenthal, 1999). They assume that the most mutually satisfying solutions demand clear communication, solid analysis, and creativity.

The third model is the interactive problem-solving approach that uses informal mediation techniques to address the needs and fears associated with varying positions (Burton, 1969; Kelman, 1972).

This nontraditional, nongovernmental third-party approach emphasizes analytical dialogue, joint problem solving, and transformation of the conflict relationship. It is designed to facilitate a deeper analysis of the problem and the issues driving the conflict, including an exploration of the underlying motivations, needs, values, and fears of the parties that are related to their different identities (Cross & Rosenthal, 1999).

It often prepares the way for more formal negotiations or enables the continuation of stalled negotiations. The interactive problem-solving approach appears to be most successful in addressing conflicts that involve unspoken needs for security, belonging, and recognition (Cross & Rosenthal, 1999).

Middle Eastern water conflicts involve issues related to sustainability, mobility, health, security, trade, economic development, and identity. They contain fears, traumatic memories, needs, and conditioned expectations within them. These psychological factors must be addressed if any type of enduring resolution is to be achieved. In our opinion, the distributive bargaining approach, rather than addressing these factors, would most likely reinforce the fear and envy at the root of already troubling disputes. The win–lose, dichotomous thinking encouraged by such an approach is emblematic of psychological immaturity and often leads to infantile reactivity. Approaching the negotiations as if they are isolated moments in time encourages the kind of memoryless and disjointed experience of the world characteristic of intensely fearful persons. From a paranoid perspective, as long as this moment is the totality of experience, then any impingement threatens to lead to one's complete destruction (Friedman, 1998). Though such claims may seem melodramatic in the context of politics or economics, they are consistent with the language of the psyche. The distributive bargaining approach highlights the need for clear boundaries and limits and acknowledges that a sentimental solution is not possible in the context of intense hostility. However, it sabotages attempts to promote cognitive flexibility and ego-mediated responsiveness and engenders a historical and envy laden stance.

The first stage in promoting the resolution of a protracted conflict is to identify the multifaceted and coexisting factors intensifying the dispute. The interactive problem-solving workshops may provide such a setting. By offering clear boundaries, a relatively flexible agenda, and less-immediate consequences than found during formal negotiations, both parties may better understand the complex sociological, economic, and psychological variables influencing their respective positions. The content of the workshops will be essential to constructing informed interventions; and the process will model ways to think flexibly and tolerate complexity. These workshops are not group therapies—such an approach would inevitably trigger corrosive, persecutory fears—but rather methods of analysis that serve to broaden both parties' perspectives. Once prenegotiation work has begun, more formal negotiations can be pursued. Obviously, the process of negotiating will lead to the emergence of additional factors and myriad threats to the negotiation's continuation. Therefore, the mediating party will need to contain the ensuing fears and needs through structural entities (e.g., enforced cease-fires) and symbolic gestures (e.g., Sadat shaking hands with Israeli officials) and continually refine their formulation of the conflict, given the presence of new data.

The present chapter is an attempt to demonstrate the complexity of psychological factors influencing Middle Eastern water conflicts and, in so doing, justify the use of interventions that recognize the interdependency of the conflicting parties. In highlighting the psychological factors complicating these disputes, one must develop a detailed understanding of the sociohistorical basis of the conflicts. These factors and the perceptions associated with them provide the foundation for a psychologically based approach. Psychologists trade in details. They integrate data into comprehensive case histories and then construct preliminary formulations. Within the context of theoretically informed formulations that account for the available information, they strive to design effective interventions. In the present chapter, we will begin by providing background information concerning Middle Eastern states and then describe three case histories that illuminate pertinent psychological dynamics. Given that most Westerners are unfamiliar with Middle Eastern politics and diplomacy, we will describe the historical context for each study in relative depth. These case histories will not only provide the foundation necessary to build thoughtful interventions but will also be a type of intervention themselves. As an individual expresses previously unnamed intrapsychic conflicts in service of greater psychological health, our attempt to move beyond shallow representations of international disputes may lead to greater clarity. Intersocietal tensions obviously differ from intrapsychic conflicts in salient ways; however, the present comparison likely holds true. The verbalization of historically grounded case histories is a type of preliminary intervention.

BACKGROUND

Our use of the label "Middle East" to describe the region bounded by Turkey on the north, the Gulfs of Aden and Oman on the south, the Iranian border with modern Pakistan on the east, and the Mediterranean Sea and northeast corner of Africa on the west is itself illustrative of the region's modern political and social evolution. The largely Arab and Islamic area was middle and east relative to the colonial expanse of the British Empire, whose use of the term for military purposes during the Second World War soon made its way into common international discourse (Hillel, 1994). Perhaps no region in the world has been as much a focus of European, and later American, intervention than the Middle East; and certainly no region in the postcolonial world has maintained such a high level of Western political penetration into its putatively regional affairs (Brown, 1984). From the perspective of Westerners, the volatility among Middle Eastern states may seemingly reveal communal sadomasochistic or at least self-destructive tendencies; however, the fact that even the region's name has been imposed by Westerners suggests that this volatility is partially due to resentment toward foreign intervention and a lack of ownership for societal structures constructed by foreign powers. Westerners often seem to forget what Middle Easterners are forced to remember—that foreign nations have been directly impacting Middle Eastern affairs for centuries.

European interest in the Middle East dates back to 1798, when Napoleon invaded Egypt, partly in an attempt to block British access to India. Though the area was at that time dominated by the Ottoman Empire, Napoleon's militarily unsuccessful expedition confirmed the strategic importance of the Middle East to the European Great Powers. European influence began to grow markedly thereafter. The vacuum created by the Ottoman Empire's decline and eventual dissolution following the Allied victory in the First World War removed any lingering barriers to European involvement in regional power struggles. As Western, and heretofore alien, notions of nationalism and statehood came to predominate throughout the area, Britain and France considered the establishment of state boundaries and the selection of national governments too important to be decided by the local residents. Thus they negotiated the secret Sykes-Picot Agreement in 1916, in which Britain and France divided the Middle East into spheres of influence, with Britain claiming Mesopotamia for the Crown and France receiving Syria. Although the agreement clearly specified the economic and strategic rights and responsibilities of all parties, it "left the watersheds in the region divided in a particularly convoluted manner" (Wolf, 1994, p. 13).

The dominating parties' neglect for the natural flow of resources in the region is emblematic of their neglect of more subtle cultural and tribal currents that still complicate existing boundaries. The imposition of an externally derived structure on the region initiated the following psychological dynamics that are more or less present in most disputes: anxiety attributable to the perpetual threat of foreign impingement, resentment toward and lack of ownership of the societal structures (e.g., national boundaries) that should promote stability and prosperity but often seem insidious in their foreign origins, and low thresholds of reactivity resulting from the often chronic exposure to violence.

Four years after the Sykes-Picot agreement, the San Remo Conference institutionalized the tentative agreement between the Great Powers, and the League of Nations approved an accord granting Britain "mandatory" control of Mesopotamia and Palestine (which included much of modern Jordan), while giving France the mandate for Syria (including modern Lebanon). A general lack of regard by the Great Powers for the locations of, and access to, local water supplies would have long-lasting effects. Referring to the Jordan River Valley and its riparian neighbor states, Wolf notes that the European control and division of the Middle Eastern map led to "a river divided in a manner in which conflict over water resource development was inevitable" (Wolf, 1994, p. 19).

For Europe, the Middle East had traditionally functioned as a displaced battleground, a region where inter-European conflicts could be played out with little risk of the loss of European life and property (Brown, 1984). Middle Eastern states, however, did not have the military and economic strength to displace their strivings and resentments onto other regions, but rather manifested them locally—thereby producing a great deal of volatility. Following the Second World War, however, anticolonial momentum proved a match for imperial interests, and local populations directed their resentment toward foreign presences in the region. Most major states had achieved nominal independence by the early 1950s, though the establishment, backed by Britain, of the state of Israel in 1948 extended Arab perceptions of European interference. This state of affairs—a nominally independent community of nations whose geographic and political design continued to reflect the more or less defunct strategic and political interests of European colonial powers—was inherently unstable and would lead immediately to inter- and intrastate clashes.

Two additional factors contributed to the centrality of water in Middle Eastern conflicts. The first and most obvious is the situation of freshwater scarcity, which has been growing more acute as a result of increased standards of living due to petroleum revenues, the population explosion in the Arab world, and the extended period of drought over the last decade. The second factor is the significance of water to regional political and religious ideologies, whether as water per se, or as one element in a larger system of beliefs.

Water's ideological and strategic value is clearly observed in the development of Zionism and the foundation of modern Israel. The famous statement by the first Israeli prime minister, David Ben-Gurion, that Israel would "make the desert bloom" was representative of a long-held belief that Palestine was a barren, empty no-man's-land that was destined to be recovered and reclaimed by the ingenuity and effort of returning Jews from all over the world. Conscious from the beginning of the importance of freshwater to their agricultural project, the borders proposed by Zionists for their National Home at the 1919 Paris Peace Conference exceeded the rough biblical definition of Palestine as stretching from the Dan to Beersheba. It extended well into the territory of modern Lebanon, Syria, and Jordan, encompassing every significant source of freshwater in the immediate region (Wolf, 1994). According to Wolf, "Economic security was defined by water resources. The entire Zionist programme of immigration and settlement required water for large-scale irrigation and, in a land with no fossil fuels, for hydro-power." As one would expect from a culture and a spirituality that developed in a harsh and arid climate, the value of water in the Jewish tradition is immense. According to Hillel, the Hebrew word for heaven, *shamayim*, can be interpreted as meaning "source of water." He goes on to note that

[a]ltogether, the Hebrew Bible mentions water *(mayim)* directly no fewer than 580 times and indirectly many more times as it alludes to rain and dew and river and wells. But perhaps the ultimate evocation of the spiritual quality of water is contained in Psalm 23: "He leadeth me beside still waters, He restoreth my soul." (Hillel, 1994, p. 26)

Many Zionists based their claims to *Eretz Yisrael* (Palestine) on their self-identification as the descendants of the nomadic tribes that first entered ancient Canaan by crossing the River Jordan in the twelfth century B.C. The harnessing of water resources that was a prerequisite to the foundation and survival of modern Israel was thus a religious imperative—the fulfillment of a three-thousand-year-old covenant between God and his chosen people, coming at the end of another long period of wandering, exile, and unimaginable suffering.

Water has comparable symbolic potency for Palestinian Arabs. There are over 150 references to water in its various forms in the Koran, and a popular Arab maxim describes the three most joyous things a person can behold as "water, greenery, and a beautiful face" (Hillel, 1994, p. 27). Water gained special significance to Middle Eastern and Arab populations with the rise of nationalism and the move toward independence. The need to build modern state infrastructures and to promote economic growth and security meant, in many cases, the establishment of national agricultural plans, irrigation networks, dams, and hydroelectric plants. Asserting control over disputed waterways and freshwater resources became an essential component of independence. For example, the nationalization of the Suez Canal by Egyptian President Gamal Abdel Nasser in 1956 proved to have enormous symbolic significance in the confrontation between the Western Great Powers and the newly independent states of the Third World. In terms of water's contribution to notions of national greatness and security, one can find few better examples than Turkey's ongoing Southeast Anatolia Project, or G.A.P., by its Turkish acronym. G.A.P. is a massive program to construct 13 major dams and hydroelectric plants along the headwaters of the Euphrates River in Turkish Anatolia. The plan aims to provide irrigation for agriculture and electricity for industrialization in Turkey's most politically unstable region.

The three examples just given—Israeli utilization of groundwater in the West Bank, the Suez Canal incident in Egypt, and the G.A.P. project in Turkish Anatolia—represent important aspects of the uniqueness of water as a source of contention in the Middle East. For this reason, a closer look at the circumstances surrounding each case will illuminate the psychological factors contributing to the perpetuation and potential resolution of these seemingly intractable disputes. The unique physical and symbolic properties of water inform the parameters of the conflicts engendered and the resolutions they require, and the study of these properties may inform our understanding of non–water related disputes.

ISRAEL, PALESTINE, AND THE ARAB STATES

The problem of diminishing freshwater resources in Israel and the territories under intermittent and nominal control by the Palestinian Authority has reached crisis proportions in recent years. Prolonged drought has combined with rapid population growth and increased pollution to create a situation of severe scarcity, distributive inequality, and political instability. Israeli fears of dependency on its historically hostile neighbors have led to the exploitation of aquifers underlying the West Bank and Gaza Strip and to the prolongation of its occupation of "Arab" land. This strategy represents, in the eyes of most

Palestinians and other Arabs, the theft of Palestinian natural resources. Israeli water policy is viewed by Palestinians as one more weapon used to crush their hopes of a viable, independent Palestine.

Approximately 67 percent of Israel's available freshwater resources are ear-marked annually for agricultural use, though agricultural products account for only 4 percent of Israeli GDP and less than 2.6 percent of employment (CIA World Fact Book, 2001). An investment in domestic crop production so dis-proportionate to its economic return suggests that agricultural self-sufficiency is not only a security issue, but also a cultural imperative—an attempt to make the desert bloom, whatever the costs. The urgency of Israeli efforts to acquire additional water is most likely matched by the intensity of the fear that their water will be taken away by hostile neighbors. From such a standpoint, they will never have enough water to assuage their fears. The perceived threat of annihilation that is undoubtedly reinforced by the horrors of the Holocaust does not permit moderation or temperance. It produces a restlessness that de-mands chronic vigilance.

Palestinian access to water resources contrasts starkly with the relative abun-dance made available to Israeli farmers and other citizens. According to the Israeli Information Center for Human Rights in the Occupied Territories, "Per capita water consumption in the West Bank for domestic, urban, and industrial use is only 26 cubic meters a year, which translates into 70 liters per person per day," whereas average Israeli use is "five times Palestinian per capita con-sumption." The center goes on to note that the World Health Organization's recommendation for individual daily water consumption is one-third the amount of Israeli consumption. Palestinian anger at this inequity is exacerbated by the fact that although 40 percent of Israel's water is drawn from under Palestinian land, Israel has typically denied West Bank Palestinians permits for digging nondomestic wells. Water withdrawals for Palestinian agricultural use in the West Bank and Gaza have been capped at 1968 levels, whereas a number of new wells have been sunk to provide water to Israeli settlements (Dillman, 1989 cited in Wolf, 1994). Conditions have only worsened since the outbreak of the current intifada more than two years ago. The recent reoccupation by the Israeli Defense Forces (IDF) of major West Bank towns like Jenin, Hebron, and Nablus has severely limited the freedom of movement of water tankers, which are often the sole source of water to surrounding villages. Another scorching summer in 2002 increased demand for water, while tankers, which once made several trips per day to a given community, are now often limited to one trip or none at all. Currently, approximately 30 percent of Palestinian homes, or about 200,000 Palestinians, are not connected to a central water network, and many of these are found in smaller villages that depend entirely on small-scale livestock—and thus a ready supply of water—for economic sur-vival. It is not unusual for villages and larger communities that are connected to a water network to be given access to water for only 24 hours every week or two (Israeli Information Center for Human Rights in the Occupied Territories).

Israel receives more than half of its water from sources shared with Syria, Jordan, Lebanon, and the Palestinian Authority (Drake, 1997). In a highly polarized environment rife with serious conflict and recalcitrant positions, it is ironic that the key to basic survival is a water system so intimately shared between opposing forces. To understand the Israeli position regarding the safeguarding of its scarce water resources, it is important to evaluate the role water has played in past conflicts between Israel and its neighbors. The chain of events that led to the Six-Day War in 1967, for example, can be traced to questions of water access and consumption, just as many of the current conflicts between Israel, the Palestinians, and its other Arab neighbors, are the lingering consequences of that war.

In 1964, Israel completed work on its National Water Carrier, a system designed to channel water from Lake Kinneret in the northeast corner of the country to the Negev Desert in the south. Fearing this action would jeopardize the flow of the Jordan's waters to both Syria and the severely water-taxed Kingdom of Jordan, the Arab League met in Cairo to plan a response. The league decided on a counterdiversion of the Hasbani and Banias waters through a tunnel across Syria and into the Yarmouk tributary, thus guaranteeing the Jordan's supply and greatly diminishing that of Lake Kinneret. This particular summit also decided on the formation, under Egyptian direction, of the PLO, as well as the establishment of a unified Arab military command (Shlaim, 2001). The preamble to the list of decisions taken by the Arab League illustrates the tensions that the Jordan conflict created.

The establishment of Israel is the basic threat that the Arab nation in its entirety has agreed to forestall. And since the existence of Israel is a danger that threatens the Arab nation, the diversion of the Jordan waters by it multiplies the dangers to Arab existence. Accordingly, the Arab states have to prepare the plans necessary for dealing with the political, economic, and social aspects, so that if the necessary results are not achieved, collective Arab military preparations, when they are completed, will constitute the ultimate practical means for the final liquidation of Israel. (cited in Shlaim, 2001, 229–230)

Thus the escalating conflict over water resulted in the first official, collective Arab declaration of the Arab nations' desire to see the state of Israel "liquidated" (Shlaim, 2001). What followed was a series of events, including Israeli military assaults on the Arab diversion project, which led to full-scale war in June 1967. The Six-Day War ended not only in total victory for Israel, but also in its wresting control of the Gaza Strip and Sinai Peninsula from Egypt, the West Bank from the Jordanian administration, and the Golan Heights from Syria, along with the important sources of water that came with them.

Control of water remains the primary reason for Israel's continued occupation of the Golan Heights, which continues to be one of the main obstacles to progress in the Middle East peace process. Successful negotiations are unlikely between rival nations that view concessions on basic issues of water sharing as threatening their respective survival as entities. A 1990 memorandum from the Israeli Ministry of Agriculture all but cemented the link between Israel's identity and water supplies.

It is difficult to conceive of any political solution consistent with Israel's survival that does not involve complete continued Israeli control of the West Bank's water and sewage system and of the associated infrastructure including the power supply and road network essential to their operation, maintenance and accessibility. (cited in Wahdan, n.d.)

Israeli officials justify their occupation of the West Bank by positing the likelihood of mismanagement of water supplies by the technologically lacking Palestinians, the illegitimacy of Egyptian and Jordanian claims to the region, and the acuity of Israeli need (Wolf, 1994). The Palestinians, however, argue in public edicts such as the PLO Statement on Water, that Israeli occupation is a blatant violation of international law.

Both the Israelis and the Palestinians are psychologically invested in these protracted conflicts. They envision water to be not only a means to survival but also a source of independence and security in a world populated by hostile neighbors and intrusive foreign powers. These factors contribute to the vigilance with which both parties defend their water sources and the cognitive rigidity with which they cling to their competing positions. At the center of these layered interests, however, is a psychological theme uniquely prominent in this conflict: the centrality of water to the identities of both parties. Specific bodies of water, such as the Sea of Galilee, are considered sacred ancestral places. They are holy sites that define who the people are and from where they have come. Water not only is linked to the origins of life but also demonstration of the ongoing blessing of their God.

Water plays a similarly prominent role in the national identities of both parties. In a study of nearly 2500 Palestinian and Israeli youths, Sagy and colleagues (2001, p. 24) concluded the following: "These two national groups consider peace to potentially set off a severe crisis of national identity." The conflict itself has become a buttress to their communal identities. Furthermore, not only their endurance but the "other's" demise is necessary to their survival. Kelman observes, "Fulfillment of the other's national identity is experienced as equivalent to destruction of one's own identity" (Kelman, 1999, p. 355). Given the centrality of water to religionational identities in the region, it is little wonder that they pursue the acquisition and defense of water supplies with such intensity. Drives for sustenance and economic viability are expressed in the context of enduring belief systems.

THE SUEZ CANAL

The importance of water to the smooth functioning of human civilization is not limited to its necessity as an agricultural input, a source of hydroelectricity, or a drink. Water is unequaled as a means for delivering large amounts of goods to the marketplace, and thus as a lubricant for the human economic machine. Though the oceans and seas are open and available to nearly anyone with the material resources to navigate them, the man-made canals that join them are often the focus of intense proprietary and nationalistic feelings.

Post–WWII Egypt, home to the Suez Canal, was such a place. The modern Suez Canal stretches from Port Said on the northwest tip of the Sinai Peninsula, into and out of the Great Bitter Lake, and down again into the Gulf of Suez, where it connects the Mediterranean and Red seas. The importance of the Suez Canal as an international waterway dates back over two millennia. In various forms, the canal has been dug, fallen into disrepair, and been redug on numerous occasions. It was not until the middle of the nineteenth century that a definitive attempt to dig the canal in its present form was made by Frenchman Ferdinand de Lesseps. Work began in 1859 and continued until 1867, costing the lives of over 125,000 Egyptians who labored in slaverylike conditions. From 1867 until 1956, the Suez Canal was operated by the Suez Canal Company, whose stock was owned primarily by Great Britain. The Anglo-Egyptian Treaty of 1936 also gave Britain the right to station troops within the Suez Canal Zone.

In the Egypt of the 1950s, however, militant anticolonialism due to British occupation of the Suez Canal base and the ongoing hostilities between the Arab nations and Western-backed Israel led to a military coup by a group of young Egyptian officers. Gamal Abdel Nasser eventually came to power and challenged the hegemony of the European Great Powers with his support for the doctrine of pan-Arab nationalism. Britain withdrew its troops from the canal base, and completely evacuated the state by 1956. This move, however, was not enough to diffuse the growing tensions between dying Great Power colonialism on one hand, and nascent Third World independence on the other.

Having failed to negotiate an arms purchase with the United States in the early 1950s, Egypt turned instead to the Soviet Union and, in 1955, made a deal to buy Czechoslovakian arms. In response to this and other Egyptian overtures to the Soviet Bloc, the United States and the West withdrew financial support of the Aswan High Dam on the Nile. Nasser's reaction to this Western vote of no confidence was to nationalize the Suez Canal by unilaterally buying out all the European shareholders.

It was a triumphant moment for Egyptians everywhere the night late President Gamal Abdel-Nasser stood in Alexandria's Manshiya Square and defiantly announced the nationalization of the Suez Canal. The Egyptian people had suffered deeply to bring the canal into being—hundreds of thousands died digging the channel virtually with their bare hands under the corvée system. They had seen little reward for their efforts, however, as control of the enormously valuable resource was wholly enjoyed by foreign powers. (Abdel-Razek, 2001)

This action provided Britain and France—both already intent on the overthrow of the nationalist Nasser regime—with the *casus belli* they had been looking for. The two countries began preparing for an invasion of Egypt and were soon joined by Israel, whose government saw the "tripartite collusion" as an opportunity to strengthen relations between itself and powerful Western states and to deal a blow to the leading Arab power in the region (Shlaim, 2001).

On October 29, 1956, Israeli troops advanced on the Canal Zone, and Egyptian troops followed suit to defend their newly nationalized asset. The Israeli move was a ruse designed in advance to give Britain and France a pretext for action. Britain subsequently issued an ultimatum to both armies to withdraw from the Canal Zone, which Israel promptly did. Nasser's refusal to recall his troops resulted in a French and British invasion of the Canal Zone on October 31. However, the Anglo-French war against Nasser was short-lived: strong opposition to the European intervention was voiced by both the United States and the Soviet Union, and on November 6, a cease-fire was declared. Within less than two months, the French and British troops had pulled out of the Canal Zone under UN supervision.

The canal's value was not simply the sum of its economic and military utility. It, like so many of the themes explored in this chapter, carried a type of psychological valence. The canal represented independence. It reflected Egyptian nationalism in the face of decades of colonial rule, and evoked images of industrious traders and courageous explorers. It also represented generativity as both the product of one of the most ambitious projects in the region and the link to previously inaccessible technologies and cultures. For Britain, it represented the last potentially British stronghold in the region and an attempt to counter the diminution of British influence in international politics. Whereas the Israeli–Palestinian conflict hinged largely on issues of identity, the Suez Canal incident called forth themes of independence, mobility, and freedom. Though Egypt eventually prevailed, the United States and the Soviet Union were largely responsible for the victory. Therefore, this triumphant assertion of Egyptian independence was clouded by the sense that the United States and the Soviet Union had allowed it to be so.

THE EUPHRATES BASIN

Mesopotamia (Greek for "land between two rivers") is widely recognized as having been the cradle of civilization, the place where many of the basic societal paradigms we cling to first developed. There are a number of reasons why this precocious social evolution occurred first in Mesopotamia. The Fertile Crescent's Mediterranean climate, along with its wide variety of domesticable animal and plant species, its varied topography, and its seasonal weather changes, provided an environment appropriate to the development of sedentary agricultural practices. Of particular importance to early farmers were the Euphrates and Tigris Rivers.

Nearly 10,000 years later, these waters remain essential to neighboring peoples, though industrial progress and population growth have created problems of a distinctly modern character. Perhaps more than any sources of water in the Middle East, these rivers highlight the inescapable interdependency of riparian countries and the psychological dynamics such situations trigger. Turkey's planned construction of a system of dams and hydroelectric plants along the Tigris and Euphrates headwaters has set into motion complex, transactional processes that extend beyond the fervent protests of its downstream neighbors.

Whereas the first case studies highlighted the role of water as identity, pathway, and independence, this case study demonstrates the unavoidable and yet seemingly intolerable interdependence of countries sharing water systems. Turkey, Syria, and Iraq have struggled to dwell together. The proximity of the threat each party poses to the others, the inevitability of their interdependence, and the primacy of water as a resource have led to repeated escalations.

Both the Tigris and Euphrates originate in the mountainous area of southeastern Anatolia, and from there remain on divergent courses before conjoining again nearly one hundred miles from the head of the Persian Gulf. Roughly 78 percent of the Tigris's course lies inside Iraq, with almost the entire upstream remainder flowing through Turkey and the Syrian border. About 25 percent of the Euphrates's course lies inside Syria, 35 percent in Iraq, and about 40 percent inside Turkey, which contributes about two-thirds of the total combined flow of both rivers. Syria provides no water to the Tigris, though it contributes to the Euphrates; conversely, Iraq contributes nothing to the Euphrates, though it has tributaries that feed into the Tigris (Hillel, 1994). These countries' interdependence is carved in the bedrock.

Although all three are Middle Eastern countries, the hydrological situation of each is quite distinct. Turkey enjoys a temperate climate, with rain-fed farming in much of the 32 percent of its territory that is arable. Turkey's water supply is so secure that it has sold water to Israel, as well as discussed plans for a "peace pipeline" to deliver water as far away as the Arabian Peninsula. However, the area surrounding the Tigris and Euphrates headwaters is semi-arid, and the need to irrigate the land to increase its agricultural productivity was part of the inspiration for the Southeast Anatolia Project, or G.A.P. by its Turkish initials.

Syria, however, is in dire hydrological straits. Nearly 86 percent of Syria's water comes from the Euphrates alone, and the current water infrastructure has not been sufficient to provide for the growing needs of the country. Drought and significant depletion and pollution of groundwater threaten Syrian agriculture, which accounts for 30 percent of its GDP and about 40 percent of its total employment (CIA World Fact Book, 2001). With such a significant portion of the national economy directly dependent on scarce water, the outlook is grim.

Downstream from Syria is Iraq, which is also highly dependent on the Euphrates for agriculture. However, only about 6 percent of its GDP comes from agricultural production (CIA World Fact Book, 2001). Dangerous levels of salinity in the soil have been caused by outdated flood-irrigation methods, and

Iraq, in spite of its agricultural potential, has long been a net importer of grain. Iraq's water scarcity problems have only been aggravated by eight years of costly fighting in the Iran–Iraq war of the 1980s and the destruction wrought during Operation Desert Storm, the combined effects of which have erased much of the industrial and public health infrastructures built up since the 1950s. The one advantage Iraq has over Syria is access to the underutilized Tigris (Lowi, 1999).

Turkey's G.A.P. project has been a catalyst for recent conflict over the waters of the Tigris and Euphrates. G.A.P.'s main component is a system of 22 major dams and 19 hydroelectric plants, which, when completed, will regulate 28 percent of Turkey's water potential, increase the area of irrigated land by 40 percent, and provide up to 25 percent of Turkey's electrical power supply (Nissman, 1999). The project's stated objectives are, among others, "to achieve accelerated economic and social development" and "to alleviate disparity between the [G.A.P.] region and other regions by increasing production and welfare levels." The eight provinces included within the G.A.P. region are home to a large concentration of Turkey's Kurdish minority and serve as a base of operations for the KPP, or Kurdistan Workers Party, which has been fighting a low-intensity conflict against Ankara for decades. Turkey hopes that industrialization, heightened agricultural productivity, and improved living standards will undermine the KPP's appeal to its Kurdish residents (Nissman, 1999).

Turkey claims that G.A.P. will actually benefit downstream riparians by allowing storage and release regulation during periods of flooding and drought (Drake, 1997). In spite of Turkey's assurances, Syria and Iraq have responded with fear and suspicion, and perhaps justifiably so. According to Lowi, the distributional question of the amount of water to be released is less important than the danger that the water's quality will have already been compromised by the time it is re-introduced into the system. Much of the water that is released will already have been used for irrigation in Turkey and will therefore contain large amounts of salt and other contaminants. But potential shortfalls in the flow could reduce the rivers' level, hurting both Syria's and Iraq's ability to irrigate crops and leech salinated land. Estimates of the potential reduction in intake from the Euphrates are about 40 percent for Syria and up to 80 percent for Iraq (Hillel, 1994).

As a result, conflicts related to G.A.P. have increased in severity and frequency since the late 1980s and have pushed Turkey and Syria "to the brink of war several times" (Berman & Wihbey, 1999, p. 46). In 1990, for example, Turkey implemented a planned, month-long impounding of the waters of the Euphrates to fill the Ataturk reservoir. Although Turkey had informed Syria and Iraq of its plans and had laid out a detailed plan of compensation to the two countries, a major diplomatic incident ensued, and Syria and Iraq—historical enemies because of Syria's support for Iran during the Iran–Iraq War—joined together to denounce Turkey. They called for equal access to the waters of the Euphrates as well as a shortened impounding period.

Syria and Iraq again registered their objections with the Turkish government in 1996, when Turkey began construction of the Birecik Dam, designed to regulate the flow of the Euphrates while hydroelectricity was being generated at the Ataturk Dam. Kibaroglu and Ünver (2000) note that attempts to solve these problems through negotiations failed because the parties could not agree on basic principles to be reorganized as a basis for negotiation." The levels of fear and distrust were simply too high to allow even minor concessions. Furthermore, the laws governing riparian access to shared waterways have very little to say about the obligations of the ultimate upstream riparian (Nissman, 1999).

At the center of these conflicts is the sense of powerlessness felt by the downstream riparian nations. Turkey has the military, economic, and geographic advantage and, therefore, is free to invest energy and resources in broad, future-oriented projects. Syria and Iraq, however, have to remain vigilant in protecting their interests and therefore have less mental, emotional, and physical resources to pursue long-term development. To varying degrees, however, the conflict forces all parties concerned to focus more on past grievances and memories of betrayal than future possibilities (Bar-Tal, 1998). The feeling of powerlessness has led Syria to forge a more extensive partnership with Iraq, including the establishment in 2000 of diplomatic ties between the two countries for the first time in 20 years. More ominously for regional stability, Syria also began, in the 1980s, a program of military, economic, and political support for the PKK in its operations inside Turkey—a clear attempt to utilize whatever means to power are at hand. In 1987 Syria and Turkey signed a protocol that amounted to an overt linkage between security and water, with Syria agreeing to help limit PKK activities in exchange for guaranteed water flows from Turkey. However, Syrian "brokerage" of the PKK continues and was increased in response to the launch of a program of military cooperation between Turkey and Israel in 1996 (Wihbey & Berman, 2000).

Given the lay of the land, Turkey, Syria, and Iraq are dependent on one another. Rather than this situation leading to mutuality and reciprocity, it has most often produced mistrust and defensiveness—a type of negative interdependence (Kelman, 1999). Each party behaves as if the threat of destruction is omnipresent and, therefore, creates fleeting alliances based on fear and fantasies of independence. Within such a context, participation in a "peace pipeline" or joint regulatory project most often provokes feelings of vulnerability rather than hope.

CONCLUSION

When considering international conflicts, water is never simply water. It is a resource with unique physical and symbolic qualities that shape the disputes it engenders and the resolutions it demands. Middle Eastern water conflicts often seem inevitable and self-perpetuating. From within the region, they are associated with centuries of strife concerning identity, independence, and even survival. From outside, they are represented as chaotic manifestations of irrationality and aggression. Attempts to approach resolution in these cases, however, are more than simply nods toward sentimentality. They are possibilities and, if we accept the forecasts of hydrologists, necessities.

In an insightful book, *Rivers of Eden*, Daniel Hillel writes the following:

Considering the intense rivalry over water, in [the Middle East] as well as elsewhere, we can readily understand how the very word *rival*, originally a neutral term used in Roman law to designate a neighbor sharing with another the waters of a *rivus*, has acquired the negative connotation of competitor, adversary, even enemy. Sharers of so vital a resource as water may choose either to cooperate or to compete. Somehow, our language has forgotten the first option and has retained only the second. (Hillel, 1994, pp. 36–37)

The case studies presented here are both the products and stories of this forgetting. Impulsive, fearful reactions to situations of scarcity have often dominated the narratives. Whereas some efforts to promote cooperation initiated gradual, everyday progress, these ordinary murmurings have been overwhelmed by the cacophony of extreme events. They have lacked the saliency necessary to demand attention, shape expectations, and neutralize persecutory anxiety. Therefore, they have been forgotten. Memories of intense, corrosive conflicts, however, have been retained and relived, thereby shaping each new encounter.

Why has the destructive quality of these conflicts often overshadowed creative attempts at reconciliation? The answer may partially be explained by the demands of living peaceably. Whereas anyone can react violently to a perceived adversary, only those persons who have enough intrapsychic and environmental resources can provide ego-mediated, tempered responses (Friedman, 1998). Cooperative initiatives demand higher levels of functioning such as cognitive flexibility and emotional regulation. The qualities that allow a person to negotiate and interact with perceived enemies—self-awareness, perspective, and patience—are not givens but rather developmental achievements.

The case studies provide an additional answer to this troubling question. The following formulation is an integration of the themes addressed throughout the chapter and a potential template for subsequent attempts to promote resolution. At numerous pivotal periods in Middle Eastern history, powerful foreign entities have imposed dramatic and sweeping changes in the region, thereby overwhelming self-determined attempts at development. Even during periods of foreign inactivity, the absence of external powers has been a sort of ominous presence in itself. Local actors, who work gradually to build empowering societal structures, must struggle against the widespread perception that foreign intervention could (re)transform the region and topple these structures. The feelings of helplessness associated with such perceived disempowerment and discontinuity undoubtedly lead to desperate attempts to claim power through extreme means.

Similarly, protracted volatility leads actors to fear being dependent on hostile neighbors. These fears most likely trigger compensatory efforts to remain independent at any cost. Such efforts inevitably fail, however. Water flows across the same boundaries intended to provide cohesion and security. Despite innovative attempts at damming and irrigation, the geography of the bedrock determines the flow of water more than the wishes of riparian societies. Therefore, attempts to deny interdependency through reactive assertions of independence tend to have escalatory rather than soothing effects.

As these conflicts persist, agitation and fear spread and, in some cases, become traumatic (especially when paired with overt violence). As circles of suffering expand across societal groups through direct experience, informal communication pathways, and formal media outlets, the trauma can take on a collective quality. It may trigger obsessive and compulsive symptoms such as repetitive acting out or intrusive remembering. These reactions are conscious and unconscious attempts to contain the anxiety associated with knowing that a trauma has occurred and may likely occur again. They only bind anxiety for short periods of time, however, and become maladaptive if not replaced with high-order processing, such as verbalization.

Whereas some people attach words to their experiences to understand their cognitive, emotional, and behavioral reactions and thereby change maladaptive patterns, many persons construct systems of beliefs (e.g., the people who have died in the conflict are martyrs for a greater cause to which I must commit myself) in an attempt to make meaning out of their suffering. This coping process often leads people to externalize their interior dynamics and become psychologically invested in the conflict's perpetuation (Bar-Tal, 1998). The belief system feeds on the adversarial relationship. If persons seek resolution, they may have to relinquish their beliefs. And, if they relinquish their beliefs, they fear they will be overwhelmed by their reactions to the original trauma (through repeated acting out and intrusive remembering) without the buffer of the belief.

Identity issues further complicate efforts to promote cooperation. Water is integral to the religionational identities of numerous groups in the region. Furthermore, the conflicts themselves are essential components of group identities (Sagy et al., 2001). Therefore, to resolve the conflict is to lose one's sense of orientation in the world. If I am not your enemy, who am I? Threats to identity often provoke particularly intense anxiety. When coupled with the perception that one's enemy wishes to destroy one's group (through either overt violent means or hoarding life-sustaining water supplies), fear of dependency becomes diffuse annihilation anxiety. A lack of vigilance in defending one's water supply is no longer associated with temporary deprivation but with fragmentation of one's sense of self. In the midst of such anxiety, the desire for water is insatiable. No amount of water will ever be enough to soothe the restless wanting.

The case formulation highlights some of the multifaceted psychological factors that bring intensity and stubbornness to these conflicts. Until these factors are identified and addressed, attempts at resolution will either be singed by the climate of reactivity or disregarded as foreign impositions (even if originating within the Middle East). No intervention will be effective and durable without initial exploratory work. Kelman (1999) has described ways in which interactive problem-solving workshops could facilitate the emergence and identification of these factors. The informal and analytic tone of the workshops promote higher-level coping. They allow participants to acknowledge the interior experiences of their supposed adversary and themselves and, in so doing, recognize their mutual humanity. They also help illuminate the psychological undercurrents that may steer the negotiations so that mediators can anticipate resistances. Lastly, they model ways of thinking flexibly and responding moderately to tense issues.

Along with conducting problem-solving workshops, societal structures need to be more securely in place to contain the anxiety associated with these issues. In the face of intrapsychic and intersocietal volatility, some entity needs to absorb a portion of the anxiety. A judicial structure would be fitting because it ostensibly would provide nonescalatory and equitable procedures for mediating future conflicts (and therefore preventing future traumas). No entity will be able to neutralize the persecutory anxiety fully; however, a stable judicial structure could limit subsequent escalations. International water laws have thus far not addressed the specific concerns of arid, developing countries. "There is no legal international obligation to share water resources; in a region such as the Middle East, where intrastate rivalries remain strong and tend to rule out peaceful management and cooperation, the potential for conflict over this vital resource is great" (Morris, 1992, p. 36). Thus, functioning, enforceable laws related to shared water resources could provide the clarity and predictability necessary to ground some of the free-floating anxiety.

The primary challenge in developing a stable framework will be agreeing on the method by which it is constructed. The World Bank and United Nations agencies in the realms of food production (FAO), sustainable economic development (UNDP), environmental protection (UNEP), public health (WHO), and meteorology (WMO) have attempted to facilitate cooperation among Middle Eastern riparian nations with moderate success (Elhance, 2000). In order for the legal framework to be accepted within the region and not perceived simply as another product of foreign imposition, however, representatives from Middle Eastern countries will need to take leadership roles in writing just guidelines. After a workable framework is in place and problem-solving workshops have been conducted, formal diplomatic efforts may be more effective.

The severity of water crises in the Middle East both motivates people to cooperate and leads them to respond in rigid and destructive ways. In addressing the needs and fears complicating these crises, the hope is that a dynamic and generative balance will be struck—a balance that recognizes the inevitability of tension and yet uses that tension for creative means. Civilization is thought to have originated in the Fertile Crescent largely because of two factors: there was enough water to sustain a sedentary, agricultural lifestyle; and yet there was not so much water that persons could rely on fishing rather than turning to agriculture (Diamond, 1999). Similarly, if the tension surrounding these conflicts is sufficient to promote innovation, and yet not so extreme as to produce hopelessness and fatalism, cooperative efforts may initiate realistic progress. Perhaps rigidity can give way to flexibility and destructiveness can give way to cooperation, and our inescapable interdependency can be more fully acknowledged in word and deed.

REFERENCES

Abdel-Razek, Sherine (2001, July 26–August 1). Rites of passage. *Al-Ahram Weekly Online, 544.* [Online] Retrieved October 19, 2001, from http://weekly .ahram.org.eg/2001/544/fe1.htm

Bar-Tal, D. (1998). Societal beliefs in times of intractable conflict: The Israeli case. *The International Journal of Conflict Management, 9*(1), 22–50.

Bar-Tal, D. (2001). Why does fear override hope in societies engulfed by intractable conflict, as it does in the Israeli society? *Political Psychology, 22*(3), 601–627.

Bartos, O. J. (1995). Modeling distributive and integrative negotiations. *The Annals, 542,* 48–60.

Berman, I., & Wihbey, P. M. (1999). The new water politics of the Middle East [Electronic version]. *Strategic Review, 27*(3), 45–52.

Brown, L. C. (1984). *International politics and the Middle East: Old rules, dangerous game.* London: I.B. Tauris & Company.

Burton, J. W. (1969). *Conflict and communications: The use of controlled communication in international relations.* London: Macmillan.

CIA World Fact Book. (2001). http://www.cia.gov/cia/publications/factbook/

Cross, S., & Rosenthal, R. (1999). Three models of conflict resolution: Effects on intergroup expectancies and attitudes. *Journal of Social Issues, 55* (3), 561–580.

Darwish, A. (1994). *Water wars.* Lecture given at the Geneva Conference on Environment and Quality of Life.

Diamond, J. (1999). *Guns, germs, and steel: The fates of human societies.* New York: W. W. Norton.

Dillman, J. (1989). Water rights in the occupied territories. *Journal of Palestine Studies, 19*(1), 46–71.

Drake, C. (1997). Water resource conflicts in the Middle East [Electronic version]. *Journal of Geography, 96,* 4–12.

Elhance, A. P. (2000). Hydropolitics: Grounds for despair, reasons for hope. *International Negotiation, 5,* 201–222.

Fisher, R., & Ury, W. (1991). *Getting to yes: Negotiating agreement without giving in.* New York: Penguin Books.

Friedman, J. A. (1998). *The origins of self and identity.* New Jersey: Jason Aronson.

Hillel, D. (1994). *Rivers of Eden: The struggle for water and the quest for peace in the Middle East.* New York: Oxford University Press.

Israeli Information Center for Human Rights in the Occupied Territories. http://www.btselem.org

Kelman, H. C. (1972). The problem-solving workshop in conflict resolution. In R. L. Merritt (Ed.), *Communication in international politics.* Urbana: University of Illinois Press.

Kelman, H. C. (1987). The political psychology of the Israeli-Palestinian conflict: How can we overcome the barriers to a negotiated solution? *Political Psychology, 8,* 347–363.

Kelman, H. C. (1990). Applying a human needs perspective to the practice of conflict resolution: The Israeli Palestinian case. In J. Burton (Ed.), *Conflict: Human needs theory* (pp. 283–297). New York: St. Martin's Press.

Kelman, H. C. (1999). The interdependence of Israeli and Palestinian national identities: The role of the other in existential conflicts. *Journal of Social Issues, 55*(3), 581–600.

Kibaroglu, A., & Unver, I. H. (2000). An institutional framework for facilitating cooperation in the Euphrates-Tigris river basin. *International Negotiation, 5,* 311–330.

Lowi, M. R. (1999). Water and conflict in the Middle East and South Asia: Are environmental issues and security issues linked? *Journal of Environment & Development, 8,* 376–396.

McGuire, D. (2001). *Cadillac desert.* http://www.pbs.org/kteh/cadillacdesert/water.html

Morris, M. E. (1992). Poisoned wells: The politics of water in the Middle East. *Middle East Insight, 8*(2), 35–39.

Nissman, D. (1999, April 9). Turkey denies confrontation with Arabs over Euphrates. *Iraq Report, 12*(19). Retrieved October 9, 2001, from http://www.rferl.org/iraqreport/1999/04/14–090499.html

Palestine Liberation Organization Negotiations Affairs Departments Web site http://www.nad-plo.org/permanent/water.html

Postel, S. (1992). *Last oasis: Facing water scarcity.* New York: W. W. Norton.

Pruitt, D. G., & Carnevale, P. J. (1993). *Negotiation in social conflict.* Pacific Grove, CA: Brooks/Cole.

Republic of Turkey Ministry of Foreign Affairs Web site http://www.mfa.gov.tr/grupd/dc/dcd/gap.html

Sagy, S., Orr, E., Bar-on, D., & Awwad, E. (2001). Individualism and collectivism in two conflicted societies: Comparing Jewish and Palestinian-Arab high school students. *Youth and Society, 33*(1), 3–30.

Shlaim, A. (2001). *The iron wall: Israel and the Arab world.* New York: W. W. Norton.

Wahdan, H. (n.d.). *Water conflict.* Retrieved October 15, 2001, from http://www.jmcc.org/new/1999/water.html

Walton, R. E., & McKersie, R. B. (1965). *A behavioral theory of labor negotiations.* New York: McGraw-Hill.

Wihbey, P. M., & Berman, I. (2000). The geopolitics of water [Electronic version]. *Institute for Advanced Strategic and Political Studies, 10,* 1–17.

Wolf, A. T. (1994). A hypdropolitical history of the Nile, Jordan and Euphrates river basins. In A. Biswas (Ed.), *International waters of the Middle East* (pp. 5–43). Oxford: Oxford University Press.

World Bank Report. (1996). *From scarcity to security: Averting a water crisis in the Middle East and North Africa.* Washington, DC: Author.

10

Applied Anthropology and Diplomacy: Renegotiating Conflicts in a Eurasian Diplomatic Gray Zone by Using Cultural Symbols

Ignacy Marek Kaminski

INTRODUCTION[1]

Since the unilateral declaration of global war against terrorism by the United States, the diplomatic means used to accelerate the processes of interstate peace negotiations and of intrastate cross-cultural conflict resolution have become for international observers far less transparent than before.[2]

Uncovering cross-cultural dynamics of international diplomacy at work requires study of the governments' policy declarations and the actual activities in the diplomatic gray zone within which the foreign policy makers and their associates often operate in the field and a closer examination of the level of congruency between the policies and the operations in real life.[3]

RENEGOTIATING PEACE IN A DIPLOMATIC GRAY ZONE

Today, Japan and Russia remain still at war legally over territorial issues. This is despite the long series of peace negotiations for a long period of time. And it is despite the great expansion of activities in the emergent diplomatic gray zone.

The post–Cold War changes in the geopolitics called for new interstate alliances, and the post-9/11 changes have further necessitated rapid formation of new alliances. This allowed greater freedom for the introduction of innovative conflict resolution. And this led to the increased danger for uncontrollable escalation of cross-cultural frictions in the communities divided by territorial borders and among the displaced people (e.g., the Japanese nationals [incl. Ainu tribesmen] expelled by the then Soviet Union from the disputed Northern Islands). The problems over disputed Northern Territories have brought about new regional conflicts in the very process through which both sides tried to resolve the old conflicts across the territorial borders.

Theoretically the Japanese minister for foreign affairs appointed by the prime minister and held accountable to the Diet is in charge of diplomacy. However, in practice, Japanese diplomacy in the field was often practiced by others, without the prior knowledge of the foreign minister. In some cases processes were initiated and promoted even against the prime minister's political directives and official declarations. As will be shown in the following section of the chapter, some of Japan's foreign policy operations might have been carried out at times outside the government's legal mandate and even against the parliament's recommendations.

Diplomacy, peace, and economic restructuring were among the major themes of Japanese prime minister Koizumi's policy speech to the parliament on February 4, 2002. In the section devoted to the "Basic Posture on Diplomacy," he focused on the choices of diplomatic means that Japan wished to use to respond to the post-9/11 global changes. The preferred means included economic and humanitarian assistance to the post-Taliban Afghanistan, an improved relationship with North Korea, and the new diplomatic initiatives to finalize the peace treaty with Russia. However, Prime Minister Koizumi, in the speech, did not spell out the specifics of the latest negotiation with Russia for this end.

The overt and covert strategies that have been used for resolving the issues concerning the disputed Northern Territories over the past decade will be examined later in this chapter.

The prime minister, in his policy speech, referred to the Tokyo International Conference on Reconstruction Assistance to Afghanistan, CRAA.[4] Mr. Koizumi declared in his policy speech that "our nation will implement the assistance measures across a broad spectrum, with priority focused on sectors such as reintegration of refugees and displaced persons, rebuilding communities health and medical care." In addition to the already well-established Official Development Assistance (ODA) projects sponsored by the government, there have been a large number of Japanese international aid programs carried out by the nongovernmental organizations.

For the purpose of our discussion in this chapter, we will classify the Japanese NGOs working overseas into three broadly defined categories.

1. The self-financed NGOs that are voluntarily run by nonpolitical associations operating outside the Japanese government's administrative controls and focus on the humanitarian aid programs and on the projects at the community level.

2. The NGOs that are financially dependent on the state funding and often managed by former government officials, and at times set up by the Japanese government to advance its foreign policy goals through the combination of humanitarian and economic development aid programs.

3. The NGOs that have emerged as self-financed local voluntary groups and had so successfully expanded projects that they required professional management and state

funds to sustain their activities. Subsequently some of them began to operate in the gray zone of aid diplomacy by advancing the governmental policies in the field. They sometimes diverge from the initial politically neutral humanitarian aid programs.

Let us examine the field activities of globalization that fall into these three categories in the context of Japan's diplomatic initiatives toward the community-oriented peace negotiations with Russia, which the prime minister had shown Japan's commitment to in his policy speech (Feb. 4, 2002, TV Broadcast from the Japanese Diet).

LEGAL AMBIGUITIES[5]

Legally, the world's second largest economy, Japan, and one of the world's largest countries, Russia, are still at war even in the early twenty-first century. This is the fact that most Japanese today find hard to believe, especially with the international developments they have been observing in the last decade.

For the last several decades, the main objectives of Japanese diplomacy toward Russia have been to formally end the state of war between the two countries by signing the peace treaty. The only remaining obstacle is the issue of sovereignty of the four Russian-held northern Japanese islands, the so-called Northern Territories located to the southeast of Hokkaido in the Pacific.

In addition to the official negotiations being carried out between Japanese and Russian foreign ministries, there has been significant expansion of "aid diplomacy" carried out through the NGOs that have been operating within the ambiguities of the diplomatic gray zone.

While the successive Japanese prime ministers have been actively promoting humanitarian aid to Russia, the Japanese Foreign Ministry has been consistent in refusing to consider the Russian-held Northern Territories to be foreign soil during the past decade. Thus, officially the Japanese Foreign Ministry could not contribute any of its international aid programs to the four disputed islands. But in practice, the Japanese Foreign Ministry has been providing aid to the disputed territories through an affiliated organization *(Shien Iinkai)*. The actual size and the scope of the aid programs have been increased substantially during the past years.

Shien Iinkai (SI) was officially established under a post–Cold War international agreement and affiliated with the Foreign Ministry in 1993. In addition to its overt objective of managing overseas assistance programs for the former Soviet Republics, SI has been providing some politically motivated humanitarian assistance to the disputed four northern islands: Habomai, Shikotan, Kunashiri, and Etorofu.

Technically the *Shien Iinkai* has always stood outside the Foreign Ministry's administrative structure. In organization, however, it heavily reflected the structure of the ministry. The head of the SI's secretariat has been a former official of the Ministry for Foreign Affairs. Furthermore, among the SI's dozen staff members, there are former governmental officers with links to the law-makers from the ruling Liberal Democratic Party (LDP), the party that advo-cated the so-called two-track peace negotiations for some years.

The "two-track formula" implies that Russia returns Habomai and Shikotan islands, while simultaneously continuing negotiation on the return of remain-ing Kunashiri and Etorofu islands. The proposed formula was based on the 1956 joint declaration that Habomai and Shikotan would be returned to Japan following the signing of the peace treaty between Russia and Japan. Its latest modification also implied that even after the peace treaty was signed, the ne-gotiations for the return of the remaining islands should be continued between the two countries. This was at least what the Japanese public was led to believe.

Among the long-time advocates of the two-track negotiation approach have been two LDP lawmakers. One was Mr. Yoshihiro Mori, the former prime minister and the head of a leading faction to which the current prime minister Koizumi belongs. The other was Mr. Muneo Suzuki, a former cabinet minister in charge of Hokkaido and Okinawa Development, who had also served as parliamentary foreign secretary and had belonged until March 2002 to the LDP's largest intraparty faction, called the Hashimoto Faction (led by the for-mer prime minister Ryutaro Hashimoto).

The two-track formula often challenged the ministry's foreign policy, and subsequently it was branded by the then foreign minister Makiko Tanaka as a destructive "dual diplomacy." Both Mori and Suzuki have continued to use the combination of symbolic and financial means to pressure the post-Yeltsin Russian government to modify its position on the return of the Northern Territories.

MANIPULATING SYMBOLS: DOUBLE BURIAL SITES

Let us examine Japan's unorthodox diplomatic overtures and the use of cul-tural symbols. Yoshihiro Mori's father had been for decades mayor of a small village in the prefecture of Ishikawa, the prefecture facing the Japan Sea. (When one visits the village today, one sees numerous Russian signs on stores and restaurants as well as on the streets.) Mori made the arrangements to make double burial sites for his father. Mori personally asked for Russian president Putin's presence in creating the second burial for his late father and tried to involve Putin in the two-track peace negotiation formula.

Mori's father, a Japanese Imperial Army war veteran, had, according to his son Yoshihiro Mori, asked in his last will to have his cremated body used to advance the peace negotiations between Japan and Russia. Mori Sr. requested his ashes to be divided, and then a part of them to be buried in his native country and the other part in Siberia, near the town of Irkutsk.

In spring 2001, young Mori (Yoshihiro Mori), in the capacity of the prime minister of Japan, arranged that the working meeting with President Putin would take place in Irkutsk. Between their official negotiations, Putin (himself a son of an injured World War II veteran) agreed to accompany his Japanese guest in the limousine to Mori Sr.'s Russian burial site. After leaving the prime minister post, Yoshihiro Mori disclosed that during their long trip to the grave he and Putin had not only shared their late fathers' war memories and desire for peace but also discussed in the car's privacy the two-track peace negotiation formula.

The subsequent official March 2001 Irkutsk Agreement between Putin and Mori generated a framework to settle the territorial dispute by return of Habomai and Shikotan islands as stipulated in the 1956 joint statement, while at the same time continuing negotiations regarding the remaining islands of Kunashiri and Etorofu.

Simultaneous with Mori's efforts to personalize the interstate negotiations— by bringing cultural symbols of death into political peace process—the other influential LDP lawmaker, Mr. Muneo Suzuki, has continued to use the cross-border humanitarian community aid projects to link his Hokkaido constituency with the communities on the Russian-held islands.

TWO-TRACK FORMULA AND CROSS-BORDER
AID PROGRAM

Suzuki, a long-term Lower House member representing the Hokkaido constituency of Nemuro (since 1983), had become the first postwar cabinet minister to make an official visit to the Northern Territories and establish working relations with the islands' community leaders. During his subsequent meeting with the then newly elected president Putin (April 2000), Suzuki outlined his cross-border community exchange and aid programs. In post–Cold War negotiations when successive Japanese foreign ministers failed to advance their peace negotiations with Russia along legal ambiguities, Suzuki continued to practice his own regional foreign policy. He employed both overt and covert approaches.

Suzuki's local influence in his Nemuro constituency was based on his public insistence that the Northern Territories should be returned to Japan. However, in other contexts he contradicted himself by expressing the view that Japanese government should not be preoccupied with the return of the islands.

Suzuki (according to documents declassified in March 2002), during consultations with the Japanese Foreign Ministry's officials, made his views on the territorial issues very clear. He stated that "[i]f, in fact, the islands were returned, there would be no benefit at all to the nation. We should put an end to the calls for a return of the territory and proceed with economic exchange with four islands."

The basis of Suzuki's power structure has been multiple networks of informal alliances. In reality the networks were of contradicting interests involving cross-border local community leaders with the governmental and party bureaucracies as well as, in some cases, with the Russian intelligence's operatives. This allowed him to gain access to different levels of both Japanese and Russian power structure. He was able to manipulate contradictory interests through informal and often covert means. However, as will be shown later, the Russian foreign intelligence operatives could have been manipulating the other side without Suzuki himself being aware of it.

Now let us examine the legal, economic, and sociocultural background of Suzuki's "humanitarian efforts."

1. Suzuki stood on ground different from foreign ministers. The foreign minister is an appointed cabinet member in Japanese politics has often been reshuffled after a short term by the prime minister. The foreign minister's power in reality has been determined and often restricted by the ministry's elite bureaucracy as well as by the prime minister's office.

Suzuki, on the other hand, has been an elected grassroots community leader from Hokkaido, to which prefecture the disputed islands administratively belonged. Suzuki's electoral district, Nemuro, consists of numerous voters whose families had been resettled by force from the Russian-held islands to Hokkaido. He could remain representative from the district for any duration of time as long as the voters continued electing him to the office. In the eyes and the minds of the local people, Suzuki, by officially visiting their "native islands," has personified a link between their parents' past in the Russian-held islands and their present life in Hokkaido.

Suzuki has also acted to link to the future by purporting the return of the islands with an ongoing economic benefit scheme for his exiled constituency. Suzuki has proven his resourcefulness as a local leader by increasing the economic benefits for the border-divided communities in his position as the cabinet minister in charge of Hokkaido and Okinawa (the northernmost and southernmost islands of Japan). Suzuki has continued to exert his influence in the matters concerning the programs between the two countries of Japan and Russia long after he left the official post.

2. Suzuki continued to involve himself in the cross-border programs by going back and forth between his cabinet position and the LDP platform. In fact, Suzuki could continue exercising his unconstitutional influence over the successive administrations long after he had left his cabinet post. This was possible because the Japanese prime minister concurrently serves as the head of LDP, and as an LDP member of the Diet, Suzuki could continue to operate through the LDP channels.

Suzuki, while occupying the cabinet position, could use dual channels, the foreign ministry's official channels as well as the LDP channels and the parliamentary committees, which traditionally have had strong ties with the government bureaucracy. Having left the cabinet position, he could continue to exercise his power in the latter channels.

Although the Japanese constitution stipulates that the administrative authority lies de jure with the cabinet, de facto influential LDP lawmakers, who, like Suzuki, have chaired the "right" committees, could continue influencing the administrative process without being a part of the cabinet.

At one point, Suzuki had served at the same time as the chairman of the LDP's Special Committee on External Economic Cooperation (SPCEEC) and the chairman of the House of Representatives' Rules and Administration Committee. In practice he combined his influence through parliamentary position and the position within the LDP party. In fact, he was aggressively exerting his influence over the allocation of the country's entire foreign aid programs. By doing so, he used the foreign aid to advance his version of regional foreign and economic policies along the "two-track diplomacy" line. Among the evidence of influences exerted over successive foreign ministers, the Diet investigation found the following cases documented. Suzuki, questioning the then foreign minister Kono at the Parliament (May 31, 1995) was dissatisfied with Kono's cautious response regarding the construction of a medical clinic at Shikotan Island (that Suzuki had openly lobbied for). The following day (June 1, 1995) Suzuki and Kono had a working breakfast. At the breakfast Suzuki secured support for building the medical facility. (The building contract was awarded to the contractor from Suzuki's constituency, which was a regular contributor to Suzuki's electoral fund.)

3. The Japanese government's rapid expansion of the aid programs to the Northern Territories, from a small-scale food aid to a huge economic assistance measured in billions of yen, has coincided with Suzuki's ambitions to regionalize the peace process and to generate a cross-border virtual constituency.

The regionalization that almost ended in de facto establishment of the visa-free cross-border community financed by Japanese ODA and foreign ministry funds was carried out at three levels simultaneously. First was the political mobilization of the local community through manipulation of symbolic means to reinforce and politicize a shared identity among exiles. Second was the illegal redistribution of foreign development aid to benefit the domestic economic interests of Suzuki's constituency. Third, an unconstitutional use of party influence was used to advance regional foreign policy against national interests and governmental declarations.

REINVENTED MEMORIES AND POLITICAL MOBILIZATION

At first Suzuki succeeded in activating his Nemuro constituency's collective memory by referring in his election campaigns to the Russian-held islands. In doing so, he always used the regional dialect, not the language of abstract political declarations. Many resettlers who joined Suzuki's *Koen kai* (Election Support Organization) have gradually reactivated their past through their participation in the postelection festivities. They were actively sharing their collective memory. Suzuki's local support groups have continued to meet informally between the parliamentary elections and attracted resettlers across different generations. These meetings have become a natural occasion to revive the islands' dialect by sharing such common things as seasonal dishes. The use of regional names for the seasonal dishes made from the fish that had been traditionally caught at a particular time of the year near the islands' waters reinvented the memories of their birthplaces, even for those generations who never lived in the islands. Those dishes served during the postelection festivities have become symbols for their past, present, and future hopes. Suzuki used them as means for political mobilization.

The collective past has thus become once again an integral part of the resettlers' community's shared consciousness and social activities. The symbolic exchange of reinvented memories during the gatherings strengthened their double identities: as members of the local Nemuro LDP constituency and as displaced islanders.

Suzuki had succeeded in reinventing the displaced people's past in positive symbolic terms; it was only a matter of time before Suzuki incorporated the exiled islanders' collective expectations for the return of the Northern Territories into his own political agenda. To promote his agenda by steering the Foreign Ministry's peace negotiations with Russia through the "two-track formula," Suzuki had to continue generating economic benefits to his constituency of Nemuro during a period of economic recession.

For his regional peace process, Suzuki had to operate across the border to mobilize the local leaders at the Russian-held islands. Suzuki had to achieve several results simultaneously.[6]

He had to secure the flow of public funds that would meet contradictory local interests of the "Japanese exiles" and the "Russian occupiers." The funded projects had to be legitimate enough to solidify his leadership position at both the national and international levels. By investigating into Suzuki's cross-border economic activities, one could uncover the mechanics of foreign policy making within the diplomatic gray zone.

BROADENING THE DIPLOMATIC GRAY ZONE AND ECONOMIC AID

The Japanese Foreign Ministry's policy of managing the humanitarian aid programs to the Russian-held islands not through the ministry's Russian Support Section but through the ministry-affiliated organization *Shien Iinkai* made the aid selection process hard to trace. In fact, the entire aid financing and contract awarding structure has been built around the artificial political reality (of Northern Territories being part of Japan) and therefore gave room for further manipulation by political operatives. Suzuki (and his aides) were not the first to invent creative use of foreign aid for their political purposes. He exploited the Foreign Ministry's structural weaknesses to broaden the diplomatic gray zone so that he could benefit economically from it and could deliver benefits to his Hokkaido constituency and his local support group (*Koen Kai*).

Here is how the diplomatic gray zone was broadened and how the de facto aid diplomacy functioned.

In November 1997 (two months after Suzuki had taken his cabinet post as the director-general of Hokkaido and Okinawa Development), Japan's then prime minister R. Hashimoto, and the then Russian president Yeltsin met in Siberia and reached the so-called Krasnoyarsk Accord. The working meeting ended with an informal pledge by both sides to sign a Russo–Japanese Peace Treaty by the end of the year 2000. The pledge, though never fulfilled, generated a framework for successive Japanese governments to link informal peace diplomacy with humanitarian assistance to the Northern Territories.

After Hashimoto's successor, Prime Minister Kenzo Obuchi, made Suzuki his deputy chief cabinet secretary (that de facto coordinates cabinet policies), the overt economic aid to the Russian-occupied islands jumped from about 0.5 billion yen in 1998 to over 3 billion in 1999. Among the aid projects promoted that year by the *Shien Iinkai* was the construction of an emergency evacuation facility on Kunashiri Island. In May 1999, two months before *Shien Iinkai* officially awarded the 417 million yen worth of contract (July 99), Suzuki conferred with the Foreign Ministry's officials regarding the bidding requirements and procedures. On Suzuki's request, the ministry illegally limited the contractors eligible to place the bids to those from Hokkaido's Nemuro region and with certain business experiences in the past.

According to Suzuki's explanation, the change that narrowed the contractors to his Nemuro constituency was necessary because it would integrate national foreign policy interests with the community interests of the displaced people. Awarding the contracts to the two Nemuro firms would generate work and at the same time the emergency evacuation facility on the Russian-held island could also be used as the lodging for the Nemuro residents visiting their "native" Kunashiri Island.

The consular agreement between the governments of Japan and Russia that allowed the former Japanese residents of the Northern Territories to cross the interstate border without a visa had further expanded Suzuki's regional influence across the border. But these visits also expanded the possibility for the manipulations of cross-border diplomacy. For example, Suzuki, with the Nemuro group of Japanese resettlers, visited the Russian-held islands visa free to plant cherry trees as the symbols of peace, and the Russian government used this as an opportunity to spell out its own territorial claim: The Northern Territories, in spite of the expanding humanitarian aid programs by the Japanese government, are still under Russian sovereignty. To make the point, the Russian border authorities demanded that while Suzuki and his group could cross the border freely, the live cheery trees they had brought with them had to undergo quarantine because they were brought from abroad.

The Japanese Foreign Ministry's armchair diplomacy to achieve a diplomatic breakthrough (by transporting the cherry blossoms as if they were transported within Japanese territory) yielded no result. What seemed most offensive for the Japanese parliamentarians investigating (in March 2002) the country's foreign policy making was that during the time of Suzuki's "regional diplomacy," there was no substantial change in the Russian government's position on the disputed Northern Territories. And yet the Japanese government kept providing funds for both sides of Suzuki's "virtual constituency."

ACTIVATING CULTURAL SYMBOLS IN THE DIPLOMATIC GRAY ZONE

Suzuki has continually worked on linking economically his Nemuro constituency with the disputed islands' communities through regional aid projects. The Japanese and the Russian governments have continued their gray zone diplomacy through reactivating myths and utilizing symbols rich in cultural meaning. In contrast to Suzuki's down-to-earth exchange programs, the message exchange followed a sophisticated scheme based on a nonverbal but very precise communication. Let us examine what cultural symbols each side used during the indirect peace negotiations and what diplomatic messages they have intended to convey to the other part.

Whenever Suzuki and his group arrived by boat to the disputed Kunashiri Island, the Russians used to welcome the Japanese visitors at the harbor with a freshly baked local bread that was later followed by a vodka drink and more substantial refreshments. Many Japanese resettlers were familiar with the Russian habit of treating visitors to a glass of vodka and a piece of bread with salt. For them it was only natural that Suzuki, being a head of the Japanese group, was invited to share the bread first. In a similar manner, the head of a Russian group revisiting Suzuki's Hokkaido constituency usually was invited to be the first to be toasted with *sake* and offered a piece of rice ball.

However, what Suzuki and the visiting resettlers did not pay attention to was the symbolic significance of the bread, salt, and vodka, as well as the order in which these entrées were served. The Japanese group (without being aware of it) had become involved in an ancient and highly structured ritual that was not just a simple snack (as many thought it was).

The ancient community ritual of offering the guests a loaf of home-baked bread conveyed the message of peace by the fact that there was no knife. Only bare hands were used to share it. The status of the guests and hosts were confirmed by the order of the offering: it was always the host, or his representative, who offered a visitor the honor of breaking the bread loaf and eating the first piece. Both sides were involved in performing the ritual. The ritual confirmed to the community their positions and the roles they played during the social intercourse. This ritual was the most familiar one among the Slavic people, as this left no room for doubt as to who visited whom (as the visitor could never offer the bread-sharing to the host or master of the house).

Traditionally, this bread and salt–sharing ritual was celebrated during the important community and family rites of passage. For example, when a newlywed moved to the groom's household, the head of the groom's family would welcome the bride with a loaf of bread. By sharing the bread in public, she would confirm her transition from a daughter to a daughter-in-law with all the duties and privileges accorded to her new position in the new household and in the community. She was expected to be treated with respect and awarded protection according to her new status.

The bread sharing also symbolized gratitude for past kindness and hopes for the future. It was therefore frequently used during the harvest rituals and welcoming receptions of particularly esteemed guests from outside the community or the country.

The community members of Kunashiri Island that had gathered at the harbor to witness the ritualized welcome of Suzuki and his group knew the importance of the order: bread first, followed by salt, and only then by a sip of vodka. When a representative of the Kunashiri community, a young Russian female wearing a Russian folk dress, offered Suzuki a loaf of bread on the tray, Suzuki followed the ritualized order, and thus publicly confirmed for the Russian community his status as a Japanese member of Parliament (Diet) from the neighbor Hokkaido Island paying, together with his group, a courtesy visit on Russian soil.

Because neither Suzuki nor the other members of the Japanese group accompanying him seemed to have understood the significance of this ritual as a political statement confirming the Russian sovereignty over the disputed territory, they willingly followed the order.

In contrast, Russian government officials were well prepared to obstruct the Japanese Foreign Ministry's attempt to use the Japanese symbols of the cherry plants to assert sovereignty over the Northern Territories. Therefore, only after the bread was shared in front of the TV cameras and the welcoming ritual completed in the Kunashiri harbor did the Russian authorities invoke international medical considerations and request their Japanese guests to fill out the quarantine forms for the overseas cherry plants to be brought into their country.

What seemed to have been a routine procedure that caused just a minor friction between the Russian hosts and their Japanese guests during a 1996 courtesy visit on a tiny and impoverished northern island had actually evolved in the next six years into a major political crisis. This further developed into a series of parliamentary investigations in Moscow and Tokyo that resulted in the dismissal of the Japanese foreign minister Makiko Tanaka (in January 2002). The prolonged crisis effectively ended Suzuki's regional peace diplomacy, and the "double track" finally closed down in March 2002 when Suzuki was forced to leave the ruling LDP. Suzuki's manipulation of the peace process and economic aid could have been prevented (and the peace treaty signed) at an earlier stage, had the peace negotiators understood all the symbolic implications made by both sides and the meaning communicated covertly through the ritual. However, both the Russian and Japanese foreign policy makers and the intelligence analysts paid no attention to the increasing miscommunication at the symbolic level and the growing personal misconduct among the operators of the diplomatic gray zone.[7]

When the Kunashiri's regional authorities requested the Japanese visitors to complete the quarantine procedures before the cherry roots could be planted, Suzuki was willing to follow the procedures. However, Mr. X, an official from the Japanese Foreign Ministry who accompanied Suzuki's group, refused to comply until receiving an approval from his superior in Tokyo. The Japanese Foreign Ministry's official stance was that they always considered the Northern Territories to be Japanese soil, and therefore the ministry instructed Mr. X to not fill out the Russian quarantine forms and thus not to legitimize the Russian government's claims to sovereignty over the island.

The cherry trees that were supposed to symbolize peace were not planted. According to the Foreign Ministry's documents (declassified in March 2002), Suzuki had not only accused Mr. X of undermining his regional peace efforts, but he had also physically attacked Mr. X during the group's return trip onboard the Japanese vessel. Although the official's facial and leg injures required a week to heal, the Foreign Ministry suppressed the incidents caused by Suzuki. The reason that the ministry tolerated Suzuki's excesses will be examined in detail in the next sections, but let us here put the issue in a broader international context by asking two practical questions.

- How have the U.S. foreign policy makers, including the U.S. national security adviser, used plants as political symbols to openly challenge the Iron Curtain without offending their communist hosts?

- How could Suzuki have saved himself from the trap set up by the Russian counterpart and his own Foreign Ministry without endangering the peace negotiations and offending the local community leaders?

Dr. Zbigniew Brzezinski, a Polish-born U.S. national security adviser, who accompanied U.S. president Jimmy Carter during an official visit to Poland, used his profound understanding of Polish cultural symbols to ritualize the U.S. support for the anti-communist opposition. Brzezinski is credited (together with the Polish-born pope John Paul II) for preventing the Russian army's invasion to crush the Polish anti-Communist Solidarity movement while at the same time offering a symbolic framework for reconciliation between the adversaries.

Understanding Brzezinski's strategic use of community symbols might be instructive for those who have to carry out their duties in culturally and politically tense environments. It might also be helpful for those serving in the field who are not trained as anthropologists but have to deal with contradictory political interests while carrying out some reconciliatory activities across the communities divided along cultural and political boundaries.

Dr. Brzezinski, in his results-oriented cross-cultural diplomacy, used the symbols of death and ritualized bread sharing as political statements to regain the symbolic territory occupied by a regime supported by Russia. Brzezinski was careful not to transgress the diplomatic arrangements the U.S. State Department and the Polish Foreign Ministry had agreed on in advance for Carter's visit in Warsaw. But he simultaneously carried on semiprivate activities in the diplomatic gray zone. Let us examine in detail how the U.S. national security adviser (during his brief visit to Warsaw) expanded the diplomatic gray zone and liberated the anti-Communist symbols from a private space of Polish homes and churches into a public space that was still controlled by the Russian-imposed ideology.

Although the U.S. president had to pay attention to his protocol and attend official luncheons with his hosts, the U.S. national security adviser attended the ritual of bread sharing at a Polish church. Brzezinski's meeting with the Polish Christian leaders and his participation in the act of communion were not only religious but political acts as well. Brzezinski and the U.S. president's wife, Rosalynn Carter, paid a private visit to the head of the Polish Catholic Church, Cardinal Stefan Wyszynski. The church, led by the former political prisoner Wyszynski, was the core of the Polish civil society at the time. It was also the only organized anti-Communist opposition in a nation consisting of over 90 percent Catholics.

After the unofficial meeting with the de facto leader of Poland (the cardinal), Brzezinski honored the Warsaw official monument of the Polish World War II freedom fighters with a wreath made of flowers in the Polish national colors. The wreath he delivered was in the shape of an anchor. The anchor's upper arm was shaped to form the letter P, and the lower main part formed the letter W (NOTE: P = *Polska*/Poland, W = *Walczaca*/Resistance). Both letters made of red and white flowers overlapped each other, forming an anchor-shaped symbol. The Communist rulers of Poland realized only too late that the wreath symbolized the Polish World War II resistance forces of the National Army (AK) that was allied with the anti-Communist Western Alliance. Brzezinski brought a symbol that was forbidden during Communist rule into public view. He used the state visit and the dignity of his office as the U.S. national security adviser to ritualize the display of the armed resistance symbols (PW), which until that time were only displayed in the privacy of Polish homes at best. Although the state-controlled media largely ignored the ceremony with Brzezinski's wreath, it became instantly known nationwide through the church network.

Subsequently, the act had a strong impact on the mobilization of Polish civil society, which 10 years later (1990) resulted in national reconciliation, free elections, and finally the liberation of Poland from Russian domination.

Brzezinski's extensive experience of Eurasian politics (as a U.S. member of the Trilateral Commission), as well as his academic fieldwork in Japan (as a Ford Fellow), helped him place Polish–Russian bilateral relations in the broader multilateral context of Eurasia. Brzezinski pointed out in his book on Japanese politics (1972) that many Japanese politicians whom he had interviewed in the course of his fieldwork had difficulties in viewing geopolitical changes in a broader cross-cultural context. In contrast to Brzezinski, who so carefully orchestrated the covert symbolic rapprochement between the community leaders and the governmental leaders before confronting the Russian geopolitical interests in Eurasia, the Japanese officials negotiating a compromise peace formula with Russia did not understand the geopolitical significance of the rituals performed by the community leaders on the Russian-held islands.

Both the Suzuki group's attempt to use the cherry trees as symbols for peace and then prime minister Mori's subsequent attempt to use his late father's double burial site as a symbol of reconciliation between Russia and Japan did not advance anything. On the contrary, the prospects of solving the Northern Territory issues through the "two-track formula" and regional diplomacy seems to have yielded very little. Less than a year after Mori left office in a voluntary retirement as prime minister, the parliamentary investigation of Muneo Suzuki as a witness under oath disclosed massive irregularities in foreign policy making. It resulted in Suzuki's departure from the ruling LDP. Let us discuss an alternative scenario for diffusing the confrontational attitudes between Russia and Japan.

MOBILE THINK TANKS: AN ALTERNATIVE SCENARIO AND USE OF ANTHROPOLOGICAL THINKING

Let us now discuss a possible alternative scenario for diffusing the confrontational attitudes between Russia and Japan. If one looks at the disputed Northern Territories from a longer historical and cultural perspective, it becomes clear that these islands had neither belonged to the Russians nor to Japanese governments but to the Ainu people. The Ainu, the northern aboriginal tribes whose physical features and culture are distinct from both the Japanese and Russians, have traditionally lived on the lands of northern Japan and Sakhalin and Kurile islands.

The control over the northern Ainu tribal lands had frequently shifted between Russia and Japan throughout the twentieth century. Many Ainu had to be repatriated after the Russo-Japanese War (1904–05) and in 1945. As a result, the Ainu tribes have continued to reside on both sides of the Russo-Japanese border. My earlier fieldwork among the Ainu tribesmen indicated that many Ainu resettlers identified themselves as Ainu living as Japanese or Russian citizens.

Now, bearing this in mind, let us try to outline an alternative political scenario involving culturally meaningful symbols and a broader multiethnic approach. The Japanese Foreign Ministry could have used a different set of symbols in making political statements on the Northern Territories and promoting regional economic cooperation. In place of Japanese cherry trees and the ethnic Japanese member of Parliament chairing the Hokkaido group, the visits to the Northern Territories could have incorporated the Hokkaido Ainu leaders and their cultural symbols. Had the Japanese strategists structured their peace negotiation around a pluralistic regional identity and utilized the politically neutral Ainu rituals, the outcome of bilateral negotiations might have been quite different.

Such a pluralistic approach to bilateral negotiations might not only have depoliticized the sovereignty issue, but shifted the focus from legal issues involving state border regulations (such as the quarantine procedure) to cross-cultural exchange in a truly regional context. Among the Ainu symbols that could travel freely across the Russo-Japanese border were potent cultural expressions of peace such as tribal rituals in the Ainu community. An equally important fact was that although Suzuki had monopolized the regional diplomacy, an Ainu leader, Shigeru Kayano, might have been a better speaker for the former islanders, both native and Japanese. He was from the Ainu community Nibutani Piratori. I interviewed him in his native Ainu village in the mid-1970s. Some 20 years later, he was elected from the same Hokkaido constituency to the Japanese Diet in the 1990s. For the first time in Japan's parliamentary history the divided Ainu aboriginal communities were represented in the Japanese Diet. Kayano, an Ainu cultural activist, accomplished writer, and fluent Ainu speaker, has been considered by both Japanese and Russian scholars to be one of the most distinguished living authorities on the Ainu culture (based on my interviews with the scholars attending an international conference on B. Pilsudski research of Ainu culture in Krakow [Cracow], Poland, August/September 1999).

Kayano has preserved the unwritten Ainu history that has been transmitted in the form of tribal songs from generation to generation. By writing down the songs he had learned from his illiterate grandmother, he recorded their oral history. Among the old Ainu epic songs were some songs that referred to the Ainu land (Ainu Mosir) located across the vast territory, not in political terms of interstate boundaries, but in spiritual dimensions of Ainu gods living in nature. The epic songs often referred to the tribal rituals known on both sides of the Russo-Japanese border and frequently made symbolic reference to local fish, regional animals, and trees with which the Ainu tribesmen could communicate. The Ainu myths preserved by Shigeru Kayano, Bronislaw Pilsudski, and other international authorities or scholars of Ainu culture all stress the peaceful coexistence of men and nature and thus could have been used in ritualized exchanges. Kayano could have easily advanced the point by bringing the branches of Kunashiri willows to perform the sacred Ainu rituals in tact of ancient Ainu epic songs about the Northern Islanders' past. The point is that displaced settlers, old or new, suffer greatly from the loss of their homeland and wish for reconciliation.

These complementary elements (the epic Ainu songs and the willow branches) could have been unified into a more culturally comprehensive message, strengthening regional unity across cultural boundaries.

There are several questions.

- Why could the officials from the Japanese Foreign Ministry not come up with such an alternative political scenario?
- Why did the Japanese prime ministers not use the regional and cross-cultural expertise of the Ainu member of the Japanese Diet?
- Why could they not utilize the cultural resources in the way the U.S. president sought using the cross-cultural expertise of his Polish-born national security adviser (Brzezinski) to neutralize Russian influence over its Polish neighbor?
- Why did the Japanese government fail to engage such a valuable human resource as Kayano in the process?

The simplest answer would be that Kayano, in contrast to Suzuki, represented a minority party (Social Democrats), and therefore his influence over shaping the political process was limited. Furthermore, although Kayano was older than Suzuki, Kayano was considered a junior parliamentarian without cabinet experience and therefore lacking informal networks among the ministerial bureaucrats.

As of March 2002, not all the internal documents related to Suzuki's exercise of illegal pressure over the foreign ministry's diplomats had been declassified. There was, however, already enough evidence to point to a pattern. Suzuki, contrary to his public stance demanding the return of the Northern Territories to Japan, according to the documents disclosed during his parliamentary testimony, did not believe it was in Japan's national interests to demand the return of the Russian-held islands (Sources: Japanese Foreign Ministry's investigation declassified in March 2002).

What seems at first glance a contradiction in his beliefs or conviction is actually logical in terms of Suzuki's own political and financial interests. He could secure his reelection by continuing to bring the nation's financial resources to his Nemuro constituency. The Japanese government's humanitarian aid to the Northern Territories could be redirected to his own supporters, the Nemuro-based contractors, by granting them the building projects on the Russian-held islands. As long as the islands were being held by Russia, and the grassroots movements among the resettlers for their return persisted, Suzuki could continue his political career. Not only could he maintain his parliamentary advancement by chairing the important committees, but he could also expand his influence in the diplomatic gray zone and pressure the Japanese Foreign Ministry to continue providing the funds.

Prolonged negotiations with Russia and the indication of progress (through the media reports) in the cross-border community exchange programs simply prolonged his own political career. The two-track negotiation formula provided Suzuki legitimacy to practice his alternative diplomacy. The parliamentary investigations of Suzuki's activities proved that the aid projects were awarded to the contractors from Suzuki's Nemuro constituency. But it brought no jobs to the Nemuro residents (as the subcontractors were hired from 2000 km away in Yokohama). Nemuro contractors who won the contracts diligently contributed money to Suzuki's political funds. In other words, it was a simple fraud disguised as grassroots diplomacy and the most upsetting scandal for the people in his electoral district.

The second question is: Why were the Russian operatives working in the diplomatic gray zone interested in helping Suzuki in his fund-raising scheme?

One of the answers might be that by engaging Suzuki in the regional diplomacy, the Russian government agents could use him as a direct channel to manipulate the Japanese ruling LDP. The Japanese Foreign Ministry's latest internal investigation confirmed that Suzuki had private meetings with a certain Smirnov of the Russian embassy in Tokyo. Suzuki was aware that Smirnov was an intelligence official. But he pressured the head of the National Police Agency (NPA) not to pursue his meetings with Smirnov. A report written by Colonel Nikolai Pietrowich Koshkin, a resident Russian intelligence official working under diplomatic cover in Tokyo in the 1990s, revealed an interesting fact. Colonel N. P. Koshkin, a fluent Japanese speaker and a lawyer by training, has described the disinformation techniques and manipulation he used on the issue of the Northern Territories through his meetings with an anonymous, high-level Japanese official.[8]

Our next question is: Were Suzuki (and his aides) the only operators in the diplomatic gray zone that grew around the Northern Territory issue and Nemuro? Additional Eurasian materials seem to imply a broader geopolitical context and more complex cross-cultural strategies that supported the process of Japanese–Russian peace negotiations.

AN ALTERNATIVE EURASIAN PEACE STRATEGY

In the report on the peace keeping operations (published by United Nation University Press, 2000, Tokyo) there is a comparative chapter devoted to the transformation of Eastern Europe and referring to the Polish foreign and defense policies in context of NATO and Kosovo crisis (Talas & Valki, 2000).

The authors refer to Janusz Onyszkiewicz, the then Polish minister of defense, who facilitated Poland's NATO membership and the foreign policy implications in this framework.

Now, let us search for the structural and personal connections that involved the Polish defense minister in the gray zone diplomacy surrounding the Ainu resettlers and the disputed Northern Territories. For most observers Onyszkiewicz's personal involvement in the Ainu resettlers' affairs, including his participation in a cross-continental reunion of the divided Eurasian clans, escaped notice, and his involvement seemed improbable. But here is why the Polish defense minister and his family found themselves attracting the Japanese public media's interests.

NHK (the Japanese Public Broadcasting Corporation, similar to the British BBC) had arranged a meeting between an Ainu resettler from Hokkaido and the Polish defense minister Onyszkiewicz in the fall of 1999.

The Japanese interest in Onyszkiewicz had become more pronounced after the former Solidarity activist became, through his third marriage, a cousin to an Hokkaido Ainu, Mr. K.

In 1945 the K. family, together with the other Ainu families, were resettled by force from the territories then invaded by Russia to Hokkaido. Mr. K.'s Sakhalin-born grandmother belonged to an Ainu clan whose ancestors' hunting and fishing grounds covered the large area including the disputed islands. Mr. K., who had left Hokkaido for a community in close proximity of the Tokyo metropolitan area in the 1970s, never openly referred to his Eurasian Ainu roots. Although Mr. K. had known that his Ainu grandmother married a Russian political prisoner in Sakhalin at the beginning of the twentieth century and thus his father inherited the Slavic family name of Pilsudski, Mr. K. (like his late father) had been using the Japanese family name.

During the last decade Mr. K. became my neighbor. Then I gradually discovered that he was indeed a cousin of my Polish schoolmate from Warsaw. Mr. K. often visited me at home, and on Mr. K.'s request I became an intermediary between the cousins. Gradually I became well versed in the family's Eurasian history. The history gave me the inspiration to write a three-volume book manuscript, which was in due course passed on to the people at the Japanese public broadcasting corporation, NHK, in the mid-1990s.

In 1999 Mr. K. informed me that the Japanese NHK had invited him to fly to Poland for a reunion with the Polish side of his family. In Warsaw, the Japanese-Ainu kin was greeted by his cousin, Mrs. Pilsudski-Onyszkiewicz, and her husband, Mr. J. Onyszkiewicz, the then Polish minister of defense. Although Mr. K.'s visit to the land of his grandfather was a private matter arranged by the Japanese Public Broadcasting Corporation (NHK), there were a number of current and former employees of the Japanese and Polish foreign ministries who became involved in various aspects of his visit to Poland. Because Mr. K.'s knowledge of the Polish language was very limited, both sides provided their interpreters during the family reunion.

The qualifications of the interpreters may provide the insights and the importance that each side attached to the visit.

The Polish/Japanese interpreter was Mr. H.L., (Japanologist and the former official interpreter of both the former Communist Prime Minister and the former Solidarity Labour Union Chairman, Mr. Lech Walesa during his visit to Japan in 1981). Mr. H.L. served as Poland's first post-Communist ambassador in Tokyo during the President Walesa's State Visit to Japan in 1994. (The anthropological scenario of the state visit was published by The Japan Times, December 4, 1994; see Kaminski, 1994b.)

The Japanese/Polish interpreter was Mrs. Y.Y., the former Japanese employee at the Polish embassy in Tokyo during the Communist regime, who had subsequently served as an interpreter during many high-level "informal" Japanese visits to Poland, including the "private talks" between the chairman of the major Japanese labour union and the chairman of the Polish Solidarity Labour Union.

Mr. K., during his private trip to Poland, paid a courtesy visit to the Polish Defense Ministry where Minister Onyszkiewicz welcomed him at his office. While at the office, Mr. K. videotaped the portrait hanging on the wall near the defense minister's desk. The portrait featured his paternal granduncle, Marshal Jozef Pilsudski. Mr. K.'s grandfather's younger brother, Jozef Pilsudski, the first head of the recreated Polish state after World War I, remains a household name in Poland. During the Communist rules (1945–90), the Pilsudski name was considered a taboo because of his victorious war against the Soviet Army in 1920. In the 1990s, Jozef Pilsudski retained his historical status as the most potent symbol of anti-Communism. And it was, therefore, as soon as the former Solidarity activist, Onyszkiewicz, took over the office of Poland's defense minister that he began displaying his wife's grandfather's portrait at his office to make the family's military tradition known to the visitors. Paradoxically, on the day the two met, it was not the Polish Defense Minister but an Ainu man from Japan visiting the minister who was Marshal Pilsudski's closest male relative on the patrilineal side (Kowalski, 1997).

During the days that followed the meeting in the defense ministry, Mr. K.'s visit to Poland was more directly related to his grandfather, Bronislaw Pilsudski (older brother of Jozef Pilsudski). Mr. K. went from Warsaw to Krakow to participate in the Third International Conference devoted to the scholarship of his own grandfather Bronislaw. The Bronislaw Pilsudski Conference took place in the Japanese Center of Culture and Technology, and one of its main financial sponsors was The Japan Foundation (the semigovernmental institution that was for a period led by a former Japanese vice minister of foreign affairs and employs a number of high-ranking former diplomats). Mr. K. was introduced to the international scholarly community of experts on the Ainu culture as the only grandson of Bronislaw Pilsudski. He was greeted in Polish and the conference's two working languages, Russian and English. The Russian delegation was the largest among the foreign scholars. The group of individuals gathered together included museum officials and tribal activists from Siberia and the Kurile Islands, as well as Japanese scholars of Ainu from Hokkaido and Sakhalin. The Japanese scholars were not of Ainu background. Mr. K. was accompanied frequently by the Polish defense minister and/or the Japanese officials throughout most of his trip.

Mr. K. not only visited the historical places related to Jozef and Bronislaw Pilsudski in current Poland, but also traveled to the Pilsudski brothers' family estate, Zulow. The Pilsudski's Zulow estate, which was administratively once a northeastern part of Poland, came under the Soviet Union's occupation in the 1940s and later became a part of the newly recreated state of Lithuania.

The visit was again recorded on video by both NHK and the members of the Pilsudski family.[9]

Why did the Japanese side so carefully plan a private visit of an Ainu Japanese to all these places, which were once under Russian/Soviet control? The reasons may be several.

One, it might have been simply the timing. It was considered the perfect timing. Mr. K.'s visit coincided with the Krakow conference that gathered Russian and Japanese scholars specializing in the cross-border Ainu cultures. On the other hand, it took place during the time that the very Japanese politicians were promoting the "two-track" diplomacy for the return of the Japanese Northern Territories from Russia. Indeed, during this very time, Mr. M. Suzuki was expanding his influence over the Japanese Foreign Ministry.

Does it mean that Suzuki, the Japanese member of Parliament, was involved in an effort to use Mr. K. and his Eurasian Ainu links for his Northern Territories aid scheme? There were no such indications in the documents declassified by the Japanese Foreign Ministry. Suzuki's sworn witness testimony in the Japanese Diet in March 2002 disclosed no such intentions; however, Polish documents suggested linking economic aid, Ainu, and return of Northern Territories to Japan. The 1990 internal memorandum, drafted by a field anthropologist specializing in leadership studies (on the request of a high-ranking official from the Solidarity-led government) furnished an alternative political scenario and possible other reasons Polish foreign policy should consider supporting Japan's claims for the Russian-held islands.

The memorandum had foreseen the gradual regionalization of Japanese diplomacy and the emergence of the visa-free cross-border communities along the Northern Ainu lands linked together through socioeconomic and cultural exchange programs that would be rapidly increasing.

It suggested that it was a good opportunity for Polish diplomacy to restructure bilateral relations with Japan and adjust it into multilateral relations involving other countries. It was a chance to weave Poland's needs for broadening its economic relationships with Japan with Japan's needs to gain broader international support to finalize the peace treaty with Russia and regain control over the Northern Territories.

The fact that this memorandum pointed to the possibilities for weaving several issues became of practical value to the post-Communist Polish government. The opportunities to link somehow the issue of the Northern Territories with the Pilsudskis' regional Ainu research and with the visit by the delegation of Japanese industrialists (Keidanren, The Association of Industries) that was concurrently taking place in Warsaw (autumn 1990) suggested by the anthropologist caught the immediate attention of the government.

Within hours after his memorandum was read by the minister of industry and the minister of culture, the field anthropologist was invited to consult both ministers on the practical advantages of turning the Polish–Japanese bilateral diplomacy into more pluralistic relations.[10]

The two ministers were not familiar with Japan's most powerful organization of industrialists (Keidanren) nor with the historical fact of the Northern Territories being an ancient land for the Ainu tribes. Even though the ministers had been unaware of the information presented by the anthropologist, they could immediately grasp the idea that Pilsudski as a national symbol could serve as a structural link to Japan at several levels. In fact, what they learned was how they could weave the diplomatic, economic, and cultural issues together.

The key to the policy suggestion made by the anthropologist was the active use of symbols, the very focus of this chapter.

How could the Polish, or any other, government identify the symbols, what each symbol meant to each of the parties involved, and how the meanings conveyed by different symbols could be brought to paint a comprehensive picture that has the power to influence? Such a picture can carry strong and powerful meanings, a product of multiplication of cultural symbols rather than a mere product of additions. This is one of the ways field anthropologists, not armchair anthropologists, render expertise to the practice of diplomacy and facilitate the process of international policy making in the field.

What caught the government officials' interest in this particular context was that the Pilsudski family's Eurasian link could increase the prospects of bene-fiting from strengthening economic ties with the world's second-largest econ-omy, both in the forms of investment and aid.

In another context, the names might have been different and the symbols applied could have been as simple as an anchor-shaped wreath made of flowers or the plants of cherry trees brought by a Japanese parliamentarian to a small northern island or offering a loaf of bread with salt.

Although in each of these cases the symbols and the reasons they were used (or abused) to bring an immediate solution for diplomatic issues generated far more complex messages and long-term processes. The effect is long lived. It has the longevity that it outlives most of the political actors involved in real life. Rituals encapsulate meanings, and in the capsule, meaning is communi-cated instantly and vividly. The effect of ritualized exchange often extends much beyond what many could have ever imagined.[11]

In contrast to mainstream political scientists, field anthropologists who have continuous access to both grassroots communities and governmental leaders could foresee how these symbols may easily lead to miscommunication and mistrust as well as to an improvement of cross-cultural communication and innovative conflict resolution on the global scale.[12] How difficult it is to act and react within what seems to be just a simple sharing of bread and salt or planting of trees? It might be a fact that the world's second-largest economy and the world's largest state territory remain in the legal state of war, while the world's most powerful nation continues its war against global terror.

When we are confronted with the failure of conventional methods of conflict resolution,[13] we have to search for a more creative and sometimes unconven-tional means. The unorthodox means for conflict resolution might be found outside mainstream foreign policy and opinion makers.[14] It is in such cases that field anthropologists can be brought in to find opportunities for cross-cultural conflict resolution by effective use of cultural symbols.[15]

CONCLUSIONS AND RECOMMENDATIONS

What an international community may need is the establishment of a highly mobile field think tank network[16] that can respond to the emergencies brought by the conflicting use of symbols in the field.[17] The recommendations by such a network of field anthropologists may help prevent these, often minor, inter-cultural conflicts from being turned into massive military and economic con-frontations as a result of armchair diplomacy.[18]

If these field think tanks would be able to attract the cooperation of the internal community leaders (like the Ainu cross-cultural activists operating across the state boundaries) rather than elected external leaders (like Suzuki-style parliamentarians operating in the diplomatic gray zone) there is a possi-bility for furnishing global policy makers and nongovernmental organizations with an innovative conflict resolution framework that could be continually updated in the field.

NOTES

1. This chapter was originally submitted on March 31, 2002. Background information and several updates had to be added to reflect the following unexpected developments that have taken place in the meantime: (a) the arrest of a Japanese parliamentarian, Muneo Suzuki (in June 2002), whose activities in the Eurasian diplomatic gray zone have been among the main issues discussed in this chapter; (b) A failure of traditional diplomacy to prevent the outbreak of the war in Iraq (March 2003) and a subsequent urgency to depoliticize conflicting intercultural symbols while facilitating the post-Saddam reconciliation process in the field.

2. Dr. George Packard (a former U.S. intelligence officer turned diplomat, journalist, and scholar) in his private lecture to the members of the Asiatic Society of Japan (ASJ) and the International House (Tokyo, December 2002) offered new insights into the workings of gray zone diplomacy.

Packard served as a special assistant to John Kennedy's ambassador to Japan, Edwin O. Reischauer, during the height of the Cold War and growing anti-Americanism in Japan. He pointed out that Reischauer was born and educated in Japan, where his Austrian-born father worked as an American protestant missionary. Reischauer had first applied his prowess of navigating within the contradictory systems of cultural symbols as a young Lt. Colonel responsible for the intercultural training of U.S. Army officers during his World War II service. Later in his career these practical skills helped him to further his postwar field research and spot early signs of forthcoming major conflicts and forecast the global geopolitical changes, for example that nationalism would prevail over Communism in Asia (1956), that U.S.-occupied Okinawa should be re-turned to Japan (1962), and finally that weapons of mass destruction including germ warfare would be available to poor and backward nations in the twenty-first century (1973). Packard stressed that Reischauer's predictions that were based on his extensive field research through networking among the Japanese and non-Japanese operators in the diplomatic gray zone were frequently challenged by both scholarly and diplomatic critics during his lifetime. The 2003 Iraqi crisis, the growing tension on the divided Korean Peninsula, and the unsolved territorial issue between postcommunist Russia and Japan have proven Reischauer's projections to be correct (see Baker & Frost, 1992; Kaminski, 1982a, 1994a, 2001; Ogata, 2001; Vargo, 1992, 1997, 1998).

3. One of the most experienced operators in the Japanese diplomatic gray zone is a former U.S. Navy officer turned diplomat, Neal Henry Lawrence (see references). I have been extensively interviewing him since 1987. Lawrence's wartime and postwar experiences in Military Government (MG) in Okinawa and diplomacy, as well as my own anthropological research in Okinawa, Hokkaido, and Tokyo, provide complementary arguments for the necessity of developing a multiethnic field network of impartial individuals with access to the international policy makers directly from the field. It should be a cross-border network of people with diverse professional and religious experiences and willing to utilize their life experiences of cultural symbols for ethnic reconciliation and peacekeeping emergencies.

How gray zone diplomacy has been evolving in Japan (1945–2003) could be studied in depth by analyzing the extensive life experiences of its actors. Among the oldest and still influential field operators (I have been interacting with in the field 1987–2003) is a former business executive turned U.S. naval officer and diplomat in Japan, Rev. Dr. Neal Henry Lawrence (1908–). Lawrence participated in the 83-day Battle of Okinawa (assigned to Marines as a field officer in charge of refugees) in 1945. He then joined the U.S. Military Government as a chief fiscal officer and director of economic affairs. As early as September 17, 1945, Lawrence envisioned a native Ryukyuan administration and drafted a memorandum, Political and Economic Plan for Okinawa (see references). After completing his field mission in Okinawa (Lt. Commander, USNR), he became a foreign service officer in the Diplomatic Section of Gen. Douglas MacArthur's HQ (SCAP). Lawrence left the U.S. State Department after serving as director of USIS in Singapore, Malaya, and Taiwan and became a Benedictine monk (entered the priesthood, being ordained a Catholic priest in 1960). He then returned to Tokyo as a member of St. Anselm's Priory and reactivated his interest in the influential Asiatic Society of Japan (ASJ), which he had come to know in 1948 during his years in the diplomatic corps. Lawrence became ASJ vice president in 1978 (like Ambassador E. Reischauer's missionary father who served as ASJ vice president during the pre-wartime). Lawrence is Vice President Emeritus now. In this context, Lawrence has continued to interact with the Diplomatic Corps in Tokyo, Imperial family members (who are the ASJ patrons), as well as the leading Japanese opinion makers and multicultural academics who are ASJ members. His perspective as a monk has made him more sensitive to the importance of symbols in cross-cultural communication. Lawrence, in his interpretation of international affairs that he has witnessed as a member of the U.S. Navy, diplomat, and university professor, succeeded in integrating his past military and diplomatic insights (see references) with his more recent ecumenical focus on reconciliation through an active use of cross-cultural symbols. Although his activities in the Japanese diplomatic gray zone remain informal, his structural influence is comparable to an aged wise man in tribal society. Lawrence is a man who links the past with the present through his multigenerational and multicultural network of personal contacts with former and current leaders as well as their offspring. In contrast to the career diplomats who must follow their governments' directives in the field and exercise their roles within the protocolar limitations, Lawrence can freely reshape his roles utilizing his accumulated diplomatic and spiritual life experiences. His advanced age combined with his still sharp intellect and a prestige of the Order of the Rising Sun (bestowed by the Japanese emperor) enable him to function as an informal adviser to the frequently changing diplomatic operators, global opinion makers, and field researchers. His advice does not have a political but a spiritual clout. It has allowed Lawrence playing in the Japanese diplomatic gray zone a role similar to a tribal catalyst (see Kaminski, 1987; Okely, 1996; Seelye & Wasilewski, 1996).

4. The CRAA hosted by the Japanese government between January 21 and 22, 2002, was cochaired by Sadako Ogata. Professor Ogata, the Japanese scholar of international relations and the former head of UNHCR, was offered by PM Koizumi the foreign minister's post a few weeks after the conference, but she declined to take over the position from the dismissed Makiko Tanaka. (The official reason for Ogata's decline was her earlier international commitments as a Ford Fellow.) The dismissed Japanese foreign minister Makiko Tanaka had pointed out in an interview with a South Korean TV station in March 2002 that the Koizumi administration, like the former administrations, had continued to manipulate and influence foreign policy operations through secret funds. Tanaka's accusations were broadcast several months prior to the arrest of her main parliamentary adversary, Muneo Suzuki.

5. My main sources of information used in this chapter are based on the Japanese Foreign Ministry's internal investigations on Muneo Suzuki's illegal activities. Most of my information is based on public records and was disclosed in the Japanese Diet's debates in March 2002. For example, at Suzuki's insistence his informal meetings with Russian embassy intelligence official Smirnov were not formally or officially monitored by Japanese counterintelligence. (Compare the note on Col. Koshkin, another Russian diplomat and intelligence operative in Tokyo. He was actively involved in misinforming Japanese officials regarding the Northern Territories.)

6. Translation of the interviews with the Russian community leaders on Russian satellite TV as a broadcast program stated their genuine appreciation for Suzuki meeting medical care of individuals as well as delivering food for their communal festivities. At the same time, the Japanese internal investigation proved that the joint venture made with the two Nemuro contractors continued to provide donations to Suzuki's local support organization. (During the 1995–2000 period the two contractors donated over 9 million yen to Suzuki's Koen Kai.)

7. Foreign Ministry officials often accompanied Suzuki during his frequent overseas trips. Among them was Mr. S., a currently demoted official from the Foreign Ministry's Section of Intelligence Analysis. Mr. S. accompanied Suzuki in 19 of 36 overseas trips Suzuki made as a member of Parliament. The examination of the Japanese and Russian TV footage indicates that Mr. S. was present during Suzuki's meeting with President Yeltsin, as well as with President Putin. He also participated with Suzuki in the community rituals in the Northern Territories. Mr. S. and his colleague from the Foreign Ministry, Mr. M., were arrested after this chapter had already been submitted to the editor on March 31, 2002.

8. Translation from the work authored by Col. Koshkin and other Russian intelligence agents and published by the Polish Ministry of Defense–affiliated Bellona Press (2000, pp. 278–289). (Compare Grajewski, 1998; MacFarlane, 2001; Soloviev, 1999.)

9. The earlier mentioned interpreters did not appear on the TV footage screened by the NHK in 1999/2000. They were recorded on the video by the family members

attending the reunion with the then Polish minister of defense, Janusz Onyszkiewicz (see: Talas & Valki, 2000, p. 208). The video film was privately screened by Mr. K. for friends, including myself, upon his return to Japan. (Compare: Kaminski, 1994b; Kowalski, 1997, 1999; Kuczynski, 1998; Pilsudski, 1999.)

10. The structural position of a researcher and his extensive intercultural experiences are more important in the multiethnic field zone than his nationality or professional position (see Horne & Kaminski, 1981, pp. 2–5). In this particular case, I happened to be the anthropologist consulting the ministers from the field, but it could have been any other anthropologist conducting field research in a very different cultural context and consulting, for example, the UN or any other governmental or intergovernmental body involved in intercultural diplomacy and conflict resolution outside Eurasia. The regional language skills and simultaneous access to both the international policy makers and local opinion leaders in the field is of utmost importance to work in the diplomatic gray zone. A direct field access to the international satellite broadcast is also essential to verify and asses the short- and long-term impact of the mass media on the intercultural strategies to resolve the ethnic conflicts or prevent their escalation across cultural boundaries (see Kaminski, 1994b, 2001; Paletz & Schmid, 1992).

11. Lt. Col. Ulf Stenback (commanding officer, Swedish Armed Forces International Center, SWEDINT), reviewing the Nordic Countries in peacekeeping operations (PKOs), outlined the 30-year-long accomplishments of the Swedish Armed Forces in the UN PKO operations. He neither mentioned the rapidly changing ethnic composition of the Swedish army nor considered the operational potential of its culturally diverse force for UN PKO's emergencies. Asked by a field anthropologist how the Swedish army uses its multiethnic resources (25 percent of Swedes are of foreign origin), the officer pointed out the security risk of involving Swedish soldiers with a Serbo-Croat ethnic background during the PKO in former Yugoslavia (Stenback, 2002).

12. During my discussions with an international group of military and police officers and academics involved in international peace keeping operations who gathered in the United Nations University in Tokyo (October 22–24, 2001), I found out that there was a need among the group members to learn how cultural symbols could be used to de-escalate community tension during the day-to-day peacekeeping operations. Some field officers, who knew how to deal with land mines, wanted to know if the hidden cultural symbols that suddenly trigger community conflicts could be also activated and deactivated in similar ways. This indicates there is an urgent need among peacekeepers to have a direct, real-time access to a practical cross-cultural anthropological field expertise out in the field. We may therefore need to consider setting up highly mobile support structures like an impartial think tank in the emerging conflict zones and link them through the satellite videophones to both tribal and spiritual leaders as well as to the 24-hour situation center within the UN Secretariat. (Compare with notes on the Iraqi crisis.)

13. The early phase of the 2003 Iraqi Freedom provides examples of how even a slight misuse of symbols in the field by the advancing U.S. troops might undermine the coalition's credibility among the tribal Iraqi leaders and fuel global anti-American protests.

The U.S. Marines, who had risen an American flag in a southern Iraqi settlement, did it without understanding that they had simultaneously short-circuited cross-cultural communication at many symbolic levels. Their action seemed to have been guided by a spontaneous re-creation of the popular images depicted in many World

War II movies and enshrined in the war monument symbolizing the U.S. victory over the Japanese army. The 2003 incident might have remained an isolated case of cultural insensitivity if it had not been captured by a camera and therefore reported and recorded permanently globally. The 2003 image of the U.S. flag in Iraq that had entered our collective perception clashed with the 9/11 symbolic message of the miniature American flag pinned to the civilian clothes of the U.S. commander in chief (CC). Via global media network the image of the victorious American flag displayed by a few Marines in southern Iraq confused the ethnically divided Iraqi people as well as undermined pro-American sympathies among many tribal and spiritual leaders. For these Iraqi the message communicated a very different meaning: "This is not the war to liberate the Iraqi people, but to subdue us all by replacing OUR national symbol with an alien one." However brief it was, the display of the American flag by a few U.S. Marines has provoked the political opponents of Saddam Hussein's regime to resist the U.S.-led coalition as a cultural threat. The symbolic miscommunication that has continued to escalate in the field has magnified distrust toward the U.S. government's policy declaration on the global scale and in real time (see note 18).

14. My comparative field research on ethnic relations in Japan (1980–83, 1987–2002) confirmed that the frequent shifts in American and Japanese diplomacy toward China and Russia have been affecting choices of political loyalties among the multigenerational Korean families residing in Japan. The third generation of politically divided Korean families has been periodically readjusting its individual loyalties to the semilegal North and South Korean immigrant associations. This has not been caused by changes in their personal ideologies. It reflects personal economic strategies to counter the discriminatory Japanese employment and educational practices. It also expands and diversifies an extensive family's network and helps broaden personal alliances across ideological and state boundaries (Kaminski, 1982b, 1994a). The field research on the domestic cross-ethnic networking and its relations to the diplomatic gray zone has been neglected by the governmental policy study groups. Currently this is recognized as an important area of field research by independent Japanese think tanks (Kaminski, 1994b) and open for public debate on the opinion pages of mainstream media (Kaminski, 1994a, 2001).

The latest intercultural dynamics emerging in the Asian diplomatic gray zone were publicly debated by the North Asian Panel at the 2003 SIETAR Japan Conference ("Intercultural Communication: New Challenges: New Directions," Tokyo). The Japan-based American, Chinese, and Russian panelists pointed at the intercultural miscommunication as one of the factors behind the Japanese–Chinese diplomatic friction over the North Korean refugees and the failure of the Russo–Japanese diplomacy to agree on the peace treaty. The North Asian Panel's chairperson, Dr. Jacqueline Howell Wasilewski (ICU) concluded that the politically and economically motivated migrations should be also examined in a broader intercultural context, including a review of the growing number of tribal claims to the oil/gas rich lands. (See SIETAR [Society for Intercultural Education, Training & Research], www.sietarusa.org.)

15. This anthropological approach might be complementary to the recent academic expertise provided by the U.S. political scientist Steven K. Vogel of the University of California at Berkeley and Michael Green, director of Asian affairs at the National Security Council, as well as the works of Ambassador Lars Vargo of the Swedish Ministry for Foreign Affairs. A latest venture in simultaneously activating the diplomatic, journalistic, and scholarly networks to gather field information on crisis management and diplomacy in Japan (1999–2002) could be found in a team work conducted by Dr.

Cecilia Ruin-Ruthstrom (a Swedish scholar turned diplomat in Japan) and her journalist husband, Pahl Ruin. The authors focused in their concluding chapter ("A More Active Foreign Diplomacy," 2002, pp. 201–220) on Japan's post-9/11 diplomacy toward its neighbors and the use of foreign aid to advance Japan's foreign policy goals (212–215). In contrast to Packard and Reischauer, who used Japanese in their extensive field interaction, Ruin-Ruthstrom's field reporting on Japan in transition is based on the personal and printed information in English they have gathered in Japan.

The Ruin-Ruthstrom team reviewed the latest Okinawan protests against the U.S. bases and summarized the English language media's observations on the Japanese diplomacy turning more independent from the United States, first (217–219). Then they provided their own generalization in Swedish (my translation authorized by the authors):

> During the past decade the Japanese political leadership has shown again and again its inability to lead the country out of its prolonged economic crisis. As a result, the Japanese leadership continues to be preoccupied with the domestic policies and economic issues first, while the foreign policy agenda comes in second.

The Ruin-Ruthstrom team concluded their field report with the following recommendations:

> A more active foreign policy role would also demand from Japan to dare a little more: If one wants to play a real role on the international stage, one cannot continue being always subdued and reconciliatory. One should dare to undertake controversial initiatives, keep challenging other countries and express strong opinions. (2002, p. 220) ("Japan i brytningstid"/ "Japan in transition")

The authors, who had lived in the Swedish embassy compound in 1998–2002, had neither substantiated their conclusions, nor examined M. Suzuki's and Y. Mori's bold but covert initiatives in the diplomatic gray zone (2002, p. 143). The publication of their field report generated a debate in Swedish media about the relevance of a Japanese expertise based on secondary sources (Dagens Nyheter & Svenska Dagbladet, 2002). In contrast to Dr. Packard and Ambassador Reischauer, whose early Japanese language skills helped them to develop their personal information networks long before their diplomatic appointments in Japan, Dr. Ruin-Ruthstrom had to depend as much on her prescribed diplomatic role and access to interpreters as her journalist husband had been during his own prearranged interviews with the Japanese speakers of English. Subsequently, although the Ruin-Ruthstrom team's recent contributions to intercultural diplomacy are largely restricted to the well-organized summaries of their personal experience through the medium of English, Packard's and Reischauer's broad range of cross-cultural information gathering in Japan's diplomatic gray zone had resulted in the development of an alternative diplomacy and the accurate long-term global policy forecasts.

16. There is already an organizational structure in place that would allow incorporation of the idea of a Mobile Field Think Tank framework (MFTT) into the work of the UN Secretariat and to coordinate MFTT's activities with the PKO's field operation through the UN satellites. Dr. Hisako Shimura (a Japanese member of the Bramini Panel and a 24-year veteran in the UN's peacekeeping) pointed out in her analysis (Shimura, 2001, pp. 46–56) that the establishment of a 24-hour situation center within

the UN Secretariat has debureaucratized the management of the PKOs and harnessed more rapid decision making in the field.

Hisako Shimura states that the center's use of its computerized satellite communication (2002, pp. 52–53) allows it to find solutions and resolve urgent problems by taking action directly in the field. The decision-making process involving everyone along the UN's administrative levels to the UN Department of Peacekeeping Operations (DPKO), the secretary-general, and finally to the Security Council takes too much time. Shimura warns, "All too often, the process ends with a Security Council resolution or statement deploring the situation" (2001, p. 53). The internal divisions among the permanent members of the UN Security Council (UNSC) regarding the authorization of use of force against Saddam Hussein's government of Iraq in spring 2003 might have indicated already the future problems in the field. If these armchair conflicts migrate from UNSC into the field, the management of peace by the U.S.-led military administration and the Office of Reconstruction and Humanitarian Assistance (ORHA) in the ethnically and politically divided postwar Iraq could become unbearably complex. A too-rapid deployment of inadequately trained ORHA officers and multinational PKOs may destabilize the region further (MacFarlane, 2001).

17. Although there is a need for standardization of the PKO predeployment face-to-face classroom and distance training, it is also essential to follow them up with a flexible, interactive education directly in the field. The current UNITAR POCI online training programs could be updated and meet the new and emerging needs in the field that are identified by the UN Secretariat's 24-hour situation room (SR). The SR wireless Internet links and inexpensive digital camera technologies could be employed to make the learning process both personal and more effective (compare Langholtz, 2002; Leijenaar, 2002).

There is an urgent need to supply the ORHA and the UN's field personnel in Iraq with the pretrained Cross-Cultural Field Interpreters (CCFI) who are able to operate within multiple regional cultures and the UN Security Council simultaneously. The earlier experiences have shown that the pretraining for the PKOs from Japan and Bulgaria operating in Cambodia or for the Swedish and Turkish PKOs stationed in the former Yugoslavia had to be structured very differently because different combinations of cultural filters were involved. For example, my interviews with a Japanese female volunteer who had worked in Cambodia prove that there were already early indications of a growing cultural conflict between Bulgarian peacekeepers and the Asian females involved in the NGO activities. The conflict gradually broadened and involved Cambodian villagers. But at the time there was no UN structure in place to forward these early warning signals from a Japanese NGO volunteer to a cross-cultural field interpreter, nor was there a way to deescalate the tension with the help of mobile field think tanks. The conflicting cultural ideas about the management of gender relations between Asian women and European peacekeepers clashed at symbolic level first. Then it escalated into the issue of the native territorial and clan duties to protect single village women from cultural strangers. Finally, it ended in a mass execution of Bulgarian soldiers by the Cambodian men (compare Akashi, 2001; Sanderson, 2001).

18. Zbigniew Brzezinski, reviewing the impact of the Iraqi Freedom's military campaign on the U.S. diplomacy, pointed out (April 2003) that the Pentagon's strategists had de facto replaced the State Department's diplomats as global foreign policy makers: "The State Department doesn't like the fact that the Defense Department takes the lead strategically, but it hasn't really formulated some alternative concept of how American

foreign policy should be conducted. And that is weakness." Iraqi Freedom confirmed that the military strategists are not always in charge of the events broadcast live from the field. Subsequently the contradictory messages broadcast by the embedded journalists have magnified distrust toward the U.S. government's policy declaration on the global scale and in the real time. The April 9, 2003, worldwide satellite TV broadcast live from Baghdad of a U.S. soldier mounting Saddam's statue before it fell and covering its face with a U.S. flag had short-circuited intercultural communication at all levels again. The pro-U.S. Iraqi exiles who guest commented on the BBC World TV (transmitted live to Tokyo) have continued to condemn the U.S. soldier's action as a symbol of cultural arrogance. The U.S. flag (for these BBC Iraqi guest commentators) portrayed a potent symbol of an upcoming U.S. cultural and military dominance of the Arab world, rather than a just a symbol of Iraq's liberation from Saddam's dictatorship. Even though the American flag was removed minutes later and replaced by an Iraqi national emblem, the misuse of symbols in the field was broadcast worldwide already. U.S. Defense Secretary Donald Rumsfeld, who seemed to have misread the interplay of the conflicting symbolic messages embedded in a display and the removal of the U.S. flag in Baghdad, later in his Pentagon briefing referred to the events of toppling Saddam's statue in Baghdad as "watching them is like seeing the collapse of the Berlin Wall." For many global TV viewers who had witnessed both events through the live broadcasts already, the Berlin Wall's symbol of peaceful power transition carried an opposite meaning to the militarily imposed symbol in Baghdad. Subsequently, the Pentagon's briefing magnified globally the already conflicting symbolic messages.

This may make a post-Saddam regional reconciliation even more complex at the intercultural level. The all-too-familiar cultural symbols exposed through a global satellite communication network showed how regional warfare may be fought in the future. It is fought in real and virtual fields simultaneously. An instant wireless access to globalized communication technology by anyone and everyone would make it almost impossible to contain the spread of globalized cultural clashes by a sheer military force. The clash has and will have true global consequences. This will in turn require an alternative foreign policy scenario from the U.S. State Department and a different strategic approach to global diplomacy and security than the one the U.S Department of Defense used during the Iraqi crisis. Brzezinski, commenting on the long-term consequences of the fall of Baghdad, used John McLaughlin's "One on One" TV program (April 2003) to caution against the prolonged rivalry between the two U.S. departments: "The Defense Department should wage war if necessary and defend our security; the State Department should make foreign policy" (compare Brundtland, 2001; Brzezinski, 1972; Ritter, 1999).

REFERENCES

Akashi, Yasushi. "The Politics of UN Peacekeeping from Cambodia to Yugoslavia." In *United Nations Peacekeeping Operations: Ad Hoc Missions, Permanent Engagement*, edited by Albrecht Schnabel and Ramesh Thakur, 149–154. Tokyo: United Nations University Press, 2001.

Baker, Howard H., and Ellen L. Frost. "Rescuing the U.S.–Japan Alliance." *Foreign Affairs* (Spring 1992): 97–113.

Brundtland, Harlem Gro. "Preparing for the Worst: Can We Give Hope to Victims in Complex Emergencies?" Presented at the Fridtjof Nansen Memorial Lecture 2001, United Nations University, Tokyo, December 2001.

Brzezinski, Zbigniew. "The Fragile Blossom: Crisis and Change in Japan." Harper & Row, New York, 1972.

Grajewski, Andrzej. *Tarcza i Miecz: Rosyjskie Sluzby Specjalne 1991–1998*. Warszawa: Biblioteka Wiezi, 1998 (in Polish).

Horne, Mary, and Ignacy Marek Kaminski. "Guests Scholars. Insiders or Outsiders? A Polyocular Approach." *Center News—Japanese Studies Center, The Japan Foundation* 6:3 (1981): 2–5 (in English).

Kaminski, Ignacy Marek. "Application of Ethnography of Law and Political Anthropology." In *Shakai jinruigaku nempo*, edited by Jiro Suzuke, 1–29. Tokyo: Tokyo Metropolitan University & Kobundo Press, 1982 (in Japanese).

Kaminski, Ignacy Marek. "Are Think Tanks Redefining Themselves?" *NIRA Review: National Institute for Research Advancement (NIRA)* (1994a): 26–30 (in English).

Kaminski, Ignacy Marek. "The Dilemma of Power: Internal and External Leadership." In *The Other Nomads: Peripatetic Minorities in Cross-Cultural Perspective*, edited by A. Rao, 323–56. Bohlau Verlag: Koln Wien, 1987 (in English).

Kaminski, Ignacy Marek. "Eurasian Sister-Relationship: The Key to Regional Cooperation?" *NIRA Review: National Institute for Research Advancement (NIRA)* (1993): 23–24 (in English).

Kaminski, Ignacy Marek. "Global Views." *Mainichi Shimbun*, 8 September 2001 (in Japanese).

Kaminski, Ignacy Marek. "Japan: From External to Internal Internationalisation." *Invandrare och minoriteter—Scandinavian Migration and Minority Review*, Nr 5(1982): 1–9 (in Swedish).

Kaminski, Ignacy Marek. "What Poland Needs from Japan." *The Japan Times*, 4 December 1994b, 19 (in English).

Koshkin, Nilokay P. "Tokio." In *Przewodnik KGB po miastach swiata*, edited by Dom Wydawniczy, 245–80. Warsaw: BELLONA, 2001 (in Polish).

Kowalski, Witold. "B. Pilsudski's Fault." In *IZVIESTIYA—Insituta naslediya Bronislava Pilsudkogo*. Yuszhno-Sakhalinsk (1999), 89–104 (in Russian).

Kowalski, Witold. *Genealogiczna baza danych rodu Billewiczow (Computer-based family tree of the Billewicz-Pilsudski Family)*. London, 1997 (in Polish/English).

Kuczynski, Antoni. "Katorznik i zeslaniec na tronie nauki." In *Zeslaniec—nr* (section on Bronislaw Pilsudski's life, 91–108). Warsaw: Zarzad Glowny Zwiazku Sybirakow, 1998 (in Polish).

Langholtz, Harvey. "Distance Training in Peacekeeping for Military, Civilians and Police." In *Reforming UN Peace Operations: New Challenge for Peacekeeping Training*, edited by Monica Blagescu and Albrecht Schnabel, 130–7. Tokyo: United Nations University Press (UNU), 2002.

Lawrence, Neal Henry. "Kurusu Saburo—Diplomat and Man." *The Transaction of the Asiatic Society of Japan (ASJ)* 16(1981).

Lawrence, Neal Henry. Memorandum to a Deputy Commander from Ascom I, Military Government Headquarters (Fiscal Department). "Subject: Political and Economic Plan for Okinawa." September 17, 1945. Records: Hoover Institute, Stanford University. (Papers of James T. Watkins IV.)

Lawrence, Neal Henry. "Okinawa: Battle & Regeneration." *The Transaction of the Asiatic Society of Japan (ASJ)* 12(1997).

Lawrence, Neal Henry. "The Unforgettable Alice J. Kurusu." *The Transaction of the Asiatic Society of Japan (ASJ)* 15(2000): 19–31.

Leijenaar, Annette. "UNDPKO's Training Initiatives." In *Reforming UN Peace Operations: New Challenge for Peacekeeping Training*, edited by Monica Blagescu and Albrecht Schnabel, 119–24. Tokyo: United Nations University Press (UNU), 2002.

MacFarlane, Neil S. "Regional Peacekeeping in the CIS." In *United Nations Peacekeeping Operations: Ad Hoc Missions, Permanent Engagement*, edited by Albrecht Schnabel and Ramesh Thakur, 77–99. Tokyo: The United Nations University Press, 2001.

Ogata, Sadako. "State Security—Human Security." Presented at the Fridtjof Nansen Memorial Lecture 2001, The United Nations University, Tokyo, 12 December 2001.

Okely, Judith. *Own or Other Culture*. London: Routledge, 1996.

Packard, George R. "Edwin O. Reischauer: Historian, Missionary, Prophet." Lecture at the International House of Japan, Tokyo, 9 December 2002. (Summary published by The Asiatic Society of Japan, *ASJ Bulletin* 1 (January 2003):4–6.

Paletz, David L., and Alex P. Schmid, eds. *Terrorism and the Media*. London: Sage Publications, 1992.

Pilsudski, Bronislaw. "Diary 1882." *IZVIESTIYA—Insituta naslediya Bronislava Pilsudkogo* 3(1999):105–33 (in Russian).

Ritter, Scott. *Endgame: Solving the Iraq Crisis*. New York: Simon & Schuster, 1999.

Ruin, Pahl, and Cecilia Ruin-Ruthstrom. *Japan i brytningstid* (Japan in transition). Stockholm: Atlas, 2002 (in Swedish).

Sanderson, John. "The Cambodian Experience: A Success Story Still?" In *United Nations Peacekeeping Operations: Ad Hoc Missions, Permanent Engagement*, edited by Albrecht Schnabel and Ramesh Thakur, 155–66. Tokyo: The United Nations University Press, 2001.

Seelye, H. Ned, and Jacqueline Howell Wasilewski. *Between Cultures. Developing Self-Identity in a World of Diversity*. Chicago: NTC Business Books, 1996.

Shimura, Hisako. "The Role of the UN Secretariat in Organizing Peacekeeping." In *United Nations Peacekeeping Operations: Ad Hoc Missions, Permanent Engagement*, edited by Albrecht Schnabel and Ramesh Thakur, 45–56. Tokyo: The United Nations University Press, 2001.

SIETAR 18th Japan Conference "Intercultural Communication: New Challenges: New Directions." *North Asian Panel: Jacqueline Howell Wasilewski, Zeng Wei, Elena Kozoulina* Society for Intercultural Education, Training and Research (SIETAR). Showa Women's University, June 28–29, Tokyo. <office@sietar-japan.org>

Soloviev, N. V. "Gas/Oil Industry and the Sakhalin Aboriginals." In *IZVIESTIYA—Insituta naslediya Bronislava Pilsudkogo* (1999): 208–9 (in Russian).

Stenback, Ulf. "Challenges of Training Peacekeepers in Europe: The Nordic Experience." In *Reforming UN Peace Operations: New Challenge for Peacekeeping Training*, edited by Monica Blagescu and Albrecht Schnabel, 81–83.Tokyo: United Nations University (UNU), 2002.

Swedish Ministry for Foreign Affairs. *Framtid med Asien. Forslag till en svensk Asienstrategi*. Stockholm: Fritzes Offentliga Publikationer, 1998 (in Swedish).

Talas, Peter, and Laszlo Valki. "The New Entrants: Hungary, Poland, and the Czech Republic." In *Kosovo and the Challenge of Humanitarian Intervention: Selective Indignation, Collective Action, and International Citizenship*, edited by Albrecht Schnabel and Ramesh Thakur, 201–12. Tokyo: United Nations University Press, 2000.

Vargo, Lars. *Den falska stillheten—Japan Da och Nu*. Stockholm: Carlsson Bokforlag, 1992 (in Swedish).

Vargo, Lars. *Den Ostra Huvudstaden—Tokyo*. Stockholm: Carlsson Bokforlag, 1998 (in Swedish).

Vargo, Lars. *Japan infor sekelskiftet*. Asienstudier Nr.11/1998 Arbetsgruppen for en svensk Asienstrategi. Stockholm: Utrikesdepartementet (Ministry for Foreign Affairs), 1998 (in Swedish).

Vargo, Lars. *Japansk organisationskultur*. Stockholm: Carlsson Bokforlag, 1997 (in Swedish).

11

Toward Conflict Transformation in the Democratic Republic of the Congo with Specific Reference to the Model of Kumar Rupesinghe

Hussein Solomon and Kwezi Mngqibisa

INTRODUCTION

From Algeria to Angola, from Sierra Leone to Somalia, violent conflict characterizes several African societies. These reinforce the picture of Africa being crisis prone. The images brought to one's living room of starving Sudanese or Rwandan refugees, thanks to CNN, simply reinforce this negative image of Africa. These images, transmitted throughout the world, then warn potential foreign investors of the risks of doing business on a continent characterized by such turbulence. This, then, results in foreign direct investments being channeled to less-volatile regions, resulting in Africa's greater economic impoverishment. From this, violent social agitation and greater political instability results. In order to break this vicious circle, it is imperative that peace researchers understand the root causes and trajectories of conflict in order to understand when and how to intervene in a conflict to achieve a successful resolution. This is precisely what this chapter seeks to accomplish by making use of the Democratic Republic of Congo (DRC) as a case study toward conflict transformation: from violent conflict to peaceful competition.

There are several factors that make the case study of the DRC quite interesting and informative from the perspective of peace studies scholars. First, the conflict in the DRC has both internal and external dimensions—it is both interstate and intrastate. Second, this is a multifaceted problem, which reflects in a microcosm all of the current maladies currently adversely affecting the African continent. Inside its borders there is corruption, ethnic conflict, poor governance, lack of a human rights culture, economic underdevelopment, and a deteriorating physical environment. Moreover, in the DRC, several attempts had been made by a variety of local, regional, and international role players to resolve the conflict—to no avail. It is very important to assess why such intervention efforts have failed and what lessons we as scholars and practitioners could learn from this to enhance Africa's conflict resolution skills so that the renewal of our continent becomes a reality.

A BRIEF NARRATIVE ON THE ORIGINS, NATURE, AND TRAJECTORY OF THE CONFLICT IN THE DRC

The Republic of Congo was changed to Zaire in 1965, almost five years after the former colony of Belgium was granted independence. Mobutu Sese Seko, who had become the president of the republic, would become the sole political player in the country for approximately 32 years. Through immense centralization of power, President Mobutu ensured, by all means, that his Popular Movement of the Revolution (MPR) was the only legal party in the country. In conformity with a dominant trend in Africa, membership of the party ensured that the system of clientelism determined the allocation and redistribution of resources in the country. This went against the grain of the existence of political opposition in the country.

The country was accorded top priority by the West due to its natural resources and regional positioning within the context of the Cold War, consequently allowing Mobutu to assume the status of an untouchable.

The politics of the country became the president's personal domain, as excesses politically and economically proved to be his speciality. Nepotism and kleptocracy ruled this Central African behemoth. Political opponents were harshly dealt with, resulting in the institutionalized abuse of political power. In the process, Zairian civil society was the biggest loser, as it was continuously marginalized from political processes through naked violence of the repressive state's security apparatus.

Attempts to highlight the suffering of the country's terrorized masses fell on deaf ears, as the international community had its own strategic considerations to contend with in an era of global bipolarity. This left Mobutu's kingdom intact at the expense of the country's socioeconomic and political system. Through increased "aid" assistance, the president managed to accord the military his undivided financial attention and therefore elevate the army into a class of its own. In return for the president's budgetary altruism, the army became a partisan tool with which to crush internal dissent from any quarter of Zairian society.

The Rwandan genocide of 1994 and the subsequent coming to power of the Rwandan Patriotic Front channeled into Zaire an estimated one million refugees, among them the Interahamwe,[1] who were organizing in and around refugee camps the attacks into Rwanda. The refugees were supported by Mobutu, who had had close relations with the deposed Kigali regime. The activities of the Interahamwe prompted the Banyamulenge, who are Congolese Tutsi, to take up arms in a bid to protect themselves in the face of the threat posed to them by the presence of the Interahamwe. This move was supported by Rwanda and Uganda and was supplemented with the creation of the Alliance of Democratic Forces for the Liberation of Congo-Zaire (ADFL), led by Laurent Kabila.

The emergence of Kabila and the rebel movement as saviors of the situation gave the uprising an internal outlook aimed at ridding Zaire of Mobutu. On the march to Kinshasa, supported by Rwanda, Uganda, and later by Angola, Kabila endeared himself to the Congolese as he introduced popular forms of governance.

On May 17, 1997, Laurent Kabila assumed control of the government when he entered Kinshasa without resistance. This was after Mobutu had fled the capital, having ceded power and leaving his followers to fend for themselves. In his bid to transform himself from guerrilla commander to national leader, Kabila changed the name of the country to the Democratic Republic of Congo and banned all political activity with the promise of elections in two years.

But the promise of elections proved to be just a mirage in the desert of autocracy. Opposition to Kabila's undemocratic impulses earned various individuals banning and reprimands. For instance, Kabila arrested and banished Etienne Tshisekedi and other politicians who were not on his side. The feeling among observers and most involved in the political process was that Kabila was systematically excluding all those who did not march with him.

When Kabila took power, he rewarded his allies with senior administrative positions in return for their loyalty. Among these were the Congolese Tutsi. The elevation of the minority Tutsi was despised by the Congolese, creating a situation to be exploited by Kabila. Responding to plummeting popularity as a result of failure to guide the country to political pluralism, Kabila ordered the expulsion of all foreign forces from the DRC. He shuffled government positions by putting in place old friends and coopting prominent politicians from opposition parties while at the same time marginalizing the Banyamulenge Tutsis. Despite all these attempts, there was still popular resistance to Kabila, coming from opposition parties, former Mobutuists, and civil society at large.

The removal of foreign troops by Kinshasa from DRC soil was not accepted by Kigali and Kampala, who believed that their national borders were only secured by their presence in the DRC. The Congolese Tutsis or Banyamulenge, meanwhile, felt that the presence of these foreign troops was their only guarantee against their continued persecution in the DRC and were against their withdrawal. On August 2, 1998, these then lifted the flag of armed rebellion against Kabila's Kinshasa. They were soon joined by other Congolese militias exasperated by Kabila's new order. This new rebellion was supported by Kigali and Kampala on what they perceived to be the best way to secure their own security interests.

Refusing to accept the internal dynamics of the rebellion, Kabila denounced it as foreign aggression purportedly by Rwanda and Uganda and therefore a

Tutsi invasion. On July 10, 1999, in Lusaka, countries[2] party to the conflict signed a peace agreement outlining the cessation of hostilities, demobilization, disarmament and peacekeeping arrangements, and democratization processes for the DRC, among other things. What was amazing was the exclusion of the rebels from the talks. The rebel groups signed the agreement on August 31, 1999, after much pressure and faced the challenge of a split in one of the major groups, the Congolese Rally for Democracy (RCD).

THEORETICAL FRAMEWORK

It has often been said that theory is a construct that assists us in selecting and interpreting facts. In this sense, theory is intensely practical. In this way, a study of conflict resolution efforts in the DRC will be of little practical utility unless this was contextualized within a broader theoretical framework that would assist us in determining the strengths and weaknesses of specific intervention efforts and allow us to draw conclusions that would have a wider applicability than the case study at hand.

Although theory is invaluable to deepen our understanding, it is also true that theoretical paradigms are often too fragmented or too rigid in their formulation to adequately interpret the many conflicts plaguing the global strategic landscape. A good example of this fragmentation occurs in Stephen Ryan's[3] work.

Peacebuilding is the strategy which most directly tries to reverse those destructive processes that accompany violence. . . . This involves a shift of focus away from the warriors with whom peace-keepers are mainly concerned, to the attitudes and socio-economic circumstances of ordinary people. Therefore it tends to concentrate on the context of the conflict rather than on the issues which divide the parties.

Such dichotomies between peacekeeping and peace building, between warriors and ordinary people, between symptoms and causes are obviously false. The truth is that at this current period in Africa where one sees a move away from professional soldiers to private militias, the distinction between *warrior* and *citizen* becomes increasingly blurred as Rwanda's Interahamwe militia could illustrate. Similarly in times of war, it is equally imperative to deal with the issues that divide the party as well as the causes and context of the conflict. At such times, both these areas need to be addressed concurrently. Clearly a more holistic model for conflict transformation is necessary.

Other models tend to be too rigid for the purpose of explaining and designing initiatives for managing conflicts. One such model has been Michael Lund's strategy for preventive diplomacy,[4] which seeks to situate preventive diplomacy within the conflict spectrum. Such a theory is useful in mapping preventive diplomacy initiatives in a given conflict environment. However, Lund is far more ambitious than this—because he advocates the use of specific preventive diplomacy initiatives to suit a particular stage in the conflict cycle, which he then proceeds to map out. The effect of this theory is that it assumes that the cycle will constantly move in a predictable way, and therefore preventive diplomacy initiatives would have to follow suit. This is not the sequence of events in real life, and using this model for the purposes of designing an intervention to manage a conflict can have limited success as issues will be dealt with in compartments ignoring the complicated cross influences. Clearly what is needed is a theoretical model that is generic enough to be broadly applicable to most conflict types.

For the purposes of this chapter, the conflict transformation model of Kumar Rupesinghe[5] will be employed. Several reasons may be put forward to justify the utility of such a model in the comparative study of conflict and conflict resolution attempts in the DRC. In the first place, unlike conflict resolution models, which cannot escape the label "Made in the West" and a product of the Cold War's emphasis on interstate rivalry; Rupesinghe's model lays its stress on internal conflicts and, as such, is more user friendly in a post–Cold War Third World environment, where such intrastate conflicts are the norm.

Second, because of the multidimensionality of protracted social conflicts plaguing much of Africa, Rupesinghe[6] emphasizes the need for an "understanding of non-linear peace-building processes. Because of the complexity of many existing and emerging conflicts, a multi-sectoral [sic] approach to conflict transformation is needed." This multisectoral approach is a far more holistic approach to conflict transformation and, as such, allows it to be far more flexible in application than most conventional models, which tend to be rigid, resulting in a gap between theory and reality. This gap between words and actions adversely affects the quality of research findings. This is an issue that Rupesinghe[7] knows full well, for he notes,

[w]e can speak of conflict processes—conflict transformation, conflict endurance and stagnation, and conflict transformation and renewal. . . . However, as with human existence, conflict development is also not solely linear and does not lend itself to neat compartmentalisation; it is rather a multi-dimensional, multi-faceted process.

Third and finally, Rupesinghe's multisectoral approach also stresses that the number of actors involved in the peaceful transformation of a conflict needs to be increased to reflect all constituencies of broader society. This is an absolutely crucial point, as we shall shortly see in the case of the DRC. Several factors account for this.

First, all constituencies of society have a stake in peace, and the peace process needs to be owned by them if it is to succeed.

Second, it is these constituencies that would be playing a key role in postconflict reconstruction. This is an important point if one considers Rupesinghe's refrain that the peaceful transfer of power is not meaningful transformation. Meaningful transformation also includes sustainable structural and attitudinal changes within broader society and the emergence of new institutions to address outstanding issues.[8]

Third, the involvement of nonstate actors is also vital in situations of intrastate conflicts in the south, where the state cannot play the role of nonpartisan broker because the state is often a party to the conflict.

Finally, the inclusion of nonstate actors also reflects a broader theoretical point that ultimately issues of peace and security revolve around people as opposed to states. In a nutshell, the conflict transformation model of Rupesinghe[9] argues that " . . . coming to an agreement on outstanding issues is of secondary importance to addressing the overall conflict process and coming to terms with the temporal aspects of conflict." The conflict transformation model of Rupesinghe has several component parts. These are:

- Prenegotiation stage
- Understanding root causes
- Ownership of the peace process
- Identifying all the actors
- Identifying facilitators
- Setting a realistic timetable
- Sustaining the effort
- Evaluating success and failure
- Strategic constituencies
- The role of outside peacemakers
- The role of local peacemakers

What follows in the next section is an analysis of the Democratic Republic of the Congo's conflict resolution processes in relation to each of the components of the model as elucidated earlier.

Prenegotiation Stage

According to Rupesinghe, the aim of this stage is to bring conflicting parties into the negotiation process with the purpose of

"the outlining of a logistical framework and timeframe for negotiations, and the setting of ambitious, yet realistic, goals for each stage of initial negotiations. The "strategic intent" of the pre-negotiation phase is to reduce intractability, to formulate and design a process that can bring parties to the negotiating table and to begin the trust and confidence-building necessary for a successful negotiating exercise.[10]

An important point to assess the success of the prenegotiation stage (and, indeed, the entire negotiation process) is why conflicting parties come to the negotiation table. Do they really want to peacefully resolve their conflict (reduce intractability) or is it just a tactical maneuver to buy time to pursue the military option by allowing one's forces to be regrouped and resupplied?

What is clear from the various failed mediation efforts thus far is that the belligerents were clearly not serious about reducing intractability. The strategies adopted by the parties to the conflict have been to make use of the negotiations process to compete for international recognition of the legitimacy of their views in the conflict. Contrary to the conviction of the need for peace, they have utilized peace efforts, and the resultant lulls in the fighting, to prepare for their next military offensive. Consider the following: On August 7, only five days after the August 2, 1998, radio broadcast of the rebellion against Kabila, a summit at Victoria Falls in Zimbabwe was called with the aim to find a solution to the conflict. After this summit, many meetings and summits at state level, regional level, and in international forums were convened to find a solution to the DRC conflict. Kabila or his envoys attended these meetings with the aim to salvage support for his cause of ending "external" aggression supported by Uganda and Rwanda on DRC soil. On the other hand, the rebels, as nonstate actors, had no direct voice in interstate meetings and forums and used this as an excuse to prolong their military escapade.

The major area of contention with the signing of the agreement was the preparation for the national dialogue that was supposed to spell out steps toward democratization in that country. The national debate has been delayed by numerous cease-fire agreement violations of different proportions reported by all sides. A prominent excuse cited by parties as to the continued delay has been the procrastination of the forthcoming United Nations peacekeeping/enforcement deployment. This has given a confusing message that gives an impression that the parties will continue to violate the agreement until a UN deployment takes place and only then can progress be expected as far as preparations for the national debate are concerned.

Rupesinghe points out that it is important to understand the motivations of the parties in entering the negotiations. In greater part, the belligerents have been forced to the negotiation table by the international community, their respective country sponsors, and by a de facto military stalemate. It needs hardly to be mentioned that this is an inadequate basis for sustainable peace. Supposing that the military balance shifts in favor of one party, would this not result in that party being encouraged to secure gains on the battlefield rather than around the negotiations table?

Understanding Root Causes

Rupesinghe[11] notes that it is abundantly clear from recent experiences in Somalia and the former Yugoslavia that there is a tremendous need for a thorough understanding of the root causes of a given conflict. It stands to reason that any successful intervention is premised on knowledge of how and why the conflict started in the first place. Addressing the sources that generated the conflict would then form the basis of the resolution to the conflict.

The current crisis plaguing Kabila's Congo relates to both internal and external dimensions. Internally, Kabila's exclusion of political players and continued disregard of basic democratic principles lies at the root of the current crisis. Externally, his fallout with former allies who are neighbors with a keen interest in the end-state of the DRC gave momentum to the rebellion. The souring of relations with former allies has been precipitated by his inability or unwillingness to ensure the border security of his neighbors.

The resolution of the DRC conflict, therefore, lies in addressing these internal dynamics, meaning the democratization of the society. One dimension of this is to find a solution to the ethnic relations in the country. The question of the Congolese Tutsi and how they relate with the other groups as far as political accommodation is concerned needs to be addressed in a manner that would ensure that all feel secure. Certainly, the need to cultivate democratic principles of government would assist in finding ways of achieving this. But the need for democratic principles also needs to be activated in relation to other, political, entities such as your Etienne Tshisikedis and your Kengo wa Dondos.[12] But this is not all. Experience has indicated that democratic governance in the absence of effective governance is useless. This means that the government has to work for its citizens—from providing homes and running water to protection against the mugger in the dark alley. This would be an essential element in securing postconflict reconstruction and sustainable peace, and the international community would need to play a key role after decades of misrule.

Furthermore, the regional security concerns of the countries involved need to be addressed. The problem of the DRC serving as a launching pad for rebel movements of neighboring countries needs to be rectified to negate the need of those countries affected venturing onto its territory by means of forward defense. Finding a solution to the rebel problem is, however, not easy because it extends to the examination of how political accommodation is exercised by the DRC's neighbors. If we are committed to finding solutions to the problem of rebel groups violating the territorial integrity of other countries, we are compelled to identify the sources of their discontent in their countries of origin.

Ownership of the Peace Process

According to Rupesinghe,[13] the sustainability of the peace process is also dependent on the "empowerment of local actors so that they become the primary architects, owners and long-term stakeholders in the peace process." International pressure, Rupesinghe notes, is not applicable in many intrastate conflicts plaguing the world today. Even when successful, such imposed settlements merely serve to postpone the conflict, as there is little internal support, and root causes of the conflict are not addressed.

After about a month of Kabila's ascendance to power, nongovernmental organizations, through a conference, were the first to sound warning bells of his government. Just like opposition parties, their main concern was centered on the political route Kabila seemed to be embarking on, especially regarding infringements of civil rights and the lack of a culture of political pluralism.

Diplomatic efforts to end the DRC conflict have had very little input from civil society, as international, regional, and bilateral efforts were largely state-centric in approach. However, the recent Lusaka cease-fire agreement gives equal status to all participants in the national dialogue that allows participation by *forces vives*. It is essential that the international community supports and empowers these local actors with financial support and the requisite technical skills to empower them to assist in the democratic reconstruction of the Congolese state. The international community must also ensure that the democratic space is maintained to allow these to continue with their efforts of peace and development. These local actors may well hold the key for long-term peace and security in the DRC.

Identifying All the Actors

Rupesinghe stresses the importance of identifying all actors (big and small) and bringing them to the negotiating table. Failure to do so could result in their alienation from the peace process, and as was experienced in Somalia and the former Yugoslavia, this could scuttle the entire negotiations. Some of the actors in the DRC process are listed following.

Laurent Kabila, the president of the DRC, is one of the main actors to the conflict. After severing ties with the AFDL that brought him to power, he expresses his will through government power in proportions comparable to Mobutu.

On August 1, 1998, a collective meeting of opponents of the DRC government created a coalition called the *Congolese Rally for Democracy (RCD)*. The coalition was made up of former Mobutuists, former opponents of Mobutu, former AFDL members, academics, and others who were anti-Kabila. The collective, led by Ernest Wamba dia Wamba, was made up of groups with different political backgrounds and interests that were conflicting and contradictory. Both Uganda and Rwanda supported this collective financially and militarily. After some extensive internal discord and acrimonious exchanges, the RCD split in two factions: one led by *Dr. Emile Ilunga* and the other by *Professor Wamba dia Wamba.*

The *Movement for the Liberation of Congo (MLC)*, led by Jean-Pierre Bemba, is another major player in the DRC conflict. This group started operations against the government of Kabila in November approximately two months after the start of the rebellion in August. This rebel group, supported by Uganda, started its contribution to the rebellion by capturing towns within the Equateur province. It is widely believed that the support given by Uganda to this movement is due to disillusionment with certain elements in the RCD coalition. After two months of the rebellion, Kampala calculated that the peace in the DRC required mass support, and the RCD had failed to achieve that.

Rwanda was first involved in the DRC conflict in 1996 with the sponsoring of the formation of the Alliance of Democratic Forces for the Liberation of Congo-Zaire (ADFL). The reason for the formation of this alliance, which had its origins in Kigali, was to give a voice to the Congolese in toppling Mobutu, who was harboring Hutu exiles who were using the North Kivu region as a launching pad into Rwanda and persecuting the Tutsi population there. The alliance was led by Laurent Kabila, who later became president. In an attempt to consolidate his power within the DRC, Kabila was forced to reduce the visible influence of Tutsis in positions of authority, especially in the military. This, in the opinion of Kigali, reduced the ability of Rwanda to satisfactorily police the activities of Hutu extremists in the DRC, and this led to him losing popularity in their quarters. Furthermore, Rwanda decided to support the rebellion against Kabila when it was established that he had integrated Hutu extremists into the newly formed Armed Forces of Congo (FAC).

There are other countries that are indirectly or minimally involved in the DRC, such as *Sudan* and *Chad*. Sudan is also part of the alliance that is supporting Kabila in the fight against Uganda and Rwanda. Sudan's motivation to get involved, it seems, relates to fears on its part relating to Uganda's support of John Garang's Sudanese Peoples' Liberation Army (SPLA) and that should Uganda control a significant portion of DRC territory then the SPLA could use this to launch a new front against Khartoum. Chad, on the other half, was receptive to appeals by Kabila to Francophone countries to help his government.

The relationship between Kabila and *Angola's* president Dos Santos is rooted in the support the latter gave the former on his march to Kinshasa. Angola also continues to support Kabila with the aim to curb the use of the DRC by the National Union for the Total Independence of Angola (UNITA) as a rear base and a conduit for supplies and illicit diamond trafficking. Continued support for Kabila's government against the rebels came naturally, with Kabila showing serious commitment to keeping his side of the bargain: adopting a hostile stance to the presence of UNITA on his territory. Thus Angola's support for Kabila was informed by the potential dangers of having a UNITA-friendly incumbent in Kinshasa.

Uganda's involvement in the DRC dates back to its support of the ADFL in its march against Mobutu. The main motivation for the support was the strategic consideration around the northern and eastern part of the DRC. Kampala was in favor of a government in Kinshasa that would stabilize the two regions and stamp out the activities of Ugandan rebel groups. The region was being used by the Allied Democratic Forces, West Nile Bank Front, and the Lords Resistance Army as launching pads to stage attacks into Uganda. During the ADFL and its allies' march to Kinshasa, the objective was achieved with the temporary forced removal of the rebels. When Kabila took over power, he paid little attention to the concerns of Uganda, and reports of fresh activities in the region by Ugandan rebels were recorded. In response to Kabila's failure to stabilize the region and growing unpopularity, Uganda sponsored the creation of the rebel movement aimed at unseating him.

The *Southern African Development Community (SADC)* coalition made up of *Zimbabwe,* Angola, and *Namibia* joined the DRC conflict when the organization was invited to do so by Kabila. The DRC had just joined the regional organization, and it was one of Kabila's targets to solicit support for his government under siege. The organization, having learned hard lessons from Lesotho, decided in 1997 in a summit to pledge itself to protect and support member governments from armed rebellion and promote peaceful engagement with all actors. It was on these grounds that this coalition involved itself in the conflict, although some commentators cite personal reasons.[14]

Other internal actors such as the various Congolese political parties also need to be brought into any peace process. The Union for Democracy and Social Progress (UDPS) is the best-known party in the DRC conflict, with its involvement dating back to moderate opposition to Mobutu and later to Kabila. Its leader is Etienne Tshisekedi, whom researchers claim is more popular than the president in their polls. This party was banned by Kabila as a result of its vocal disapproval of his governance. Other parties worth noting are the Christian Social-Democratic Party (PDSC) and the Forces Novatrices de l'Union Sacrée (FONUS). The principle of nonviolent opposition guides these parties, as they never participated in any armed activities either against Mobutu or Kabila. In addition, there is still the ADFL, which was ditched by Kabila, which prior to its current position played a crucial role in the politics of the DRC.

This identification of actors, however, is only a first step. More importantly, these actors' needs/demands and motivations at both the objective and psychological levels would need to be understood and addressed if viable peace is to be attained in the DRC.

Identifying Facilitators

Rupesinghe notes that it is crucial to identify in the design of a peace process an appropriate facilitator "who has the background knowledge, analytic and mediation skills to make a positive contribution to the design process."[15]

There were approximately 23 recorded peace initiatives of the DRC conflict,[16] which employed different facilitators to the talks about talks as well as talks themselves. The most notable facilitation attempts were those of President Chiluba, who was delegated by SADC to play such a role. President Chiluba was chosen at a time when there was a difference of opinion within SADC, specifically between South Africa and Zimbabwe,[17] to the methodology of finding a solution to the DRC conflict. The choice of a neutral party was crucial so as not to taint the process with preconceived positions. The choice of President Chiluba meant that he was to be assisted by the regional organization wherever it was possible. This is evident in the number of meetings that other SADC countries held with rebels or countries who support the rebels in an effort to augment his efforts.

President Khadaffi of Libya entered the sphere of facilitation when he held talks with President Kabila and Professor Wamba dia Wamba on December 25 and 27, 1998. Further meetings were facilitated by President Khadaffi with various players[18] in the DRC conflict that led to the Sirte Accord of April 17, 1999.

Religious groups have also played a role in attempting to find a solution to the conflict. For example, the Community of Sant'Egidio offered to mediate between the parties.

With the cease-fire agreement in place, the Organization of African Unity (OAU) was charged with assisting in the organization of the national dialogue for the country. This responsibility extended to finding a facilitator who will handle the actual negotiations. The OAU drafters of the recent Lusaka cease-fire agreement, through the contents of the agreement, displayed an understanding of the issues in the conflict and made provisions pertaining to them. The OAU had to find someone who had knowledge of the conflict and who would work to provide guidance to the process. It was imperative for the success of the process that the person chosen was one who was acceptable to all parties concerned and who could also count on the support of the international community to enforce agreements reached.

After much ado, the parties agreed in December 1999 to the appointment of Dr. Ketumile Masire, the former president of Botswana, as a facilitator. President Masire's conduct during his tenure in Botswana certainly stood him in good stead to qualify for the facilitation. So far, President Masire's facilitation has not been without problems, with the government of the DRC once refusing him access to certain parts of the country. However, he seems to be working quite well with the rebel groups in his consultation, a fact that has led to him being accused by the government of equating the rebels to it.

Setting a Realistic Timetable

Rupesinghe emphasizes the importance of setting a realistic timetable, from the identification of root causes and significant actors, through such phases as cease-fires, to the elaboration of mechanisms of political and social accommodation, for the success of the peace process. A timetable that attempts to do too much over a short period of time may result in most not being done or done very badly (such as demobilization of former combatants). This could then serve to undermine the credibility of the entire peace process. On the other hand, a timetable that results in protracted peace negotiations over a considerable period of time may result in the momentum for peace being lost. Both options are equally dangerous.

Chapter 3 of the Lusaka cease-fire agreement is a calendar of the implementation of the agreement. The total number of days set in this chapter for the full implementation from the date of signature is 270 days. It is envisaged that within this period, among things to be achieved would be the release of hostages, disengagement of forces, a national dialogue, and deployment of a peacekeeping mission.

One slippery area that draws the attention of observers in the agreement is the length of the time allocated for the disarmament of armed groups. This task has been allocated 30 days, a short period considering the number and elusive nature of armed groups in that country.

To address the international dimension of the conflict, the agreement allocated a maximum of one year to address the regional security concerns. Two hundred and seventy days after the signing of the agreement are allocated for the reestablishment of the state administration. Certainly these two processes are going to be guided by the national dialogue charged with charting the way forward for the country. The processes mentioned influence the outcome of each other; there could be no stable regional security network in the Great Lakes if the national dialogue of the DRC does not address the concerns of the neighbors of that country. It is difficult to comment whether this is a realistic time frame because conditions for success are dependent on the commitment of the parties.

There has been recognition of the limiting nature of initial time frames offered by the original agreement. With more attention being focused on the DRC, there were consultations that resulted in a Disengagement Agreement, which in turn agreed on March 1, 2000, being a new D-day for those activities not yet implemented in terms of the agreement.

Sustaining the Effort

According to Rupesinghe,[19] a "comprehensive approach to peace requires an adequate investment of financial resources, patience and a sustained commitment from sponsors."

The effort to bring peace to the DRC had been sustained by the international community through its involvement at regional, subregional, and bilateral levels. First and foremost has been the United Nations with a consistent call for the cessation of hostilities since the war began. The UN also endeavored to observe the humanitarian situation and human rights abuses in the region.[20] The UN further complemented its involvement with the appointment of Senegalese Moustapha Niasse on April 5, 1999, as a special representative of the secretary-general to the DRC.

The European Union sent Aldo Ajello as its special envoy on a trip to African states in order to find a possible solution to the conflict starting September 29. The United States dispatched its assistant secretary of state for African affairs, Susan Rice, on a regional tour to also attempt brokering peace. In November 1999, France made an important contribution toward the operation of the Joint Military Council.[21]

On a continental level the OAU made room at its summits and special meetings attempting to bring the parties to some agreement.[22] With the agreement in place, the OAU in October took a decision to assemble a Ceasefire Verification Mission to be made up of 30 persons to look specifically at the issues of disarmament and opening of humanitarian corridors, among other things. The international community has continuously pledged its support through financial commitment to the peace process, extending to the earmarked national dialogue.[23] It is important that the international community act with consistency in calling for negotiations and cessation of hostilities, even if the parties show lack of commitment to the process. By doing so, the international community gives moral support to the facilitators and a clear message to the parties of what is expected of them. It is also imperative that such international sponsors work in a coordinated fashion to prevent costly duplication and also to ensure that belligerents only get one uniform message from the international community—peace, peace, peace!

Evaluating Success and Failure

Rupesinghe[24] notes that a crucial element

of any peacekeeping design should be a process of evaluation which indicates whether the main interests of the parties are being addressed, the precedents and principles used in searching for a solution (and whether they were useful), the obstacles encountered and factors which led to progress, alternatives and missed opportunities, co-ordination with other peacemaking activities, and what could be learned from the process.

The inability of the peacemakers to identify and react to the disintegration of the RCD delayed the successful addition of the signatures to the agreement of all parties to the conflict.[25] It would have been beneficial for the peacemakers to have concurrent processes within the negotiations aimed at monitoring movements on the ground that would affect negotiation positions of the parties. If this was done effectively, there would have been early detection of the disintegration of the RCD and as such proper mechanisms devised to ensure that it impacted positively on the negotiations.

The most neglected area by the peace process has been human rights abuses. The government of Mobutu, Kabila's insurrection, and the rebellion are marred by human rights abuses[26] that the international community ignored to address with the perpetrators. When Kabila took over power, he was given recognition without the rumors of atrocities being committed by his forces ever being addressed by the international community. Although a United Nations team was dispatched to investigate the rumors, Kabila used every tactic to frustrate it, and no significant steps were taken to reverse the trend. The rebels have also been accused of committing human rights abuses, and it is highly likely that they will not be brought to book, as they may make immunity a precondition in achieving consensus in the national debate. Even with the agreement in place, local human rights groups are being persecuted with arrests and disappearances.

The cease-fire agreement (chapter 9, section 9.1, 2) makes provision for the handing over to the international tribunal mass killers and perpetrators of crimes against humanity. Mentioned in this section are the Rwandan Armed Forces (FAR), Allied Democratic Forces (ADF), Lord's Resistance Army (LRA), and others, all who are not signatories to the agreement but who have a bone to pick with some of the signatories. If we look at some of the people who are to undertake this task, they have the same background as these groups, a fact that could harden these groups to aim for total victory instead of succumbing to reason. An opportunity was missed where foundations for regional consensus could have been laid aimed at permanently laying to rest the current instability in the Great Lakes region as a whole.

The role of the UN in the DRC has been put into the spotlight as to the reaction to its envisaged role by the drafters of the Lusaka agreement. The UN has been firm on the conditionalities of its deployment, which is based on three actions: respect of the cease-fire agreement, development of a clear plan for disengagement, and a guarantee of freedom of movement for the organization. These conditionalities can be viewed against the background of the continuous reporting of cease-fire violations and refusal of security guarantees into the DRC territory. Two months after the comprehensive signing of the agreement, the UN sent an assessment team to plan and refine UN deployment in that country but experienced problems due to the lack of security guarantees.

The organization can be commended on the consistent work done by the special envoy of the secretary general to the Great Lakes, Muoustapha Naisse, and the organized visit to the region by Under Secretary Bernard Miyet. For a comprehensive and coherent approach to lasting peace in that country, we should see more cooperation between the work of the organization and that of President Masire in his mediation attempts. The current UN commitment to the DRC is an Observer Mission comprising of 500 members and a support staff complement of 5,500. Detractors argue than an Observer Mission of this size is rather small, considering the vastness of the country and the duties expected from them. On the other hand, supporters justify this small complement because they argue that it places the keeping of peace in that country mostly on the doorstep of the parties themselves.

Strategic Constituencies

Rupesinghe also identifies the need for strategic constituencies to sustain the peace processes. According to Rupesinghe[27] these include

relevant non-governmental organisations, the media, human rights and humanitarian institutions, peace institutions, religious institutions, independent scholars, former members of the military, members of the business community, intergovernmental and government officials and donors. To maximize their impact, various constituencies would form strategic alliances focused on particular conflicts, aspects of violent conflict or the overall goal of prevention.

Civil society through representation by NGOs and churches are vital actors if a lasting peace is the objective. The level of participation or lack thereof of civil society may well determine the future conflict trajectory in this strife-torn state. The attempts to silence NGOs by the Kabila government have done no favors to the peace process as well as his continued refusal to recognize them as role players.

Nongovernmental organizations in the DRC acquired elevated status over the years as a deterioration in social service delivery saw NGOs take over this function and endear themselves to society in the face of government complacency. When Kabila took over power, NGOs were organized and wielding extensive influence as far as public opinion was concerned. The NGOs lost favor with Kabila's regime because they exposed government excesses without fear or favor. Kabila attempted to silence them through banning or attempting to channel their funding.[28] But NGOs did not falter in the face of this adversity; they maintained their international contacts and continued to make their contribution to finding a solution to the conflict in the country from the sidelines.

The resolve of civil society in the DRC can be demonstrated in its organization of a national dialogue workshop in October 1999, and a Peace Forum launched on February 29, 2000. If the parties to the conflict are serious about bringing a real peace to this central African giant, then they would need to create an enabling environment in which such strategic constituencies can make their own contribution to postconflict reconstruction.

The Role of Outside Peacemakers

Rupesinghe[29] notes that traditional "diplomacy and outside nongovernmental peacemakers have important roles to play in mediating the mitigation or resolution of violent internal conflict." This was clearly borne out in the recent Norwegian intervention on the Israeli–Palestinian question that resulted in the Oslo Peace Accords.

On the other hand, the role of outside peacekeepers can also adversely affect negotiations, as was the Angolan experience. Moreover, the Angolan peace process also raises interesting questions regarding the motivations and interests of third parties who seek to mediate. Consider in this regard the short-lived Gbadolite Peace Accords. Seizing the opportunity presented by the 1988 New York Accords, President Mobutu Sese Seko convened this initiative six months later. But this initiative was as much about Angolan peace as it was about bolstering Mobutu's international image. President Mobutu's manipulation of the parties by feeding them with false information on what each had agreed to with him in private led to no agreement being secured. To the contrary, it led to the hardening of attitudes.

The role of President Chiluba as an SADC delegated facilitator was tainted when Angola, a party to the DRC conflict, alleged that Zambia was fueling the conflict by supporting UNITA. The Zambian president had to expend his time and energy in reassuring all that his country was not involved in any activity that would jeopardize the peace process. Continuous support by SADC gave the Zambian president the necessary credibility to continue with his role.

The role played by President Khadaffi to the final outcome of the peace negotiation has not been fully credited. President Khadaffi's involvement was groundbreaking, as it managed to identify areas where agreement could be reached and committed to. The Sirte Accord formed the foundation for subsequent peace talks, including the Zambian initiatives. The success of President Khadaffi could be attributed to the fact that the parties could have identified him as being far removed from the conflict and therefore genuinely committed to mediation.[30]

South Africa had played a role in the DRC from the time of Mobutu's fall. It was President Mandela who suggested a need for a negotiated settlement accommodating everyone in that country. President Mandela played another progressive role when he convinced the Rwandan vice president, Paul Kagame, to publicly admit the role of Rwanda in support of the rebellion against Kabila. The admission gave momentum to the peace process, and Rwanda was treated as one of the actors.

South Africa has continued to play a vital role in seeking the signature of the RCD when it did not sign the agreement in Lusaka with the other signatories. It was also South Africa that convinced Kabila on holding direct talks with the rebels instead of the preferred proxy talks. These attempts paid off when the rebel movement signed on the dotted line on August 31.

The one drawback of outside peacemakers in the DRC conflict has been the state-centric approach of the peacemakers. The nonstate status of the rebels has, on more than one occasion, derailed the peace process, with Kabila refusing to hold direct negotiations, and rebel-supporting countries walking out in protest. President Masire is expected to have very little problem in this regard during the national dialogue, but most eyes are on him on whether his consultations will include predialogue talks with this group.

The Role of Local Peacekeepers

Rupesinghe[31] emphasizes the role of local peacemakers who are influential "members of local communities with a first hand knowledge of conflict, actors, the political and economic situation and the cultural background who will have a distinct 'comparative advantage' over other potential peacemakers wishing to act as third-party mediators." The role of these local peacekeepers takes on added importance if one considers the sometimes erratic and ambivalent role played by outside peacekeepers, as was displayed in the Angolan case.

In the DRC case there were no meaningful local peacemaking efforts due to the mistrust that both camps had of potential peacemakers. When the rebellion against Kabila began, Tshisekedi of the UDPS offered to mediate between the parties, an offer that was rejected. The reason why no meaningful local peacemakers emerged is that belligerents did not trust such initiatives. Such trust, would, of course, need to develop if the full spectrum of peace constituencies is to be unleashed.

OMISSIONS—UNDERSTANDING THE PSYCHOLOGY OF DIPLOMACY

If there is one criticism that could be leveled against Rupesinghe's theoretical model, then it is simply the omission of those variables relating to personality and psychology. This is a damning omission, given the fact that there is a burgeoning literature that graphically illustrates the importance of psychological determinants for those engaging in preventive diplomacy. Holsti,[32] for instance, notes that "attitudes and psychological predispositions typically surround any serious conflict or crisis. These frames of mind help to explain the propensity to use violence in attempts to achieve or defend collective objectives." Meanwhile, Jones[33] illustrates how facts are a peculiar ordering of reality according to one's own personal bias, which are, in turn, determined by certain psychological drivers. More prosaically, we have seen how peace has blossomed in the absence of key personalities. The sudden death of General Sani Abacha was the catalyst needed to move Nigeria from military dictatorship to democracy. The killing of the National Union for the Total Independence of Angola (UNITA) leader Jonas Savimbi on February 22, 2002, ended a civil war that had lasted almost three decades. Similarly, the assassination of Laurent Kabila in 2000 resulted in great strides taking place toward peace under the leadership of his son, Joseph. Why is this so? Why does the leader's psychological predispositions and interests matter so much in Africa? First, polities are weak, and as such many African states subscribe to the big man theory of history. Second, given the fact that in much of Africa democracy is underdeveloped or nonexistent, there are far less checks and balances on the leader than in developed Western states. As a concomitant of the preceding points, it stands to reason that the personality of the leader matters far more in such a context. This is exacerbated in those states in which a personality cult develops around the leader.

Within the context of the DRC conflict, these psychological variables hold grave implications for preventive diplomacy if ignored. For instance it is well known that President Laurent Kabila and the facilitator of the Inter-Congolese Dialogue, Sir Ketumile Masire, never had a good relationship, and this served to delay the implementation of the Lusaka Peace Accords. The lesson that one can draw from this is that having a third-party mediator or facilitator who gels at the levels of psychology and personality with the belligerents is crucial for the success of any peace process. It is also important that the leader be in a psychologically dominant position over his followers so that he can sell them any peace agreement. The repeated changes in the leadership of the RCD on the grounds of fears that the leadership was making too many concessions to the other side suggests that this was not the case. Repeated leadership changes obviously delays the peace process further as new leaders have to develop a rapport of trust among themselves.

Mitchell[34] meanwhile stresses the importance of also understanding conflict attitudes, which he defines as: "a set of psychological processes and attitudes that accompany involvement in a conflict, particularly an intense one, where levels of personal involvement are high, and participants experience a marked degree of personal tension brought about by the existence and actions of a threatening adversary." Mitchell then goes on to explain that these include emotional orientations, such as feelings of anger and distrust as well as cognitive processes such as stereotyping.[35] Thus another objective of successful preventive diplomacy will be to break down these feelings of anger and distrust by approaching negotiations in such a way that both anger and distrust dissipate and a real rapport develops between the belligerents. Countering stereotypes by allowing parties to move from black-and-white images to see the gray is also imperative. This, however, suggests a long-term engagement on the part of third parties. Unfortunately, the various interventions in the DRC conflict have been characterized by third parties attempting to arrive at paper peace agreements as quickly as possible. What the psychology of diplomacy teaches us, though, is that the process of getting to an agreement is often more important than the agreement itself. It also informs us that often intangibles such as psychology and personality matter as much as material interests. It is therefore unsurprising that the war in the DRC has already claimed the lives of 2.5 million people, and still the carnage continues.

CONCLUSION

What this chapter has attempted to do is to understand, at the theoretical level, the conflict trajectory more holistically in the DRC with the goal of resolving the conflict. Such theoretical insights also present us with a conceptual template from which generalizations could be made that we could use in other conflict situations.

Employing theoretical insights to empirical data, several insights have been gleaned that we maintain are essential if peace is to prevail in the DRC. We have discussed how the different facilitators attempted to resolve the conflict and observed the level of participation of civil society and other actors in peacemaking. There needs to be an understanding of why the process went the way it did and what can be done to improve conflict resolution attempts (evaluating success and failure).

From a policy point of view, it is time for regional organizations to be clear of the values and principles expected from its members. Views and practices that promote human security need to be harnessed and cultivated, whereas any actions undermining this must be condemned in the most serious way. The acceptance of Kabila into the SADC fold without prior ascertaining his human rights baggage was one component that undermined its later efforts. The processes to resolve the conflict are dependent on continental and regional organizations practicing what they preach. The principles of democracy and transparent governance need to be propagated to member states, regardless of their positions within subregional and regional organizations. Principle-driven organizations will not be caught in a moral dilemma of supporting governments with dubious records of democratic practices, human rights abuse, and so forth. Regional organizations need to assume the moral high ground without equivocation. In this regard, idealism is grounded in harsh realities.

This moral high ground must inform the conduct of member states in relation to human rights, accommodation of differing views, and economic redistribution. This morality should enforce governments to recognize and carry out their duty of poverty alleviation, provision of education, and other essential social services and creating an environment for economic activity. Regional organizations need to shepherd countries out of conflict through means reflecting this morality, that is, respect for human rights, into processes that are aimed at entrenching these values into those societies. This would also contribute toward the prevention of future hostilities in countries as a culture of tolerance takes root.

The international community can support peace processes by empowering local human capital capable of peacemaking as they have the background knowledge and contacts. Africa must tap into the vast intellectual resources it has when choosing facilitators to conflicts, as states have proven not to be the safest route to facilitation because they are often involved in the conflict in one way or another. Calls by South African president Mbeki to the OAU to utilize such stalwarts as former president Kaunda and others for the purpose of facilitation needs to be thoroughly looked into. Unlike in the DRC case, the facilitators need to be untouchable by rumor of involvement in any way to ensure utmost objectivity.

Addressing root causes of any conflict needs proper identification and commitment of all, local and regional players and the international community at large. Identification of actors in any conflict needs extra care so as not to exclude potential players. External dynamics should be engaged with by including the actors affected in the process of finding a solution. Without sounding pessimistic, it is of little use identifying rebel groups and vowing to get rid of them when there are no mechanisms to assimilate their views into society.

There is a need to develop dynamic civil societies that will play a crucial role in guiding and influencing government. The development of such societies across the continent will ensure that our governments are continuously in dialogue with its people and each other, making identifying and solving problems less complex. The international community could be of assistance in funding and supporting initiatives in this regard.

This chapter began with an overview of conflict in Africa. Perhaps it would be ideal to conclude on a more optimistic note. In recent times, the South African president has popularized the term *African Renaissance* to describe the resurgence of the continent. One aspect of this Renaissance is Africans accepting more responsibility for their own actions. OAU secretary-general Dr. Salim Ahmed Salim[36] has eloquently expressed this.

OAU Member States can no longer afford to stand aloof and expect the International Community to care more for our problems than we do, or indeed to find solutions to those problems which in many instances, have been of our own making. The simple truth that we must confront today, is that the world does not owe us a living and we must remain in the forefront of efforts to act and act speedily to prevent conflict from getting out of control.

NOTES

Unless otherwise stated, all information supplied by the Early Warning Unit of the African Centre for the Constructive Resolution of Disputes. The views reflected in this chapter, however, are those of the authors.

1. A Hutu militia group organized to carry out the annihilation of Rwandan Tutsis.

2. These included the government of the DRC and its allies in Zimbabwe, Angola, and Namibia, and the other countries in the form of Uganda, Rwanda, and the facilitator in the form of Zambia.

3. Stephen Ryan, *Ethnic Conflicts and International Relations* (Aldershot: Dartmouth Publishing, 1995), p. 129.

4. Michael Lund, *Preventing Violent Conflict: A Strategy for Preventive Diplomacy* (Washington, DC: United States Institute of Peace, 1996).

5. Kumar Rupesinghe, *Conflict Transformation*, Mimeo, n.d.

6. Ibid., p. 65.

7. Ibid., pp. 77–78.

8. Ibid., p. 77.

9. Ibid., p. 76.

10. Ibid., p. 80.

11. Ibid., p. 81.

12. Etienne Tshisekedi presides over the Union for Democracy and Social Progress whereas Kengo wa Dondo cofounded with Alexis Tambwé the Union of Independent Democrats.

13. Rupesinghe, op. cit., p. 81.

14. Kabila and Mugabe, through their son and nephew, respectively, are alleged to be partners in business ventures involving the two countries.

15. Rupesinghe, op. cit., p. 81.

16. Two initial meetings in Zimbabwe, over five in Zambia, three in South Africa, and a range of meetings and summits of the OAU, UN, and SADC.

17. Zimbabwe was in favor of visible military assistance, whereas South Africa was propagating negotiations between the parties to the conflict.

18. Presidents Museveni and Kabila signed an agreement stipulating conditions for the withdrawal of foreign troops.

19. Rupesinghe, op. cit., p. 82.

20. The UN deputy emergency relief co-ordinator started investigating massacres and the humanitarian situation in the Great Lakes region on September 23, 1998.

21. The Joint Military Council is a form of self-policing mechanism comprising all signatories to monitor progress of the agreement.

22. On September 10, 1998, the OAU oversaw a meeting between the defense ministers of governments in the conflict. Secondly, the organization through a summit reaffirmed its support for peace initiatives up until that point.

23. The United States promised to contribute toward the Lusaka meeting costs whereas the EU pledged to support the national dialogue and costs.

24. Rupesinghe, op. cit., p. 82.

25. The alliance disintegrated with the unseating of Wamba dia Wamba and him setting up his own faction. This resulted in two RCDs, one based in Goma led by Emile Ilunga, and the other based in Kisangani led by Wamba dia Wamba. This occurred while the peace process was in motion and close to signature.

26. Arbitrary arrests, illegal detentions, ethnic persecution, harassment of human rights defenders, and extrajudicial executions are reported as some of the charges against both sides.

27. Rupesinghe, op. cit., p. 82.

28. The biggest human rights nongovernmental organization, AZADHO, was dissolved; NGO leaders were arrested; and funding was forced to be channeled through the state. Government-sponsored NGOs were formed, such as the Congolese Union for the Defence of Human Rights.

29. Rupesinghe, op. cit., p. 84.

30. This was the case, even though everyone knew of Khadaffi financing Chad's intervention in the DRC on Kabila's side.

31. Rupesinghe, op. cit., p. 85.

32. K. J. Holsti, *International Politics: A Framework for Analysis* (London: Prentice Hall, 1983), p. 405.

33. W. S. Jones, *The Logic of International Relations* (Chicago: Scott Foresman and Company, 1988), p. 238.

34. C. R. Mitchell, *The Structure of International Conflict* (London: Macmillan, 1981), p. 71.

35. Ibid., p. 29.

36. Salim Salim, *Address by the Secretary-General of the OAU at the Second Annual Meeting of the Chiefs of the Defence Staff of Member States of the OAU Central Organ.* Harare, October 25, 1997.

12

The Making of a Nonviolent Revolution: The 1985–1994 South African Banking Sanctions Campaign

Terry Crawford-Browne

Exponential growth in international communications will transform the psychology of diplomacy in the twenty-first century. Human security relating to people will take priority over traditional notions of military security related to states. No longer will diplomacy be the preserve of professionals in support of governments but, instead, will become an increasing function of churches, nongovernmental organizations (NGOs) and other voices of civil society.

Moreover, the nation–state—the driving force of diplomacy and of wars for the past 350 years—will become increasingly irrelevant.

The international campaign to ban land mines illustrates the point. NGOs linked by e-mail and the Internet soon overwhelmed hesitant government securocrats. The Jubilee 2000 campaign for cancellation of Third World debt has already become part of mainstream economics and has forced itself onto the agendas of G8 meetings of heads of governments.

London-based Global Witness identified diamonds as the means for funding wars in Angola and Sierra Leone and soon obliged the United Nations Security Council to suspend the trade in "conflict diamonds."[1] Because of rising public opinion associating "blood-on-your-finger" with engagement rings, De Beers and the diamond market now take measures to prevent diamonds from being a source of funding for weapons.

At issue is the will and commitment of the international community to find peaceful alternatives to the use of war as the ultimate instrument of diplomacy. Other than the confrontation between the United States and the Soviet Union, no conflict during the second half of the twentieth century attracted as much attention and effort as South Africa's political structures of racial segregation, apartheid.

That seemingly intractable system collapsed relatively suddenly and peace-fully. Ironically, massive military expenditure intended to maintain the status quo became instead the means to engineer its demise. South Africa's apartheid government might have lasted another 50 years, except that the militarists bankrupted the country. The military response to opposition to apartheid had ranged from development of nuclear weapons to the deliberate destabilization of neighboring countries.

The consequent financial strains made possible the successful international banking sanctions campaign and South Africa's relatively peaceful transition to democracy. It is, therefore, instructive to examine the South African banking sanctions strategy and the psychology of that campaign.

The Indian government had objected to South Africa's racial segregation policies at the United Nations as early as 1946 because of the treatment of South Africans of Indian origin. It will be recalled that Mahatma Gandhi lived in South Africa from 1893 until 1916, during which time he developed his passive nonviolence strategies.

By the 1960s and 1970s, world revulsion against apartheid was already such that South Africa was being expelled from most international organizations, including the Commonwealth and the Olympic Games. Most countries main-tained trade boycotts against South Africa, which were, however, mere token gestures and easily circumvented.

South African businessmen became the world's experts in phony documen-tation and sanctions busting. Chambers of commerce and banks—in the so-called "national interest"—happily colluded by supplying false certificates of origin and fraudulent letters of credit. Trade sanctions, especially, were regarded as a farce.

In November 1977 the United Nations Security Council designated apartheid South Africa to be a threat to international peace and security and imposed an arms embargo. The government until then had successfully resisted interna-tional criticisms of apartheid with the argument that article 2.7 precluded in-tervention in "matters which are essentially within the domestic jurisdiction of any state."

The decision to override article 2.7 of the UN Charter by determining that severe abuses of human rights constitute threats to international peace and security ranks as one of the major developments of twentieth-century diplo-macy. Human rights issues were back on the international agenda. More im-portantly, diplomacy had become an open arena.

South Africa had intervened in Angola in 1975, reportedly at the behest of CIA agents as America's proxy in the Cold War. The uprising of schoolchildren in Soweto protesting against apartheid education followed in June 1976. Tele-vision coverage and the fact that English is the language of South Africa's print media ensured that debates about apartheid reverberated around the world.

Whereas British commentators considered apartheid as a decolonization story gone wrong, American journalists saw it in the context of racial problems in the United States. As opposition to apartheid within South Africa mounted in late 1984 and early 1985 and news of riots was shown on television screens, international bankers became increasingly nervous about their loans.

The World Council of Churches in Geneva and the National Council of Churches in New York had for many years been monitoring bank and other foreign loans to South Africa and had become active lobbyists. In response to pressures from the Municipality of New York, Chase Manhattan Bank announced on July 29, 1985, that it would recall its loans to South Africa, which were estimated at about US$500 million. The announcement caused a stampede among bankers.

Two weeks later, President P. W. Botha—in front of a television audience, which had been primed for an announcement of major reforms—told the world instead to go to hell and to do its damndest. South Africa's future, he blustered, would be decided by South Africans, not foreigners.

Reaction to Botha's "Rubicon Speech" was dramatic. Overnight, the rand lost 16 percent of its value on foreign exchange markets. By the end of August, South Africa had defaulted on its foreign debt of US$24 billion. Having precipitated the debt standstill, American bankers actually had a relatively small exposure to South Africa. At US$3.4 billion, it was very substantially less than that of their British and European counterparts.

Uncertain about South Africa's rapidly deteriorating financial circumstances, Bankers Trust in New York then compounded the crisis by seizing a payment of US$59 million being transferred through Nedbank's account. Bankers Trust applied a rather dubious doctrine and pretext of setoff against outstanding loans to South Africa of US$200 million to justify its action.

In the process, however, the whole New York bank clearance system virtually unraveled. Companies without the slightest connection to South Africa became ensnared as the carefully constructed American payments mechanisms temporarily collapsed. The Chase Manhattan decision, inadvertently, had become the greatest single blow against apartheid.

It also proved the limitations of raw military power—even for a pariah state such as apartheid South Africa—as an instrument of last resort in international diplomacy. Whereas the government was militarily impregnable, the pivotal role of the U.S. dollar as settlement currency in foreign exchange markets now offered anti-apartheid activists an effective nonviolent instrument against the government.

The military structures created to defend apartheid were proving utterly useless against actions 9,000 miles away in New York City.

With most South African political leaders in opposition to apartheid either in jail or in exile, the task of organizing a revolution fell to church leaders. In September 1985 the "Kairos Document" challenged mainline churches to take action on behalf of the oppressed. If the state was tyrannical, it declared, then the church rather than "give legitimacy to a morally illegitimate regime . . .

must be prepared to be involved in civil disobedience . . . to confront and to disobey the State in order to obey God.[2]

Pop stars began dedicating their songs to Nelson Mandela and Bishop Desmond Tutu and conscientized the public at large into a reinvigorated and worldwide anti-apartheid movement. Tutu, who less than a year earlier had been awarded the Nobel Peace Prize, used his international acclaim to rally foreign support and to bolster flagging spirits at home.

Tutu's message was direct and simple. "Any struggle for liberation from the yoke of oppression," he declared, "was blessed and ordained by God, for God himself had taken a huge political step in leading the oppressed Israelites out of the house of bondage that was Egypt. God hated oppression then, and there is no reason to believe he might have changed his mind about oppression since."[3]

Church leaders were quick to seize the opportunity presented by the default on foreign debts. A statement issued by Tutu and Dr. Beyers Naude (then general secretary of the South African Council of Churches) to New York bankers and United States congressmen requested that

[r]escheduling of South Africa's debt should be made conditional upon the resignation of the present regime and its replacement by a government responsive to the needs of all South Africa's people. We are of the view that such a government must involve the participation of recognized black leaders, and necessitates the immediate release of all political prisoners, the return of exiles and the lifting of banning orders of all banned political organizations. We, together with other Church leaders, offer our services as facilitators to ensure the transfer of office to a government commitment to the goal of democracy.[4]

The *Washington Post* noted that this was the first time that the tenure of the South African government had been seriously questioned. Suddenly, prominent Americans were demonstrating outside the South African Embassy on Massachusetts Avenue and offering themselves for arrest.

The debt rescheduling offered an opportunity for a much more effective sanctions campaign and pressure for constitutional change within South Africa. But it was the American payments system—much more than the loans themselves—that really mattered. Without access to U.S. dollar bank accounts in New York, South Africa's trade and financial structures would collapse.

The U.S. Congress responded to the rising public outcry against apartheid by passing the Comprehensive Anti-Apartheid Act (C-AAA) and, in October 1986, confirmed it over President Ronald Reagan's veto. In conjunction with church and other anti-apartheid activists, New York had become a city with a foreign policy. Did the New York banks really prefer the banking business of apartheid South Africa to that of New York City? The bankers would be forced to choose.

After the passage of the C-AAA, the South African Reserve Bank reluctantly conceded that "should the world banking community effectively exclude South Africa from international trade and payments systems, it would be much more effective than trade sanctions applied by governments."[5]

Other American municipalities and states were also beginning to apply their own sanctions campaigns against apartheid in defiance of the Reagan Administration. Banks throughout the United States were being pressured by public opinion to close the accounts of South African correspondent banks. Even payments to and from third countries such as Japan and Germany became increasingly difficult because of the role of the U.S. dollar as settlement currency in international foreign exchange markets.

Could apartheid be defeated without resort to violence? Had the South African government passed the point of no return that resort to violence was both justified and inevitable? P. W. Botha believed that a communist "total onslaught" against his government justified a "total response," including draconian repression.

In common with Christian theologians—and as exemplified by the American Declaration of Independence—Tutu believed that there might be circumstances in which the use of violence may offer the only solution. He, however, was obliged to seek a nonviolent solution, and the banking sanctions campaign was the last option before violence became inevitable and justifiable. Although not a pacifist, he was and remains one of the world's leading campaigners for both human rights and peace. Botha publicly and foolishly challenged his Christian commitment and accused him of acting on behalf of the South African Communist Party. Tutu replied:

Apartheid, the policy of your government, is shown to be unbiblical, unchristian, immoral and evil in its very nature. Apartheid teaches the fundamental irreconcilability of people because they belong to different races. This is at variance with the central teaching of the Christian faith about the reconciling work of our Lord and Savior, Jesus Christ.[6]

Abroad Tutu was feted. At home, the white community was conditioned by the state radio and television service to consider him as an ogre—a communist with blood dripping from his hands!

Tens of thousands of people were detained without trial after 1985 as the apartheid government struggled to maintain its political ascendancy. Torture was all but routine, a University of Cape Town study reporting that 88 percent of detainees experienced some form of torture.

By late 1988 the United Nations, the Commonwealth, and other international organizations were increasingly determined to bring an end to the apartheid system. They now considered the banking sanctions campaign to offer the most likely instrument for success.

The Commonwealth heads of government were scheduled to meet in October 1989 in Kuala Lumpur, Malaysia, and the matter of tightening banking sanctions was intended to head the agenda.

In January 1989 George Bush succeeded Ronald Reagan as president of the United States, but was viewed with considerable suspicion by South African liberation leaders, who considered him to be tainted by his association with Reagan.

Advice from Afro-American activists in New York and Washington such as Randall Robinson was that Bush was endeavoring to develop a "kinder, more caring America." Most pertinent, however, were their suggestions of tying banking sanctions to constitutional negotiations. Constitutional negotiations toward a nonracial and democratic South Africa would be a concept to which Americans could relate.

Robinson had arranged for the church leaders to meet President Bush in Washington during May 1989, which proved a watershed in the sanctions campaign. Bush declared that he was "very, very angry at what was happening in South Africa" and expressed the hope that he could be a catalyst for change. Back in Johannesburg, *The Citizen* newspaper raged: "Perhaps President Bush will learn like his predecessors that there is no way in which Uncle Sam is going to force South Africa to do its bidding."

Five points became the core demands of the sanctions campaign.

a. The end of the state of emergency.

b. The release of all political prisoners and detainees.

c. The unbanning of all political organizations.

d. The repeal of the Group Areas, Separate Amenities, Population Registration Acts (and other flagrantly racist legislation).

e. Negotiations for a new constitution for a democratic, nonracial and united South Africa.[7]

The South African business community huffed indignantly and embarked on a massive campaign to discredit the growing momentum. Sanctions were suddenly becoming serious. How dare the Americans apply sanctions against apartheid! Domestic political considerations in the United States, it was said, should not influence American financial and foreign policies—or prevent South Africa from borrowing American money.

What became known as "rolling mass action" within South Africa coincided with the mounting international campaign and had the government bewildered. From "beach picnics" in midwinter on beaches designated as "whites only" to disruption of the segregated hospital services, the tactics of civil disobedience were also gaining momentum.

At hospitals, doctors were challenged to consider their Hippocratic oaths against the legal stipulation that first considered the patients' racial identities.

Given the stigma that still hung over the medical profession after the 1977 Biko case, the medical profession buckled. White South Africans are passionate supporters of the game of rugby. A 20-minute blockade by activists of a banking hall in Cape Town caused First National Bank to cancel its sponsorship of the "rebel" 1989 World Rugby XV tour.

At a United Nations conference in Geneva, Switzerland, in September 1989, South Africa's business elite tried unsuccessfully to convince the panelists that sanctions, rather than weakening apartheid, actually helped to entrench the system. Sanctions were also said to be impoverishing the poor. After years of ridiculing sanctions as ineffective, this was a new admission.

A study conducted for the Commonwealth had found, however, that banking sanctions impacted primarily on the rich and politically influential. Half of South Africa's black population lived outside the money economy. The other half was at the bottom of the economic ladder and had gained little benefit from South Africa's development.[8]

The United Nations panelists thoroughly debunked all notions that sanctions were not working. The General Assembly went even further and condemned apartheid as a crime against the conscience and dignity of humanity. The secretary-general, Perez de Cuellar, was instructed to report back by July 1, 1990, on the progress made in South Africa to abolish apartheid.

The minister of foreign affairs, "Pik" Botha, declared that the United Nations declaration was fundamentally flawed, bizarre and unacceptable to the South African government. Nonetheless, June 1990 was now being established by a variety of international organizations as the deadline for the abolition of apartheid.

Four years to the day after the "Rubicon Speech," a palace coup led by F. W. de Klerk and "Pik" Botha removed President Botha from office. Botha had suffered a minor stroke during December 1988 and was now ousted under the pretext that his memory was failing. Botha's stroke and the subsequent coup has gone down in South Africa's political lexicon as "the stroke of good fortune!"

The first weeks of President F. W. de Klerk's administration were among the most violent of the period. To his white constituents, the new president was endeavoring to reassert his right-wing credentials with a tough security crack-down ahead of the election on September 6. The election was limited to whites, "coloureds," and Asians, with the blacks representing 74 percent of South Africa's population being excluded. To the international community, de Klerk pleaded for a chance for reform. The two postures were completely incompatible.

On the night of the election the police in the "coloured" area of Mitchell's Plain attacked residents with tear gas, sjamboks, and bullets and killed at least 23 people. Their behavior was such that one distraught policeman described his colleagues as a "pack of wild dogs."

The response was Cape Town's "March for Peace" one week later—on September 13, 1989—to protest the barbarity of the security forces. Church leaders and the new mayor of Cape Town announced that they would be marching. Diplomatic representatives were instructed by their governments to participate.

Such a protest was, of course, illegal. Yet there was no way that the security forces could use tear gas and bullets in downtown Cape Town against foreign ambassadors, the mayor, and church leaders. De Klerk capitulated under the pressures and "legalized" the march as a "procession." Tens of thousands—an estimated 35,000 people—marched from St. George's Cathedral to the city hall. It was like a purging of the soul as Capetonians of all races reacted as one community to turn their backs on more than 40 years of apartheid.

The *Cape Argus* newspaper noted:

The august Cape Town City Hall shook to its foundations as a wildly cheering crowd linked hands and celebrated a brilliant victory for justice and peace. Archbishop Tutu challenged the State President to come and see the peaceful people. "Come and look at the Technicolor people, we are the rainbow people—the new people of the new South Africa. De Klerk, you have already lost.[9]

A month later there were similar marches in Leipzig and other East German cities. Tutu delights to this day to proclaim "we marched in Cape Town and the Berlin Wall fell down!" and even he remains astounded by the ramifications of the march he initiated without wider consultation.

The African National Congress (ANC) was undoubtedly caught off guard by the speed of events within South Africa. Nelson Mandela's first and only meeting with P. W. Botha in Cape Town in July 1998 had convinced some ANC members that there was a possibility of negotiations. There was also massive distrust that Mandela was cutting a deal without authority from the ANC in Lusaka. The ANC was split between hard-liners of Umkhonto-we-Sizwe (MK) committed to an armed struggle and a segment around Thabo Mbeki.

MK had repeatedly proved to be militarily incompetent and absolutely no threat to the South African Defence Force. Mbeki prevailed, and in August the Organization of African Unity accepted the Harare Declaration setting out the five preconditions for negotiations. Six weeks later the American assistant secretary of state for African affairs, Herman Cohen, told the Senate Foreign Affairs Committee that the Bush Administration had taken note of both the banking sanctions campaign and the March for Peace.

To the fury of the South African government, which lodged two sharp, diplomatic protests, Cohen declared that the United States expected compliance with the first three conditions by the beginning of the Parliamentary session scheduled for February 1990. In addition, the United States expected repeal of apartheid legislation by the end of the parliamentary session in June together with movement toward constitutional negotiations for a nonracial and democratic South Africa.

Cohen had also informed Tutu that if by June President De Klerk had not responded to these deadlines, the State Department would consult with Congress on how best to step up the banking sanctions campaign.

There were howls of protest about the nine-month deadline from newspapers such as *Business Day*. It berated the blunderings of American foreign policy and editorialized under the headline "The Beast Moves" that "the Americans— heaven help us from the righteous—have all the finesse and intelligence of a beach invasion by the US Marines."[10]

In an op-ed article for the *New York Times,* Archbishop Tutu wrote:

Let us see what Mr De Klerk achieves in his first 100 days. Then we should evaluate carefully what he tells the opening session of Parliament next year and give him, say, three months after that to make the necessary legislative changes.

I desperately hope that Mr De Klerk will have demonstrated by then that the sanctions campaign can be put on hold. And, of course, once a truly democratic government is guaranteed sanctions can be lifted and South Africa will take its rightful place as a respected member of the international community.[11]

Mrs. Thatcher announced in Kuala Lumpur that very day that South Africa's foreign debt had been rescheduled for another three and a half years until December 1993, and without concessions on the political conditions. The timing was quite clearly intended to torpedo the Commonwealth meeting. That Thatcher should make the announcement proved the collusion between the British and South African governments.

Within days, however, it became evident that even with the "Iron Lady's" support, de Klerk could no longer prevent South Africa's transition to democracy. The "March for Peace" in Cape Town had become a decisive event in winning the struggle against apartheid. De Klerk yielded to the American ultimatum with his statement in Parliament on February 2, 1990, and the release of Nelson Mandela nine days later.

The apartheid government, however, was not yet defeated. During a telephone conversation that evening, he told Tutu: "Now you tell the Americans to call off their sanctions." It soon became apparent that de Klerk had not undergone a "Damascus conversion"! His speech had been merely a ploy to buy time and to get his government off the hook.

The government reportedly allocated R2 billion to efforts to break the banking sanctions campaign in the United States. Morgan Guaranty was commissioned to raise US$150 million, ostensibly to build clinics and schools for the poor. After all, who could object to such noble objectives? Fortunately, activists in New York saw through the ploy and worked hard and successfully to derail the Morgan "road show."

Relative to its worldwide involvements, South Africa was merely "small change." Morgan's exposure to South Africa in September 1989 amounted to

US$195 million compared with US$260 million at the time of the debt stand-still in 1985. Whatever the attractions of "getting on the right side of history," Morgan's immediate problem was the "Pandora's box" of the irretrievable credit disasters in Mexico and other Third World countries. Morgan Guaranty had reported a loss of US$1.82 billion for the third quarter of 1989.

Thatcher, it transpired, had been collaborating with Morgan Guaranty and Manufacturers Hanover. The two American banks had become extremely anxious to conclude a renewal as rapidly as possible in an effort to forestall Congressional and shareholder pressures during the spring of 1990.

Yet in being party to the apartheid government's efforts to torpedo the Kuala Lumpur initiative, the banks triggered a backlash against themselves. The National Council of Churches—irreverently known as the "Godbox"—coordinated the efforts of churches, states, and municipalities across the United States to apply sanctions. As an expression of American repugnance with apartheid, state and city pension fund investments were being withdrawn from companies that maintained their South African ties.

David Dinkins had been elected mayor of New York in November 1989 and took office in January 1990. He was an old friend of Tutu and was very supportive of the banking sanctions campaign. New York City would withdraw its banking business from any bank that maintained correspondent banking relationships with South African banks. The New York City payroll was alone worth more in banking business than any dealings with South Africa. The banks themselves could decide whose business was more important to them.

In a letter to Dinkins, Tutu wrote:

We ask the banks' assistance in moving South Africa beyond apartheid to a society in which each individual is recognized as being created in the image of God. Banks do not knowingly "launder" Mafia or drug money: why are some banks prepared to "launder" apartheid money?[12]

Each of the major church denominations was assigned to target a particular New York bank and to apply whatever tactics were appropriate. Chemical Bank and the Bank of New York were the first two banks to capitulate and announced that they would sever their correspondent banking relationships with South Africa. Being identified as laundering apartheid money had become not just a hassle, but was now also bad business practice.

De Klerk embarked on a tour of Europe in the afterglow of acclaim following his February speech to Parliament. Thatcher led the way in lavishing praise on him for the steps he had taken to abolish apartheid. Chancellor Helmut Kohl implied that Germany would support the lifting of sanctions in order to encourage de Klerk.

De Klerk was praised by bankers in Frankfurt and Zurich and returned to South Africa proclaiming that the sanctions campaign had come unraveled.

Official European sanctions had actually never amounted to more than token gestures. His tour was hailed in the South African press as the "unstoppable momentum of success."

The really important visit, however, would be the United States, and Mandela's comment brought a quick end to the euphoria among the business community when he declared:

I am visiting almost every capital he visited, and I can assure you that after I have spoken there he will regret his visit to Europe. Sanctions and other pressures are designed to force the government to abandon apartheid, and have to be applied until the whole structure of apartheid is brought down.[13]

De Klerk had already suffered the indignity of having to cancel a meeting with President Bush in 1989 because of vehement objections of American congressmen. De Klerk and Mandela were also scheduled to be visiting Washington in June 1990 within a few days of each other. Mandela would be feted in the United States and honored by an invitation to address a joint session of Congress. De Klerk soon realized that he would not be welcome in Washington and canceled the trip.

The critical issue was to hold the line on sanctions until the transition to democracy was irreversible. The distinction was established that "people-to-people" sanctions, such as tourism and sport, could now be lifted, but that banking and oil sanctions plus the arms embargo should continue.

President Bush repealed U.S. federal government sanctions in July 1991, but municipalities, counties, and states across America continued their own sanction campaigns against apartheid.

Civil rights, student, and trade union groups insisted that sanctions would remain "until Mandela says so," and few local government officials were willing to challenge them. American sanctions continued even after the transition to democracy and proved critical in tipping the balance against apartheid.

P. W. Botha's nickname had been the "big crocodile"; F. W. de Klerk's became the "clever chameleon." Whereas Botha was dictatorial and blunt, de Klerk was devious but still determined to maintain white supremacy. Mandela, by contrast, considered political leadership in terms of commitment to his country. He had just spent 27 years in jail when he declared on the day of his release:

Friends, comrades and fellow South Africans, I greet you all in the name of peace, democracy and freedom for all! I stand here before you not as a prophet but as a humble servant of you, the people. Your tireless and heroic sacrifices have made it possible for me to be here today. I therefore place the remaining years of my life in your hands.[14]

De Klerk was trying to build an anti-ANC alliance in conjunction with Mangosuthu Buthelezi, chief minister of the "homeland" of KwaZulu. The country held its breath and prayed each time it was convulsed by the Boipatong massacre, by the Bisho massacre, by the assassination of Chris Hani, and finally by the fiasco of the invasion of the apartheid "homeland" of Bophutstatswana by the right-wing Afrikaner Weerstandsbeweging (AWB).

The whole negotiation process was touch and go right up until the elections in April 1994. The government was proposing the most convoluted constitutional schemes. Although the franchise would ostensibly be based on universal suffrage, the intent was to maintain a white right of veto to block any meaningful change to South Africa's socioeconomic structure. Buthelezi might even be made puppet-president, but the National Party would continue to control the country.

Archbishop Tutu had convened a consultation in Johannesburg in October 1991 to debate the Anglican Church's position. Business representatives pressed for the immediate lifting of sanctions, but the stance prevailed that the process of constitutional change would stall were banking sanctions lifted prematurely. We had not yet reached the goal outlined in October 1985 by Tutu and Beyers Naude of having an interim government that could respond to the needs of all the people of South Africa.

Again the message to de Klerk was unambiguous: sanctions would continue until the transition to democracy was irreversible. It was almost two years of talks-about-talks before meaningful constitutional negotiations began in December 1991.

Another two years passed before de Klerk was finally outsmarted by an international coalition of forces, including a lawyer who was a good deal smarter and tougher than he was. South Africa was spared a civil war, which would have devastated its economic infrastructure and which would have caused the deaths of millions of its people.

It is now generally recognized in South Africa that the American banking sanctions campaign was crucial in bringing about the country's relatively peaceful transition to democracy. The role of the U.S. dollar as settlement currency in international foreign exchange markets was decisive. South Africa's financial system—and that of every other trading country—would collapse without access to New York banks.

After years of experience that trade sanctions were themselves ineffective, the campaign was based on the premise: "no paid—no trade." Intercept the payments system of whatever commodities finance and sustain a rogue movement or government, and possibilities emerge to leverage a settlement of political conflict.

It is a lesson not lost on the South African–controlled diamond industry or the activists of the Jubilee 2000 movement. The sanctions campaign against apartheid relied on media access to oblige governments to yield to public opinion. New means of communications will vastly increase the pressures on diplomats to consider the activities of NGOs as representatives of civil society.

NOTES

1. *Mail and Guardian*, Johannesburg, July 7, 2000.

2. "Kairos Document," SA Council of Churches, September 1985.

3. Jon Qwelane, "A Tribute to Desmond Tutu: Spiritual Father of the Rainbow Nation," June 1996.

4. Statement by Bishop Desmond Tutu and Dr. Beyers Naude, October 28, 1985.

5. "The Origins and Implications of South Africa's Continuing Financial Crisis," *Euromoney* magazine, March 1987.

6. Desmond Tutu, *The Rainbow People of God* (New York: Doubleday, 1994).

7. Terry Crawford-Browne's testimony, U.S. Congress House of Representatives Subcommittee on International Development, Finance, Trade and Monetary Policy, August 1, 1989.

8. Keith Ovendon and Tony Cole, *Apartheid and International Finance: A Program for Change* (Ringwood, Victoria, Australia: Penguin Books, 1989).

9. *The Argus*, September 14, 1989.

10. *Business Day*, October 5, 1989.

11. *New York Times*, October 20, 1989.

12. Letter from Archbishop Tutu to David Dinkins, October 3, 1989.

13. *Cape Times*, May 28, 1990.

14. Nelson Mandela, *The Long Walk to Freedom* (Randburg, South Africa: MacDonald Purnell, 1994).

Fiction versus Function: The Persistence of "Representative Character" Theory in the Law of Diplomatic Immunity

Jeffrey K. Walker

THE NEED FOR INTERACTION

Diplomats and diplomatic intercourse, in one form or another, have been with us since the earliest days of human civilization. From the records of ancient Sumer and Egypt,[1] there is ample evidence that kings sent ambassadors to other monarchs for any number of reasons: to conclude peace or to make war, to demand reparation, to honor a more powerful monarch, or to negotiate for trade.

The need to interact with others is a fundamental impulse and a basic value underpinning primitive law.[2] "To be alive, to unite sexually, to possess something as 'mine,' and to live in association with others, are beginning values."[3] In the context of nations, the last of these primal impulses—the need to associate with others—is every bit as strong as with individuals.[4]

Any group of independent states with interests and ambitions of their own, living side by side and united by some community of outlook and traditions, must have some degree of formal and organized contact with one another.[5]

Although the regular interaction of states has acquired a universal inevitability, that this interaction should take the form of the exchange of ambassadors or other formal envoys is not necessarily inevitable.[6] For example, at the height of the fifteenth-century movement toward the posting of permanent ambassadors, Lorenzo de Medici relied more on bankers and merchants with well-established contacts in foreign capitals and *entrepôts* than on his official ambassadors.[7] (With the rapid growth in international economic activity over the past 50 years, there would be ample opportunity to rely on similar less-formal forms of representation.) Concerning very important matters, heads of state tend to meet face-to-face even today. Regardless of what alternative forms might be available, the standard method of diplomatic intercourse is through the exchange of ambassadors.

HISTORY OF DIPLOMATIC IMMUNITY

Just as the exchange of diplomatic envoys has a long history, so does the recognition that there was something special about them.[8] Whether as a matter of religious proscription, of sovereign immunity, or of functional necessity, diplomatic envoys have at all times enjoyed unique status and protection—in theory if not always in practice—within the community of nations.

Overview of the Theoretical Constructs

The development of the law of diplomatic immunity can be roughly divided into four main theoretical constructs. These are, in rough order of development, (1) religious or quasi-religious protections, (2) representative character, (3) extraterritoriality, and (4) functional necessity.[9] The last three of these theories were formally propounded between the late sixteenth and mid-eighteenth centuries, and each has had some influence on the development of modern diplomatic law in the nineteenth and twentieth centuries.[10]

Religious Protections

As was the case with the development of much primitive law, the original basis for the inviolability of envoys was religious. Whether envoys were viewed as honored guests who had a religiously sanctioned right to hospitality, as personifications of a divine ruler, or as earthly minions of supernatural messengers, the violation of their persons was widely considered in the ancient world to be offensive to the gods or sinful in the eyes of God.

Representative Character

Very early in the history of the use of envoys, dating back at least to the Greeks, a general norm arose based on religious precepts that envoys of all kinds (e.g., messengers, heralds, procurators, ambassadors) stood in the shoes of—indeed were an extension of the *person* of—the sovereign who sent them. This notion of an envoy as a personification of his sovereign, heavy with religious connotation, would have been quite familiar and acceptable to the peoples of the ancient world.[11] This idea that an ambassador "personif[ies] his master in a clear and unmistakable way"[12] would echo throughout the evolution of diplomatic law. As late as the mid-nineteenth century, for example, the U.S. attorney general noted that it was a tenet of customary international law that the authority of any ambassador or minister ended on the death of the monarch that appointed him.[13]

Extraterritoriality

A second theory of immunity, related to but distinct from representative character theory, developed much later as a result of the establishment of permanent embassies, beginning around the middle of the fifteenth century. Based on an extension of the canon law notion that church property and the people occupying it were beyond the criminal and civil reach of temporal rulers, the legal fiction emerged that diplomatic premises (and the people that occupied them) were not within the territory of the receiving state. The idea that diplomatic premises were considered extraterritorial from the jurisdiction of the receiving state enjoyed some prominence right through the nineteenth century,[14] particularly in major capitals such as Madrid and Rome.[15] This theory has since been generally rejected in the context of diplomatic envoys. However, the principle of extraterritoriality is still applied occasionally to the armed forces of a state residing in another state's territory,[16] although this situation is more often regulated by consensual "status of forces" agreements.

Functional Necessity

Beginning in the late nineteenth and early twentieth centuries, attempts were made, ultimately successful to a significant degree, to disregard the interesting but anachronistic legal fictions of representative character and extraterritoriality in favor of a positive, treaty-based regime of diplomatic immunities based to satisfy the needs of diplomatic missions when carrying out their routine representational functions. In order to eliminate reliance on legal fictions, the proponents of this functional necessity theory asserted that states should simply agree on what set of immunities were essential to allow diplomatic agents to perform their necessary functions and then to consent to limited reciprocal waiver of their otherwise exclusive state territorial sovereignty. Culminating in the 1961 and 1962 Vienna Conventions, this is the dominant (but not exclusive) theory underpinning diplomatic immunity in contemporary international law.

Religious Roots of Diplomatic Immunity

Envoys in many forms—ambassadors, legates, heralds, and messengers—have long been imbued with a religious or quasi-religious aura. Many commentators have noted that protections afforded envoys were originally based on religious taboos.[17] The concept of the inviolability of envoys is grounded in the sacred right of protection enjoyed by guests found in the customs of many early cultures.[18] In Judeo-Christian religious culture, the intertwining of diplomacy and religion has deep roots.

> Diplomatic agents can trace their ancestry very far into the past, all the way back to the angels, the envoys of God. [The early modern jurist Alberico] Gentili recounts that King Herod, horrified by the death of his envoy to the Arabs, called the murder a horrible act in the eyes of nations—especially in the eyes of the Jews to whom the sacred law of God had been given by the angels who fulfilled the functions of heralds and ambassadors.[19]

The classical Greeks, although never fully developing a comprehensive system of diplomacy, sent envoys between the city-states of Hellas and to the kings of Persia. Homer records the diplomatic mission of Menelaeus and Odysseus to Troy in a futile attempt to retrieve Helen and avoid war.[20] However, envoys in classical Greece were little more than messengers, and often professional orators or actors were sent. They were not particularly well trusted and constituted little more than a specialized and less-respected form of herald.[21]

Nevertheless, both the Greeks and Persians were generally in agreement that envoys should not be molested.[22] In the fifth century B.C., Darius of Persia sent ambassadors to both Athens and Sparta to demand acknowledgment of his overlordship. The Greeks promptly killed the Persian envoys. The Spartans, convinced that their slaying of the Persian ambassadors had resulted in great misfortune to the city, sent their own ambassadors to Darius's successor Xerxes with the full expectation that the Persians would kill them in retaliation. Xerxes instead returned them unharmed. According to Herodotus, Xerxes spared the Spartan envoys because he knew any abusive treatment would violate "the usages of all mankind."[23] The Romans believed envoys were "also guarded by divine law."[24]

Roman and Canon Law

Both the Greeks and Romans deemed the right of sending and receiving ambassadors as a prerogative reserved to sovereigns. Although sovereigns had the right to refuse to receive another sovereign's ambassador, in Republican Rome such a refusal was almost always a precursor to war.[25]

In the earliest days of the Republic, nearly all Rome's relations were with other Italic peoples. During this period, envoys were treated as personifications of their sovereign and were therefore treated as the sovereign himself would be treated were he invited to Rome—as guests of the Senate.[26] Cicero believed that Rome's ambassadors likewise were the "personality of the Senate" and carried with them the full authority of the Republic.[27] Therefore, at least in the preimperial Republican period, "In Rome, the ambassador was recognized as . . . a personification of the sovereignty and majesty of the State he represented."[28] This easy extension of a principle to which few would object (hospitality for a visiting sovereign) to a broader scope of application (treating a *representative* of the sovereign the same as the sovereign himself) is a good example of the practical extension of a legal principle to deal with new circumstances for which Roman jurists would become justly noted.

As would often occur in the development of the Roman civil law, the expansion of empire and the growing affluence of Rome demanded a more sophisticated interpretation of exactly what "hospitality" for the representatives of foreign sovereigns entailed. Throughout the late Republic and early Empire, Roman jurists argued the point whether or not foreign envoys should be subject to civil action before the Roman courts. Justinian's *Digest* captured this debate before pronouncing the official imperial position, with somewhat surprising reasoning for this early period:

Paul (*Plautius*, Book 17) states that Cassius [a jurist] would allow an action against a legate if the action would not interfere with his duties; whereas Julian [another jurist] said all actions should be categorically refused. Paul: "Rightly so, for the reason for not granting the action is so that he may *not be distracted from the duties* he has undertaken as a legate."[29]

Even after the fall of Rome in the West, European rulers still maintained at least a minimal level of diplomatic intercourse throughout the Middle Ages through the use of envoys. During the Carolingian period, from the eighth through the tenth centuries, the normal function of an ambassador was very rudimentary: he delivered a letter from his sovereign and returned with a responding letter. Occasionally, ambassadors would discuss general views on the subject with the foreign sovereign or his advisors, but Carolingian ambassadors had no power to otherwise speak for their king.[30]

The body of papal opinions, scriptural teachings, and conciliar pronouncements that constitute the canon law evolved rather haphazardly for the first 12 centuries of the church's existence. Nevertheless, in one of the earliest attempts to collect and roughly organize canons by Isidore of Seville in the sixth or seventh century, one of his maxims—short prescriptive statements of positive law—of the *jus gentium* (law of nations) concerned the inviolability of ambassadors.[31] The rediscovery and systematic study of Justinian's *Corpus Juris Civilis* in the twelfth and thirteenth centuries led to a systematization of canon law mainly along Roman law lines.

With the pope wielding enormous power both temporally and spiritually, it is not surprising that the papacy found it necessary to both send and receive ambassadors. Up through the thirteenth century, popes utilized *nuncii* (basically ad hoc messengers) to carry out a remarkably robust correspondence with the Christian princes. But a *nuncio* was really nothing more than a form of herald, often referred to as a "living letter." However, beginning in the twelfth

century, popes sporadically began utilizing a proctor *(procurator)* for particularly important, timely, or complex missions. A *procurator* was sent with *plena
potestas*—full powers—to negotiate on behalf of the pope. By the end of the
thirteenth century, secular rulers, too, would begin using proctors. This was
the type of envoy, a temporary representative with full powers to speak for his
sovereign, that would evolve by the end of the fifteenth century into the permanent ambassador.[32]

Canon law, therefore, developed a body of law concerning the status and
treatment of legates and other representatives of the pope and the Christian
princes. Pope Gregory VII unabashedly adopted the ancient concept of the
representative as the personification of the pontiff who sent him: "[O]ne sees
in the legate the pope's own face and hears in his voice the living voice of the
pope."[33] This somewhat overstated view was codified in the first systematic
collection of canon law, Gratian's thirteenth-century work, *The Concordance
of Discordant Canons*, universally known as the *Decretum*. Gratian, under the
heading "What the law of nations is," states that the law of nations includes
"the obligation of not harming ambassadors." In the standard gloss to this
passage, the canonist Johannes Teutonicus adds, "If anyone impedes the ambassador of an ally or enemy, he is excommunicated according to the
canons. . . . According to ordinance [municipal law], he is handed over to the
enemy to be their slave."[34]

It was not only Christian canon law that recognized the inviolability of
envoys. In Islam, the *sunna*—words and acts of the Prophet—includes Mohammed's command that envoys never be abused. Even after great provocation,
Mohammed went as far as to assert that maltreatment of an envoy may be a
just cause for war.[35] One commentator recounts the strength of Mohammed's
conviction in this matter:

In Arabia, the person of an ambassador was at all times considered as sacred. Mohammed established this inviolability. Always the ambassadors sent to Mohammed or his
successors were not harmed. [In one instance, Mohammed told an envoy who had
particularly displeased him] "If you weren't an envoy, I would have you killed."[36]

Sovereignty

Although the generally acknowledged rule that sovereigns were immune
from each other's authority and jurisdiction formed the basis, by extension,
for the immunity of envoys of the sovereign, in practice the envoys may well
have received more rigorously guarded immunity than their kings. Historically,
sovereigns were not always immune. For example, during the Crusades, Richard I of England was captured and held to ransom by Leopold of Austria.
During the Middle Ages, a king was only too aware that "if he fell into alien
hands, he might expect to be ransomed, mistreated, killed."[37] At the same time,
monarchs during this period began to recognize the importance of envoys as

symbolic extensions of their own sovereign authority outside their borders. In one early collection of national law, the thirteenth-century Castilian compilation known as *Las Siete Partidas*, all envoys of foreign rulers were granted immunity be they "Christian, Moor, or Jew."[38]

The necessary connection between sovereignty and the ability to send and receive ambassadors was universally acknowledged by the sixteenth century. The issue of whether anyone other than a sovereign could appoint ambassadors, and by extension whether such ambassadors would enjoy immunity through their special relationship to the person appointing them, was settled in English law as a result of the matter of Mary, Queen of Scots. A panel of five noted civil law jurists appointed specifically to consider the matter found that

[w]e think that the solicitor [envoy] of a prince lawfully deposed, and another [prince] being invested in his place, cannot have the privilege of an ambassador; for that none but princes and such others as have sovereignty may have ambassadors.[39]

EARLY MODERN DEVELOPMENT

Traced to the early religious notions of the sanctity of envoys, the representative character theory of diplomatic immunity has deep roots. However, as the Renaissance progressed and international legal theory developed along more secular and rational lines, the religious underpinnings of diplomatic immunity, as with much of the civil and criminal law, became less and less sustainable. Jurists sought theories deduced from human reason, rather than maxims sprung from divine inspiration. In the context of diplomatic law, the solution was found in evolving ideas of sovereignty sprung from the intellectual ferment of the Renaissance.

The Renaissance and Permanent Missions

By the early fifteenth century, the city-states of Renaissance Italy had developed sophisticated commercial and financial links between each other and with often far-flung non-Italian cities and kingdoms. As a result, the great Italian merchant cities were the first to establish permanent embassies to safeguard their commercial interests abroad. Although there is some dispute among historians, the first permanent embassy is generally thought to have been the 1450 accreditation of Nicodemus dei Pontramoli by the Duke of Milan to Cosimo de Medici in Florence.[40] The dispatch of other permanent ambassadors quickly followed, with the Duke of Milan sending a permanent envoy to France in 1460. The Venetians immediately imitated this practice, with the posting of permanent ambassadors to Burgundy (1469), France (1479), and England (c. 1500).[41]

However, during the early years of permanent diplomatic missions in the fifteenth and sixteenth centuries, the recognized primary purpose of embassies was to gather information on foreign governments. Important negotiations were left to special ad hoc diplomatic missions and were seldom undertaken by the in-place permanent mission. As a result, a "diplomat was regarded as little more than a licensed spy" and was constantly under surveillance.[42] During this time, sovereigns who received permanent ambassadors would have had little incentive to make the foreign diplomats' work easier, other than as a matter of ritual or reciprocity.

These earliest permanent ambassadors, although scrupulously respected in their persons, were universally suspected in their motives. From the earliest days of permanent embassies in the 1450s to the end of the seventeenth century, permanent ambassadors were uniformly regarded as (at best) liars or (at worst) spies.[43] Foreign ambassadors to the Sublime Porte were literally kept under lock and key within the sprawling palaces of the Ottoman sultans. Peter the Great of Russia directed that all foreign ambassadors be constantly accompanied by a Russian "guard of honor" that kept the ambassador and his retinue under constant surveillance. Henry VII of England upon assuming the throne ordered all ambassadors banished from his court.[44] Henry IV of France refused to receive ambassadors, and Poland expelled all foreign envoys in 1660. In 1651, the Estates-General of the United Provinces held extensive debate on the usefulness of allowing foreign ambassadors to remain in the Netherlands.[45] The recurrent expulsion of various diplomatic agents even today for espionage activities demonstrates there may be some persistent basis in fact for this time-honored suspicion of permanent embassies.

Several factors coalesced by the mid-fifteenth century resulting in the establishment of permanent embassies. First, the Italian city-states had developed a variety of effective forms of central government that could speak for all—or at least a vast majority—of the citizenry. Second, the establishment beginning in the thirteenth century of universities produced a class of well-educated men with the requisite linguistic, rhetorical, and political skills necessary to undertake continuous representation for their home governments. Third, ambitious neighbors anxious to interact surrounded the Italian cities on all sides. Finally, the enormous amounts of surplus wealth produced by the commercial and banking activities of the great Italian merchant cities allowed for the expensive retention of permanent professional ambassadors in far-off capitals and commercial centers.[46] By the end of the fifteenth century, there was a general movement among the Italian cities and the great trading centers outside Italy toward permanent embassies.[47] Nevertheless, the dispatching of permanent ambassadors, always an expensive undertaking, was questioned by some of the leading commentators well into the sixteenth and seventeenth centuries.[48]

Throughout this period of rapid growth in permanent diplomatic missions, the echoes of the earlier quasi-religious tenet of strict inviolability of envoys remained. One of the most influential political and legal thinkers of the early modern period, the mid-sixteenth-century French philosopher Jean Bodin held that ambassadors have a strict right to respect under all circumstances, including escort to and from the frontiers of the state to which they had been sent—not an insignificant concern when traveling in sixteenth-century Europe. Bodin stated that the person of an ambassador "is and should be sacred *(sacrée)* and inviolable."[49] The mid-sixteenth-century Spanish jurist Balthzar Ayala reiterated the notion that the ambassador was a personification of his sovereign: "An outrage offered to ambassadors is deemed offered to the king or State whose embassy they are carrying out."[50]

By the end of the sixteenth century, it was routine for ambassadors posted to key states for important causes to hold some court appointment or to stand in some other intimate relationship to the sovereign he represented.[51] This personal proximity to or familiarity with the sovereign bolstered the notion that the envoy was a personification of his king; that he personally knew the monarch's mind helped sustain this fiction. It was also at this time that the development of formal legal theory in the area of diplomatic immunities rapidly accelerated, beginning with the Oxford professor of civil law Alberico Gentili's seminal 1585 work, *De legationibus libri tres*. This was quickly followed by Francois Hotman's *L'ambassadeur* in 1603 and by Grotius' *De iure bellii ac pacis* in 1625. Of course, the many juristic philosophers of this epoch included some comment on the law of diplomatic immunity in every major work on international law.[52]

During the late Renaissance, legal theory concerning the protection of envoys developed apace with the increasing use of permanent legations and evolving ideas of sovereignty. One of the most influential writers among the Spanish Scholastics, Francisco Suarez, writing near the end of the sixteenth century, rejected the idea that the right to send ambassadors was an inherent incident of sovereignty. Instead, Suarez asserted that the right of sovereigns to send and receive ambassadors was actually based on positive state-made law within the law of nations,[53] but that once a sovereign agreed to accept an ambassador, inviolability of the envoy was a matter of natural law.[54] In short, a sovereign did not have to agree to accept envoys, but if he did agree, the envoys were inviolable under natural law. In keeping with his writings on the rights of non-Christian indigenous peoples in the Americas, Suarez extended the right of inviolability to the envoys of all sovereigns, including pagans.[55]

Enlightenment Legal Theory

In his landmark 1625 work on international law, *De iure belli ac pacis*, Hugo Grotius addressed the issue of the immunity of diplomats. Grotius realized that the Roman law provided an inadequate basis for diplomatic relations since by the first century B.C.—the period of the classical Roman jurists—such relations were nearly all intraimperial. Rather than providing a blueprint for relations between nominally coequal sovereigns, Roman law governed the relationship between the Roman *municipia* and its extensive colonies.[56] Based on his observation of state practice, Grotius subscribed to the idea that the ambassador was a direct representative of the dignity and majesty of his sovereign and was therefore entitled to the same privileges and immunities. However, in attempting to explain this theory, Grotius compared the effect of the receiving state's lack of legal control over the ambassador to the ambassador being physically outside the territory of the receiving state. This unfortunate choice of metaphor, misunderstood as a literal principle by some subsequent commentators, resulted in the confused notion that Grotius endorsed the extraterritorial principle of immunity for envoys.[57] Although a novel fiction, Grotius's apparent support of an extraterritorial principle, coupled with his enormous general influence in international law, led by 1750 to a wide acceptance of the extraterritorial principle, particularly in the context of diplomatic premises.[58]

From Grotius's work in the early seventeenth century onward, what originally had developed as a quasi-religious notion that an ambassador was inviolable as a matter of religious or natural law developed into an extension of a sovereign's undisputed personal immunity to cover his formally accredited agents.[59] The eighteenth-century Dutch jurist Cornelius Bynkershoek explained this shift from personification to agency in the context of diplomatic envoys in his work *De foro legatorum*.

An ambassador does indeed represent his prince, but only in the sense that one fulfilling a commission represents the one giving the commission, and so the representation is confined to those things covered by the commission. Therefore care must be taken lest any delay or impediment be placed in the way of the ambassador.[60]

Christian Wolff, a contemporary of Bynkershoek, concurred in this more restrictive view of the relationship between ambassador and sovereign.

Therefore, it does not belong to this right to extend the representation to the dignity itself of the sender, or his majesty, consequently by the law of nature an ambassador is not the same moral person as the sender.[61]

This extension of agency theory to the envoy–sovereign relationship, by then widely known as *representative character*, was a characteristic Enlightenment exercise in recasting fundamental legal constructs like diplomatic immunity in reason, rather than divine mandate.[62] Nevertheless, the purging of the religious basis of immunity left undisturbed the legal fiction that the ambassador stood in the shoes of his sovereign by agency if not by supernatural personification. Equally, this shift did not lessen the emotive force of the representative character of ambassadors—princes still strongly held as a matter of honor that an insult to their ambassador was a personal insult to themselves.[63] This was not, therefore, quite the same as the well-developed principal–agent relationship found in the law merchant or in the developing law of contract.

The universal acceptance of the principle of diplomatic immunity by the end of the eighteenth century was also manifested by the actions of the nascent U.S. government. One of the first acts passed by the newly constituted Congress was a statute recognizing the immunity of foreign envoys from the jurisdiction of U.S. courts.[64]

Modern Development

The law concerning immunity of diplomats enjoyed universal acceptance by the second half of the twentieth century. So much so that the International Court of Justice, when considering the potential culpability of the government of Iran for failing to protect the American diplomats taken hostage at the U.S. embassy in Tehran in 1979, found that the principle of inviolability may have matured into a peremptory norm of international law or *jus cogens*. As such, the principle of diplomatic inviolability would be binding upon all states—with or without their consent—and cannot be abrogated by treaty or other agreement.[65]

The Modern Idea of Sovereignty

The representative character theory of diplomatic immunity was based on an extension of sovereign immunity from the *person* of the sovereign to *representatives* of that sovereign. But what exactly does sovereignty entail? What rights and privileges appertain to sovereign states, however defined?[66] First and foremost, states have the right to autonomy, independence, and liberty—in short, *to exist as an entity* within the community of nations.[67] Second, states have the right to sovereignty (in terms of exclusivity) and jurisdiction within their borders—put simply, *internal autonomy*.[68] Third, states are entitled to *legal equality* within the international community.[69] Finally, states are entitled to representation within the international system, particularly within international institutions[70] and bilaterally with the consent of other individual states.[71]

The idea that state sovereigns enjoy absolute immunity from another sovereign's jurisdiction began eroding with the 1917 Russian Revolution and has accelerated since the end of World War II due to the widespread state ownership of airlines, shipping lines, and other purely commercial enterprises.[72] Governments quickly recognized that absolute immunity from their own domestic civil and criminal processes gave an enormous competitive advantage to foreign state-owned enterprises at the expense of competing domestic privately owned companies.[73] Therefore, as the customary attributes of sovereignty have constricted, so have the hitherto near-absolute immunities of diplomatic agents.

The Triumph of Functional Necessity Theory?

One of the more innovative jurists of the Enlightenment, Emerich de Vattel, was the first to suggest the stripping away of legal fictions from the law of diplomatic immunity. Vattel, with impeccably rational deduction, reasoned that one could observe from history and current state practice that nations universally recognized the necessity of diplomatic intercourse. Based on this recognized necessity and the fact that sovereigns could not possibly conduct any but a small fraction of their relations with other sovereigns in person, nations must send and receive envoys. Therefore, reasoned Vattel, if you must have ambassadors, reason dictates that states should not interfere with ambassadors lest they be unable to accomplish their mutually agreed upon functions.[74] This utilitarian argument—immunity for the sake of diplomatic efficiency—was in keeping with the overarching secularization of thought throughout the Enlightenment. Why base something as important as a waiver of sovereignty on religious or quasi-religious grounds when a rational basis would do nicely? Because, as Vattel recognized, the sending and receiving of ambassadors was an "indispensable obligation" to promote the common welfare and safety of nations, provide a means to peacefully settle disputes, and to facilitate general intercourse among states,[75] it was perfectly rational and efficient to ensure diplomats could go about their work protected from local interference.

In 1926, a senior legal counsel from the British Foreign Office, Sir Cecil Hurst, declared the representative character theory of diplomatic immunities a dead letter. Hurst was bemused by the extensive amount of written debate between authors on the matter.

In fact, it is a very simple thing. Privileges and immunities are founded on necessity: they are indispensable to maintaining international relations. . . . [Representative character] theory could have had some usefulness, but it did not accord with the facts. It came in the end to absurd consequences and it was definitively repudiated by modern authors and court decisions.[76]

In the flush of internationalist fervor that followed the victory of the Allied Powers over fascism in World War II, many legal commentators rushed to proclaim the end of old notions of sovereignty, including strict diplomatic immunity as an extension of sovereign immunity, in favor of the new international repository of sovereignty, the United Nations. One of the leading international law scholars of this period, Hersch Lauterpacht, systematically dismantled the traditional supports for a theory of sovereign immunity: the assumed *sovereignty, independence, equality,* and *dignity* of states.[77] Lauterpacht dismissed concerns that limiting sovereign immunity, and by extension diplomatic immunity, would offend the principles of *independence* and *equality.* Why should these principles prevent a state being brought before a foreign court if subject to the same procedures and substantive law as citizens of the foreign state?[78] In addition, Lauterpacht could not see how *sovereignty* could be offended if a state were brought before a foreign court as a party to a contract made within the foreign state or as a defendant in a tort action that arose within the receiving state's territory. In fact, Lauterpacht argued, there is a greater affront to the foreign state's sovereignty because it is denied the traditional sovereign authority to enforce contracts that were made or redress injuries that had been incurred within its borders.[79]

It was with the least tangible of these concepts that Lauterpacht had the most difficulty. Having disposed of the other three traditional bases for sovereign—and by extension diplomatic—immunity, Lauterpacht conceded that the only remaining rational basis was *dignity*. However, he found that basing any legal principle on anything as anachronistic as dignity was quite ill-advised.

[Dignity is] alien to the conception of the rule of law, national and international, and to the true position of the State in modern society.[80]

How, reasoned Lauterpacht, could any state's dignity (while not conceding this was even a valid basis for concern) be offended as long as equal due process was available in the foreign court? After all, state governments routinely submit to the jurisdiction of their own national courts.[81]

Although a perfectly rational argument, Lauterpacht missed a significant point. States, particularly new states emerging from the yoke of colonialism, cared deeply about *dignity*. In the case of many new and desperately poor states, the seemingly equal dignity within international organizations such as the UN General Assembly afforded to each state, no matter how small or powerless, provided significant political validation. Even in the face of economic and political backwardness, new states could claim a seat at the table, even if the meal was someone else's treat.

Developing State Practice

Beginning in the immediate aftermath of World War II—but really harkening back to the Russian Revolution—many states began asserting a more restrictive interpretation of the heretofore absolute theory of sovereign immunity. In 1952, the acting legal advisor to the U.S. State Department issued a landmark memorandum setting out a restrictive interpretation of immunity as the official U.S. position.[82] The U.S. codified the so-called Tate Letter's restrictive immunity in the 1976 Foreign Sovereign Immunity Act.[83] Fearing that important U.S. business centers like New York City would now gain an advantage over London in attracting commercial activities, the British Parliament followed the American lead in 1978 with the State Immunity Act.[84]

Vienna Conventions

The opening for signature of the 1961 Vienna Convention on Diplomatic Relations (and its companion the 1962 Vienna Convention on Consular Relations) represented a triumph for the functional necessity theory of diplomatic immunity.[85] The immediate and resounding acceptance[86] of the 1961 Vienna

Convention was a result of the confluence of several factors. First, diplomatic law had remained fairly stable for some time. Second, there was a keen interest among states in clear rules of reciprocity of treatment, particularly with the rapid expansion of the number of new states in the late 1940s and the 1950s. Finally, there was mutual interest in reaching a compromise on uniform rules between states, the International Law Commission, and the United Nations Sixth Committee (International Law).[87]

THE PSYCHIC VALUE OF REPRESENTATIVE CHARACTER

So with the broad acceptance of the Vienna Convention, including its codification of the functional necessity theory of immunity, one would have expected representative character and its baggage of legal fictions to have slipped from the scene without a ripple. However, although diplomatic law may have rejected the idea that ambassadors personify their sovereigns, diplomatic practice has not.

Of course, representative character is a legal fiction—the ambassador does not corporeally represent anyone but himself. Nevertheless, it is hardly the first such legal fiction to influence the development of positive law in important ways.[88] The fiction that the envoy personified his sender, in law and dignity if not in fact, served as a mechanism allowing diplomats to carry out their functions free from the threat of interference by a host nation's coercive institutions while leaving intact the emotive force of the principle of absolute territorial sovereignty.[89] Given the great flurry of controversy over the perceived erosion of the internal sovereignty of state governments in the face of foreign interventions in domestic humanitarian crises or internal civil conflicts, territorial sovereignty still carries substantial emotional weight. With international institutions in the early stages of development and international society still grasping at consensus regarding even the most fundamental issues, the fiction of representative character still holds appeal. As Sir Henry Maine observed in regard to primitive societies, "It is not difficult to understand why fictions in all their forms are particularly congenial to the infancy of society."[90] In the infantile society of nations, the fiction that the envoy is a physical personification of his sovereign has likewise proven a durable myth.

If it is true that humans, and nations as an aggregation of humans, act toward each other either with *egoism* (self-interestedly at the expense of others) or with *sociability* (in cooperation with others, self-interestedly or not),[91] to which impulse does one attribute the universal acceptance of diplomatic immunity? Realists would not—indeed cannot—accept that states act out of sociability for any reason.[92] But is the legal regime of diplomatic immunity purely a tit-for-tat exchange of self-interests? On the other hand, can we presume that states waive the exercise of a fundamental sovereign prerogative—control of those within their borders—out of nothing more than an impulse to sociable coop-eration? The truth, as is often the case, lies somewhere between. In an increas-ingly interconnected world, there is substantial psychic value to be gained from ensuring the continuous and safe presence of diplomatic envoys within the borders of other states.

Even during the age of industrialized war with millions of lives at stake, the sanctity of diplomats has generally been respected.[93] The question is, of course, why? At least part of the answer lies in the fact that diplomatic envoys fulfill a complex need for intrahuman contact between sovereign states, both by pro-viding a human face to national policies and by supplying a tangible way to directly affect the "person" of a foreign sovereign, be it a monarch, a dictator, or an elected assembly.

Physical Control

Once diplomats are formally received within a host state, they are in many ways subject to the whims of the receiving government and the winds of po-litical change in the relations between the host country and the envoy's home country. As such, they represent a tangible object against which governments can react to express pleasure, rebuke, or warning. One of the mechanisms used to some effect as a form of diplomatic signaling by both the United States and the Soviet Union throughout the Cold War was expulsion of diplomatic per-sonnel or the use of the persona non grata designation. Under accepted legal principles, diplomatic personnel may be declared non grata and expelled for any reason or no reason, and the host state is under no legal obligation to provide an explanation.[94] This mechanism proved to be an effective form of registering displeasure between the two superpowers whose nuclear arsenals rendered more aggressive forms of signaling unacceptably dangerous.

One of the earliest and most infamous cases of a host state declaring another sovereign's envoy non grata and immediately expelling him was the case of the sixteenth-century Spanish ambassador to England, Don Bernadino de Men-doza. Caught assisting in the plot of Mary, Queen of Scots to overthrow Eliz-abeth I, a treasonous act for any subject of the realm, Don Bernadino was immediately expelled, his well-honored diplomatic immunity from criminal prosecution all that stood between him and the same fateful end met by his English and Scottish coconspirators.

After the Napoleonic Wars, a period within which European Great Power diplomacy was developed to a subtle and highly nuanced art, expulsions were normally accomplished with little notice and as discretely as possible. That is not the case in modern practice; the expulsion of diplomats is as often intended to serve as a public remonstrance of a foreign government than as a rebuke of an individual diplomat's peccadilloes.

Talleyrand once advised his diplomats, "Above all avoid an excess of enthu-siasm."[95] Diplomacy is and always has been a nuanced business. Signaling in diplomacy is highly stylized and the often-ossified rituals of diplomatic intercourse can often severely limit the availability of nonverbal or unscripted signals. However, international mass media, in particular television, has probably changed this forever.[96]

Dignity and Prestige

The elaborate trappings of diplomatic precedent and protocol developed in response to the fiction that all sovereign states are equal within the community of nations. This is factual nonsense—there have always been stronger and weaker states—but the pretext of sovereign equality has been enshrined in the constitutional documents of international society.[97] That the ideal of sovereign equality (and its visible diplomatic manifestations) has proven persistent, even in the face of vast disparities in the political, military, and economic power of states, is hardly surprising, for "the cost of sovereignty is low and the psychic satisfaction it provided was high."[98]

Sovereignty is the fantastic representative of infantile pride . . . As *individuals*, we usually have to abdicate our "absolute sovereignty" . . . by the second or third year of life. But individually we retain, and collectively we luxuriate, in expressing [in the form of state sovereignty] traces of these early forms of thought which represent us as free and independent in *all* our actions.[99]

Since the rapid decolonization that followed World War II, and again after the dissolution of the Soviet Union, small and new states, as well as national, religious, and ethnic movements, have often found self-validation and international recognition, even in a purely ritualistic form, through the rites of diplomacy. It is often these newest and smallest states (or even substates) that most crave the ritual expression of equality among state representatives, regardless of the actual strength or weakness of their respective nations.

If the doctrine of sovereignty helps fulfill deeply-rooted emotional needs, then arguments alone—no matter how valid—cannot convince sovereignty's champions to abandon it.[100]

It is within this highly stylized milieu, wherein the pretense is tentatively maintained that states are coequal sovereigns, that even the smallest states can find recognition, the façade of equality, and some full measure of dignity within international society.[101]

Ritual is used to resolve what may be one of the greatest areas of conflict for the developing individual, that is, what is inside and what is outside? This is, in effect, to define the individual, to separate one biological unit from the mass that is the remainder of the species.[102]

From the earliest days of diplomatic intercourse, ritual and prestige were inextricably mixed. Because the theory of diplomatic capacity was grounded in the notion that the ambassador was a direct proxy of his sovereign, complex rules of precedence and protocol emerged very quickly.

The crux of this matter was that appearances—the right to a place of honor in public ceremonies; coats of arms; the grant by one ruler to another of some particular title . . . clearly and indeed brutally symbolised power and status. Any change in ceremonial indicated a rise or fall in the standing of a state or its ruler; diplomats therefore watched with a jealous eye the formalities observed on any great public occasion.[103]

Therefore, in an environment where even a seemingly meaningless change in protocol might lead to a nasty diplomatic imbroglio, the ability to use direct manipulation of protocol and ritual to communicate meaning is greatly restricted.[104] Although vigorously monitored and enforced, rights of precedence based on the relative importance of states obviously change over time. Shifting alliances can also cause a reworking of the diplomatic pecking order.[105]

Short of physical assault, the ultimate insult to the dignity of an ambassador or chief of mission, and by extension to his sending state, is a declaration of him or her as persona non grata. During negotiations preceding the 1961 and 1962 Vienna Conventions, one of the leading members of the International Law Commission warned that declaring a head of mission persona non grata without clear cause would likely lead to the sending state feeling "its dignity affronted and relations between the two might suffer" as a result.[106] Keep in mind this succinct exposition of the personification implicit in representative character theory is from a member of the very commission that sought to jettison what they found to be the anachronistic representative character theory. This is a strange way to support functional necessity theory.

THE SOCIAL PSYCHOLOGY OF DIPLOMACY?

What then is the present state of diplomatic immunity? Although much of the international legal community, led by the International Law Commission, has sought to stamp out what may seem an anachronistic legal fiction, representative character theory has proven remarkably resilient. The reason for this is that the permanent posting of diplomats and maintenance of embassies abroad is a twofold enterprise. First, the day-to-day functioning of diplomacy at the microlevel is undeniably important to the nitty-gritty work of international relations. The economic role of embassies greases the wheels of international trade. Increasing numbers of foreign nationals living abroad have placed growing demands on consular services. Low-level exchange of information between government agencies, usually facilitated by embassy staff, helps ensure uniformity in regulatory and enforcement activities. In order efficiently to perform these often mundane but important functions, diplomats must remain unhampered by fear of interference by receiving state agencies or courts. Undeniably, this free exercise of traditional diplomatic activities creates a functional necessity for diplomatic immunities. These are the purposes the Vienna Conventions were intended to advance.

However, stripping the purpose of permanent envoys to the barest utilitarian functions misses much of the traditional sociological role fulfilled by diplomatic representatives. The mutual exchange of and respect for diplomats represents an important mechanism for bolstering solidarity within the society of states. As in any social relationship or grouping, maintaining solidarity is necessary to fostering the desire "to remain together at work or play, in trade, or under the same flag and government."[107]

Ritual plays a powerful role in social groups, particularly "primitive" societies like the international community.[108] The ritual exchange of diplomats, like any ritual, can be a powerful tool for creating and perpetuating social solidarity.[109] Ritual, after all "demarcates, emphasizes, affirms, solemnizes, and also smoothes over critical changes in social relationships."[110] The sending and receiving of diplomats is not merely a utilitarian function to smooth trade and communication between states. Like other rites of intensification,[111] the ritual of diplomatic interaction is intended to reinforce among states an intense awareness of the existence of a "community of nations" and their status as nominally coequal members of that community. In short, this diplomatic ritual of intensification helps ensure that a nation—or worse, whole classes of nations—do not become alienated from the basic tenets and goals of the international community. When states become alienated (North Korea seems an apt example in this context), dire consequences can accrue to their own people and to the international community at large. As with alienated individuals within a social group, such states "live incomplete, normless, and relatively meaningless lives."[112] And as with highly alienated individuals in society, highly alienated states can wreak havoc within the larger community of nations. There is, therefore, a cost to excluding states from the diplomatic rituals.

The nineteenth-century English political economist Walter Bagehot analyzed this same kind of utilitarian–ritualistic dichotomy in his influential study of the English system of government, *The English Constitution*.[113] Bagehot acknowledged that the Crown performed two seemingly contradictory roles in English society—one functional (the day-to-day business of government through the Cabinet, Privy Council, and the "Queen-in-Parliament") and one ritualistic (the traditional ceremony of monarchy). Bagehot described these separate roles as the *efficient parts* and the *dignified parts* of the English Constitution. The efficient parts consist of the actual mechanisms through which the government "works and rules," whereas the dignified parts include "those which excite and preserve the reverence of the population."[114] Much the same kind of bifurcation of purpose appears to be at work in diplomatic immunity, although as Bagehot pointed out well over a century ago, "There are indeed men who reject the dignified parts."[115]

CONCLUSION

Diplomats, rather than existing as mere functionaries, represent in a universally acknowledged way the sovereignty of their sending state—a real-time presence in a foreign country of the presumed equality and dignity of their state. The persistence of seemingly archaic forms of protocol, the deference paid to heads of mission at social functions, even the presence of a foreign state's flag in another nation's capital—all demonstrate an essential symbolic representative character inherent in the presence of permanent envoys that cannot be reduced by positive law to a mere efficient function. Because the importance of diplomatic intercourse cannot be quantified merely in numbers of trade contracts signed or amounts of foreign aid received, states will continue to engage in the ritual of representative character diplomacy to allow some tangible (albeit ritualistic) mechanism for directly manifesting honor, disdain, or anger toward a nominally coequal sovereign in an intrinsically personal and human way.

NOTES

1. See, for example, McCoubrey, Hilaire, *Natural Law, Religion, and the Development of International Law* 177–89.

2. See Bederman, David, *International Law in Antiquity* 135–36 (2000). The inherent sociability of humans has been the subject of much interest and comment by philosophers for many centuries. In Book I, Part II, of his *Politics*, Aristotle makes his famous assertion that man is, by nature, a political animal. He continues:

> The proof that the state is a creation of nature and prior to the individual is that the individual, when isolated, is not self-sufficing; and therefore he is like a part in relation to the whole. But he who is unable to live in society, or who has no need because he is sufficient for himself, must be either a beast or a god: he is no part of a state. A social instinct is implanted in all men by nature. . . .

The seventeenth-century philosopher and jurist Samuel von Puffendorf stated in a chapter entitled "On Natural Law" from his 1673 work *De Officio Hominis et Civi (The Duty of Man and the Citizen)*, I.iii.7:

> Thus then man is indeed an animal most bent upon self-preservation, helpless in himself, unable to save himself without the aid of his fellows, highly adapted to promote mutual interests; but on the other hand no less malicious, insolent, and easily provoked, also as able as he is prone to inflict injury upon another. Whence it follows that, in order to be safe, he must be sociable, that is, must be united with men like himself, and so conduct himself toward them that they may have no good cause to injure him, but rather may be ready to maintain and promote his interests.

This is not to say that the idea of inherent sociability is not without its detractors, with equally notable thinkers like Jean-Jacques Rousseau and Emmanuel Kant among them.

3. Davitt, Thomas E., *The Basic Values in Law: A Study of the Ethico-Legal Implications of Psychology and Anthropology* 9 (1968).

4. It is of course possible to make too much of this Platonic notion that states are just men writ large, but there is undeniably some organic texture to the behavior of states—or any human collective—discernible from their interaction with other similar entities. This is not a completely uncontroversial position, however. The great French sociologist Emile Durkheim in his 1912 work, *The Elementary Forms of Religious Life*, boldly asserted that society is a reality *sui generis*. Quoted in Scheff, Thomas J., *Bloody Revenge: Emotions, Nationalism, and War* 75 (1994).

5. Anderson, M. S., *The Rise of Modern Diplomacy* viii (1992).

6. See Professor Bederman's discussion of personal diplomacy in the ancient world, *supra* note 2, at 90–91.

7. Anderson, *supra* note 5, at 9–10. The practice of using bankers or merchants to perform duties as official envoys was, by the nineteenth century at the latest, considered very bad form. Denza, Eileen, *Diplomatic Law: Commentary on the Vienna Convention on Diplomatic Relations* 382 (2d ed. 1998). The possibility of using such persons as formal representatives was extinguished formally by the 1961 Vienna Convention on Diplomatic Relations, which specifically forbids diplomatic agents to engage in professional or commercial activity. Vienna Convention on Diplomatic Immunity, article 42, in Brownlie, Ian, *Basic Documents in International Law* 226 (3d ed. 1984).

8. The preamble to the Vienna Convention on Diplomatic Relations states, "Recalling that peoples of all nations from ancient times have recognized the status of diplomatic agents." *Vienna Convention, supra* note 7, at 213.

9. For a broad discussion of each, see, e.g., Barker, J. Craig, *The Abuse of Diplomatic Privileges and Immunities: A Necessary Evil?* 35–55 (1996).

10. *Id.*, at 49. See generally, Henkin et al., *International Law* 1201–02 (3d ed. 1993).

11. The myths of the Olympian pantheon, for example, were replete with stories of any number of deities assuming human or animal form to manifest themselves to—and cavort with—mortals.

12. Anderson, *supra* note 5, at 12.

13. Dreener, David R., *The United States Attorneys General and International Law* 266 (1957). Attorney General Cushing also noted that this customary rule did not apply to the American republics because the executive power is continuous and there was therefore no need for a custom to reappoint ambassadors with a change in presidents.

14. See, e.g., the Austro-Hungarian Empire's 1895 law on civil jurisdiction, exempting, "Persons enjoying extraterritorial status by virtue of the principles of international law." Act of 1895 to Establish Rules Governing Jurisdiction, art. 9, cited in *Laws and Regulations Regarding Diplomatic and Consular Privileges and Immunities* 15 (UN Legislative Series, vol. VII, 1958). U.S. Attorney General Cushing wrote in 1855 that extraterritoriality of diplomats "is the unanimous doctrine of all publicists, and is recognized in England, as it is in the United States, by statute." 7 *Opinions of the Attorney General* 386 (1855).

15. Barker, *supra* note 9, at 39–45. In practice, immunity from the criminal and civil jurisdiction of the receiving state often extended to whole sections, known as *franchises du quartier*, of the capital. Some of these diplomatic quarters were quite large and extended for many blocks around an embassy. The modern analogy to *franchises du quartier* is the occasional granting of asylum by an embassy to a national of the receiving state. See, generally, *Department of State Bulletin* 50 (Oct. 1980) (U.S. policy on asylum in embassies).

16. Strisower, Leo, "L'exterritorialité et ses principales applications," 1923 *Recueil des cours de l'academie de droit internationale* 911 (Walker's trans.).

17. Barker, *supra* note 9, at 33–34. The author specifically cites to works by De Martens (1866 *Le guide diplomatique*) and Alberico Gentili (1585 *De legationibus*).

18. Van der Molen, Gesina H. J., *Alberico Gentili and the Development of International Law* 92 (1968).

19. Stuart, Graham, "Le droit et la pratique diplomatiques et consulaires," 1934 *Recuil des cours de l'academie de droit internationale* 463 (Walker's trans.).

20. Barker, *supra* note 9, at 15.

21. *Id.*

22. Bederman, *supra* note 2, at 91–94.

23. Hosack, John, *Law of Nations* 3 (facsimile reprint 1982) (1882) (citing Herodotus, Book VII, v. 136).

24. Cicero, "On the Response of the Soothsayer," *quoted in* Grotius, *De jure bellie ac pacis* bk. II, chapter xviii, §1 (1646) (*Classics in International Law* series, F. W. Kelsey trans. (1925) at 939.

25. Phillipson, Coleman, *International Law and Custom of Ancient Greece and Rome* 309–10 (1911). For example, the Romans refused to receive ambassadors from Rhodes in 169 B.C. and from Ptolemaic Egypt in 161 B.C. In both instances, Rome went to war with these states shortly after refusing their ambassadors.

26. Frey, Linda S. and Marsha L. Frey, *The History of Diplomatic Immunity* 37 (1999).

27. Phillipson, *supra* note 244, at 330.

28. *Id.*

29. D. 5.1.24–28. Paul was one of the most influential jurists within the collection of juristic writings assembled into what would become known as Justinian's *Digest*.

30. Ganshof, Francois L., *The Middle Ages: A History of International Relations* 42 (1953, Remy Inglis Hall trans. 1970).

31. Doyle, John P., "Francisco Suarez on the Law of Nations," in Mark W. Janis and Carolyn Evans, eds., *Religion and International Law* 109 (1999). The *Etymolgies* of Isidore of Seville included the maxim *legatorum non violandorum religio* at v. 6. This maxim was also incorporated by Gratian in his later *Decretum* at D. 1, c. 9.

32. Brundage, James A., *Medieval Canon Law* 116–17 (1995).

33. Frey & Frey, *supra* note 26, at 78.

34. Gratian, *Decretum*, D.1, c. 9 (in "The Treatise on Laws," DD. 1–20, A. Thompson, trans., with the Ordinary Gloss, J. Gordley, trans. 1993).

35. Frey & Frey, *supra* note 26, at 88.

36. Echid, Ahmed, "Islam et le droit des gens," 1934 *Recuil des cours de l'academie de droit internationale* 421 (Walker's trans.). Citing the International Court of Justice's *US Diplomats* decision, 1980 ICJ 41, regarding the seizing of U.S. diplomatic personnel in Iran, one commentator states that Islam has continued to contribute to the development of the law of diplomatic immunity. See Gamal M. Badr, "A Survey of Islamic International Law," in Janis and Evans, *supra* note 31, at 99–100 (1999).

37. Lewis, Charles, *State and Diplomatic Immunity* 15 (3d ed. 1990).

38. *Las Siete Partidas*, part 7, title 25, law 9 (quoted in Frey & Frey, *supra* note 26, at 86).

39. *Quoted in* Hosack, *supra* note 23, at 157–58.

40. Barker, *supra* note 9, at 21. A nineteenth-century historian, Otto Krauske, claimed that the first permanent ambassador was sent by the Duke of Milan, but to Genoa in 1455. Van der Molen, *supra* note 18, at 88.

41. Van der Molen, *supra* note 18, at 88.

42. Anderson, *supra* note 5, at 13.

43. Van der Molen, *supra* note 18, at 89–91.

44. *Id.*

45. Hurst, Cecil, "Les immunités diplomatiques," *Recuil des cours de l'academie de droit internationale* 119 (1926). A noted jurist of the seventeenth century, Richard Zouche, quotes another commentator, Paschal, on the matter of the honesty of ambassadors:

> I would have an ambassador rely on truth, the most certain of the virtues, and her faithful comrade reticence. Yet I am not so simple or rude as to exclude the diplomatic lie altogether from the mouth of an ambassador.

Zouche, *An Exposition of Fecial Law and Procedure* pt. II, § iv.17.21 (1650 ed.) (J. L Priestly trans., in the *Classics of International Law* series [1911]) at 97.

46. Anderson, *supra* note 5, at 2–3.

47. *Id.* at 8–9. Oddly, the greatest power of the age, France, was the last to engage to any significant extent in the sending of permanent embassies abroad.

48. Alberico Gentili did not think much of permanent embassies and steadfastly asserted that sovereigns retained the right to refuse to allow permanent embassies. Hugo Grotius likewise thought that rulers could easily do without them, relying instead on special envoys or other ad hoc representatives. Van der Molen, *supra* note 18, at 98.

49. Gardot, André, "Jean Bodin: sa place parmi les fondateurs du droit international," 1934 *Recuil des cours de l'academie de droit internationale,* 655 (Walker's trans.).

50. Ayala, Balthazar, *De jure et officious et disciplina militarii,* bk. I, ch. ix, §2, *quoted in* Brown, *infra* note 53, at 269. The 1582 edition translated by J. P. Bates is also available in the *Classics of International Law Series* (1912).

51. Anderson, *supra* note 5, at 12. The U.S. attorney general stated in 1855 that diplomatic immunity extended to all diplomatic personnel with a "direct putative relationship to the sovereign" regardless of their title. 7 *Opinions of the Attorney General* 210–11 (1855).

52. Barker, *supra* note 9, at 22–23.

53. Suarez, Francisco, *De legibus,* bk. II, ch. xix, §7, *cited in* Scott, James Brown, *Law, the State, and the International Community* 269 (1939). This would also be the explicit position incorporated into the 1961 Vienna Convention on Diplomatic Relations. Article 2 of this convention states, "The establishment of diplomatic relations between States and of permanent diplomatic missions, takes place by mutual consent." *Vienna Convention, supra* note 7, at 214.

54. Doyle, *supra* note 31, at 108. This is still the accepted rule today and few commentators have questioned the prerogative of state sovereigns to refuse ambassadors from particular states. *But see,* Wolff, *infra* note 75, at ch. ix, §1045 (p. 528) ("Those who claim that it is merely a matter of choice whether or not anyone wishes to admit ambassadors, comes to a rash decision . . .").

55. *Id.* at 112.

56. Barker, *supra* note 9, at 22–23.

57. Barker, *supra* note 9, at 39–45.

58. Denza, *supra* note 7, at 113. See also, Grotius, *De iure pacis ac belli,* II.xviii. vii–ix.

59. Barker, *supra* note 9, at 35–39.

60. Bynkershoek, Cornelius, *De foro legatorum,* ch. vii (1744 edition of the 1721 G. Laing trans.) (*Classics of International Law* series, 1995 reprint, at 37). Nevertheless, Bynkershoek recognized the emotive appeal of the idea that ambassadors actually personified their sovereigns. In answering the question why there was need for diplomatic immunity, Bynkershoek wrote, "[B]ecause they are the representatives everywhere of their prince, because they are messengers and negotiators of peace and treaties, and because without them the association and blessed tranquility of nations cannot be preserved." *Id.* at ch. v (p. 27).

61. Wolff, Christian, *Jus gentium methodo scientifica pertratatum,* ch. ix, §1055 (1737) (J. Drake trans., in the *Classic of International Law* series (1934) at 532–33).

62. Wolff rejected outright any quasi-religious or natural law notions of immunity, finding the basis of immunity in the consent of states. "Those who claim the sanctity of an ambassador is a part of the common law of all nations *(jus gentium)* imagine a right which does not exist." *Id.* at ch. ix, §1062 (p. 536).

63. Bynkershoek, *supra* note 60, at ch. v (p. 27).

64. Statutes 118 § 26 (1790), *cited in* Dreener, *supra* note 13, at 156.

65. Hannikainen, Lauri, *Peremptory Norms in International Law* 193 (1988). However, as Professor Haanikainen points out, the English text of the ICJ decision does not exactly track the language of the Vienna Convention on the Law of Treaties, article 53, that deals with the non-derogability of *jus cogens* norms. Whereas the English text uses the term "imperative" rather than peremptory, the French text of the decision uses identical language to the French text of article 53.

66. *See generally,* "Declaration on principles of international law concerning friendly relations and co-operation among states in accordance with the Charter of the United Nations," UN Doc. A/2625 (1970); Fiore Pasquale, *International Law Codified* 62 at 107 (1918); Louis Henkin, "International Law: Politics, Values and Functions," 216 *Recuil des Cours* 26–27 (1989-IV). *Cf.* Martti Koskenniemi, "Sovereignty—Prologemena to a Study of the Structure of International Law as Discourse," 4 *Kansainoikeus Ius Gentium* 71, 106 (1987).

67. *Charter of the United Nations,* art. 2, para 4. The International Court of Justice's opinion in the 1949 *Corfu Channel Case* stated that within the international community, "The sovereignty of States has now become an *institution,* an *international social function* of a psychological character . . ." *United Kingdom v. Albania,* 1949 I.C.J. 43 (opinion of J. Alvarez); Henkin, *supra* note 66, at 28.

68. Pasquale, *supra* note 66, at 107.

69. *Id.,* at art. 2, para 2.

70. *Id.,* at art. 4.

71. *Vienna Convention on Diplomatic Relations,* art. 2, *supra* note 7, at 214.

72. Hsiung, James C., *Anarchy and Order: The Interplay of Politics and Law in International Relations* 100–101 (1997).

73. This economic reality was one of the driving forces behind the issuance of the Tate Letter in 1952. *See* note 82, *infra.*

74. Cited in Barker, *supra* note 9, at 46–49.

75. Vattel, Emerich, *The Law of Nations or the Principles of International Law* bk. IV, ch. v (1758 ed., Charles Fenwick trans.) (*Classics of International Law* series, 1995

reprint, at 362). This view that there was a moral obligation on states to send and receive ambassadors was endorsed by Vattel's contemporary, Christian Wolff, who stated that ambassadors were necessary

> according to that duty imposed by nature by which one nation ought to contribute what it can to the presentation and perfection of another in that in which it is not self-sufficient, so that they may promote the common good as members of the supreme state.

Wolff, *supra* note 61, at ch. ix, §1044 (p. 527).

76. Hurst, *supra* note 45, at 121–22, 145 (Walker trans.).

77. Barker, *supra* note 9, at 194–97.

78. *Id.* at 196.

79. *Id.*

80. Lauterpacht, Hersch, "The Problem of Jurisdictional Immunities of Foreign States," 28 *British Yearbook of International Law* 220 (1951).

81. See, e.g., the Federal Tort Claims Act, 28 U.S.C. §§2671–2680.

82. Letter from Jack B. Tate, acting legal advisor, Department of State (19 May 1952), 26 *Department of State Bulletin* 984 (1952).

83. 28 U.S.C. §§ 1330, 1332(a), 1391(f) and 1601–1611 (1976).

84. State Immunity Act (1978), c. 33.

85. Hsiung, *supra* note 72, at 99.

86. According to the official UN treaty database, there are currently 179 states party to the Vienna Convention on Diplomatic Relations. The list of states is available at http://untreaty.un.org.

87. Denza, *supra* note 7, at 1–3.

88. The systematic development of modern tort and contract law, for example, depended in many ways on the acceptance of certain fictions. Fuller, Lon L., *Legal Fictions* 52–53 (1967). For example, implied consent, assumption of the risk, trespassers as invitees to attractive nuisances, and last clear chance are all examples of legal fiction introduced to mitigate otherwise unwanted results from strict application of legal maxims. Historically, the Roman jurists built an elaborate body of civil law from a handful of archaic rules and procedures through the use of legal fictions.

89. *Id.*

90. Maine, Henry Sumner, *Ancient Law* 24–25 (14th ed. 1891). Maine saw three primary mechanisms for legal change: legal fictions, equity, and legislation. He believed that law developed through these three phases in roughly historic order.

91. Carr, E. H., *The Twenty Years Crisis: 1919–1939* 177 (1939).

92. See, e.g., Waltz, Kenneth, *Theory of International Politics* 91 (1979). Waltz states, "[N]o state intends to participate in the formation of a structure by which it and others will be constrained."

93. Nussbaum, Arthur, *A Concise History of the Law of Nations* 231–32 (rev. ed. 1962).

94. *Vienna Convention*, art. 9, *supra* note 7, at 215–16. Article 9 states, "The receiving State may at any time and without having to explain its decision, notify the sending State that the head of the mission or any member of the diplomatic staff of the mission is *persona non grata*."

95. Cohen, Raymond, *Theatre of Power: The Art of Diplomatic Signalling* 7 (1987).

96. *Id.* at 7.

97. UN Charter, art. 2(1).

98. Levi, W., *Law and Politics in International* Society 116 (1976), quoted in, Schoenfeld, C.G., *Psychoanalysis Applied to Law* 122 (1984).

99. West, Raynard, *Conscience and Society: A Study of the Psychological Prerequisites of Law and Order* 55 (1945).

100. Schoenfeld, *supra* note 98, at 127.

101. Nafziger, James A. R., "The Functions of Religion in the International System," in Janis and Evans, *supra* note 36, at 160.

102. Group for the Advancement of Psychology, *Us and Them: The Psychology of Ethnonationalism* 37–38 (1987).

103. Anderson, *supra* note 5, at 18.

104. Cohen, *supra* note 95, at 143.

105. Anderson, *supra* note 5, at 61–62.

106. Barker, *supra* note 9, at 102.

107. Honigman, John J, *Understanding Culture* 75 (1977).

108. The world community as a primitive society is an old idea, tracing back at least to Thomas Hobbes in the seventeenth century.

109. *Id.* at 169.

110. Lewis, I. M., *Social Anthropology in Perspective: The Relevance of Social Anthropology* 136 (2d ed. 1985).

111. *Id.* at 171.

112. Oldenquist, Andrew, "Autonomy, Social Identities, and Alienation," at 54 (in Geyer and Heinz, eds., *Alienation, Society, and the Individual: Continuity and Change in Theory and Research* 51–60 [1992]).

113. Bagehot, Walter, *The English Constitution* (2d ed. 1873).

114. *Id.* at 44.

115. *Id.*

Index

About the Editors and Contributors

TERRY CRAWFORD-BROWNE is a peace activist resident in Cape Town. He is a former banker who, during 1985–1990, advised Archbishop Desmond Tutu on the application of banking sanctions as a strategy in the campaign against apartheid. He is chair of the South African affiliate of Economists Allied for Arms Reduction (ECAAR-SA), currently engaged in litigation for cancellation of South Africa's proposed purchases of warships and warplanes from Germany, Britain, and Sweden.

JEFF DANIELSKI is a freelance writer living in Los Angeles, with a particular interest in the history and politics of the Middle East. He has conducted research at the Institute for Research and Study of the Arab and Muslim World in Aix-en-Provence, France.

HERBERT C. KELMAN is the Richard Clarke Cabot Research Professor of Social Ethics at Harvard University and Director of the Program on International Conflict Analysis and Resolution at Harvard's Weatherhead Center for International Affairs. He has been engaged for many years in the development of interactive problem solving, an unofficial third-party approach to the resolution of international and intercommunal conflicts, and in its application to the Israeli–Palestinian conflict. His writings on interactive problem solving were recognized with the 1997 Grawemeyer Award for Ideas Improving World Order.

HARVEY J. LANGHOLTZ is an associate professor at The College of William and Mary and a Senior Special Fellow at the United Nations Institute for Training and Research. He served as a delegate on the U.S. Delegation to the United Nations from 1991 to 1993, where his portfolio included peacekeeping, The UN Convention on the Law of the Sea, and other issues in the Security Council and the General Assembly.

IGNACY MAREK KAMINSKI is a Polish-born Swedish citizen and a permanent resident of Japan, where he teaches Cultural and Applied Anthropology and Intercultural Negotiations and Conflict Resolution at International Christian University (ICU), Tokyo, and Warsaw University. His specialty is the comparative study of political cultures, leadership, and conflict resolution among ethnic and social minorities, and his globally oriented research includes long-term fieldwork among Okinawans, Ainu, Roma-Gypsies, Inuit, and other transnational groups.

KWEZI MNGQIBISA is currently head of the Peacekeeping Program at the African Center for the Constructive Resolution of Disputes (ACCORD). In this capacity, he trains African peacekeepers in conflict mediation throughout the continent. He also writes on issues of peacekeeping, conflict management, and African regional organizations.

ARIE NADLER is the incumbent of the Argentina Chair for Research on Social Psychology of Conflict and Cooperation at Tel Aviv University. His research interests include the study of interpersonal and intergroup helping relations and emotional processes in conflict and its resolution. He was the head of the Department of Psychology and, later, the dean of the Faculty of Social Sciences at Tel Aviv University. He established the Institute of Diplomacy and Regional Cooperation at Tel Aviv University and was its first head.

LINDA A. PRICE is professor of psychology and specializes in counseling and educational psychology. She teaches at NOVA Southeastern University and critiques medical proposals prior to submission for funding as a member of the Nemours Children's Clinic Institutional Review Board. Professor Price serves as a certified group leader and facilitator for race relations with the Jacksonville Human Rights Commission. She is a member of the American Psychological Association and Peace Psychologist. Her publications include a book on *Existential Psychology* and numerous journal articles. She travels and lectures internationally.

TYRONE F. PRICE is a consultant and graduate professor at Florida Metropolitan University. He has held numerous academic and administrative positions. His publications include book critiques, journal articles, and book chapters on social psychology, clinical sociology, and justice systems. He has traveled and lectured in the Caribbean and internationally. Professor Price has also served on the Editorial Board for the *Journal of Social and Behavioral Sciences* and specializes in conflict resolution strategies.

TAMAR SAGUY received her M.A. degree in social psychology from Tel Aviv University. Her research focused on motivational influences of status differences between groups. She has also conducted research on trust building between Israelis and Palestinians who cooperated on joint projects. She is a group facilitator in dialogue groups between Israelis and Palestinians.

STUART SELDOWITZ is a career U.S. diplomat, currently serving in the State Department's Office of Israeli and Palestinian Affairs. His previous assignments have included the U.S. delegation to the United Nations and U.S. embassies in Mexico City and Israel.

MATTHEW F. SHAW presently works within the Department of Psychiatry at the Yale School of Medicine and for the state of Connecticut's community mental health system. He conducts research, provides direct clinical services, and consults with various states concerning the organization and administration of their service delivery systems. He has served three years as a National Service Award fellow within the Agency for Healthcare Research and Quality and one year as a Veteran's Administration Health Services Fellow.

BETSIE SMITH is a career diplomat serving with the Department of Foreign Affairs of the Republic of South Africa. She is currently assigned to South Africa's embassy to Singapore, and she was most recently the deputy-director of South Africa's National Office for the Coordination of Peace Missions (NOCPM).

HUSSEIN SOLOMON lectures in the Department of Political Sciences at the University of Pretoria, South Africa, where he is also Director of the Center for International Political Studies (CIPS). His research interests include conflict resolution, religious extremism, and political psychology.

CHRIS E. STOUT is a licensed clinical psychologist and holds a joint governmental and academic appointment in the Northwestern University Medical School and at the University of Illinois College of Medicine. He is a Fellow of the American Psychological Association, past-president of the Illinois Psychological Association and is a Distinguished Practitioner in the National Academies of Practice. He produced the critically acclaimed four-volume set *The Psychology of Terrorism* and 25 other books.

JEFFREY K. WALKER is a Ph.D. candidate in Georgetown University's Program in International Relations. He has served as an adjunct professor of law and judge advocate, International and Operations Law Division, Headquarters U.S. Air Force. His areas of specialization include air and space law, treaties and status of forces agreements, law of war, rules of engagement, information warfare, peacekeeping operations, war crimes, and antiterrorism. He has taught international military education programs in Bolivia, Chile, El Salvador, Mexico, Nepal, Paraguay, Uganda, and Uruguay.

MICHAEL WESSELLS, Ph.D., is professor of psychology at Randolph-Macon College and senior child protection specialist for Christian Children's Fund. He has served as president of Psychologists for Social Responsibility and as president of the Peace Division of the American Psychological Association. In war zones around the world, he helps to establish community-based, culturally grounded systems of support and reconciliation for war-affected people, with a special focus on children.